PLYMOUTH
THE
WATERFRONT
CITY

By

JOY DAVID

Illustrated by

SHIRLEY HOLE

ACKNOWLEDGEMENTS

The author would like to thank Hilary Kent for her patience and her efforts for this book. Jamie Macleod for his instinctive knowledge of how it should look. Sonia Donovan for her faith in me and for the excellent work she has done to produce the prints which have added so greatly to the look of the book. To Plymouth artist, Shirley Hole for the cover and the many original prints within the covers. I am indebted also to The Evening Herald and Western Morning News for the pictures of Plymouth in the Blitz.

I would thank also the many people who have generously given their time and help in the compilation of this book, especially Mike Pallot, of PricewaterhouseCoopers; Andrew Huckerby, of Kitley House Hotel; Neill Mitchell, of the Chamber of Commerce; Commander Charles Howeson and John Ingham.

ISBN:0-9540974-0-8
Copyright Joy David
All rights reserved

All information is included in good faith and is believed to be correct at the time of going to press. No responsibility can be accepted for error.

The book is sold subject to the condition that it shall not by way of trade or otherwise be lent, re-sold, hired out, or otherwise circulated without the publisher's prior consent in any form of binding or cover other than that in which it is published and without similar condition including this condition being imposed on the subsequent purchaser.

Printers: Allen of Derby
Typesetter: Mick Devereux

The Mayflower Steps. The Barbican.

CONTENTS

Acknowledgements

Foreword by the Rt. Hon. Lord Owen, C.H.

House of Lords,
Westminster,
London SW1A 0PW

PLYMOUTH –THE WATERFRONT CITY
FOREWORD BY THE RT HON LORD OWEN CH

As a Plymothian born and bred I have read the "Waterfront City" with fascination. However well one thinks one knows Plymouth I challenge anyone to say that they have not learnt new facts or insights from this remarkable book.

"Nothing was ever achieved without enthusiasm" wrote the famous American writer, Ralph Waldo Emerson and Joy David's enthusiasm radiates out from every page. Encyclopaedic in its range, it is nevertheless surprisingly intimate in the way personalities are woven into the text.

It is hard to pick and choose from the many gems but to try to give you a flavour of her writing look up Chapter 12 where she tells you about Cremyll Ferry across the Tamar with a short account from a crossing in 1698 and a poem published by the Evening Herald in 1946. Then in Chapter 17 she takes you into Mount Edgcumbe Park "to revel in its quiet beauty and its splendid walks and the chance to explore the house". Here, though in Cornwall, you have the best view of the City.

Another vignette is in Chapter 2 on the Barbican, itself the very essence of the City, where the old building which houses Plymouth Gin, the only English gin still made at its original distillery, is open for daily tours. The reader is not given the 200 year old closely guarded recipe. But the famous monk on the label is now back on the bottle, but this time on the inside so that you know "when his feet get dry it is time to buy another bottle". In the Barbican the old fish market is now where you can buy Dartington Glass and see it being made in the Studio workshop. The extraordinary educational experiment that Dartington Hall in Totnes, under the Elmhirsts, represents is well described.

The book gives an excellent and up to date account of the restaurants, hotels and shops in Plymouth and in the surrounding area and any first time visitor to Plymouth will find here far more information than in any General Guide Book.

Throughout the book history is interweaved with modern developments in an informal and chatty style that mixes the essential and the trivial. For anyone who wants to know more about every aspect of the City this book will be a constant and treasured companion whether as a short term visitor or as a resident dipping in over the years ahead.

Sir Francis Drake. From a Painting by Shirley Hole.

Chapter I

First Impressions

I am not generally an indecisive creature. In fact my family would tell you I make up my mind to do something and then normally go for the jugular without hesitation. It was the thought that the glorious autumn day was a reminder that winter was not far off, and far too good to be wasted, made me turn my car towards Plymouth Hoe and the sea rather than driving directly back through the city to home. I did hesitate because I knew that I should be sitting behind my laptop and getting on with writing this book, rather than indulging in an intense desire to look at the sea. How glad I was that I hesitated only momentarily. The panoramic view of Plymouth from The Hoe is the first impression of Plymouth that should be mandatory for every first time visitor! How could they fail to appreciate all that we have, having taken in such glorious surroundings.. The weather is almost immaterial, although I have to admit that a blue sky, and an equally iridescent sea does make the picture perfect.

This particular autumn morning was idyllic. Visitors strolled along obviously revelling in the beauty around them and frequently contentedly leaning over the rails enjoying an ice cream from one of the vendors. To my right was Drake's Island wrapt up in its own secretive life and out beyond that I could see Mount Edgcumbe Park. Round the point I could just make out Cawsand Bay. To the left the busy Cattedown and the newly developed Mount Batten, once the base for the magnificent Sunderland Flying Boats. Before me was Rennie's famous Breakwater built with the help of Napoleonic prisoners making Plymouth a perfect, protected harbour, and there, steaming slowly out to sea were three ships of the Royal Navy, line astern, making their graceful way towards the open sea and beyond. A rare sight today, unlike the past when any number of Royal Navy ships would come and go through the course of a day, passing around one of the ocean liners lying at anchor whilst they disembarked their passengers. I could see one of Brittany Ferries ships making its way slowly towards the city, back from Roscoff or perhaps Santander. Anchored below Jennycliff, just beyond Mount Batten was a shining white cruise ship paying a brief visit to Plymouth so that its American passengers could make a quick trip ashore to the Barbican to see the Mayflower steps from which their ancestors had left these shores for their great occupation of America. Behind me was Plymouth Hoe where Sir Francis Drake reputedly played his game of bowls whilst awaiting the Spanish Armada.

So much has happened on Plymouth Hoe. In the 1940s we danced on Plymouth Hoe in sheer defiance against anything the German Luftwaffe could do to us. In March 1941 they took the heart out of Plymouth with their bombs but not the heart out of the people. It simply brought Plymothians together gaining strength from each other no matter what the adversity. As I write on March 21st 2001 inevitably I recall the night of horror that rained down on us. I remember the city burning, the buildings tumbling. I remember walking to work next morning and wondering if the Bank of England where I worked still stood. This terror went on night after night. Not always major raids, sometimes just a single bomber sent to make sure the city did not sleep. I remember one night standing outside our house in Mannamead with my father, watching a land mine descend slowly on a parachute, making its way towards us. We did not dive for cover but merely shook each others hand and said 'Good-bye'. Sounds ridiculous but it is true. I remember another night when I was firefighting and went to put out an incendiary at the bottom of our garden, using a stirrup pump. It was one of the first exploding incendiary bombs and caught my clothes on fire. I remember being in the ABC Cinema as a raid started and advised to remain there. There were a couple of near misses which shook the building as though it was the subject of an earthquake. I remember helping to man a mobile canteen outside the dockyard after the attack on South Yard. We worked ceaselessly to keep the rescue workers supplied with mugs of tea, only to be moved on ourselves because the vehicle was standing on top of an unexploded bomb. Then it all seemed to be part of every day life. Now I look back and wonder how any of us coped. We did and still managed to have fun.

Looking down on The Hoe's green and flower decked plateau and in turn, beyond to the Sound, one wonders how the Pilgrim Fathers felt as they sailed out on the Mayflower to write their own pages of history in a far off land that we know as America. The adrenalin must have flowed through Captain Cook's veins as he upped anchor and sailed on his immortal voyage in which he found Australia and claimed it for his country. Did Captain Scott think of his birthplace and the town in which he spent all his young life and schooling at Stoke Damerel, when he lay facing death in the wastes of Antarctica?

Men and women still play bowls on the same green sward where Drake played with Walter Raleigh, Martin Frobisher, Richard Grenville, John Davis and Lord Howard of Effingham until the Spanish Armada was sighted from the Sound. They finished their game and then ran down the hill to their ships waiting below, to destroy the Spanish fleet. It was to Plymouth they returned in victory and to bow their knees in prayer in our Mother church, St Andrews, to a merciful God who had 'blown with his winds and scattered the foe'.

Plymothians stood on the Hoe and watched the French ship, Bellerophon come to anchor with Napoleon on board, a captive on his way to exile. That great Italian, Garibaldi, was a welcome guest when he was hailed as a hero for giving freedom to the Italian people. Plymothians would have stood back quietly, watching the arrival of the shy and bewildered princess Catherine of Aragon when she first set foot on the land where she was to spend the rest of her unhappy life. Widowed first in childhood and then married to Henry VIII who all the world knows treated her disgracefully. Margaret of Anjou's ship brought her to Plymouth in 1470 to marry the weak Henry VI, leaving her virtually the ruler of England and fighting the Wars of the Roses. It is probably Philip of Spain who intrigues me most. He came to Plymouth as an honoured guest, and yet I think he was already planning his great Armada. He certainly promised his Admiral, the Duke of Medina Sidonia, the lovely estate of Mount Edgcumbe as a reward for conquering the English fleet. The Admiral was to be disappointed.

It is not only centuries ago that the rich and famous landed in Plymouth. In the 20th century Royalty mixed with film stars as they came ashore from the great liners that regularly anchored in the Sound before World War II. Edward VIII, then Prince of

The Plymouth Dome is open daily in summer from 9-6pm and in winter from 9-5pm Tuesday to Sunday. For current information ring 01752 600608. The Plymouth Dome is easy to find. Follow the signs to the City Centre and to the Hoe. The Plymouth Dome is sited on Hoe Road which runs along the seafront.

From various points on the front you can take trips up the River Tamar to see the Dockyard and the ships of the Royal Navy, stopping for a while in the river village of Calstock. It is a breathtakingly beautiful trip. You can also go to Cawsand directly on one of these boats or take a cruise up the River Yealm, the entrance to which you can see to your left as you stand on the Hoe.

To appreciate Plymouth one does need to know something of its extraordinary history To more mundane matters but of vital importance to Plymouth.There is a splendid advertisement currently gracing the television screens. It shows a delightful girl of about six years old asking her mother if the sea was there because someone left a tap running! We may smile wryly at the innocent question but how many of us are guilty of assuming that South West Water just feed the water to our taps and that is what we pay for. My eyes were opened to the enormity of the task undertaken by South West Water when I spent an informative and fascinating time talking to the Customer Services Director, Peter Briens. His dedication to his work and to all that South West Water does poured out of him as strongly as the water that comes from my taps. For the first time in my life I began to view sewage as romantic! The story of the massive improvements that the company is making reads like a love story! The amount of investment reads like sci-fi! We are talking billions. Plymouth alone has had an investment of £110 million in the last few years and the majority of it has gone into the removing of sewage pouring directly into the sea off the Hoe. How has this been achieved?

Lets look at the problem before the achievement. Plymouth's sewer system was out of date by over a hundred years. Raw sewage had been discharged direct into Plymouth Sound via the outlet at West Hoe since 1902. Decades of neglect had left the sewage infrastructure in a state of decay and in dire need of upgrading. Logically if one thinks back to the war years and the Blitz when so much damage was done, almost all the repair work at that time would have been a cobbled operation looking for whatever materials were available and making repairs at the double - it could not have been satisfactory but was subsequently covered up and only looked at again when trouble occurred.

There was no doubt that there was much to be done. The water was contaminated, unsafe, and the Plymouth Sound regularly failed quality tests of the European-designated waters at East and West Hoe. A part of Plymouth vital to the city's economy was in need of urgent attention. For a city that has relied so heavily on the sea for its economy and recreation for centuries, the state of the water was letting Plymouth down.

The cavalry came to the rescue in the shape of South West Water in 1989 when it took over the sewerage services. Its immediate commitment was to the reversing of this terrible neglect and launched a 'Clean Sweep' programme. Since then around 40 schemes have provided proper sewage treatment works to over 200,000 homes, providing clean water and improved bathing standards across the region.

The Plymouth scheme was begun in 1996, and progressed steadily throughout 1998 - the first elements came into operation in June 1998 and by the end of 2000 there will be new pipelines and eight new pumping stations completing this landmark scheme. It is certainly making Plymouth a cleaner, more pleasant place to live and visit. Plymouth can rely on one of its greatest assets and be able to attract visitors to its coast. Wildlife and marine life thrive in the cleaner waters, providing an ideal home for many of Britain's native species. It will not all happen at once but by the end of this year there should be a gradual improvement in the abundance of marine life.

This is there for all of us to see and enjoy but there is much we know nothing or very little about. Underneath Plymouth lies a sewer network that until recently had not been upgraded or significantly altered since the late 19th century. Part of the 'Clean Sweep' programme involved repairing and improving the tunnels that carry the city's waste.

A completely new tunnel was built from Millbridge to Cattedown running for about three kilometres. Shafts were sunk at Millbay, Bretonside, the Barbican and Knighton Road to provide access to the tunnel works, and to house control points necessary for the operation and maintenance of the tunnel. Building the tunnels was a big task. There were 350 people involved from the civil engineers to explosive experts to miners, working deep below the surface in damp, dark and cramped conditions.
The infrastructure of the sewage network needed to be in excellent condition for the rest of it to work properly. So the tunnel was dug and lined with a concrete shell. The diameter varies from 1.5 metres at the Barbican to 2.4 metres at Millbay. It runs at a distance of 20 metres below the city, which meant disruption was kept to a minimum. The tunnels have been designed to accommodate an increased capacity to reduce the possibility of storm overflows.

The new State-of-the-Art sewage treatment works on the site of the old Cattedown power station is superb. It is modern, efficient and represents the best in treatment technology. It has to handle the tons of sewage that flows out of Plymouth, turning the contaminated liquid into water that is clean enough to be discharged into the sea. The entire works is contained within a building, and modern odour control systems have been installed to prevent the smell of sewage becoming a problem.

Raw sewage enters the treatment works from the new sewers that have been built as part of the upgrade. Preliminary treatment removes large particles and items, grit, wood, paper, rags and plastics - by passing the effluent through a series of mesh screens. Grease particles are also removed. The waste is then pumped into settlement tanks, where it is allowed to stand to let the sludge settle to the bottom. The sludge is removed, treated, and used as fertiliser. Second day treatment involves encouraging bacteria to break down the waste by pumping air through the water, as well as removing solids.
The really clever bit, and the part that has won the most admiration, is the ultra-violet light treatment. Subjecting the water to this kind of light is a natural, clean and efficient way of killing off harmful bacteria. This treatment is carried out all year round,

meaning that the water finally discharged into the sea is clean enough to help the local bathing waters meet European water guidelines.

The undertaking has been a major civil engineering project for the city, which has been carried out with minimal disruption to Plymothians. In fact, I for one, did not even know the work was taking place, directly underneath my home.

The work has not come to an end, nor will it. Places like Kingsand and Cawsand are about to have their act cleaned up. This means another enormous investment by South West Water. So when you look at your water and sewerage bills, don't get uptight. We will all benefit and whilst you may think that the company is making a fortune, this is true but it is all being reinvested with the exception of small dividend payments to shareholders without whose money the work could not be done.

The 1600 or so employees of South West Water are a dedicated team with massive knowledge and as they strive to give us perfection so should we perhaps be generous enough to appreciate them. I certainly left South West Water's offices in Exeter filled with admiration for what has been done and what is being done.

South West Water is just a tiny fraction of all that is happening in the city of Plymouth as we come into the 21st century. Every part of the city is alive with a sense of striking out and achieving and it is not just the council, industry and business, it is the people themselves who have become inspired by a desire to have a better standard of living in a great environment. Anyone visiting the city should perhaps look a bit beyond the obvious and see what is happening in the parts of the city that were run down. Communities are working together to improve their housing, the play areas, the streets, the gardens. It is exciting and an inspiration to everyone.

Plymouth is no longer living in the past, it has the future firmly within its grasp and is respected, admired, envied and frequently copied in other cities and towns.

"The Prawn."

Barbican Street Scene on The Parade.

Chapter II

The Barbican

The magic and history of the Barbican is what draws visitors here in the first place. A history that goes back to Elizabethan times when the great seafarers of the day. Sir Francis Drake, Hawkins, Grenville and Raleigh, brought their ships into Plymouth and stepped ashore to enjoy an ale or two in one of the old hostelries. The Pilgrim Fathers sailed from the Mayflower Steps on their way to the New World. The cobbled streets, old houses and the smell of history still live on but today the Barbican has a new breed of great characters and businesses. The collecting of information for this book has been full of exciting content and some of it totally unexpected. Imagine meeting up with a character who is called simply 'Jo-Jo'. He sits in the window of his first floor apartment in Southside taking constant stock of the life outside. He looks quietly studious and then you get to know he is the compiler and photographer of a book called 'Plymouth Unveiled' in which he has persuaded some staunch Plymouth citizens having divested themselves of their clothes right down to the nuddy, to permit him to photograph them for inclusion in his book. He asks them to do whatever they like doing best - playing golf perhaps - and then starts the camera clicking. The written content of the book is slender in the extreme and simply quotes how the posers - or poseurs - feel about the city. Most of their comments are not complimentary. It is the most extraordinary book, photographed with taste and sometimes style and contains no less than a hundred of these nude photographs.

Jo-Jo has had immense publicity for this book from comments by comedian Des O'Connor to the Judy and Richard show. Yet, it was compiled whilst he was totally skint and reliant on the dole. He hopes the book will replenish his coffers and lead on to other projects. His background is one of diversity as well, once a producer of documentaries he has also had dealings with the world of music. He comes across as a man who is comfortable with his own company but none too happy about his complicated upbringing. When I asked questions about that I discovered that he is the son of the well known Enrico who died recently but was once one of the Barbican's leading personalities when he owned the famous Hosteria Romana.

Enrico was an Italian who had lived in Plymouth for several decades but still spoke English with a charming Italian accent. He was a great restaurateur and I remember him particularly for his gift for looking after people so well and even going to the extent of learning Japanese - spoken with an Italian accent of course - so that he could welcome his Japanese clients in their own language. Southside Street has always been busy and yet when you walked into the courtyard of the Hosteria Romana, the hustle and bustle disappeared as if by magic. There were plants everywhere and the rough hewn walls offered shelter to the tables with their rich marble tops, and chairs where you could sit and enjoy a pre-dinner drink. Inside the restaurant was on two levels with the upper part forming a gallery. It was a warm-hearted place and one felt loved and cared for by Enrico and his Italian staff who had been with him for years. When the Hosteria Romano closed down it was a sad day for Plymouth but now, with a different owner and a different name, it has become once more a delightful backwater in a busy world. I did not see the father in the son when I met Jo-Jo but I knew I had met a fascinating and unusual personality.

Almost next door to Jo-Jo in Southside Street lives that enigmatic actor Colin McIntyre who has acquired a host of fans since he first appeared in the hospital drama ' Always and Everyone' with the delectable Martin Shaw and Niamh Cusack. One wonders, on first meeting this likeable man, why he chose to make Plymouth and especially The Barbican his home. A backwater for actors one would think and far from his North of England background. Colin soon puts you right on both these matters. Firstly with mobile phones and easy access to London, there is no need for him to live in the Metropolis and therefore he is not divorced from the opportunity to attend auditions or any other matters necessary for the success of an up and coming actor. Why The Barbican? 'I came to Plymouth for a holiday, loved it, stayed too long, ran out of money and became a salesman for a local company'. That is it virtually in a nutshell but underneath lies a deeper story. At this time becoming an actor was far from his mind but he found himself being drawn towards the theatre and thought to himself, when he watched thespians at work, that he could do that. He was lucky enough to be befriended by the Barbican Theatre and in the course of time not only acted for them but put on and directed a couple of plays. With his ability as an able salesman, Colin found he could apply the same rules of selling products to selling himself to directors and theatre managers. Slowly but surely he found himself part of a variety of television series, usually as a villain or a policeman! His public persona has come to the fore with his role as the Nurse in 'Always and Everyone' and he has now become a household name. As I write he is filming for another series of this highly popular drama.

Colin reckons he has much to thank Plymouth for and especially the Barbican where he is now accepted as 'one of them' - a difficult accolade to acquire. He loves The Barbican for its way of life. It is part of the city but an entity entirely of its own. The people look out for each other, enjoy daily communication as they wander down Southside Street or onto the Quay. I was amused by the rapid passing on of information about Traffic Wardens. The Barbican is not renowned for its parking facilities especially in Southside Street, but you can bet your bottom dollar that if you are in business here and your car is lurking where it ought not to be, then some warning will be given just in the nick of time!

The Dolphin

16

Colin and I sat talking over a cup of coffee in the little Café Pretes, where he is a regular and known to everyone. Our chatter was interrupted by an irate little lady in her sixties who loudly berated him for the noise that came from his flat two nights previously. He was partying and she had come home late from a night out. The telling off was entirely friendly and ended up with a kiss. The great thing for Colin is the ability to be himself on The Barbican. He is not famous to them anymore than the famous artist Robert Lenkiewicz or doctor, turned artist, Brian Pollard, Dawn French and Lenny Henry who are frequently to be seen here as well, usually in the much painted Dolphin, a pub that remains just that. No food, no modern accoutrements, just good ale and good local company from fishermen to the famous. Artist Beryl Cook was another regular before she left Plymouth to live elsewhere and is about to return.

The Dolphin goes back further than almost any hostelry in Plymouth. It has had the same family as licensees since the end of World War II and is still very much a family affair. Its most famous landlord was Charles Morgan, who in 1838, entertained the returning 'Tolpuddle Martyrs' Thomas and John Stanfield, James Brind and James Loveless, from Australia's Botany Bay.

One might have supposed that with the removal of the old Fish Market to its splendid new home at Coxside, many of the characters who came ashore from the incoming trawlers together with the men of the market, might have found another hostelry. This is not so, the pub is as lively as it ever was, the conversation is parochial, the floors are still bare and the beer still comes from the barrel. The atmosphere has been built up over the centuries and The Dolphin, thankfully, still remains a good old-fashioned drinking place.

There is a new publican on the Barbican and one who will undoubtedly make his mark. His name is John Buckley who with his wife Jan took over the tenancy of The Navy in Southside Street in August 2000. This fine old pub oozes history and has been a haunt of locals and service personnel for centuries. If its walls could speak then it would tell many horrific tales of nights when the Naval Press Gangs swooped down on it, rounding up unsuspecting men and without option, forcing them to join one or more of the ships lying at anchor, but short of a crew, before they set sail to confound England's enemies on the high seas. Today it is a peaceful sort of place where the beer is good and the food known for its excellence.

John spent many years in the army and retired at 45 with the rank of Captain. He spent his early retirement years in Scotland building a mini empire in Spar Shops. Although his wife is a Scot he felt himself to be a foreigner and not particularly welcome. It was a strange feeling because before he retired and simply used to go to Scotland on leave, he used to get teased about being a Sassenach but no more than that. It all changed when he went into business; the teasing became aggressive and the English unwelcome. John and Jan returned to London and bought a pub, Bradley's Spanish Bar just off Tottenham Court Road at the junction with Oxford Street. It became a huge success but commuting to it every day became a chore and so the Buckleys set out to look for something in the West Country. John liked the idea of Plymouth - its seafaring and service connection meant that whatever your race, it would be acceptable. The long and short of it is that they came to the Barbican, saw The Navy, fell in love with both, and saw the pub's potential.

The Navy needs someone like John who is a visionary but at the same time has his feet firmly on the ground. His army discipline ensures that his plans for the pub will be well constructed and feasible. He sees a new look for the pub without it losing any part of its past charm. It is a listed building and as such has certain limitations on restructuring but John hopes that he will be able to build a delightful conservatory restaurant on to the flat part of the roof on the first floor. This would look out over the docks and the water   providing Plymouth with an attractive, slightly upmarket restaurant renowned for its food and its well chosen wines. I can just imagine dining there in a great atmosphere with both the body and the mind being nourished. John also promises me that The Navy's reputation for great fresh crab sandwiches will not be lost. Hopefully he will use the bread from Jacka's Bakery across the road in Southside Street, which still bakes in the traditional manner, as it has done for centuries, and has recently been totally refurbished. The smell of the bread is enough to start the taste buds demanding refreshment. That bread combined with crab brought ashore in the Fish Market and you have the combination for a perfect sandwich..

John, quite rightly, questions some of the rules and regulations that apply to the Barbican. Some are at the behest of the Plymouth City Council. the Barbican Residents Association, the Barbican Retailers Association and finally laid down by   Sutton

The Fishmarket

Harbour plc. They own much of the property and streets. He went to a meeting of the Barbican Residents Association in The Three Crowns recently and felt that some rules should not be there. For example tables and chairs may not be placed outside any

18

establishment after 8pm. It does sound a bit daft but there is a sound reason behind it. Because of hooliganism which is inherent not only in Plymouth but sadly everywhere, the removal of tables at that hour prevents would be vandals from amusing themselves by pointlessly hurling tables and chairs and causing damage. From the residents point of view it lessens the noise. All the reasons have common sense attached to them, but what a pity it is. There is nothing nicer than sitting outside on a balmy evening listening to the gentle lap of the water against the dock, taking in the atmosphere and enjoying a quiet drink or a meal. Why is it that there is always an unruly minority element who spoil the pleasure of the majority?

Plymouth and especially The Barbican has much to thank Sutton Harbour plc for. In the last 40 years under the dynamic guidance of their Managing Director Duncan Godefroy, they have grown from quite a small company into a large, well funded plc who work constantly to make improvements on the Barbican and the surrounding area. We have the company to thank for giving The Barbican a new lease of life when in 1993 they converted Sutton Harbour into a permanent 'wet dock' creating a new lock and incorporating the new fish market complex. The lock allows water to be kept in the harbour during the whole of the tide cycle, keeping out the sea and ensuring the water level in the harbour is kept at a safe level when there are exceptionally high tides. The gates are high enough to protect the harbour against a future rise in sea level which could occur because of the greenhouse effect. It makes it possible for the fishing boats to tie up alongside, irrespective of the state of the tide. They no longer have to put up with their boats leaning over to one side at low tide. They can land their catches on a level with the Fish Market and best of all, they can sail in and out at whatever time they like, and not have to wait for the tide to be right.

Today the company owns Plymouth Airport and the Torbay Boating Centre in Paignton as well as many interests in this city. Just look at the work they have done with the Rope Walk linking Coxside with the Barbican giving us not only a walkway from Coxside to The Barbican but also one of the best seaviews in Plymouth. Then there is the land provided for the National Marine Aquarium, the refurbishment of many of the warehouses and buildings on The Barbican, the total refurbishment of the pavements and cobbled areas. The area which is now Barbican Glass was once the Fish Market. Sutton Harbour plc has also provided us with the new purpose built Fish Market, designed to look like a ship and to fulfil all the requirements of a busy fish market. Shrewdly it is also multi-purpose, so if the awful day came when fisherman no longer landed catches in Plymouth, the building could be used for other purposes. North Quay House, the company's own headquarters is also home to other offices and next door is Mariner's Court, a prestigious housing development. Next to come will be the further development of Elphinstone Car Park. The old flats in Moon Street are also due for redevelopment. The Sutton Harbour Marina is home to a considerable number of yachts of all sizes and the outer basin provides moorings for visiting yachts and motor launches. Walking around the harbour is quite fascinating. All the time, when there is a little breeze blowing, one can hear the tinkle of bells on the mastheads of the yachts and there is something very reassuring about seeing them all safely tied up in neat rows. Sutton Harbour plc is an exciting company and one that works in partnership with the City Council.

Almost immediately after turning into Southside Street from Notte Street you will see on your right hand side the old building which houses Plymouth Gin, the only English gin still made at its original distillery. The Black Friars Distillery is the oldest working

English distillery and has been on the go since 1793. The building was formerly a Dominican monastery dating back to 1431 and in 1620 was the final lodging for the Pilgrim Fathers before they sailed to the New World on the Mayflower. The British Royal Navy have been major consumers of this excellent gin for over 200 years. Plymouth Gin is documented from 1896 as the original base for the first Dry Martini and is the only gin consistently specified in the Savoy Cocktail Book - the bible of mixed drinks. Anyone who is anyone and has good taste buds cannot help appreciating the qualities of Plymouth Gin. Who are we to argue with the taste buds of Winston Churchill, Roosevelt, Ian Fleming and Alfred Hitchcock!

The recipe for the gin has been a closely guarded secret for 200 years and if you talk to Sean Harrison, the 'in situ' head stillman, who still makes his brew in the old Copper Pot Still which is now well over 155 years old., he will tell you only that one of the important factors is the softness and purity of the Dartmoor water used in the distillation which ensures that Plymouth Gin is noticeably the smoothest gin on the market. In his time in the Royal Navy, Sean tasted and tested Plymouth Gin all over the world. Now he adds a touch of this botanical and a bit of that together with the Dartmoor Water to produce a perfect dry gin which cannot be faulted and, having gone through a lean time, has now been revitalised in the market place and packaged in a replica of one of the company's earliest bottles. The label is also based on a turn of the century design. In the late 19th century no man trusted the authenticity of a bottle of 'Plymouth Gin' which did not bear the image of the monk on the label. Now the monk is back - but this time on the inside. When his feet get dry it is time to buy another bottle. The bottle has a cork finish as it did in the last century. Something that speaks of quality and is a unique feature in the gin market.

One interesting fact I discovered was that Plymouth was the first gin company to make a crystal clear dry gin. Apparently London gin makers always had problems sourcing pure water and consequently hid the impurities in green or other coloured glass.

How lucky can a man get after a career in the Royal Navy than to find himself heading the Plymouth operation of Plymouth Gin in one of the most historic buildings on The Barbican. Sean Harrison clearly loves his job.

There are daily tours of the Distillery if you would like to explore this charming old building, perhaps get a taste of gin, and come out enriched by history.

One of the most distinguished members of the Barbican Guild of Traders and one who has constantly voiced his concern about The Barbican, is Mr Foxsmith who occupies the 17th century merchants house at 53 Southside Street, and in it for the last 20 years, has run the successful and internationally respected Foxsmith Galleries. What for him started off as a hobby collecting maps, prints and engravings many years ago, has become a lifetime's work. After some years he began to buy and sell in a very small way taking stalls at craft fairs. Now he has one of the largest collections in one of the smallest galleries outside London.

Today Mr Foxsmith spends half his time seeking out, buying and selling and the other half renovating, restoring, cleaning and framing works ready for sale. It is a labour of love. All his prints, maps and engravings are genuine antiques with guarantees of age. Do not be put off venturing into this wonderful place by the thought of the cost. Of course some are fabulously expensive, but there are finds that will not hurt the bank balance too much. His

Plymouth Gin. The Distillery

The Customs House and The Jazz Café

primary interest is old maps and I get the feeling that he is reluctant to part with any of them. He will encourage you to browse because he wants you to share his enthusiasm, and also because he believes that people visiting the gallery add atmosphere. The Foxsmith trade comes not only from Plymouth and the South West but from all over the world. His busiest time of the year is not the summer when the tourists are about but in the months leading up to Christmas.

The transformation of the area surrounding Hawkins Quay on the Barbican, is one of the best things to happen in Plymouth for a long time. It has all the ambience of a fishing port in France and one wonders why anyone would bother to go through the hassle of airports or ferries to get to a destination that would certainly have nothing more delightful to offer than here. Fresh sea food and fish comes direct from the local fishing boats, the bars have tables outside, the cobbled street reminds one of the days of the swashbuckling Drake, Hawkins and Raleigh, the buildings, some of old stone and some brightly painted, have a definite continental feel and the whole is enhanced by the arrival of The Jazz Café next door to the old Customs House. It is here that two Frenchmen full of gallic charm, Vasili Dimitrovski and Eric Amann, have used their considerable talents to produce a venue which would not go amiss on the Left Bank in Paris. The building was a Wine Bar which had been operating for many years. During the Second World War it was an armoury storage on the ground floor and billeted Naval Staff on the first and second floors. Now the ground floor provides a super space which has been elegantly fitted out in a simple style with tables and chairs along the walls, a well-stocked, long bar complete with excellent wines and Belgian beers and a raised dais at the end to accommodate jazz players of all kinds in the evenings. Sometimes it may well be known musicians just enjoying making music, sometimes it may be youngsters getting their first opportunity of playing in public - I hope at some time the Jazz Band from Coombe Tec College will play here. I heard them play brilliantly for the BBC Music Live event.

Eating is a totally new experience here. The emphasis is on a family style service of trays of Charcuterie or Smoked Seafood, Continental Cheese Selections or Crudities, with perhaps a hot dish like Boeuf Bouginion or Coq au Vin. The taste of France is heightened by a delicious selection of breads and directly imported French wines sold by the carafe.

It is a sheer delight to sit outside on the harbour frontage which can provide for 60 covers. There is something very therapeutic about sitting close to water and listening to the gentle creak of the fishing boats as they lie tied up awaiting their next trip to acquire more fresh fish and scallops that have to be tasted to appreciate how good they are. The staff are both French and English. Both Vas and Eric are keen to promote the opportunity for exchanges of staff between France and England. In this way they believe, absolutely correctly, that the very best cuisine will be available either side of the English Channel.

I was loth to move from this attractive haunt, my coffee was aromatic and the patisserie superb but above it all was the delightful atmosphere that one soaks up whether you are inside at night listening to music, having a break at lunchtime or simply enjoying the morning sunshine on the quay.

Once the busy fish market which now has a new home at Coxside, the old store constructed in 1870 by Sir John Inglis has been given a new lease of life. The building has had glass walls erected around the original structure and now is the home of Barbican Glass an offshoot of Dartington Glass. Here they carry on the ethos of Dorothy and Leonard Elmhirst who came to Dartington in order to augment a clause in a will  which made Dorothy Elmhirst a rich women. The clause stated that a large proportion of her inheritance should be spent on education. Dorothy was an American and Leonard a Yorkshireman. She had an unusual degree of social awareness and Leonard was blessed with a winning combination of vision and practicality. They acquired Dartington Hall which has been the pivot of this beautiful area near Totnes since Saxon times, It flourished under the Normans, in Tudor times Sir Walter Raleigh advised the owner about the planning of the gardens and in the 17th century it was extensively modernised. It took World War I to bring it to its knees and until 1925 most of its fine farmland was derelict and the great hall was a sorry ruin but then a miracle occurred with the arrival of the Elmhirsts. It was the start of an experiment with activities spread over three thousand acres along the lovely valley of the Bidwell Brook. There were mills and workshops, the college taught the natural industries of the countryside, experts taught forestry and farming, gardening and pottery. New businesses were started - cider mill, saw mill and tweed mill. A new school was founded and an arts centre established attracting Artists and performers from around the world.

The Elizabethan house was reborn, with a fireplace sixteen feet wide in the 600 year old hall. The banqueting hall had magnificent timbers of an even earlier date. It was an estate bursting with energy and an example to everyone.

In spite of the fact that in the course of time the Dartington School was closed and the sawmills no longer exist, the Cider Press Centre remains and displays and retails beautiful crafted goods including Dartington Glass. The Dartington Hall Trust is nowadays renowned for both its glass, which is not made here, and for its excellent Courses which can be anything from the use of word processors to a residential week in making music. During the course of the year writers from all over the world gather to talk to and listen to other writers.. What started from Dorothy Elmhirst's legacy has amply justified her receiving the money and from then onwards until this day, the overriding factor has always been a standard of excellence, working together and achieving what is best for the community.

Dartington Glass at Torrington is one example of what the Elmhirsts set out to do. Bearing in mind that the Trust's purpose was rural regeneration, it was not surprising that North Devon was its chosen place for the new glass factory. Since the decline of the wool trade the working population of the area had declined at the rate of 6% a decade, and was badly in need of a broader base of industry and commerce to provide the kind of employment opportunities which local people had to seek elsewhere. It was hoped that a glass factory, making English lead crystal by hand in the traditional way, would not only provide work for local people, but also opportunities for them to develop specialised skills and improve their quality of life.

The company started manufacturing in June 1967 with a work force of 35, and it was three years later that the scheme came to fruition. It was a gamble that paid off; Dartington Crystal has become Britain's leading manufacturer of plain crystal, exporting to 50 countries, and synonymous worldwide with quality and innovative design of hand-made crystal.

With a workforce of nearly 300 and retail sales in excess of £20,000,000 per annum, the company has not only achieved its original objective of contributing to the local economy, but Dartington Crystal has also become one of the West Country's leading tourist attractions, receiving over 300,000 visitors each year.

And so we come to the latest addition to Leonard and Dorothy Elmhirst's vision and social understanding. Barbican Glass embraces all the teachings of this famous pair. Here designing is allied to retail sales but at the end of the day the ethos remains. In the Studio workshop, master craftsmen explore and refine skills handed down across the generations to make reproduction pieces using authentic methods, and undertake production work for an international field of the leading Studio glass designers of today. A number of these designers, in addition to creating their own individual pieces, work closely with Dartington on its current product range. A new dimension has also evolved in limited editions and unique pieces that exhibit the successful integration of Studio and factory skills. One difficulty that is experienced here is the lack of young apprentices coming in to learn this craft. What is seen in this light, attractive building, is a team dedicated to promoting the sale of the superb Dartington Crystal and equally not being afraid to bring in other glassmakers wares. Everything is laid out attractively and nowhere is the sign 'Hands Off'! A brave decision but one which allows visitors who may just be staying in Plymouth, or Plymothians themselves, to enjoy the enchantment of the business. In their Manager, Alison Smith, they have a lady who is a dedicated follower of the Elmhirst theory. She advocates learning, she involves Barbican Glass in all sorts of happenings in Plymouth. She and her team are very much a part of the fraternity of the Barbican. When the band plays and the Parade takes place

Cap'n Jaspers

on the Barbican at the time of American Thanksgiving you can be sure Barbican Glass will be involved and encouraging all the other businesses on the Barbican to join in the flag waving . Dorothy Elmhirst would look on with pride and say 'Well done'.

Just across the road from Barbican Glass and hidden away in an old Fish Store is the Fisherman's Museum the brain child of artist Richard Clark and a couple of his friends. Slightly hidden away in a courtyard, you will need to seek it out. Here they are slowly gathering together a collection of memorabilia of anything to do with fishermen. When I took a look at it in July 2000 it was in its infancy but still a fascinating place to explore. Richard Clark was in the middle of painting a massive mural covering the whole of one of the massive walls. It will be a tremendous focal point and is all down to the generosity of Tim Rolt of T. Rolt & Co the Mercedes distributors who have an immaculate showroom at Crownhill. It is always comforting to know how many good Plymothian citizens there are who will support such a venture as the Fisherman's Museum. Incidentally Richard Clark produces varied and sometimes highly entertaining works of art, not the least some amusing postcards dedicated to Captain Jaspers. He has painted the Field Gun Crew and the men from the Citadel; two imposing paintings, prints of which can be obtained from the Armada Gallery in Southside Street.

Now if you do not know about Cap'n Jaspers, it is time you rectified the situation. The Cap'n, John Dudley in reality, is a larger than life personality who has dominated the Barbican from his self-built wooden hut for donkeys years. It started off just as a hut from which the incoming fishermen or those working on the quay could get the biggest

25

bacon butties in huge rolls, burgers, and hot dogs imaginable, at the very best possible prices. The business grew as much because of Cap'n Jaspers personality and pronouncements, as it did. for his food. Over the years the mobile became bigger and better and then when the fish market moved away from the Barbican to Coxside, he found a new pitch closeby Barbican Glass. Now the business resides in a smart, wooden shack. The food is as good as ever, it is friendly, you will be amply fed and still for a small price. You can get a piping hot cup of tea for 25p!

The Cap'n constantly raises money for charity. In fact it was because he was asked to raise some money for charity at the Barbican Regatta that Cap'n Jaspers came into being. He borrowed £200 from friends - since repaid - and built a D.I.Y hut 6'x12'. His rent was a tenner and electricity £1 per week. He had all sorts of disasters in his first ten years but eventually built a bigger and better hut. That lasted until it nearly came to grief when it had to be moved to make way for Barbican Glass. Even 12 Gun Crew + 29 Commando couldn't move it. It took the attending SWEB lorry to give it a helping tug!. One of the best things about the whole business apart from the money that has been raised for charity, and the very satisfied and well-fed customers, is the goodwill between Duncan Godefroy and the Sutton Harbour Company and The Cap'n. Until recently no lease existed and the business relied entirely on trust. Today, thankfully, for Cap'n Jasper's customers, there is a long lease!

It is worthwhile to tell you about a few of the many achievements of this remarkable man over the years. He organised with Rod North the first Barbican Trawler Race for 90 years, funded and arranged for the return of the famous Barbican tramp, Billy Hooper, to his native New Zealand, where according to the Cap'n, he has lived miserably ever since! He won the Plymouth Marketing award for 'Best Owner run Business'. Collected thousands of pounds for the Dame Hannah Rogers bungalow appeal. Taken part in many Lord Mayor's day parades. He sponsors Jacko's Junior Football Team and in his time as Chairman of the Barbican Traders Guild, he fought hard and long to keep Southside Street open to vehicles, against very strong opposition from Plymouth City Council and Devon County Council. A great personality, unafraid and not to be deterred when he believes his cause to be right. One of the great Barbican characters.

One of the most unexpected and delightful conversations I had on The Barbican was with Karen Ciambriello, the long time partner and lover of Robert Lenkiewicz. She amazed me when she told me she was well into her forties. Looking at her beautiful unlined face with its high cheekbones, and seeing the grace and elegance of her slim figure, she seemed still a girl. It was not until I was seated in her fascinating house in a small street off Southside Street, that I was able to accept her age. She pointed out to me a large painting by Lenckiewicz, of herself and her four children, and said that the boy depicted on one side of her was now 31. Her first husband died and left her with two young children and as she struggled to bring them up, she started to paint as an escape from reality. It was not until she met Robert Lenckiewicz and fell in love with him that her whole way of life changed. Now she has almost two families, one grown up and the other still at school age. Today she is preparing for an exhibition of her work which in essence describes her life with the great artist. Her work is warm, full of meaning and as some would have written a diary of their day to day life, so she has painted it. The result is stunning and portrays so clearly how she has felt in her Lenckiewicz years. She paints in the blue bedroom with its white covered bed standing on a small platform in one corner and which you reach at the top of a steep spiral staircase that leads directly from the living room.. While we talked, I sat on the bed and fed my mind with the fascination of everything around me. It is like no other bedroom one will ever see. It is immaculately kept, everything has a place and Karen's paintings are spread around her together with her brushes, her paints, her easel and with the paintings she does on blocks and makes up into framed pictures - probably not an accurate description but they show another side to this charismatic, self effacing woman.

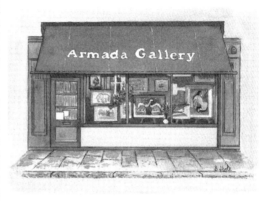

We chatted about her life today with Robert and this was an eye-opener. Here was a picture of the man renowned for his slightly austere looks, a renowned painter and philosopher. A man who has one of the most astounding libraries on philosophy housed in a chapel he has acquired close to the Barbican. Yet Karen paints a picture of him as a great family man, always understanding of his children - even if he is not known for his love of football - a man who is happy to come home, sit by the open fire in front of the television watching the soaps and eating baked beans! She also made me realise that Robert was a romantic at heart - albeit one who does nothing in the manner of anyone else. For example one evening he arrived and said to Karen. 'I am taking you out for dinner tonight.' Nothing unusual a bout that but as Robert does not drive and she acts as chauffeur, she was instructed to take the car. They drove for a while in the quiet of the evening and as darkness fell they arrived at the gates of a field. Karen was told to stop the car. They got out and all she could see ahead of her was an empty field with what looked like a white sheet a little way away in the distance. The sheet turned out to be a tablecloth on a table laid for dinner for two. There were flowers and candles and a selection of delicious foods. A lovely, unexpected romantic evening, albeit Robert had forgotten to tell her the mundane fact that they were eating out of doors and she might need a wrap!

Someone who knows Lenkiewicz very well is Sonia Donovan of the Armada Gallery in Southside Street just opposite another good, old fashioned pub, The Queens. Sonia displays Robert Lenkiewicz's large Oil paintings as well as many limited edition prints. He is a regular visitor to the gallery and every time he steps through the door his sheer aura seems to take over. A very remarkable man. Sonia is full of admiration for his ability to paint non-stop and still have time for others and an enlightening chat. Most of all though, she admires him for the way in which he has built, purely for educational purposes, one of the most extensive private libraries in the country. His philosophy library is quite breathtaking and there for the use of anyone who wants to study seriously. He never stops collecting and has an absorbing, almost obsessive love of books. His whole collection becomes the property of the City of Plymouth when he dies. Talking to Sonia I was made to realise just how much Robert Lenkiewicz means to The

Barbican. Not just as an artist, although that is a major reason for people visiting the gallery. He has to be one of Plymouth's major attractions. In the course of time the City is going to be so pleased - and grateful - that he lived in our midst. He is a man with strength of purpose, dedication to the welfare of The Barbican and its people, which has given help to so many 'Barbiconians' in a quiet, steadfast and unassuming manner. From a purely business point of view, tills ring in Barbican shops, cafes, restaurants and taxi firms whenever visitors come to see Robert's work. It would not be the same place without him. Sonia tells me that often overseas visitors are directed from her gallery to his and they come back saying that if they see nothing else it was worth coming to Plymouth for just that privilege. Whole books could be, and have been, written about Robert Lenkiewicz. I can only touch upon him lightly.

Sonia Donovan is another remarkable person who has for some years fought and never given in, to ill health. She is a respected Art Dealer with connections all over the world and her gallery is always filled with a galaxy of work by famous and would-be famous artists. Go in to the Gallery and you enter a world of beauty and romance, a place which is constantly busy and can have potential clients, temperamental artists and characters who live on the Barbican, all united in odd conversations. I love being there, it is inspiring at many moments but can be just like visiting your next door neighbour for a cosy chat. Whatever the content, the conversation is always interesting and frequently hilarious especially when Sonia or her staunch assistant Christine, are trying to persuade an artist to do what they want and on time. The latter is a very hard option. The Gallery is a living entity, full of subtle colour and exhibits which emphasise the superb number of West Country Artists, past and present. It is Sonia's enthusiasm, aligned with her vast knowledge, that has made the Armada Gallery so prestigious. Sonia will travel anywhere at a moment's notice in search of business for the Gallery and a buzz for her!

Working with Sonia Donovan in whatever capacity is never dull! For this reason joining her as 'Resident Artist', Len Norrish will find life lively, full of interest and will no doubt add zest to his already stylish paintings. He paints with the decision of a draughtsman and with the intrinsic skill and artistry of one who loves light and shade. His work is exciting, original in concept, colourful and pleasing to the eye.

I felt very privileged to have a painting done specially for my 75th birthday by one of Sonia's young artists, Mic Chambers, whose work has almost the feeling of the old masters. His colours are rich, the texture tangible and the subjects always very human. My birthday present from my three children, was of a madonna like mother and child - in fact Mic's wife and son. I treasure it and look at it every day. Sonia supports up and coming artists in the best possible way. She chivvies them, she advises them, she encourages them and she gets them known. A prime example is the constant help she is giving to Shirley Hole, who is painting, and will have painted all the illustrations in this book. This will be followed by an exhibition of Shirley's work in the Armada Gallery when the book is published. Liz Jones is another of Sonia's stable. Her work is fun, beautifully constructed and a pleasure to see. Karen Ciambrelli and Richard Clarke are two more I have written about in this chapter.

Sonia likes to specialise in 18th and 19th century watercolours but when you look at the work around her you realise how wide is her interest. Sonia came into the art world having been a bursar in a private school at Mothecombe. She was born in Oreston in Lucas Boatyard, I am told. Her parents were well known licensees for many years of The Royal Oak at Hooe, and her grandfather, a ferryman plying between Oreston, Turnchapel and the Barbican.

Her first venture was in 1985 when she opened a shop, called Connections, selling gifts, jewellery and paintings. Her ambition was to have a gallery where she could handle lots of large dramatic oils. This she has achieved and spending time in the Gallery with so much colour, strength and beauty around you is something not to be missed. As well as the Gallery she also found a small shop in Southside Street from which she now deals with Picture Framing.

An example of her acumen is the purchase of the whole collection of the works of Albert Bardsley, the water colourist, which was exhibited in Plymouth, Cawsand, London, Dubai and Beirut. These water colours have gone into some very good collectors' homes.

Alan Halliday, the Theatre Artist for the Royal Shakespeare Company also displays his work in the Gallery. Sonia has taken exhibitions of his work to Dubai, London and Beirut and when visiting the Caracalla family in Baalbeck. Prior to the pictures going to the Middle East, Vospers of Plymouth sponsored an exhibition in their showroom. Alan painted these pictures in Beirut whilst they were there in the Theatre dancing an Arabian version of Midsummer Night's Dream. She also exhibited his work in Plymouth's Theatre Royal, sponsored by T.C. Rolt when the RSC came on their first residency to Plymouth.

Sonia organised an exhibition of the private collection of David Shepherd in the Gulf to raise money for Arabian wildlife, particularly the Arabian Leopard. She obtained patronage of the deputy Ruler of Dubai, HRH Sheik Hamdam, HRH Prince Michael of Kent who flew out for the Gala dinner which Sonia organised for 500 people. Also in Dubai she exhibited a very fine collection of David Roberts R.A. in the Majis Gallery.

In November 1999 Sonia achieved almost the impossible. She organised artists from all over the world to make the journey to Dubai and once there to take part in painting the world's longest canvas, 10km. The artists came from London, Glasgow, Japan, Venezuela, Russia, France, South Africa, Australia. Oman and India. Once the canvas was stitched - a mammoth job in its own right - it had to be rolled out. As this was being done a sandstorm erupted and picked up one end of the canvas sending it spiralling out of control but Allah was watching and the day was saved - the storm subsided as quickly as it arose.

Sonia is an amazing lady with an enormous heart and a wish to help people. It is her efforts that have provided this book with its beautiful, worthwhile prints. Her warmth and appreciation of the needs of Plymouth's underprivileged children has made her work for many years for the Battisborough Trust and also with Cos Cosway who runs the Horizon Charity - more about him elsewhere..

The Barbican Gallery on The Parade is owned and run by Bill and Sheila Hodges And their son, Robert. Housed in an old Georgian warehouse which was converted in 1979, it is a treasure trove. The Hodges specialise in the sale of watercolours by living painters. The range also includes paintings by Gerry Hillman and Clem Spencer together with other Westcountry artists. One of whom, is a particular favourite of mine. His name is Nicholas St John Rosse and it is his ability to communicate a delightful escape from reality that is so appealing. He makes you feel good and on a grey day puts a smile on your face. I could become addicted to his paintings.

Brian Pollard, a doctor from the Midlands who made Plymouth his home some years ago, finds time to paint. His work is better than any medicine he prescribes! He has never had a painting lesson in his life but he has developed a remarkable style all of his own. The paintings are bright, cheerful and with that degree of simplicity that only the great can achieve. A painting of his is always a worthwhile investment.

Prints have become a part of life at the Barbican Gallery since they became members of the Fine Art Trade Guild. They publish paintings by artists whose work has a particular interest or appeal to people living, working or visiting the West of England. Much of the work load on this side falls on Robert Hodges. In his own right he is the agent for Beryl Cook's limited edition prints and books.

Bill Hodges is a mine of information about The Barbican. He is passionately aware of its constant need for preservation and upkeep. His enthusiasm fires the Barbican Traders into action whenever they feel threatened by some outside intrusion. The Barbican Gallery is always worth a visit both for its treasures and its artistic appeal and for a chat with Bill.

Two residents of the Barbican must never be overlooked. One is the venerable Crispin Gill, whose books on Plymouth have delighted readers for a long time, both for their beautifully descriptive content and for their enormous detail. He lives quietly in retirement now in an apartment just off Sutton Marina. The other is Chris Robinson who is both a writer and an artist whom you will find in New Street at Number 34 where he has a shop Plymouth Prints. This is a man to whom most Plymouth people, and many from around the world, have reason to be grateful. He evokes feelings of nostalgia amongst so many with his beautifully drawn pictures of Plymouth. His books written about the City are gems. Go into the shop and you will be thrilled with the hundreds of local views, framed and un-framed, and cards, all originating from his own pen. It seems fitting that a man with so much love for Plymouth, should be housed in a building which dates back to 1650.

New Street is full of interest and houses, and an eclectic mixture of businesses in old warehouses. I am particularly fascinated by the change wrought in what was The Green Lanterns restaurant, and is now a splendid Indian Restaurant. The food is excellent, the building, dating from the 17th century, is anything but Eastern and yet it has adapted itself to a totally different culture. A good place to seek out.

At Number 32 New Street you will find The Elizabethan House. A feeling of Elizabethan England touches your heart as you take in the oriel windows, the low ceilings, the roofs and floors of massive timbers. An old stairway winds round the weathered oak-mast of an old ship. As I climb up the stairs I am always reminded of a true story I was told by a man called Wynn Scutt, a keen historian, He told me that one day he was in the house waiting for a group of people. Never a man to stand idle he decided to climb to the top of the house. The early evening was still, there was no wind but as he approached a room at the top he could hear something creaking rhythmically. He could also feel the hairs at the back of his neck coming to attention! Quietly he slipped into the room expecting to surprise an intruder. He could feel a presence but all he saw was a low slung baby's cradle rocking gently to and fro. What had started it he never discovered. Unseen hands from the past maybe?

Do wander through the house and enjoy the beautiful fireplaces with pebble-patterned hearths. Maybe you will find the cradle still rocking. The narrow garden behind the house is planted with old English herbs and flowers and a cutting of rue from Shakespeare's garden. Sage, thyme, sweet scented balm, lavender, sweetbriar, golden rod and the simpler wallflower, all strive to reach up for the sun that shines down on this hidden treasure of old England.

Number 36 New Street is another old building which also has a delightful garden. It is the home of the Tudor Rose Tea Rooms. This is definitely a Tea Room and not a restaurant. It serves wonderful home-made cakes and scones in good old fashioned surroundings. On fine days you can sit out in the garden, enjoying the peace and the perfume whilst relishing a true afternoon tea. Inside the atmosphere is great and I especially liked one doorway which is made from an old ship's mast with a carving of a Tudor Rose on it. You may also be tempted by a filling all day Breakfast known as the Henry VIII. I am not surprised. Too much of this succulent fare and one could end up as large as the revered King. For those who keep to sensible diets the menu offers an array of super salads and there are also excellent toasted and open sandwiches.

Eating on the Barbican has a cosmopolitan flavour about it. In addition to the venues I have already mentioned one should not miss the opportunity to dine at Piermasters, a favourite haunt of the yachting fraternity or taste some of the best fish in town at Platters which is best described as 'earthy' in the nicest possible way. No frills, no pretension, just honest, well cooked fish served on platters. Delicious! Quieter is The Bella Napoli which is delightfully Italian and old fashioned with perfectly laundered napery, sparkling glass and attentive waiters. The food and the wine are Italian in essence and presentation. Every guest is treated with respect and deference. Presided over by Michael the Tailor, as he is known on The Barbican, this is dining at leisure at its best. If you are a lover of pasta then you cannot do better than go to the Barbican Pasta Bar almost next door to the Bella Napoli. Fresh pasta, delicate sauces and enormous helpings at sensible prices, are the hallmark of the restaurant.

The National Marine Aquarium at Rope Walk just off The Barbican is nothing short of spectacular and the realisation of a dream which filled the life of Doctor Geoffrey Potts who headed the old Aquarium and Laboratory. For years he had wanted to see a world renowned Aquarium with laboratories and teaching facilities. He had models and plans drawn up but at one time almost despaired of getting the required funding to achieve his dream. His story needs to be recorded for posterity.

I first met Geoffrey Potts when I was writing 'Invitation to Plymouth' in 1992. At that time a Plymouth Visitor Survey showed that the Aquarium attracted more repeat visits than any other facility, more overseas visitors and was of great appeal to young persons. It was owned by the Marine Biological Association (MBA) and Geoffrey was the Curator..

He devoted some twenty five years of his life to his work as a biologist and behaviourist, to the promotion of the MBA and the improvement of the Aquarium.

A man for all season is perhaps how I would have described this likeable man. Not because he was remotely like Thomas More, but because he had the ability to be all things to all people in the world of Marine Biology. His role demanded that he was centre stage most of the time, whether in the day to running of the then Aquarium or the world-wide part he played in the fight to conserve marine life. He donned many mantles, that of lecturer in far distant countries, as a provider of data for eminent scientists around the world and a host to the distinguished visitors who came to research a specific subject.

His deep commitment to his job was legendary. I suggested to him that he must wake up in the morning to find the adrenalin flowing immediately; his response was that the same adrenalin stopped him sleeping. A man of tremendous vision and courage, unafraid to tackle the world of commerce with his begging bowl in order to get sponsorship for his projects. He gained the respect of the top people in his own profession both here and abroad and with those in the world of commerce and industry who understood what he was trying to do.

Just after I had been to see him in 1992 he was awarded grants by the computer software firm Oracle UK and the Fisheries Society of the British Isles. This was to pay for a complex database that would provide a full annotated list of Britain's estimated 330 species of marine fish. This has added even more prestige to the Institution which is seen as a world leader in marine science. The fish database is a valuable research tool and of great interest to researchers from home and abroad as well as the UK fishing industry. Experts find it an indication how the seas around Britain are affected by global warming. As we know from the news, fish have been found in our waters which are usually found in warmer seas.

You probably do not know, anymore than I did, that the scientific work carried out in the Marine Laboratories in Plymouth has produced no less than seven Nobel Prize winners since 1888. What an achievement and what a good reason that it should continue as Geoffrey Pott's dream is realised. No comparable facility exists in Europe, so what an opportunity has been given to Plymouth.

Geoffrey Potts also saw the National Marine Aquarium, built on the Coxside land, providing and increasing spending in the city of some £10 million a year. The creation of between 728 and 1118 jobs directly and indirectly, new roads and a catalyst for a regeneration programme. He knew that in Aquaria around the world wonderful results were being achieved and that each one had produced significant social, cultural and economic benefits without there being a down side. All of this added substance to Geoffrey's dream. His dream has come true in parts and even now new extensions are planned for Plymouth's own National Marine Aquarium.

I remember asking Geoffrey Potts what would it take to build and operate such a project? First of all it cannot be done without an army of biologists to keep the livestock in good condition. Plymouth provided this. Secondly it would have to be in a recognised centre of excellence. Plymouth was that centre because Plymouth qualified with its Marine Biological Association, the Plymouth Marine Laboratory and the University of Plymouth with its extensive marine interests. It had to be sited somewhere that would attract visitors and again Plymouth qualified with its strong maritime tradition and historic links going back to Sir Francis Drake, the Armada and the Pilgrim Fathers. It must not be in a backwater. Plymouth is dynamic and right at the heart of the United Kingdom's largest tourist region from which the primary market for the National Marine Aquarium comes. Finally Geoffrey believed that no other attraction would entail such a mix of cultural prestige, international research, educational excitement, genuine quality and straightforward crowd-pulling appeal as the National Marine Aquarium.

Eventually the funding became available and the plans started to materialise as buildings. It lives up to the dream. 'What will the public see?' I asked. 'First of all the building will be quite remarkable. It will have the drama of a modern theatre with the servicing complexity of a chemical factory. The building will be of such architectural merit that even Prince Charles would happily except. It will also be designed with care to retain synergy with the Barbican and the foreshore position.'

Our discussion continued even further whilst we sat in Geoffrey Potts' tiny Dickensian office. We were talking about a vast megamillion project bigger than this country has ever seen, yet the telephone was constantly ringing whilst we were speaking and he was patiently answering queries from the public. What to do with a toad that had been abandoned was just one of the questions. He treated this as seriously as he did his dream project.

So finally this astonishing man has got his dream, or at least part of it, but he is no longer in the driving seat. Today Mike Leece, formerly the Managing Director of DML is the Chief Executive. A man who has the same drive and energy and who will continue to achieve the dream in its entirety.

The way forward came after much heartache and with the continued, unflinching support of the aquarium sub-committee consisting of Dr Michael Whitfield, Professor Anne Warner, Professor Mike Land and John Fry as well as Geoff Potts. The Devon and Cornwall Training and Enterprise Council came to the rescue in the mid 1990's and they together with the West Country Development Corporation provided a grant which enabled English Partnership to commission a further feasibility study into the funding opportunities. This was well received and led to an approach to Plymouth 2000 Partnership Ltd which resulted in the first major public sector funding from the Single Regeneration Budget. Soon to follow was the offer of grant aid from the European Regional Development Fund. The public sector recognised the value of the project, not just for its own sake, but as the catalyst to urban regeneration, increased employment and boosting the local economy. With such support and enthusiasm an approach, which proved successful, was made to Barclays Bank. The future of the National Marine Aquarium was now assured.

What does the National Marine Aquarium offer today? Firstly it is a stunning building standing proud in Rope Walk, linked to The Barbican and Coxside and with a stunning view of the water and the activity of the harbour ahead of it. Within the complex there are several magnificent viewpoints which put the Aquarium experience into context with the historic and natural surroundings of Plymouth. It's colourful literature says 'where truth is stranger than fiction'. A statement that brooks no argument.

In its first trading year the NMA attracted 475,000 visitors from throughout the UK and Europe. As a national facility, it is a significant addition to the infrastructure of the tourism industry in the South West, offering all year round entertainment and education of the highest quality.

Local people too play an important role in the life of the NMA as volunteers, members and customers. Approximately 2000 people have joined the Aquarium's membership scheme. In addition, many specialist groups are likely to become affiliated to the Aquarium, not least anglers, divers, fishkeepers and naturalists.

The National Marine Aquarium is a whole world of underwater learning which is designed to give the visitor an entirely new outlook on the underwater environment and the threats and challenges it faces. The breathtaking journey across the planet will reveal a strange and secret world that is both bizarre and beautiful, both wonderful and weird. Exploration will take you through stream and river, along the shoreline, across the reef and down into the deepest ocean. You come face to face with thousands of marine creatures, some pretty and peaceful, others sinister and deadly. An awesome wall of ocean 15 metres wide and five metres high, a shark theatre set in over 700,000 litres of water, the dazzling brilliance of the living coral reef, a seawater wave-tank and much, much more. It is a journey one never forgets, one of thrilling discovery. When you finish the journey, your mind will be full of all sorts of information; sharks for example can detect the tiniest drop of blood in seawater, enabling it to home in on its prey from a great distance. Seahorses pair for life and it is the male that gives birth to the young, often producing hundreds of babies at a time. Newborn trout can double their weight in three weeks, some species reaching an adult weight of up to 16kg.. equivalent to 16 bags of sugar!

To get the very best out of your visit to this superb aquarium, take your time. Maybe after a while you will want a rest. The café on the Quay which overlooks the Barbican and Plymouth Sound, is the ideal place to relax before you go back to take another look at the sharks or the myriad of exotic sea creatures. The only people I have ever known who have not enjoyed a visit here, have been those who just walked through, glancing around them as they went. Inexplicable!!

Education facilities feature prominently in the life of the NMA. Throughout the school year children come here not only to visit but to be taught in the classroom, by an Aquarium Teacher. The variety of themes incorporated in this world of underwater learning, ties in with the key areas of the National Curriculum. The NMA team have special evenings for teachers. If schools are planning a marine based topic and need some ideas for arts and craft activities then the Aquarium can supply a member of staff with extensive experience of arts projects to organise and lead a creative day in school. Themes can be tailored to suit the needs of children and can be adapted to suit all ages.

Barbican Rooftops

At a later stage in education the National Marine Aquarium is an ideal case study for students of business and tourism covering many issues relevant to the leisure and tourism industry today. During a visit students are given an insight into this unique operation. The visit begins with a slide show outlining the origins of today's aquarium and explaining how it was funded and developed. This is followed by a guided tour, focussing not on the fish but on the business itself. Students meet the staff and have plenty of opportunity to ask questions. They are also provided with several information sheets to take away.

Away from education the National Marine Aquarium offers superb facilities for corporate events, whether it is entertaining clients or rewarding staff. The venue is unique, innovative and superb. It is available all year round for receptions, dinners, meetings, presentations, product launches, shows and exhibitions.

It was one of Plymouth's greatest moments when the National Marine Aquarium came into being. A dream realised for Geoffrey Potts, fought for with much the same spirit as Drake, Grenville, Raleigh and Hawkins in Elizabethan times, and how appropriate that it should have its setting on The Barbican.

Cap'n Jasper's by Liz Jones.

Sadly, after this book was finished, Cap'n Jasper, John Dudley, died. His character and enthusiasm will be sorely missed on Plymouth's Barbican *(Author)*.

The Barbican Fishermen 2000
by
Robert O. Lenkiewicz.

Phoenix Wharf-Turnchapel-Oreston Ferry.

Tinside, Plymouth.

The Pier, Plymouth.

40

The Old Fishmarket – Albert Bardsley 1912-1990. In the Crispin Gill collection.

Duke of Cornwall Hotel.

Chapter III

Hotels, Guest Houses, Restaurants and Pubs

The sweet smell of success emanates from Plymouth's premier hotels and almost all of them have something special to talk about. One of the interesting factors I have discovered unfolds as you discuss the wedding scene. In every case it is reported that the size of wedding receptions has shrunk from 150 guests down to 50 or sixty and each reception is almost invariably followed by an evening party for a bigger number. It is not that 'small is beautiful' but comes down to the more mundane matter of cost. Weddings are not cheap. Many of the hotels are now licensed to hold the marriage ceremony which is an added bonus; everything can take place in the hotel cutting out the anxiety of transporting people from the church or registry office and creating a cohesive atmosphere for the big day. These venues are especially popular with second time marriages. About the only hotel which cannot hold a licence is the dignified Grand Hotel standing right on Plymouth Hoe. The reasons are simple; this delightful old hotel simply doesn't have the space to accommodate the event and it has no means of adding additional accommodation to achieve the stringent rules laid down. I had no idea that if you wish to hold such a licence you must have a special room set aside which will not be used for any other purpose than the ceremony for at least three hours on either side of the hour of the marriage.

In point of fact this does not prevent people from using The Grand for wedding receptions, quite the contrary. Plymouth Registry Office is just around the corner and the city centre churches just down the road. Assuredly they would not find a more beautiful position with Plymouth Sound stretched out ahead of them and inside the hotel the modern touches marry happily with the old atmosphere. The restaurant leading out to the enclosed terrace is one of the prettiest anywhere with its soft pink and green colour scheme and a profusion of greenery everywhere. Talking to Janet Powell, the Sales Executive, I learned of the time and care spent making sure that every wedding comes up to the expectations of the bride and groom. From the food to the music and dancing, to dispensable cameras on the tables for guests to take photographs, or perhaps an arrangement of balloons from Celebration Balloons a company I will tell you about later. Every small detail is taken care of and innovative ideas suggested to the wedding party. Special occasions like birthdays and anniversaries are regularly held in the hotel. Plymouth people have discovered what a super place it is to hold something that one wants to be memorable. Mark you everything about the Grand is well organised and the fact that it can only claim 3 stars does not justify all that it has to offer. The reason that no more stars can be awarded is because they do not have lifts to all floors and there are no Leisure facilities. In a hotel built almost three centuries ago and with no room for expansion, it would be impossible to add these requirements. What is so nice about the hotel is that every beautifully furnished bedroom is different, every corridor has an unexpected turn and from the moment you enter the hotel you are aware of its majestic proportions, its warm atmosphere and its attentive, friendly staff.

This beautiful building stands a mere bowl's throw away from where Sir Francis Drake played his famous game. It was built in 1879 by John Pethick who was also the first owner of the hotel. It has known two setbacks in its time; the damage done by the German Luftwaffe in 1941 and the severe shock to its system when it was taken over by the Berni Group who did their best to destroy its character. Fortunately they did not stay too long. It is now under the expert managership of Andy Thomas and is a credit to Plymouth.

The Grand is a hotel which attracts many overseas visitors who love its ambience and are mesmerised by the glorious views over the sea. It offers excellent weekend breaks which frequently include interesting activities. Supper dances with live music are regularly held on Saturday nights. It is also very popular with people coming to Plymouth on business.

I have always wondered what the politician William Ewart Gladstone had that few others of his ilk ever achieved. Whatever it was he was capable of drawing 100,000 people to Plymouth Hoe in 1889. By this time he was a frail, old man of eighty, serving as Prime Minister for his third term in office and enjoying a stay at the Grand Hotel. A crowd gathered on the Hoe getting as close to the hotel as possible. Some of them would have heard him address a meeting in the Drill Hall earlier in the evening and they wanted to hear more. Finally Gladstone came out onto the balcony of The Grand, on a cold, wet November evening and spoke to them. Whatever he said must almost have gone unheard for there were no such things as microphones or Public Address Systems. His voice would have carried on the wind and been passed along from one row of people to another almost like Chinese whispers. Imagine our current Prime Minister, Tony Blair conjuring up that size audience anywhere let alone Plymouth Hoe on a winter's night.

The best site on The Hoe is where you will find The Post House. I cannot pretend to like the building but the views from the windows are unsurpassed. There is nothing I like better than sitting in the lounge overlooking the patio and beyond to the glory of Plymouth Sound. In recent years the hotel has suffered hugely from the upheaval caused by Granada's take over of the Forte Group. No one could make up their minds about what was to become of the hotel. Rumours of its imminent sale disturbed the staff and the hotel began to look run down, tired and unloved. Now I am delighted to report, the hotel is not to be sold, money is to be spent on it and it is to have a whole new look on the ground floor with a new bar, a sense of continuity as you enter the hotel. New conference and meeting rooms will replace the existing bar and upstairs ten new bedrooms are to be added on - not newly built but opening up rooms that are currently closed. The first floor restaurant will take on a more dominant role and, as always, it will be one of the most popular places in Plymouth for weddings. The hotel will carry on its tradition of offering excellent value breaks for visitors and a very commercially viable rate for business people coming to the city. The news of the investment in the hotel seems to have put a spring into the step of the staff and I look forward to seeing the reborn hotel.

Just a short way away and also looking over Plymouth Hoe with magnificent views beyond to the sea, is Plymouth's largest hotel The Moat House. Modern in design and without the character of The Grand, it nonetheless has a warmth and welcome internally that endears it to everyone who stays here. It is a favourite stopping place for the many tours which come through Plymouth, usually bringing Americans and frequently Germans. Much money has been spent recently in the refurbishment both of the public rooms and the bedrooms. Visitors love the spacious bedrooms, which have all the extra touches provided by a first class hotel. There is an excellent restaurant which offers them not only exceptional food but unsurpassed views as well.

Throughout the year The Moat House is host to many Conferences both big and small. Their function rooms are equipped with everything any company or delegate could wish to have. The service is efficiently and quietly carried out and the whole environment is conducive to listening and learning. There are rooms specially designed for smaller meetings as well and these are frequently used for parties, dinners, wedding receptions, christenings and any other special occasion one can think of. Attention to detail is one of the hallmarks of success at The Moat House.

I have been there on many occasions for big and small parties and in recent years have enjoyed a beautifully presented meal and a very good evening out.

One of the excellent improvements in The Moat House is the Leisure Centre which is well equipped, has a great swimming pool, sauna, gym and much more. It is managed by Dave Thomas and his staff whose expertise helps members and guests to make the very best use of the equipment. They will work out a routine for you if you are a member, or ensure guests, who have free use of the Leisure Club, use the equipment safely.

The Moat House has acquired that welcoming atmosphere that is sometimes missing in an hotel of this size and is a really happy place in which to stay. Some Australian friends of mine have just been visiting Plymouth, one of the many places they were visiting in their whirlwind tour, and they could not speak highly enough of the way in which they were greeted, treated, fed and housed.

Plymouth is very lucky in having such a varying array of hotels. Anyone with a sense of history could not fail to appreciate the turreted and castellated Duke of Cornwall Hotel in Millbay Road. The one time Poet Laureate Sir John Betjeman described The Duke as one of the finest buildings in Plymouth. It is definitely different both on the outside and within. Entering it you  are aware of a sense of well being. It has that almost intangible aura of the past with its magnificent proportions, the superb, sweeping grandeur of the staircase. The bedrooms are charming, the old blending happily with the modern requirements of today's travellers. The Duke is much loved in Plymouth and is the venue for many weddings. Almost every Saturday you will see the red and white striped awning up over the steps leading into the hotel awaiting the arrival of the bride and groom. Inside they will find a superbly organised reception in a flower filled room, with food that delights every palate. In the evening the ballroom will be alive with the sound of music and the fun emanating from happy guests enjoying every minute of the couple's memorable day.

From the glamour of a wedding to the more mundane matters of business meetings and conferences. The Duke provides an excellent service for the business community who have long recognised the hotel as a place to be if they want quiet efficiency and sufficient comfort to encourage delegates to absorb the content of the conference or meeting.

The Duke of Cornwall is situated close to the City Centre and within striking distance of Millbay Docks where Brittany Ferries' ships tie up. About sixty years ago the trade would have been very different. The hotel catered for people arriving in this country from the States and Europe on the liners that called in to Plymouth to disembark the famous and the immigrant. On top of the building there is a look out from which the hall porters used to watch for the arrival of those great colossi of the ocean, the Queen Mary, Ile de France, Normandie, Mauretania and a host of lesser known passenger ships. The moment a ship was sighted it was helter skelter for the porters down to the docks, complete with trolleys to await the arrival of the tenders bringing the passengers ashore. It was then their task to suggest - or perhaps fairly forcibly put across the idea -that the Duke of Cornwall was the best hotel in town for people to stay . The hotel must have seen more baggage with stick on labels from across the world, than anyone can imagine. The aeroplane was a thing of the future whilst these great ocean liners ruled supreme.

In addition to the business from the sea, it was also built to cater for the increasing number of people travelling by rail. It was advertised as such in one of its earliest brochures. 'It possesses the great advantage of being close in proximity to the Millbay Terminus of the Great Western Railway and also being within a short walk of the Great Western Docks, where the ocean liners embark and disembark passengers and merchandise from all, parts of the world.'

Millbay Station was situated directly opposite the site for the hotel and was built in 1849. It was nicknamed the 'Shabby Shed' although if it still existed today it would probably be considered a unique and ornate building. The stone pillars from its entrance have now been incorporated into the Pavilions which stands opposite the hotel.

Reading the records of the hotel you can see that when the need for the hotel was first recognised, a group of railway officials were appointed as the original Board of Directors and selected 'Honest John' of Messrs Hall and Pethick to construct this large and luxurious building. The cost totalled £40,000 including the excavation work required to clear the site where The Saracen's Head Public House and Millbay Grove Terrace then stood. The hotel's function rooms are still named after some of the men originally involved in the design and running of The Duke of Cornwall. Looking at the price of £40,000 for the construction of the whole imposing building and then looking at the cost of £60,000 for simply putting up scaffolding today to clean the front, one realises the enormity of difference in money nowadays. A third more for scaffolding than for the whole hotel - frightening isn't it?

More differences in cost shows up when one looks back through the first minute books written in 1862. Bed and Breakfast seven shillings and sixpence or 37p in today's money. A cold bath would cost you a shilling and your dog, an expensive item, at three shillings and sixpence a day. The manager however was supremely well paid at £125.00 per annum.

Few of the places of interest advertised in the early brochures have altered. The Barbican, Burrator Reservoir, Eddystone Lighthouse, Mount Edgcumbe and the

Dockyard were all featured together with Plymouth Pier and its Pavilion which came to an untimely end in the 1940s.

My greatest memory of the hotel is of the daily lunches enjoyed by myself and my Bank of England colleagues who were all sent across from the Bank during the war years to have lunch. We were well cared for and welcomed the break. Even then the service was good and the food, though restricted by the necessity of rationing, was as appetising as any food during those tough times. I wonder how many people even remember that the Bank of England had a branch in the city! More of that later.

Jeremy Palmer is the General Manager of the hotel. He spent some time in the hotel in his early days as a Manager, and then took off for pastures new, only to return when he was offered by new owners, the opportunity to take on the task of bringing the Duke of Cornwall back to its rightful place in Plymouth. A task he has relished and the results shine out as the hotel goes from strength to strength.

Close to the Duke is The New Continental which is an establishment playing an important role in the city. It caters for business people and largely for tours, offering good, comfortable accommodation at reasonable prices. It has become a popular place for weddings and has lively bars, one leading to the entrance to Plymouth Pavilions, home to ice skating, swimming, concerts of all kinds and a great meeting place. My greatest memory of the hotel stems from the owners, the Greek Cypriot family Hajiyiani who have long been associated with anything to do with catering and leisure in the city. The founding father, Steve Hajiyiani was respected by everyone. It was he who first took the family into the hotel business, which today, after his death, is still family run and family owned. The memory in question was the wedding reception of the daughter of my best friend who married the son of Steve Hajiyiani's sister. It was a day of great joy and celebration in true Greek fashion. Music, laughter, the pinning of money on the bride and groom all made it memorable and whenever I have had occasion to enter the hotel since, it has always reminded me of the warmth of that occasion and it is a warmth which is, I am sure, extended to everyone who stays here.

In the very centre of the town at the top of Western Approach and close to Plymouth Station is The Copthorne. No one could call it architecturally pleasing but once inside it has an air of well being, somewhere that makes you feel at ease. It is efficient, capable of catering for people at any level. The hotel is part of a major group, each hotel having a different character but offering throughout a standard of service that is hard to beat. It attracts custom from the United Kingdom and from Europe. It is the ability to answer the needs of different nationalities that has made it such a success in Plymouth. Interesting and famous people stay here. Two different stories about staying in the Copthorne have stayed in my mind. The first was when the hotel received a booking from France. It was from a coach party touring the gardens of Devon and Cornwall. Nothing very strange about that but when the guests arrived the staff soon realised it was very different! The coach party consisted mainly of millionaires including the Baron de Rothschild! The guests were charming and no trouble but in an unexpected way they stretched the hotel to its limits. Everyone one of them wanted breakfast in their rooms at exactly 8.15am! Imagine that number of breakfast trays! Needless to say the order was carried out on time, as one would expect.

The second tale is about the Royal Ballet Company when they stayed. They dined late, they rose late and needed a great deal of pampering. Delightful to have them - and prestigious - but a strain on almost every department in the hotel.

47

On the Plympton side of Plymouth there are three very different hotels. The first is The Novotel at Marsh Mills where the excellent, efficient and charming hotelier Iain France is at the helm. In keeping with the first class staff training which is the hallmark of Novotels anywhere in the world, it runs as smoothly as clockwork and over the years it has grown a personality of its own which was sadly lacking in its early days. Now it has warmth and charm and a reputation for providing food and first class accommodation at realistic prices. Its situation, just off the Expressway, makes it a popular rendezvous for business people, a great stopover for visitors going deeper into Cornwall and a super base for those who simply want to explore all that Plymouth and the surrounding areas have to offer. To reach it as you come into Plymouth you take the slip road at Marsh Mills roundabout off the A38 marked City Centre and then take the third exit signposted Plympton. The entrance to the hotel is almost immediately on your left.

It is probably a compliment to General Manager, Iain France that his staff stay in their jobs for some number of years, only changing when promotion or opportunities within the group arise. Opportunities come thick and fast with Novotel opening more and more hotels worldwide. Glasgow and London were to open shortly when I met with Iain France in July. Novotel is part of the French Group Accor which also owns Carlson Wagonlit and is one of the World's largest Hotel Companies.

This is the third time that Iain France has come back to the Novotel and each time it has been a time of exciting growth. He confirmed my earlier findings that weddings were getting smaller in size, largely down to cost. More couples were opting for smaller receptions and bigger evening parties. He also told me that a large part of the hotel's business comes from conferences and small meetings for which the hotel is well equipped with all the modern equipment required. With 100 bedrooms the hotel can accommodate a large number of delegates.

One of the most buzzing establishments I have come across in a long time is The Elfordleigh Hotel Golf & Country Club at Colebrook, Plympton where the ebullient Tam McHale is the General Manager. He arrived direct from the Royal Naval College at Dartmouth and has brought to the whole place a sense of excitement, wellbeing and motivation that is evident immediately. This is helped by having a brilliant assistant Margaret Stone, a redoubtable and very capable lady who apart from the many other things she has done was once Mayor of Totnes. She is the Marketing and Sales Manager as well as being Tam's right hand.

Elfordleigh is now owned by a private individual who is prepared to invest millions in making Elfordleigh one of the finest Hotels and Country Clubs in the country. He is aided by the fact that the hotel stands in wonderful grounds and is encompassed by superb scenery. 16 new bedrooms are being added, making 34 in all, the golf course is being extended to 18 holes as opposed to the existing 9 hole course and a whole new Leisure Complex is being built which will include a super swimming pool with a separate pool for children, sauna, two spas, steam room, fully equipped gymnasium, dance studio, beauty therapy, hairdresser and solarium. There will be two tennis courts, a jogging track and a children's outdoor play area.

Stay at Elfordleigh and all these facilities are included in the price. For those who live in the Plymouth area what a heaven sent opportunity to join a thriving club and enjoy all it has to offer which will include social events. For golfers the course is well-designed and sufficiently challenging to please the most experienced and the beginner. Tam McHale tells me that football teams have discovered the pleasure of staying at Elfordleigh. When I was there Birmingham City were arriving the following evening for a week's pre-season training which would include the use of the Leisure facilities and diets as required by the Manager. This also applies to teams coming to Plymouth to play Plymouth Argyle. They arrive on a Friday night, have a meal which is a mixture of fish, chicken and pasta - definitely no chips. Breakfast is substantial but nothing fried and lunch before the match is chicken and pasta. The only thing one has to worry about is that if they are too well cared for they may beat Argyle!!

On the domestic side, the panelled Churchill Restaurant with its adjoining conservatory is such a delightful place in which to enjoy the superb food prepared and presented by a Chef who was part of the Royal Yacht Britannia and now, with his team, adds his skills to the Elfordleigh for everyone to relish. The Bars are busy and on a warm day sitting out on the terraces enjoying a drink has to be one of life's more pleasureable experiences.

Licensed for weddings, which are performed in the Conservatory, Tam and his staff have achieved almost perfection in the management of these important occasions. Everything is planned down to the last detail and most Saturdays there are two weddings taking place in the hotel and usually one mid-week as well.
Sunday lunch is a Carvery and served in one of the function rooms, allowing families to enjoy a great meal at a give away price - as I write in July 2000 the price is £4.95.
I cannot think of a better way of spending a Sunday, well fed and in beautiful surroundings.

I found it exhilarating to be among such motivated and dedicated people who had success written all over them. One wonders what the Langmead family who originally owned the old house would make of today's activity. They were a fascinating family in their own right producing three Mayors of Plymouth in the early 19th century one of whom, Philip Langmaid was also an MP for Plymouth.

Boringdon Hall is a magical place with a wonderful history. You reach it by taking the Plymouth Road towards Plympton at Marsh Mills, taking a left turn at Larkham Lane, just past the Unicorn pub, continue along Crossway and at the junction you turn left. You will find the drive into the hotel clearly marked on the left hand side as you climb the hill.

The small approach road lined with trees leads you to the house which was first mentioned in AD956 when Kind Edgar granted the manor of Boringdon and Wembury to St Peter of Plympton. Henry VIII granted it to his friend, the Earl of Southampton, in AD 1539 at the dissolution of the Monasteries. Ten years later the Earl sold it to the Duke of Suffolk, father of the ill-fated Lady Jane Grey. Queen Elizabeth I slept in one of the bedrooms in 1588 by which time the house had come into the hands of John Parker.

John Parker spent a great deal of time and money in restyling the house and on completion he gave one of the greatest banquets ever seen in this part of the country. His guest of honour was Sir Francis Drake who brought with him Sir John Hawkins, Sir Richard Grenville and Sir Walter Raleigh. There is no doubt that it was a magnificent occasion and one your imagination can conjure up when you dine in the

Gallery Restaurant which overlooks the Great Hall, where these famous men would have been so royally entertained. A later Parker commissioned the magnificent Coat of Arms of King Charles I which dominates the Great Hall to this day. The loyalty of the Parker family to the Crown lost them the ownership of the house during the Civil Wars.

Boringdon Hall has had many changes of fortune in the ensuing centuries, and even today, as I write, it is about to change hands once again. It must have been very expensive to run in Elizabethan times and this is still the case today. Much money has been spent on it in the last decade and more will have to be spent if it is to retain its grandeur. Nonetheless it is a delightful place in which to stay with modern comforts and luxuries the Elizabethans could not even have dreamed of. It is perfect for seminars and small conferences and excels as a romantic place for weddings.

Just as you enter the porch of Boringdon Hall, there is a little plaque to the right of the front door which says, 'Please take care and note the unevenness of the floor'. Floors that have been there since the day Boringdon Hall was first built. They would give a spirit level apoplexy but for me I simply love the history emanating from the building.

I have to admit to being biased in favour of Kitley House Country Hotel and Restaurant at Yealmpton. This is for two reasons. The first is that it is a house I have known since my childhood days when the Bastard family lived there as they had done for centuries. In my day it was Colonel Reggie Bastard and his wife Lulu who were in residence. Two charming, if eccentric people, much loved by their friends. The house, Nicholas Pevsner tells you in  his book 'The Buildings of England - South Devon' 'is one of the earliest in England showing a sympathetic approach to the Tudor style. The House is not specially imaginative or fanciful in its detail but exquisitely set off by the freshwater lake in front separated by a dam from the creek'. In Reggie Bastard's time Kitley was full of wonderful antiques, superb silver and a comfortable, well loved, well-lived in atmosphere. My second reason is that I am an admirer of the talents of Andrew Huckerby. Having become an hotel, Kitley had a rough ride in its early days when nothing seemed to go right but in the last few months it has been under the slightly unorthodox but highly successful management of Andrew Huckerby whose ability to take any hotel out of the doldrums seems to be his stock in trade. Most of us will remember him a few years back as the General Manager of the Moat House when he took that ailing establishment by the scruff of the neck and left it shining brightly. He achieved the same success with a hotel in The Crescent in Bath amongst others and then having searched for a hotel in the Plymouth area he came across Kitley quite by chance. It was a lucky day for Kitley but beneath the genial, welcoming bonhomie of this out of the ordinary hotelier, one knows that it is far more than a friendly approach

50

that makes a hotel shine, especially one that had acquired an appalling reputation for its food and its service. Andrew is a man who is not afraid to roll up his sleeves and get stuck in and this is exactly what he has done at Kitley. Now the hotel is vibrant. Its rooms are full most of the time and the functions diary shows bookings for balls, parties, wedding receptions, meetings, dinners, in fact every occasion you can think of, stretching way into 2001.

Inside the hotel there is an immediate warmth in its welcome. The outstanding feature is the magnificent staircase with its 18th-century oak carpentry, the diverging flights, the hanging balusters, three to each step, two of them spiral and one fluted. The bedrooms are charming, immaculate and each is furnished differently. The restaurant which is housed in the library of the old house, has character and is conducive to the enjoyment of good food and wine from a well stocked cellar. Morning coffee, afternoon tea, a casual drink..they are all on offer and overall is the beauty of the surrounding grounds which have a well-ordered wild look! This summer has seen many outdoor occasions including a barbecue for 1000 people. Last summer Kitley hosted 'Seascape' in the grounds. A concert performed by the Royal Philharmonic and solo artists; a superb evening out. One wonders what Kitley will give us next. Somehow I feel that Andrew Huckerby will get itchy feet and want to tackle something bigger. I wish he might tackle my bete-noir, the Post House on Plymouth Hoe and turn that architectural monstrosity into the sort of seafront hotel that would be the envy of Europe. It could be done but it would need the Huckerby energy, vision and imagination - and a lot of money. Meanwhile do not miss the opportunity of going to Kitley which is only about 15 minutes from the city centre and is a place in which to recharge lethargic and worn batteries.

Going back to Nursery days you will remember the well-loved nursery rhyme 'Old Mother Hubbard'. This was written by Sarah Catherine Martin whose sister married Edmund Pollofox Bastard, MP for Totnes in the late 18th century. Sarah wrote the rhyme when she was staying with them and got her inspiration from the servants' quarters below stairs. Here the Kitley housekeeper had her sitting room and this is where the cupboard referred to in the rhyme is situated. Sarah sent her manuscript to John Harris, a London publisher of children's books. And as we know, it has remained a firm favourite since and hardly a year goes by without a new issue being printed.

Sarah Martin was one of the loves of William Henry who became William IV. Had she accepted his proposal of marriage in 1785 when she was 17 years old she might have become Queen of England and her children would have taken precedence over Victoria who would not have come to the throne and so the whole course of history would have been changed.

On the edge of Dartmoor is The Moorland Links Hotel near Yelverton. One of the things I have taken great pleasure in over the years is the increasing beauty of the gardens here. Perhaps not the most obvious reason for visiting a hotel but in this case it certainly adds to the pleasure of staying here. The lawns, the richness of the colour of the shrubs intermingled with the brilliance of roses and poppies, makes a perfect stage for the hotel and has the added beauty of Dartmoor behind it as the backdrop. This is an hotel which has been embedded in the life style of Plymouth albeit it that it is a little way out of the city on the Plymouth to Yelverton road. You come to it about halfway from Roborough to Yelverton where you will see a sign telling you to turn off. It is a little way down this moorland road.

For me it is a place of nostalgia. During the war years and immediately afterwards I used to come here with my friends on a Saturday night when it's atmosphere was club like and we all knew one another. It was a place of fun and enchantment where the blinds were drawn keeping out the ravages of war. Evening dress was de riguer and in spite of the necessity for clothing coupons to purchase anything to wear, all the girls managed to find sufficient to buy pretty dresses that were a foil to the uniformed men. Frequently the dresses were made from gowns worn by their mothers and grandmothers, or even from materials found in the attic, old damask curtains or chintz that had lain mothballed in trunks for years. Sometimes one dined there, sometimes we just went to dance to the music of the much loved Frankie Fuge and his band. Romance was always in the air, accentuated no doubt by the urgency of war. These were nights when we firmly shut out the thought that the very next day some of these men and women, would be sailing or flying into battle, perhaps never to return.

Sixty years later much has changed as the hotel has been brought up to the requirements of the 21st century but not its intrinsic charm. The foyer has not changed much in all those years apart from beautiful new carpets and impeccable décor, the ladies cloakroom still reminds me of the shared secrets when the girls got together to powder their noses. Gone are the small sitting rooms that filled the space from the reception desk to the dining room and ballroom. Now there is a beautifully appointed restaurant immediately to your left looking out over the manicured lawn fringed with oak trees, and leading onto the ballroom. The ballroom has recently been refurbished and has a delightful bar added on. Ideal place for private parties and wedding receptions. Talking of which The Moorland Links now has a licence for Civil Weddings and what could be a better venue. It has everything and nowhere could produce a more romantic setting for photographs. Every bride and her anxious mother can leave all the details to the hotel and everything will be carried out in an efficient way that makes the day perfect.

One of my favourite places in the hotel is the Gunroom Bar to the right of the entrance. With its warm autumnal colour scheme and sofas and chairs that just insist you relax, it is an ideal spot in which to enjoy a drink, a bar meal or just relax with coffee.

The whole hotel has a cherished feeling about it and this is largely down to one man, Michael Jenkin who was General Manager here for thirty years and never lost his enthusiasm for the hotel or for the well being of the guests. In addition to being a highly respected manager, he has a talent for interior design, which is evident everywhere. You have only to look at the bedrooms to see this gift at work. Some of the beds are crowned with pretty drapes that match those at the windows, and nice pieces of furniture together with some pretty ornaments and comfortable armchairs, make the rooms very welcoming. Michael has now handed over the reins of management to Nicola Quinn, a talented lady whose friendly attitude aligned to her ability makes her a worthy successor. He, himself, is now in overall charge of the interior design of all the group's hotels.

As in many good hotels today, great emphasis is put on the facilities for conferences and seminars. There are special conference rooms and smaller ones for meetings. Irene Brown is in charge of this side of the business as well as weddings. She is a calm, efficient lady who has been at the hotel for fourteen years and seen much in the way of advancement when it comes to what is needed for business people today. Every piece of equipment is available, including a helicopter landing facility. One must always remember that Plymouth Airport is only five minutes away.

All sorts of people enjoy the Moorland Links. Frequently the visitor's book will show that the guests are business people relocating to Plymouth or down on business at one of the industrial estates which are a short drive away. If I had worked flat out all day, I can think of no more charming place to return to in the evening. The food is excellent - the restaurant has recently been awarded a Rosette, the wine list is intriguing and the staff are here to cosset you.

Business is by no means the only use for the hotel. Many people have discovered the excellent Leisure Breaks that are available. It is so relaxing here, and of course the surrounding countryside offers a variety of choice. You can play golf, walk across the moors, ride, visit historic Tavistock or Plymouth, take a look at Buckland Abbey, the home of Sir Francis Drake or just simply sit on the lawn and contemplate. I have discovered too that people from surrounding areas find that dinner here on a Saturday evening accompanied by a first class bottle of wine, or two, a stay overnight and a walk in the morning to blow away the cobwebs, is a perfect way to spend a weekend and the icing on the cake is a delicious, traditional Sunday lunch before returning home.

How many proprietors of small hotels can have two claims to fame other than that of running a welcoming, well-cared for 10 roomed hotel - not many. Keith de Bruin, the ebullient owner of Smeatons Tower Hotel on Grand Parade, Plymouth Hoe, is such a man. Sitting on the small patio in front of the hotel, enjoying coffee on a sunny June morning, I learned a great deal about this big man who has been so much a major player in the pub scene in Plymouth for many years. What comes over strongly is that he may not be a publican anymore but it is an industry he will love until his dying day. His friendly small bar in the hotel is a mecca for people who stay in the hotel - many of them here on business who love the informal attitude and the humour as they enjoy a drink at the end of the day. Keith is Chairman of the South West Region of the British Institute of Innkeeping, an organisation dedicated to making professionals of anyone coming into the business. Gone are the days when anyone could decide to become a publican, fulfilling a dream of being the owner of a pretty country hostelry. Today it is a profession requiring knowledge and skill as well as the essential bonhomie required in landlords and to achieve these standards, the British Institute of Innkeeping is there to assist.

Keith's second claim to fame is as the Good Samaritan in a tale of the sea. Plymouth has been the starting point for the single-handed Transatlantic Race and it was the Sunday night before the start of this year's race that disaster struck the trimaran, 'Spirit of Belgium' as she tried to enter Plymouth Sound at night and in strong winds. Sadly the boat foundered on The Breakwater and the two man crew sent out a Mayday signal. In the meantime the wife of one of the men who was booked into the hotel, rang Keith about midnight and asked for help. He immediately informed the Coastguard who said they had picked up the signal and rescue was at hand. Keith reported this to the woman and then took her and her small child firstly to the Mayflower Marina where the men were supposed to be landed and having discovered that was a wild goose chase they then set forth for the other side of the city and the Marina at Queen Annes Battery. Here amid relief and tears the husband was reunited with wife and child and the other man was profuse in his gratitude to the rescue services. Keith's part did not end there. The two men stayed with him and he provided them with clothing from his own wardrobe. All in a hotelier's night's work? Not really but that is the sort of guy he is. Something else I learned from him about the Transatlantic Race is that all competitors are allotted 'helpers/minders' who are at hand to assist when needed and one named Richard from Saltash was that man for the 'Spirit of Belgium' and certainly did his job well.

Its when you are talking to a man like Keith De Bruin with such a wealth of experience in the licensed trade that you pick up some amusing stories. He told me that quite frequently, when he is discussing people with his wife, he won't call them by name but for example 'Whipitquick' was the name for a drinker who used to come in almost every day with a carrier bag containing two empty screwtop Guinness bottles. He would order a beer, slap the empties on the counter, whip two new ones in the bag and before you could say 'Guinness' be gone. Hence he became Mr Whipitquick'

The De Bruins are a couple who make staying in their hotel a pleasure and enjoying a drink with Keith is to relish the drink and the flow of stories that go with it.

Also on The Hoe is The Bowling Green Hotel looking right over the Bowling Green, a place much loved by its members who can be seen playing there almost daily throughout the season. The Hotel is a tall, elegant building, kept immaculately by David and Paddy Dawkins. It is light and airy, prettily furnished and very comfortable. You can only get Bed and Breakfast here but with the wealth of eating houses in walking distance this does not pose any problem.

The house is very much alive but has that restfulness that is so important after a busy day. Equally it provides a stimulus for the day to come when you arrive downstairs after a good night's sleep, to sit in the attractive dining room awaiting one of the best breakfasts in Plymouth.

Many visitors have made The Bowling Green their second home whenever they come to the city. People appearing in the Theatre Royal for example find it ideal. Nobody fusses them or remonstrates when they get up late. The Dawkins both have friendly natures touched with a keen sense of humour, making them so easy to get on with.

Plymouth has a wide selection of places to eat and at varying price levels. Some I prefer to others, some because of the standard of their cuisine, and some because the atmosphere is right, relaxed and friendly.

Tanners is a restaurant tucked away in the Prysten House in Finewell Street. Owned and run by Chris and James Tanner it is a culinary experience in enchanting surroundings.

These two young men are refreshing to meet. They always cherished the dream from their very young days, that one day they would have a restaurant of their own. That dream became a reality on 17th July 1999 when Tanners opened its doors. Their vision was an affordable, exciting restaurant where they could develop their own individual style and concept. Fine food, fine wine and an ambience to match. They source the very best in local suppliers to ensure each meal is a memorable one. They make everything on site, fresh each day. Their backgrounds in the food world are synonymous with great restaurants in London, Bath, France and New York.

That explains their ethos but the rest of their story tells of the hard work, dedication, singlemindedness and a little bit of luck. The brothers hail from Kent and both started their careers at 12 years of age. After college they each moved into full time cooking and were able to benefit from training and working under the Roux Brothers at quality restaurants in England, France and the United States of America. Most recently Christopher Tanner was Head Chef at the Kitley House Hotel achieving 3 AA Rosettes within 14 months of his tenure. Meanwhile James Tanner was working at a fine 2 star Michelin establishment in Bath, Restaurant Lettonie. Their experience has been wide and varied

The Tanner brothers wealth of experience gained at home and overseas in top establishments combined with their skills, enthusiasm, flair and imagination have seen a most successful start to their own fine food restaurant which has already been awarded 2 AA Rosettes.

Fine food and wine are vital to a successful restaurant but the finishing touches come from the place itself and from the friendly,welcoming atmosphere that prevails. Chris and James instinctly know how to treat their clientele and that rubs off on their small, efficient staff. The icing on the cake comes from the good fortune the brothers had in acquiring a lease on The Prysten House which oozes history and provides a ready made atmosphere. It was built in 1498 of limestone with granite doors and windows, around 3 sides of a courtyard with the 4th side originally open and then enclosed by stables and in the 1890's by the addition of the Abbey Hall. The Abbey Hall now serves as the Parish Hall for Plymouth's mother church St Andrews, which dates back at least to the 8th century. St Andrews acquired the Prysten House in 1923 and instigated a mammoth restoration of the 3 storeys.   It was far luckier than the church itself which was destroyed by German bombers in World War II. The house suffered no damage at all.

Inside is the Bar Room with a massive tree mural on the remains of the old kitchen fireplace painted by local artist, Gary Ryan whose work continues to cover the walls of the bar and rest room areas with a sprawling, linked tapestry of vinery and ancient sayings which all adds to the unique ambience that is Tanners Restaurant. The Well Room has a fine water well which is one of the many limestone holes that provided water to Plymouth before Sir Francis Drake diverted water from the River Meavy and built his leat to bring water from Dartmoor to the reservoir on North Hill in 1591. The Prysten House makes a superb, intimate restaurant and at the same time remains a great example of domestic architecture of the medieval period.

In a very short time Tanners has become very successful and a mecca for Plymothians who enjoy the ambience, the good food, the excellent wines and the quiet service. The Tanner brothers are ambitious and have great plans for the future which include the possibility of a short term exchange between a first class American restaurant and themselves. That should be an interesting experience both for them and for Plymouth. They have also set about broadening interest in fine food, to develop a wider customer base and to use their innate acting skill. To do this they have started cookery demonstrations, which achieved immediate popularity and enabled many people to discover how to produce delicious meals in their own homes with a slight twist from the norm. This successful venture achieved local recognition when the Brothers were asked to demonstrate their skills at Plymouth EXPO 2000. If any television company reads this maybe it might suggest to them that a cookery programme called simply 'Tanners' would not come amiss. It would be both fun to watch and demonstrate how one can adapt restaurant recipes to home-cooking.

Young men like Chris and James Tanner deserve to succeed and Plymouth, gastronomically, is enhanced by their presence.

Across the road from Tanners, is an interesting bar/restaurant which has changed several times in the last few years. It was originally Rackham's Wine Bar, Pissarios and now The Deck. Run by the likeable chef Joseph, the food here is more than acceptable. In fact you will find the best Mez here; its only problem is that there is so much of it, that you need to make sure you take a doggy-bag with you. Good value and a pleasant friendly atmosphere.

There are two ethnic restaurants in particular which are outstanding for their cuisine and each undoubtedly successful. At the Baba Indian Restaurant, 134 Vauxhall Street, The Barbican, you will meet Baba Laskar who is a culinary legend in his own lifetime. You dine in the most comfortable circumstances. Not always the case in an Indian restaurant. Here the atmosphere is created by the rich panelled walls, deep red tablecloths, sparkling silver and gleaming glass, every table has small posies of flowers and in between there are large vases of lilies throwing off a delicate and refreshing scent. The long room is part of a building that is one of the oldest in Plymouth. Once you get to know Baba you begin to understand why his restaurant has such a good name. He spent many years learning his trade before he ventured into ownership. There is no job in the restaurant that he cannot personally undertake and will do, if the need arises. This keeps his friendly and efficient staff - some of whom are family - constantly on their toes as they see to the needs of customers.

Baba is well aware that with supermarkets selling all kinds of ready made Indian food or the ingredients from which to make a dish, he needs to stay ahead of the game. His creative mind is always thinking up new additions to the menu or a variation of something existing. The menu is wide ranging and invites you to taste the flavours that are as varied as the climate of India and as exotic as its people. Fragrant, pungent and warm spices, from the four corners of the country are delicately blended in meticulous proportions to create the dishes of your choice. Each dish will have its own distinctive flavour and aroma which cannot be produced from any Curry Powder but only from spices which have to be separately prepared each day afresh for each individual dish. The blending and preparation of spices is a centuries old craft, indispensable to Indian cuisine and one that Baba has perfected. It is no easy matter to select dishes from the menu - everything is tempting. If you find it difficult then Baba himself, possibly his grandson or another waiter, will happily recommend dishes to suit your taste and temperature! For wine lovers, the list is well chosen, the house wine very acceptable and the prices sensible.

On the first Tuesday in every month there is a 9 course banquet which once sampled would never be forgotten. There are two sittings, one at 6pm and the other at 9pm. Booking is essential. Sundays there is a family buffet from 12 noon to 4.30pm. There is also an excellent Take-Away Service with free delivery within four miles for orders over £10. It is easy to order either by telephone or on the Internet, another Baba innovation keeping up with the modern trend. The telephone number is 01752 250677 and the website www.babas.co.uk.

I expect by the time this book is published Babas will be able to boast 'Egon Ronay recommended'. I understand there were two inspectors there recently who thoroughly enjoyed their meal whilst they remained incognito. Whatever the accolade it will be well deserved. You will not get a better Indian meal in Plymouth.

A completely different but equally relaxed atmosphere is to be found in The Thai Palace, Elliot Street, The Hoe. There is something so attractive and elegant about the Thai people as a race, and that is evident in the grace and charm of Mrs Stanton and her family who run both this restaurant and the Thai Restaurant in Notte Street. Do not wonder why Mrs Stanton sounds so English; she acquired the surname when she married an Englishman! Whilst she still uses that surname that is the sole concession to this country. Once you enter the doors of the Thai Palace you are enveloped in the mystique of the Orient with all its fascination. The restaurant set in a fine old house, is the epitome of peace and the sense that nothing will be rushed. You order your meal from a selection of dishes which change regularly and are frequently dependant on what is available. The food is perfectly cooked and presented, the service smiling and silent. A wonderful place to enjoy an evening out.

Talking with Mrs Stanton who has been here for some years now but not always in Elliot Street - she once owned the Bangkok Palace at Yelverton - I found out how much easier it has become for Asian catering businesses to buy their requirements in Plymouth. Something I did not know is that there are two Asian Importers operating in the city. For ingredients that are still not available here, a journey is made to London once a month and enough to fill a van comes back to Plymouth for the two restaurants. I was equally interested to discover that the clientele in the two restaurants is totally different. The restaurant in Notte Street deals with passing trade, largely visitors, whilst the Thai Palace has its own regular patrons together with people who come from the hotels on the Hoe, usually business people working in the city. I wondered why they had taken on the restaurant in Notte Street when they were already so busy. The answer was simply that they wished to keep a good name for Thai restaurants and they also saw no reason to invite competition! Mrs Stanton has made many friends over the years but has little time to socialise. Like all Thais, she and her family are incredibly hard workers, putting the business before everything. It is probably this family unity and desire that makes the business so successful.

No one can say that Plymouth does not have a wide range of ethnic restaurants. Leaving the world of Thai and moving into the city centre proper Mayflower Street is the home of The Positano owned by two Italians. Luciano Constantin and Sabato Cinque from Positano on the Amalfi coast, near Sorrento, who came to England for six months to perfect their English, fell in love with the country and for almost thirty years have made Plymouth their home. Originally they worked for an Italian restaurant on The Barbican and then eight years ago took the bold step of starting their own restaurant. Unafraid of hard work, they have achieved a successful business, where the Italian influence is strong, and Pizzas are as close to the ones you would find in Italy as they can possibly be, Pasta is home-made and the various dishes on the wide menu are exciting and delicious. Their clientele are almost all regulars who have learned how good the food is and now seldom consult the menu because they would rather find out what the specials are for the day. It is not just for the food that people come here; they enjoy the friendliness of Luciani and Sabato, the lively personalities of the two girls who run the bar and the essentially intimate atmosphere of the restaurant. It is frequently difficult to get a table unless you have booked but the option of enlarging the restaurant does not appeal to the two men. They feel it would take away the intimacy and the personal touch. Commonsense prices both for wine and food have ensured that people can use the restaurant without it of necessity being a special occasion.

For the lover of Cuisine spontanee, there is no better place to lunch or dine than Chez Nous in Frankfurt Gate, where Jacques Marchal is Le Patron ably assisted by his wife, Suzanne. There are no obvious signs from the outside that this is a restaurant. Once outside the door you will notice a discreet sign tucked away proclaiming the restaurant's identity.

The interior is a pleasant discovery. Typically French, elegant, informal and friendly, a reflection of Jacques style of cooking. Jacques has been here ever since 1980. He had previously trained in his native country getting various culinary experiences under his hat. After a stint at the Café Royal in London he was ready for a change and chose Plymouth.

There is no leather bound, flamboyant menu to illustrate the selection of food available - rather a simple blackboard menu at the back of the restaurant. This is because cuisine spontanee is based on fresh, local produce, according to season and availability.

Jacques is a pleasant contradiction, typically gallic, with an arrogant charm and dry humour, yet without the 'snobbish' prejudices one might expect. He appreciates a personal regard for style but no one is condemned or judged by their manner or dress - only their appreciation of the meal once tried. Chez Nous provides the opportunity to try something different, to gently break local habits.

The 28 cover restaurant relies upon the business world for a large part of its trade. Jacques looks to them for approximately 10 covers at lunchtime and in the evening the theatre crowd is a popular market. He encourages his customers to eat as they please, possibly to enjoy a pre-theatre starter and to return at the end of the evening for their entrée. His approach works as the majority of his customers, approximately 70% from out of town, are repeat business who come again and again, introducing on occasion new converts. Indeed this has resulted in many a famous face from far and wide, sitting in discreet corners of the room, sampling and delighting in the food. No fuss is made and no publicity is sought - word of mouth is sufficient for the Marchals.

I have lunched and dined at the Trattoria Pescatore at 36 Admiralty Street, Stonehouse, for some years and never without appreciating its cuisine and ambience. I dined there again this summer on a quiet Wednesday evening in the company of my son and my eldest grandson. Rita Caligari, as always was there to welcome us, and offered us a choice of table in the intimate restaurant or in the passage leading to the courtyard garden. We opted for the passage which does not fairly describe its charm. It stretches down one side of the building and was once just open to the skies with rough unadorned walls and used for nothing else than a journey to the loos. Now it has a roof and the walls are decorated with hand painted flowers which look so real you can almost smell them and hear the breeze soughing through their leaves. There is a profusion of flourishing greenery which appears to thrive on the tantalising aromas of delicious food and hoping perhaps for a sip of Valpolicella or one of the excellent wines on offer. Had we been there at lunchtime we might well have decided to lunch in the small walled courtyard. Indeed on some fine evenings people do sit outside for pre-dinner drinks, and if it is warm enough, stay there to enjoy an alfresco dinner.

Piero Caligari is the chef/patron and his undoubted talents have never been better. Here is a man who has a delicate touch when he produces some wonderful sauces and seems to instinctively know when ingredients marry well. I started with Calamari accompanied by a light garlic sauce and then probably the best salmon I have ever eaten. It was perfectly cooked, wrapped in pancetta, unbelievably moist and served with an excellent salad. My son had the same starter but then chose one of the house pasta specialities, again with a superb sauce. My grandson ordered Parma Ham but was insistent it should not be accompanied by avocado and prawns - a more than generous plateful of Parma Ham appeared. His fillet steak was medium rare as he had ordered, tender and succulent and with saute potatoes completed the perfect meal for him. We drank a white house wine of a high quality and a sensible price. The evening was one of contented enjoyment in lovely surroundings with food that was memorable, service perfection and from the moment we stepped through the doors we felt welcome and cared for.

Trattoria Pescatore is just outside the centre of the city, close to the Ferry Terminal and almost on top of the river. Make a determined effort to go there. I promise you will not regret it.

Plymouth has, under the ownership of Andy and Helen Hobbs, two brilliant new places in which to indulge ones taste buds in the best coffee, the richest chocolate and a range of teas as well as enjoy light meals, rich cakes and other tempting delicacies. Both places are called Hobbs Chocolate and Coffee House. The first one was opened in Eastlake Street where passers by are constantly enticed inside by the simply elegant interior and the look of quiet, satisfied, contented expressions on the faces of the customers sitting at the attractive pine tables. The second is recently opened and is where Perillas Fish and Chip restaurant used to be, next door to the Positano in

Mayflower Street. Equally elegant and restful, it has a first floor which is spacious not only in size but in the amount of room between every table. It has sofas and armchairs into which one can sink. The colours of the decor are like a woodland in spring, light, airy, with touches of cream, brown and green. The pictures on the wall are works of art and in the main originals which are being exhibited on behalf of the Armada Gallery in Southside Street. They add distinction to the walls. The essence of the whole place is one of well-being. You know you will never feel you have outstayed your welcome. You can be as private as you wish - business people find it ideal for a quiet meeting. If you want to talk  then Andy Hobbs, who simply enjoys people, will always find the time. He, like his wife, Helen, is a person of many parts and a wide range of experience from being a policeman to an Engineer at Wrigleys and a dedicated chocolate maker. With the same innovative dedication, Helen makes cakes which are delectable.

Like Hobbs in Eastlake Street, this one in Mayflower Street serves something in the order of 17 different coffees, a range of chocolate and teas. The food is delicious and beautifully presented. Above all it is the place itself which is so cleverly designed and built to engender in every customer the desire to become a regular - many Plymouth people are rapidly becoming addicted. Incidentally, apart from the electrics which definitely do not come into Andy's field of expertise, the whole design and work was carried out by him. This way he knew it would be exactly as he wanted it.

Originally after leaving Wrigleys, Andy wanted to become a full time chocolate maker and to own a chocolate shop, much like the excellent one, Chesters, which used to be in the Armada Centre. He could make something like 1500 chocolates a day but unless he employed others, this was not enough to sustain a shop or make a sufficient living. You realise how serious he is about chocolate making when he tells you of the way he adapts various recipes from his vast chocolate making reference library. He will never lessen his standard and never buy in anything that will not please both his sense of perfection and his customers' tastes. At Easter and at Christmas the Hobbs Coffee and Chocolate Houses will have stocks both of Andy's own chocolates and those of top class makers from elsewhere, together with very special ornaments to compliment the chocolates or to house them. Exclusive is probably the word I am seeking.

It was in a busy, small and popular coffee place in the city that Andy and Helen decided that if they could not have a chocolate shop then running a Coffee and Chocolate House, as they believed it should be run, was the answer. From that moment they set about looking for suitable premises. Not an easy task in the City Centre. By good fortune they were just in time to acquire the Eastlake Street premises before it became a Soup Kitchen and Helen happened to notice that the Mayflower Street premises looked as if they were closing, whilst she was having her hair done in the Cutting Garden across the road. Two good sites and two great places for Plymothians to enjoy.

Not far away in Richmond Walk, at Mayflower International Marina is The Brasserie where one can eat superb scallops cooked to perfection in a variety of guises but always absolutely fresh every day. The Hadlingtons, who are the proprietors, specialise in fresh fish but they recognise that perhaps it is not everyone's choice so the menu also has tender lamb and succulent steaks. The Brasserie is essentially a comfortable place to be and caters largely for the yachting fraternity who use the Marina, but the quality of the cuisine and the warmth of the welcome suggests to me that it should be far more widely used by non-nautical Plymothians! Great all the year round it has a cosy feel in winter and is enhanced by the patio overlooking the water in summer. Here one can enjoy a sandwich at lunchtime or dine alfresco at night.

Plymouth has a host of hostelries, certainly enough to find one to suit one's taste. In recent years more and more of the big chains have appeared. We now have a lively Yates Wine Bar at the top of Royal Parade and at the bottom by the junction of Union Street and Western Approach there is a very large Witherspoons serving probably the cheapest pint in town. In between there are a number of smaller pubs, all serving good pub grub and catering for a shifting population. Some of course have their regulars.

One of my favourites is The China House at Marrowbone Slip, Sutton Harbour which has graced the waterfront in various guises since the 17th century. It is a curious building which, from the other side of Sutton Pool, looks like an old wooden ship that has somehow found its hull stripped of wood, leaving only the ribs to hold back the water. It is surrounded by water on three sides and if you wonder why it has such an odd name, it is because it was built on the site where William Cookworthy set up his china factory. In its restoration it lost all the evils of the intervening centuries - including concrete floors and an old tin roof. Brought back were the old wooden floors and an interior that would not have been too unlike those of the days of William Cookworthy. There are flagstones from the north of England, panelling and old pews from a church in Bristol. Everything has a sense of age and history.

For anyone with an interest in old Plymouth, a vast collection of old Plymouth photographs, maps and prints decorates the walls belonging to the writer Crispin Gill. It is worth going to the China House to see these. There are views of the Barbican regattas, the old fish market, Tar barges and pictures of William Cookworthy himself, Joshua Reynolds, Captain Cook and Smeaton. David Cheyne was the architect and it is a building of which he should be justly proud.

Good food in the bistro style, well-kept ale and live Jazz on Sundays - what more can you want?

The Bank at Derry's Cross was once exactly that. In fact, it was the main branch of Lloyds in Plymouth. I remember it as such when I worked just across the street in the Bank of England. Today it is a popular venue, stylish in décor and providing both good food and live entertainment. It is a next door neighbour of the Theatre Royal. The façade of the building is as it has always been and so are some of the internal features which remind one of its former occupation. One excellent addition is the large conservatory which is a popular meeting place.

Just behind the Magistrates Court in St Andrew Street is Bigwigs, a wine bar and bistro. Attractively fitted out, it is a venue where many people from the Law Courts are to be found plus many legal beagles and accountants.

The true English Pub is almost a rarity and especially in city centres but lo and behold in Coxside there is not only the very best type of pub but as a bonus it has its own prize winning brewery attached to it. The Thistle Tavern and Sutton Brewery housed in a a bright primrose yellow building stands on the corner of Sutton Road opposite CD Bramall and just across the way you come to the National Marine Aquarium and the other way to the new Warner Centre. Walk inside the door and you are immediately in the main bar complete with church like pew seating around the walls, nice old polished tables, walls covered with pictures or blackboards telling you what is available food wise or what the Tuesday night live entertainment is going to be. It has atmosphere, a contented landlord and landlady, cheerful, friendly bar staff, a regular clientele who do not object to the advent of visitors, a simple bar menu and above all superb beer. Quinton Styles is mine host, a South African and a true man's man who enjoys the company of men and especially those of a sporting ilk. Debbie, his wife, has that essential quality in a pub, she is a good listener and happy to talk with anyone. One of the things that impressed me about The Thistle was that the clientele came from every walk of life from Bankers to Fishermen, Solicitors to Market Traders, and all of them were happy in each other's company. Apparently you can book an evening's visit to the brewery for no more than ten people, where Steve, the dedicated, and one might rightly say, passionate brewer, will tell you about his brew and how it comes about. This is followed by an invitation to sample the beers in the pub followed by food and a genuinely social evening. It is a good excuse for a small party and a great deal of fun.

Sutton Brewery has been in business since 1993 when Quinton realised a dream. He had always dreamed of owning a brewery but until then the opportunity had not presented itself but suddenly there was an additional building next door that could be added on to The Thistle and Quinton grasped the chance with both hands. It has been a hard slog to get it going but the rewards today are satisfying. You will find the brew on sale all over Devon and some in Cornwall. Some has even found its way to the House of Commons. You can choose from XSB, Sutton Comfort, Plymouth Pride and six other brews, each as good as the other. In winter a particularly good Porter is produced. The small team in the brewery apart from Quinton and the Brewer consists of a Brewery Rep who also delivers and a couple of other guys who all have the same attitude towards the nectar. Quinton will tell you that always using the best quality hops is one of their secrets of success but there is much more that has enabled them to win prestigious awards including CAMRA's 'Beer of the Season' which had just been awarded when I was there in October 2000.

Plymouth has a great cross-section of hotels, guesthouses, restaurants and pubs. Each and everyone of them striving to serve their customers well - and generally succeeding.

The Elizabethan House.

Derry's Clock. The City Centre

Chapter IV

The City Centre

Plymouth led the way in the building of new city centres after the German Luftwaffe destroyed it in continuous air raids during World War II. What has become known as the Abercrombie Plan set the scene for the new city centre, the first in England to be rebuilt, which started to rise from the ashes. It was an exciting time and the plans looked marvellous but as the years have gone on so much has changed that what appeared brilliant in the 1940s has almost caused the centre to self destruct at the beginning of the 21st century. However with the same determination that the city showed when it needed to rebuild so is the same spirit in evidence almost everywhere you go in the centre and with whomever I have talked to. One can feel the get up and go spirit, the genuine excitement and the sincerity with which people speak of their love and belief in Plymouth. Oddly enough though, I have to admit that the most enthusiastic believers in the future of Plymouth are not Plymothians by birth but have adopted the city when their jobs have brought them here. Plymothians tend to sit back and believe that the city sandwiched between the awesome glory of Dartmoor and the magnificence of one of the finest harbours in the world, is enough to make people come here.

That philosophy does not wash with Steve Lobb of the Estate Agents and Property Developers Chesterton. For the last eight years he has patiently worked on the plan for the redevelopment of Drake Circus Shopping Centre and the multi-storey car park at Charles Cross - surely one of the worst possible eyesores as you approach the city from Exeter Street. This car park is the first which most incoming traffic encounters, a great, barren, concrete monstrosity from which one emerges, as a visitor, with no idea where to go. With the vision and planning of Steve and the other members of his client's project team, all this will change. The final result will be a superb modern shopping Mall encompassing an enlarged Marks and Spencers and Boots (probably in a wholly new store) at one end and the up market department store Allders - a newcomer to the city - at the other. A further 80 retail shops and over 1,200 car parking spaces will be included, all of it under cover in a light and airy environment.. I have seen a scale model of the site and it has grace and charm as well as every modern facility. Its up market features will offer shoppers a far better range of goods and fashion than at present, in a transformed environment. Instead of people in the South Hams and other areas outside of Plymouth - together with the city's wealthier residents - going to shop in Exeter or Truro, it is hoped they will turn their cars in our direction. It is a superb plan and deserves success but Steve Lobb will not be happy until he sees the first building work commence in 2002 and then come to fruition 30 months later.

Talking to Steve and absorbing his enthusiasm which is at the same time based on down to earth common sense, I began to realise how much more there is to regenerating a city than just putting up buildings. It tied in well with the conversations I have had with educationalists, people in the sports field and hoteliers as well as the lawyers, accountants and the hospitals. To create a healthy, vibrant city and one which attracts people to come and live and work here, all the ingredients have to be in place. As Steve says, you have to sell a package not just sun, sand and sea. His firm recently put together a research document which attracted   Orange before they decided to move here and in so doing, create more jobs for local people.   The document included everything from labour availability, qualifications and wage expectations, to house prices and availability, public transport, schooling, healthcare, shopping, recreation and social life - the whole enchilada! Gone are the days when families used to take off for a bucket and spade holiday every year and expect no more than a good beach, a comfortable hotel or guest house offering full board. Today they want much more and so do companies relocating.

Before the Drake Circus project started, Steve Lobb had been looking for another area of the city centre on which to develop the major covered shopping centre which Plymouth lacks, and he conceived a project known as "The Quays' This admirable and ambitious project foresaw redevelopment of the entire block of the city centre between Dingles (the only building which would have remained, albeit with three levels of mall penetrating what is presently its rear wall) to the west, Old Town Street to the east, New George Street to the north and Royal Parade to the south.   Steve amused me when he told me that when the idea first came to him, he took his girl friend (now his wife), plus a clipboard, paper and a tape measure and spent a long evening measuring the external dimensions of every property he envisaged being demolished to make way for his grand plan. The process, an essential part of the estimating viability, even involved clambering around flat roofs! The initial design, not much different from the finished article, was in place by the following dawn! 'The Quays' reached the milestone of receiving detailed planning permission (no mean feat for a proposal of this size, valued at £200 million) at the end of 1988, but then fell victim to the British commercial property funding market collapse in 1989 - the first harbinger of the coming recession. Drake Circus now has pride of place in the city's priorities and God willing will soon be part of the life of the city.

Chesterton play a very big role in attracting business to the city and they are fortunate in having enthusiasts like Steve Lobb and his colleagues. I can't wait to see the new Drake Circus. Even the thought of it is making other stores in the centre look to their future.

There was something else that grabbed my interest when I was talking to Steve. The lack of residential property in the city centre has made it almost deserted at night apart from the pubs and the theatre. The advent of the new Warner Village at Coxside has made it even worse. The objective has to be to try and get more people actually living in Royal Parade, Old Town Street etc. To this end we know that there are now flats above the Halifax building at Derry's Cross but what I did not know is that Steve Lobb is trying to get the fine old Pearl Assurance House building in Royal Parade turned into residential accommodation. He also explained to me how many of the shops in Old Town Street and other city centre streets, have empty rooms above the shop. Originally these were part of the premises and designed to be used as storage, nowadays the movement of transport up and down the country is so much simpler and quicker that the need for keeping large stocks has gone and therefore many of these upper floors remain empty - more wasted residential space. Just imagine how many more people would pop out of their front doors to go into the market to shop, make one of the pubs their local and genuinely make the centre feel lived in.

While I am writing about live wires in the city like Steve Lobb, let me introduce you to David Draffen, The City Centre Business Manager comparatively newly appointed, he is someone who cannot fail to enthuse anyone about the City Centre and in so doing makes one realise how much he relishes the challenge of his role. Funded partially by the businesses in the City Centre and partially by the Council, his role is to attract new life to the City Centre and to get the existing businesses to work together, think up new marketing ideas that are beneficial to all the businesses and to the people of Plymouth as well. It is a mammoth task but the reaction of the business people he deals with, is anything to go by, he is one of the best additions to the future of the city that has come our way for a long time. I am told that when they were interviewing to find someone to undertake this role, he stood out amongst the many good interviewees, and the decision to appoint him was unanimous. Probably the finest thing to occur, not only from David Draffen's appointment, but from the sort of things that are happening generally, is the sense of community and continuity that I am finding everywhere. You talk to Sue Goode in Boots, Neill Mitchell in the Chamber of Commerce, Commander Charles Crichton OBE of the Plymouth Naval Museum, Steve Dudley of Dingles, Mrs Tombs of Derrys,Andrew Huckerby of Kitley House, Alison Smith of Barbican Glass, Sonia Donovan of the Armada Gallery, Sainsbury's and Plymouth Library, to name but a few and each and everyone of them is in someway linked to things that are beneficial and exciting for the City and which will attract more people to come to Plymouth and use the City Centre. The varying activities I will talk about elsewhere in the book.

For any writer there can never be exactly the right time to produce such a book as this, especially when one is writing about a city which is sprouting new buildings, new businesses, new thoughts, new ideas for the improvement of the life of Plymothians. Every day I hear about something new. In this week alone in October 2000 I read that a new hotel is to be built on the site of the existing Derry's Cross Car Park. It has people who think it is a brilliant idea and will help to enliven the Derry's Cross end of the town. There are others who can see that the loss of a car park may prevent people from coming into this part of Plymouth. Talk to the Manager of the adjacent cinema and you will see how upbeat she is about the idea of having more potential customers on her doorstep. She rightly says that with the advent of the Warner Complex in the Barbican Leisure Park, much of her trade has vanished. Then the old Drake cinema, still at the moment proudly displaying its golden galleon above its darkened doors, is to be demolished and will make way for a casino and restaurants. It is all happening.

At the other end of town we are promised new developments in the east end. This could see a whole street of post-war stores demolished to make way for regional giants. Firstly if Welbeck Land Limited fulfil their plans we will lose H Samuels, the newsagents O'Briens, the Framing Shop and for me I will miss the two cafes including Les Jardins de Bagatelles with their outside tables and chairs that have become so much loved by workers and shoppers in the town. I have had many a good cup of coffee in these pleasant surroundings watching the passers by. You never know who you might see there. In one morning I spotted Olympic Swimmer Sharron Davies and her small son and on another Ian Stirling of Carlton Television. One hopes that these places will arise again when the dust and drilling has ceased.

The next block of shops between Mr Minute in Old Town Street, Pete's Place and McDonald's in New George Street would all disappear and be replaced by five large stores and a new car park entrance. In many ways it is time this end of the city was rebuilt. It was one of the first areas to be rebuilt after the Blitz and compared to other cities, it does look a little beyond its sell-by-date.

All this added to the Drake Circus development with which it would dovetail, will provide the large units necessary to attract the big name retailers. You can already feel the vibrancy in the city but these developments would provide Plymouth with the opportunity to compete with Exeter and Truro when it comes to shopping. At the moment there is no doubt that Plymouth does lose out to its neighbours.

Another piece of good news that came my way was that the derelict land next to the Grand Hotel is to be sold for £2 million and that together with the money raised from the sale of Derry's Cross car park will be ploughed into the restoration of Tinside Pool and the Hoe foreshore. In October 2000 architects will be chosen to do the work, the preparation work will start in April 2001 and an expected completion date is September 2003. If this comes about what a boost it will be to the city and what a relief to see the eyesore which Tinside Pool has become, finally making a recovery. I do hope the plans will include a roof over the pool which can be removed in warm weather, thus making the pool and its facilities usable all the year round.

By the time this book is published Staples the national stationery store and the Gala bingo hall will have opened just opposite Charles Church leading down to Bretonside bus station.The whole building will undoubtedly enhance the look of Charles Cross. It already has a certain stylish look about it. There is a whisper that there might be a restaurant in the Rotunda and shop units are also planned. At the moment there is great activity with the building of a luxury apartment block on Discovery Wharf and Sutton Harbour Holdings tell me that they are considering making allotments into a block of flats with community areas.

A fascinating and somewhat curious shopping expedition to find the unusual can be experienced by visiting Worldwide Trading tucked away behind the Kings Head Pub by Bretonside Bus Station. In fact to reach it from the bus station you come down to the roundabout go straight across and take the first turning left. It has a large car park so that makes a good enough reason for coming here if, in the first instance, you only want to browse. The building is not remarkable but once through the doors you are in a fantasy world looking at heaven knows what. There are items from the exotic isle of Bali, the plains of South Africa, the bazaars of Istanbul, the hills of Romania, mysterious Persia and the Far East. The warehouse is full to the brim and what is remarkable is the unbeatable price. Open every day except Tuesdays and Thursdays from 10-5pm and Sundays from 11-4pm. Definitely worth a visit. It is owned and run by John Henning and his partner. John made his name in Plymouth when he built the highly successful Hennings Estate Agency and subsequently sold to the Black Horse Agency. A very different way of life for him but he obviously revels in the acquisition of his extraordinary stock.

On the Barbican the Mayflower Visitors Centre will be completed in the spring of 2001 and opened in the summer. It will tell the history of the Barbican, with emphasis on the Mayflower. Its opening will herald a new era for the Barbican Theatre which is becoming more and more prominent in the Arts field in the city. They will have a new entrance leading to a café bar which will be open all day to the general public.

A major player in the life, future and current well-being of the city has to be the suave, charming, shrewd Chris Freegard, the Director for Regeneration, whose office on the 8th floor of the Civic Centre with its superb views, must compensate in some measure for the enormous ugliness of the building as a whole. He has acquired so many roles and with them a wealth of titles since he came to Plymouth five years ago, that I was forcibly reminded of Gilbert and Sullivan's Lord High Executioner! His post seems to encompass everything from Redevelopment to Highways, Regeneration to Housing and much more. It is evident that he relishes his role and brings to it an enthusiasm that is infectious. He tells me that his driving ambition for Plymouth makes him carry in his mind a list of all the things he wants to achieve for the city and for him it becomes a perfect day when he can positively cross one of them off. When you listen to him you cannot fail to become equally addicted to plans for the resurgence of Devonport, the delight he has in knowing that the next step towards the new Drake Circus is underway, the thrill of expectation for the Plymouth Naval Base Museum, the reclamation of land, the partnership with the 20-20 Partnership and a host of other plans, some of which are still firmly under wraps.

The word 'Partnership' is constantly used and that is something that is becoming stronger and stronger in Plymouth. No longer are new ideas isolated to one business or person. New thinking is shared by a whole range of people who have the same goal in mind. This sharing is without doubt one of the most important parts of Chris Freegard's joy in his job and bodes well for the future of us all.

The man himself is interesting. His background stems from a father who came back from World War II as a very young Major and decided he never wanted to work for anyone else again and eventually founded a successful business in the Rag Trade. Chris was well educated and finished off with degrees from both Portsmouth and Cardiff which launched his career into the realms of Planning and Development taking him to several parts of the country including Sheffield, Dorset and Nottingham, where incidentally he was at the time of City Challenge in which Plymouth lost out to Nottingham. When the Plymouth job came up he was none too sure about coming here and even less sure when he arrived on a wet winter's evening attending one of the series of meetings through which he had to progress to get the job, and which ended up in the Grand Hotel where he stayed the night. He awoke to bright sunshine streaming through the bedroom curtains and when he pulled them back there was Plymouth Hoe and the gleaming, sunlit waters of Plymouth Sound ahead of him. He was hooked from that moment and couldn't wait for the post to be offered to him.

For me, the hour I spent in his office simply added to my layman's desire to see that Plymouth is recognised as one of the most important cities in Britain and has the respect of the world. My sadness since writing this piece is that Chris has been lured away from Plymouth by Newport where he is to be the Chief Executive. Their gain is our loss but at least he leaves us with firm foundations on which to build and he also leaves behind his very able assistant, Nigel Pitt, whose quiet strength serves the city well.

If you want to get a feel for the future of a city, for finance at the highest level then there is probably no better source than International Accountants, Pricewaterhouse Coopers. Their offices in Plymouth are quiet, somewhat sedate and yet there is a sense of power. The highly qualified staff led by the two partners, Mike Pallot and Francis Drake look after a comparatively small number of clients but when you know who those clients are you realise how accountants at this level are perhaps beyond the reach of small businesses. Since I wrote the first 'Invitation to Plymouth' book published in 1993, there have been many changes to the firm. In those days they were Coopers & Lybrand and had recently swallowed up the old firms, DeloitteHaskins & Sells and Cork Gully. Since then Coopers have lost the name Lybrand and joined forces with PriceWaterhouse In so doing the force of this new firm can be experienced world wide. I believe there are something like 170,000 partners and staff throughout the world. To this great firm they bring expertise is so many fields. Their professionals include economists, engineers, IT and telecommunications specialists, strategists, marketing professionals, lawyers, actuaries, human resource and recruitment specialists, insolvency practitioners, educationalists, public sector advisors, corporate finance and acquisition specialists. Slightly overwhelming isn't it?

However, all this might disappears when you talk to the senior partner in Plymouth, Mike Pallot. You are immediately aware that behind his very pleasant, easy going manner, there is one of the shrewdest brains in Plymouth. He has a finger on the pulse of almost everything and a keen interest in making things happen. PricewaterhouseCoopers do much to cultivate good business relationships in the city including running regular debating occasions when various business people are invited to debate on any given subject. This is a chance for people to speak their minds in an environment that is not going to lead to outside reporting, it allows for fun and acrimony, but its purpose in getting people together to discuss issues, is highly successful.

However large the firm is, Mike Pallot and Francis Drake maintain a personal contact with all their clients, constantly looking for ways for them to expand their business, or how to cut cost if the scale has swung downwards. They do not pretend to look after very small businesses. It is neither sensible nor financially viable. Their field is definitely corporate. It' s abundantly clear when you realise what resources are needed to provide big companies with the expert advice and assistance they need. One only has to look at many opportunities there are in Europe and around the world and how constantly regulations are changing.

Insolvency Practitioners tend to be part of these big accountancy firms. It is always sad to see a company needing this help but sometimes through the expertise offered a company can be salvaged. This happens when a good receiver pinpoints the good areas of an ailing business and finds a buyer or an investor willing to take on the challenge. It is an expensive business and one that no firm of accountants would touch unless the company could upfront sufficient money to make the work entailed viable. The lack of these funds is frequently why small companies go the wall even though they might well be salvageable. The advice for anyone in this situation or teetering towards the brink is to ask for a meeting, which is free of charge, and then take the advice given. Most small businesses tend to struggle on until it is too late when perhaps by approaching PWC or a similar firm at an earlier date, might have saved the day. In today's world there are all sorts of Business Angels out there looking for good companies who need help.

Mike Pallot has worked in four offices during his thirty one years with the firm and in 1981, he set up Coopers & Lybrand's first Plymouth office in 1981 at a time when working anywhere outside London might have been considered a lost cause but he has steadily proved how successful a provincial office can be. He comes from a banking family in Jersey and originally was not over enthusiastic about the long years it would take to become a Chartered Accountant. In fact he rebelled against it but eventually saw what a good career it could be and he has certainly proved how valuable he is both to his own firm and to many businesses in Plymouth.

When I first visited Coopers, I chose to do so for two reasons. Firstly it was a familiar name to me because when I married my first husband I acquired Henry Benson, their senior partner in London, as a cousin and this time I was intrigued to hear that Henry had kept his office and desk at the London office until the day he died at the age of 82. Secondly it was because Francis Drake was a partner and I could not resist the chance of meeting a direct descendant of our great explorer Sir Francis Drake. Coopers' Francis Drake was amazed at the furore his arrival in Plymouth had caused. He was regularly in demand for photo calls alongside Sir Francis Drake's statue on Plymouth Hoe and was interviewed endlessly. The fuss has died down but it is good to know that we have one of the illustrious man's descendants gracing the city, especially as so recently we have lost, at the ridiculously young age of 53, Andrew 'Spud' Spedding who was also a direct descendant and lived in one of Drake's old manor houses at Sampford Spiney.

Two of the most imposing and important buildings in the City Centre and part of Drake Circus are Plymouth City Museum and Plymouth Central Library. These buildings are important not only because of their architectural value but for the part they play in the life of Plymothians. If you had ever thought that the Library was just there for the purpose of borrowing books and CD's as one is apt to do, then read on and find out, as I did, how much goes on within the doors of the Central Library which also controls all the other libraries, static and mobile around the city. Here in Drake Circus, Alasdair MacNaughtan is in charge of the whole Library Service. A personable, friendly Scot he is a comparative newcomer to the job and the city, but has settled into life in Plymouth happily - his wife has a number of relatives here so it was not quite such a wrench to leave Scotland. Since his arrival in the Library he has quietly taken stock of all his 'kingdom' had on offer and then set about bringing in some of his own innovative ideas, with a little help from outside sources like Sainsburys.

Knowing how to use the library is so important and then discovering all that it can offer. For example it has a Key Information Service looked after by a number of intelligent and well informed people. The service provides information for businesses, students and members of the public, it encompasses printed directories, company reports, statistical sources, on-line databases. You can find technical information which will help you protect your ideas and inventions or enable you to research ideas and inventions of others. If you are going to a job interview and want to learn something about the company you are hoping to join, then you have the opportunity of digging up some information. If you are in business you can seek out information on what your competitors are up to. You may just want to enhance your studies. Whatever it may be Key Information is there to help, and wherever possible this help will be free. Needless to say in today's market place On-Line database and Internet searches are also on offer; as with obtaining specialist reports from other locations and other research activities, however, there is sometimes a charge for these services.

Have you ever thought where you might turn for the elusive answer to that question which has been annoying you all day? You could do far worse than start with the very friendly and helpful staff in the Reference Department. They seem to be able to find out almost anything about everything or put you in touch with someone who will know. From benefits and rights to butterflies and bytes, very little seems to stump them. If you need to know more about Plymouth or the history of your own family, there is a mass of information, photographs and other items available in the Local and Naval Studies Department. Staff there are also in close contact with colleagues in the Museum and Archive services for a more specialised enquiry. All you need to do is drop in to the Central Library, or make contact on (01752) 305907/8 (Reference Department) 305909 (Local and Naval Studies Department)

The importance that Alasdair MacNaughtan and his staff place on ensuring that the young are encouraged to love books from an early age, is evident both in the colourful and frequently lively, Children's' Section with its wide range of books and the many special occasions for children which are held here. Working with Schools, and supporting the National Curriculum, has become increasingly important. There is an open invitation for teachers and playgroups to arrange visits to the library, and classes are often invited to listen to talks from authors and a huge array of other happenings. School libraries themselves can purchase excellent book and project support packages from the Schools Library Service based at Chaucer Way, whose helpful and knowledgeable staff can be contacted on 01752 780713.

Part of the encouragement to youngsters to read is fed by the excellent 'Feed Back' magazine which is attractive, glossy and full of reviews from schoolchildren. It is a brilliant concept inasmuch as it is the passing on of what they have read and enjoyed to Plymouth's young readers, their counterparts in fact. I was not in the least surprised to discover that it was edited by Libby Allman who works at 'In Other Words' on Mutley Plain (a business you can read about in Chapter 15) and has revolutionised their Children's' Section. Believing too that books should become part of a child's life almost from the cradle, there is the splendid Bookstart which is a National concept originally sponsored by Sainsbury's. It is all about parents sharing books with babies and so, at the 9 month hearing test, parents receive a free bag with lots of goodies including two free books and a special invitation to join the library. The goody bag is not sent through the post but is personally delivered by Health Visitors who enjoy the task of handing the bag over and giving parents some handy tips on sharing books with babies. The babies begin with simple board books and they love looking at pictures and listening to the reader - even if they do not understand the words. It should be said that they also love to touch, hold and frequently taste the books! The scheme has proved enormously successful and without doubt helps babies to begin reading sooner and stimulates their imaginations. It also gives the parent a chance for an extra cuddle time!

One interesting fact has emerged from Bookstart and that is the encouragement it has given parents to start reading. It also helps the older children in the family who improve their reading ability by reading to the baby. From the age of five, extra encouragement is offered through the 'Turning the Pages' reading programme. This has the incentive of wonderful bookmarks and badges to collect as the children share the fun and joy of reading with Browser Bear and Reggie the Veggie Dinosaur. At the age of nine the programme takes on a new dimension in the form of 'Out of this World'.

Babies can join the library from the day they are born and you will find libraries have wonderful books for babies and toddlers. Joining is one of the few things that is free to us today and a visit to the Children's' Section can be fun for the whole family. I haven't been to one but I believe there are even Bookstart parties held at local libraries and family centres. You should look out for 'Under Fives story times', Holiday funtimes' Library clubs, Special Displays and visits from authors, illustrators, storytellers, puppeteers and musicians who are very happy to share their lives with the young of all ages! If you want more information ring the Bookstart Co-ordinator on 01752 306791 or the City Children's Librarian on 01752 306799.

Take Music and Drama for instance. This is a service for everyone. You might be learning an instrument, singing in a choir, studying GCSE Drama, or just interested in the performing arts. You can borrow music and plays at the Central Library where you will find Songbooks, Playscripts, Vocal scores, Books on music, Instrumental music, Books on theatre, Music tutors and Books on dance. Groups can benefit from the wide range of music sets and playsets which are available to local groups and societies from full-length plays to Choral works, Shows and librettos and much more. These sets can be borrowed for long loan periods to cover rehearsal and performance. Advance booking is strongly recommended especially for popular works like 'Messiah'.

For someone like myself who is always digging for information and has a great need of help I find the specialist staff superb. They seem to be able to find anything from an artist's address, to the name of a tune, from a crossword clue to copies of a play with just the right number of characters to match the people you have available If you enjoy music, but can't read or perform it, you might like to relax with a CD from the huge range available. The Music and Drama Department is the place to contact Tel: 01752 305914

Yet more facilities include photocopying in black and white or colour. There are reader-printers for reading and copying microform material and a fax bureau service. The Business and Technical Department has a CD-Rom workstation for patent searching and so it goes on. Many people are either not able to read or prefer not to. This doesn't mean that the library doesn't have anything to offer. Books are available in large print and can be listened to on cassettes, and there are several available to help develop the basic skills needed by anyone of any age who is learning to read for the first time. If you want pure visual stimulation, easily absorbed information or simple relaxation you might want to try the wide range of videos and DVDs in the library. For the more adventurous, the library offers several language courses on cassettes, and many books in Chinese, French, German, Italian, Russian and Spanish.

Why more Plymothians do not join the Library and benefit from all that it has to offer, I fail to understand. My fortnightly visit to the Peverell Branch of the Library is one of my great pleasures in life. It is a light, airy place with a friendly, helpful staff and in many ways I prefer it to the Central Library because it is smaller and less daunting when it comes to seeking out what one wants to read. You can always order anything you cannot find here so one does not miss out on anything one especially wants to read. There is a computer which allows you to search for information. Videos and music are also available. These smaller libraries are dotted all around the city and for those who are unable to visit a library, the WRVS 'Books on Wheels' volunteers can be contacted through the Library, and they operate a home delivery service. Books and cassettes are delivered to residential and nursing homes, and sheltered accommodation and regular visits are provided by library staff. If you want to know more, you can find the addresses of all libraries in the City under 'libraries' in Yellow Pages. If you are connected to all the latest technology, a mass of useful information appears on the library website at www.plymouth.gov.uk/star/library.htm. So there is no reason why anyone should be deprived of the joy of reading and the services the library offers.

As Plymothians we tend to take for granted that we have a Museum and Art Gallery but I wonder how many of us realise what a tremendous operation it all is. Just for starters lets look at the sort of exhibitions it has staged in the year 2000 and then I want you to take a look at the work that goes on behind the scenes. This will reveal to you the amazing complexity of storing, repairing, restoring and mounting exhibitions. It is another world.

In the year 2000 over 80,000 people have visited Plymouth City Museum and Art Gallery. The variety of displays has been mind boggling. Much of the attraction for visitors today, especially youngsters, is the interactive displays which allow them to press buttons, pull things and listen to many different noises. The major summer exhibition 'Claws' attracted over 40,000. The locally produced 'Tales of the City' was a winner and was put together using old photographs, letters and objects, contributed by more than 1,000 city people. Probably the largest number of people who have ever contributed to one exhibition. They are all local stories and make you realise what colourful lives Plymothians have - some of them completely unexpected. The Chinese Artist Chan'Ky-Yui was here at the beginning of the year and certainly helped to forge new links with the Chinese community in the city.

An exhibition called The Jews of Devon and Cornwall' has brought another dimension to our lives. It tells of their history, their lifestyle and displays many of their treasures not seen before.

As I write a display of the costumes, scripts and props that went into the Theatre Royal's Union Street production, is about to be mounted. Amongst the busy programme for next year will be an exhibition of Plymouth Unveiled' photographed by Jo-Jo of whom I have written in the Barbican chapter. His book has gained itself National publicity producing, apart from anything else, an award winning television documentary for Carlton TV.

The year 2001 will also see a complete revamping of the Museum and Art Gallery's natural history gallery with new fully interactive facilities

The Museum and Art Gallery's Outreach programme in the capable hands of Jo Loosemore is reaching new audiences and is now visiting schools, community centres and libraries.

I revel in the wind of change that has occurred in the Museum over the last decade. It has an air of excitement about it.which is infectious. Not only are you able to absorb modern and ancient history, all displayed in a manner which does not alienate anyone, the Museum is also the venue for lectures and a regular series of lunch time concerts organised by the indefatigable Jeannie Moore, who since she retired after many years of service with the Prince's Trust for which she received the MVO, seems to have worked even harder in making music readily available to the public. If you have never been to a lunchtime concert make the effort to do so. The Museum will provide you with dates and times.

Just below Plymouth Library and the Museum there is a small row of shops which seem to change hands on a fairly regular basis but they will only increase in consequence when the new Drake Circus comes into being. However, one that has been in the same place for many years is the well established and highly regarded

75

Maison Terry, a unisex hair dressing establishment founded in 1932 and purchased by the grandmother of the present owner, Jonathan Howe in 1935.

If you were to ask most of the salons in the city today where their staff were trained you would probably find that in almost every case at least one member trained at Maison Terry, highlighting the service this establishment has paid Plymouth for roughly 70 years. There was even a time when the apprentice stylists were sent to Nazareth House, an orphanage run by a group of highly dedicated nuns, where they would cut the hair of all the children - willing or not! Within half an hour of their arrival every child had a very similar hairstyle a la Maison Terry!

Times have changed and so, obviously, have fashions. Maison Terry has always been innovative and led the way, setting trends for other salons to follow. For example in the 1950's a coffee bar was installed and boasted the very first Espresso coffee machine in Plymouth, and in 1972, again leading the way, Maison Terry became the first unisex hair salon in Plymouth. Today the establishment is changing again to include a section for beauty treatments as well as hair dressing. Now it has become a 'one stop shop' to pamper oneself totally, offering therapeutic massage, manicures, eyelash and brow curling/dying and much more. Something that has never changed since the time of Jonathan Howe's grandmother is the courtesy with which clients are greeted and treated. Something that is frequently lacking.

Old Town Street bears no resemblance to the street of the same name that I knew so well before the Germans decided to flatten it. Its only reminder to me is that it still runs from St Andrews Cross towards Drake Circus. It is always busy leading from Royal Parade past the Post Office, the Royal Bank of Scotland, HSBC and NatWest and on into New George Street. On the other side there is, amongst the shops and with a pedestrianised area outside, Les Jardins de Bagatelle at Number 11. It is somewhere that outlines the ability of its owner Vasili Dimitrovski who hails from Cannes in the South of France, to find the right spot to site his ventures in Plymouth. I have already told you about the exciting Jazz Café on the Barbican which he owns in conjunction with Eric Amann and here in Old Town Street is another touch of authentic French lifestyle. The small patisserie and coffee shop offers its customers everything that has a taste of France. The bread is wonderful, the French tarts out of this world - the strawberry ones are the best I have ever tasted. All through the day there is a constant stream of people beating a path to his door to purchase the super Baguettes, filled with French ham or chicken and a variety of mayonnaise and Fallot mustards. The additional Continental touch is the tables and chairs which grace the pavement outside with a backdrop of leafy trees. Here, in the heart of the city, you can sit and watch the world go by simply enjoying coffee or a glass of wine.

Vasili is a man full of surprises with a fertile mind and an appreciation of all manner of things. For example he is one of the sponsors of the Chamber Concerts held in the old Sherwell Chapel, now part of the University. His love of music covers a wide range. If you are given a lift in his car you probably listen to the glorious sound of Mozart. If you visit the Jazz Café, it is Jazz from all around the world that will assail your ears. Vas will tell you he had no intention of opening a business in Plymouth until he came here to play golf and fell in love with the city. From the time he made the decision to open the Bagatelle it took just four months. The speed was down to his own hard work all of the interior of the shop was created by his staff and himself. He also gives high praise to Plymouth City Council who could not have been more helpful in ensuring that everything was made as easy as possible and nothing was held up because of red tape.

I have a sneaking feeling that his exquisite French manners and Gallic charm helped his cause!

Bastille Day, July 14th 2001 will see the triumphant opening of Le Café D'Azur in the Royal Building, St Andrew's Cross. Vaz and his partner Eric have fought long and hard to open a true French Brasserie in the City Centre. Originally they hoped to have one on the Barbican but that came to nothing. Now they have created a truly delightful, perfectly appointed Brasserie on the ground floor of this spacious building. Everything about it is minimalist, providing an elegant brasserie in the true French style. Beech floors, pale blue décor, glass partitions to produce intimacy; it is all there. The menu is to die for, with succulent French dishes combining wonderful ingredients. The wine is perfectly chosen and the coffee includes Illy, a brand unobtainable in England which will send coffee epicures into raptures. Apart from being open every day, seven days a week from 8am-midnight, Le Café D'Azur also has its own Deli providing customers with perfect sandwiches, every imaginable cheese and deli requirement

Boots stands on the corner of Old Town Street and New George Street, I am not sure when the giant chemist first arrived in Plymouth but I expect it will have been at the beginning of the 20th century. I remember it, strangely enough, as a place where, before World War II, my Mother changed her library books on a Saturday morning and then adjourned to the Boots café for morning coffee with her friends - other mornings in the week would have found her either at Pophams or Dingles, not changing books but putting the world to rights with her friends over coffee. Now the lending library and café have gone and in Boots you have a modern, well laid out store offering far more than just a chemist although they have never forgotten their roots and never, ever, stinted on the quality of their products. Talking to the Manager, Sue Goode, she stressed, in her quietly persuasive way, that Boots would never stoop to the 'Pile it High, Sell it Cheap' philosophy. In fact listening to her you realise that it would not be possible for Boots to contemplate such a practice whilst they maintain their very high degree of service to their customers. Boots Plymouth, for example, employs a talented and dedicated lady, whose sole job it is to advise customers on skin care products, irrespective of the brand. She has been supremely well trained for the task and is constantly being sent away on refresher courses to bring her up to speed with everything that is new in the market place. This is an expensive operation and just one of the many facets of the business that keeps the standard so high.

In order to provide an even better laid out store, based on what customers tell them they want to buy from Boots, they are dispensing with some of their goods; for example music and video, children's wear from 2-5, because this has become apparent it is not their market place and does not attract enough custom to warrant the space, staff and time these products take up.

Sue Goode was very interesting on the difference between one end of New George Street and the other. Most Plymothians she believes are very value conscious but this becomes more apparent in their shop at the Market end of New George Street, a shop which seems to have a totally different clientele from the main store.

Boots are very involved in Chestertons Drake Circus project and when it comes to fruition they will have an outstandingly modern store making them even more of a major player in the regeneration of the City Centre.

Half way down New George Street and turning right into Armada Way you will come to The British Home Stores, a store which has weathered many different ownerships in the last twenty years, some have successfully taken the store forward and others almost killed its true identity but today having just changed again it looks set to have a sparkling future. What people like about BHS is its consistently high quality and its consistently realistic prices. The store is light and bright, shines with cleanliness and has a staff who are well-trained, well-informed and courteous. Whilst I waited to see Mr Max, the General Manager and his assistant Rose, I listened to people coming up to the Customer Service desk and heard the response to queries and complaints. Both were dealt with politely and the one complaint over goods that were not satisfactory could not have been handled better; the customer went away totally satisfied. Oddly enough it is this sort of thing that one remembers. For years you can shop and be satisfied and probably not think about recommending the establishment but when something is wrong and you get treated so well, it is never forgotten. I have told several people since how good BHS is.

Plymouth's premier department store is without doubt Dingles part of The House of Fraser. It has a sense of well-being as you walk through its doors and find yourself amidst merchandise that shrieks quality. Not the store to venture into if you want the cheap and cheerful but at the same time it is not expensive for what it provides and the thought that it is only for those with well-lined pockets, is totally wrong. It is a store to wander through, enjoy and when you find something you would like to have you will find the price is not outrageous but sensible. I am not a shopper but I love the beauty of the store with its wealth of exciting things for sale from simple necessities to the grandest ball gown. It has a staff who are dedicated and proud to call themselves Dingles' people. You can browse around without being bothered but you will always find a member of staff at hand to help you make a wise decision and unearth your credit cards! It is nice, for example, to spend time amongst the glassware and then be able to talk to someone who knows about Waterford glass, or the beautifully designed, modern Dartington Glassware. In china you will find the staff knowledgeable about all their range whether it is the Royal Doulton or the more mundane articles. It is that sort of pride in their work that pervades the store.

A store as efficient as Dingles, must have a great leader and that is so in the friendly, enthusiastic General Manager, Steve Dudley, who has recently taken over from Stuart Collins, Peter Fairweather's successor. Stuart has now gone to the House of Fraser,

Reading and Peter is now in charge of Dingles, Exeter, bringing to that store the same desire for progress that he instilled in Dingles, Plymouth in his tenure which has provided the groundwork for Stuart Collins to start his campaign to bring the store into the 21st century. Now, with Steve Dudley at the helm it will undoubtedly be ready for the competition that will undoubtedly come from Alders, when they arrive in the new and eagerly anticipated Drake Circus complex.

When I went to see Steve Dudley, he was in the throes of tweaking the final touches of the total refurbishment of the Restaurant on the top floor. An exciting project and one that was long overdue. Much more change and refurbishment is also in the pipeline. Currently as I write the whole of the Hairdressing Salon is being revamped to produce something very special for their current clients and enticing for anyone who wants to sample the very best in styling and beauty. I have since been back to the new restaurant and it is super. Having been to see Steve in his fourth floor office - a gracious place in its own right and an oasis of peace away from the bustling store, I got into the lift and met two complete strangers who without any prompting told me that I must try the new restaurant because it had so much space, was so friendly and had such nice staff. Nothing like unsolicited testimonials. A great meeting place for Plymothians and also for the many cruise ship visitors who land at Millbay Docks for a quick visit to the City. They are greeted by an army of buses which transport them into the city centre, depositing them outside the Theatre Royal and letting their passengers loose amongst the shops.

No business can afford to stand still in these days and there is no doubt that with the constant updating of the departments within the store, the consistency of staff training and the pride that every Dingles employee feels about the Store, Alders will have to do something very special to be in any way superior to this House of Fraser flagship.

Seeing how busy and prosperous Dingles is today reminds me that the store was almost brought to its knees on the evening of December 19th, 1988 when a mindless. militant rights group set the store alight because they objected to Dingles selling furs.

It happened almost forty years on from September 1st 1951, when the resurgent Dingles opened its doors in Plymouth, after the Blitz of World War II - the first major store to emerge. Indeed it was the first new department store to open in Great Britain since 1938. It was, and is a prime site, and on the opening day nearly 40,000 people came through the doors of the store. Nylons, groceries and tinned fruits were in great demand - still hard to buy after the deprivation of the war years. Some people came simply to ride on the escalators, a novelty in Plymouth, and the first to be installed in a West Country shop.

Peter Fairweather was General Manager then and will tell you that the morning after the fire, having helped the police with their enquiries, he returned to the building at mid-day. Uppermost in his mind was the wellbeing of his staff who had turned up for work to find desolation and possibly no jobs. His practical mind was telling him that with the looming recession, the main board in London might well decide that the high market value of the prestigious site, together with the insurance would be a better option than rebuilding. With a heavy heart he waited for the board to arrive. His anxiety was needless. Almost the first words spoken to him by Mohammed Al Fayed were ' How soon can we re-open?'

From that moment it was all systems go. Peter and his staff rolled up their sleeves, started clearing away the debris, and just like the war years, found a way to carry on. After the bombing raids of 1941 Dingles' building was destroyed and various departments were housed in large private houses around the city. Ingleside - now a Residential home - on Mutley Plain housed the haberdashery and millinery. The shoe department found a home in a shop close to what is now Somerfields. John Yeos - now part of the Debenhams group - occupied what is now Somerfields; they too were homeless. Charlton House on Mannamead Road housed Dingles' children's clothes and babywear.

This time it was slightly different. On January 19th 1989, 5,000 people queued up for Dingles' fire-clearance sale, in temporary premises secured at Estover. The old Habitat premises in Campbell Court were purchased as an outlet for furnishings and electrical goods, whilst the staff and contractors worked all out to get the ground and first floors at Royal Parade opened by the end of March.

There was no question in Peter Fairweather's mind that the intense loyalty of his staff this would never have come about. He is a modest man and not given to blowing his own trumpet but whereas he is absolutely right about his staff, many of whom have been with Dingles for years - whole families of them - it was his ability to lead from the front that was the catalyst.
It was not until September 1990, that the store was fully operational. Even for a non-shopper like myself, it is a good place to be. One feels pampered and cosseted by its comfort. Dingles' staff do their bit for the community as well. They support many charity events throughout the year including abseiling down the outer walls to the street - a horribly long way to my mind. Dingles' itself is always willing to give a helping hand to any worthwhile cause.

One of the major changes in the City Centre in the last few years has been the emergence of what was Co-operative House in its new format Derrys. It has been a bit like a caterpillar shedding its skin and becoming an attractive butterfly, although in the case of Derrys something slightly more substantial! In its new image it has shed quite a lot of its building which in turn has re-emerged as a pub, Argos and a Post Office - the latter a very welcome addition for those of us who found it daunting to have to go from one end of Royal Parade to the other to reach the main Post Office. Inside the refurbished Derrys is an up to date department store far more in line with the shopper of the year 2000's requirements. It caters for every taste and has found a new niche in the market place with its improved image.

The Society is one of the largest private sector employers in the city and second only to DML. What makes it different from other stores is that apart from its dividends to shareholders it is bound under co-operative values and principles to plough money back into the business and more especially to provide all sorts of extraneous functions for the good of the people of Plymouth as well as its 108,000 members. For example it has an excellent educational centre now part of the Derrys building which runs three Pre-School Playgroups as well as other activities.

I talked with Gill Tombs, who has been with the Society for well over twenty years and now runs a department which deals with education, charitable events of all kinds, many of which support local schools and provide them with all kinds of equipment. Her office is a bit like Aladdin's Cave with an ever changing quantity of goods which are designed to grace various occasions. When I went to see her there were baby clothes everywhere being collected for the Special Care Baby Units at Derriford and Torbay Hospitals - The Co-operative's Charity of the Year. That Gill loves what she does is apparent and her sense of enthusiasm and fun rubs off on the people who work with her. If you look at the Calendar of Members' Events you would be amazed to see what a diversity of subjects are covered. A Consumer evening held in the Pioneers Room on the third floor of Derrys Department Store may well cover the various aspects regarding the importance of making a will, and the significance of Funeral Bonds, all on an informal basis without any feeling of pressure and lightened by the provision of wine and cheese. Members can, on another evening, meet the Managers perhaps at Kingsteignton Homemaker, when they can find out more about the store and be taken on a behind the scenes tour. Wine and cheese tasting is all part of the fun of the evening. The Annual Sunday Fun Day, Concerts, social evenings are all on the agenda for Members, providing Gill Tombs with a constantly demanding job that she takes completely in her stride. One task she never minds is overseeing the annual Art Competition for young people which grows every year in its number of entries and in talent. There are 4 different age groups with the first being for Infants - 7 years and the senior 16-18 years. Qualified adjudicators are asked to choose the most imaginative, apt and skilfully, executed entries for awards. Exhibitions of prize winners and other entries are staged at Derrys Department Store and various Plymco Food Stores. In judging the aim is to provide an opportunity for children of all abilities to display and receive public recognition for items of artwork which they have proudly produced. In addition to prizes being awarded to the winners of each category, every entrant receives a gift voucher and certificate.

One other important role Gill Tombs has is the running of the Community Grants Scheme. The Society believes, and after 140 years they should know, that if they co-operate with others who share their values then they can achieve something special. Through the retail outlets they want to help achieve an improved community for members, customers and their families.

Community Grants is a partnership with the local community aimed at established voluntary groups; community action groups, churches, schools, youth clubs and residents associations, who have plans to carry out a specific community project that will benefit their local environment. Together they can work towards a better environment and a better world.

Suitable projects are not difficult to find. For example; collecting bottles and cans for recycling, removing graffiti and picking up litter, planting flowers and shrubs. Schools for example could include nature gardens or safe play areas. Indeed Mrs Tombs told me that any project which will help the local community and is within five miles of a Plymco or Normans Food Store, or within ten miles of a Homemaker Store or Funeral Home, is eligible. The value of grants ranges from £100 -£1000. Application forms have to be completed by a member of the Plymouth and South West Co-operative Society Limited and their share number must be included on the application form.

If you are not a Co-operative Member and would like to be one, joining is simple. Apply to The Member Relations Department, Plymouth & South West Co-operative Society Ltd, Third Floor, 88 Royal Parade, Plymouth PL1 1HA.

What happens on the busy Third Floor of Derrys Department Store is an eye opener to the uninitiated. I was amazed and excited by the work for the community that occurs daily and all because of a caring society which at the same time is professional and commercial as evidenced in Derrys itself and all the other Plymco's and associated shops and facilities.

Just a little way up New George Street from Derrys and next door to W.H.Smith is the only independent store left in Plymouth, Lawsons. Known and beloved by its fans this family business sells an amazing range of goods. It is modern, well laid out and in a comparatively small place displays its diverse wares extremely well. Here you will find a range of kitchen and cookery ware to delight the heart of any chef, glass to complement the china, a new lighting department which sheds its soft, becoming rays, and in keeping with its beginnings in 1904, it has a range of tools and machinery and every size of nail and screw. Its most recent addition is the arrival of Castle Kitchens who have found a home in one corner just inside the main entrance. It seems fitting that one family business should have this marriage of convenience with another. I have written about the fascinating story of Castle Kitchens at length in Chapter 16.

Recently Liz Lawson has been made the Managing Director of Lawsons and has brought to her role a new brand of management which upholds the tradition of the past but is well placed to deal with the onset of the 21st century. When I called in I met with her father, John Lawson, who remains Chairman but supposedly has partially retired. He was there standing in for Liz who is on maternity leave and I have a sneaking suspicion that he was enjoying every minute of emerging from the wings and once again running the business. He has as much enthusiasm for the store as he had in his younger days and I thoroughly enjoyed talking about the past, the present and the future of Lawsons with him.

Lawson started in 1904 when F.T.B. Lawson became a tool merchant and rented a shop from a Mr Winnacott at 13, Frankfort Street. From day one he set out to give service to his customers and a letter of his, that I have been privileged to see, and which I have copied here, illustrates the point. It also underlines the fact that service and quality remain important to Lawsons today.

Dear Sir,

I have pleasure in submitting to you my latest illustrated Catalogue of Engineers' and Joiners' Tools and Machines.

The tools herein listed are made by manufacturers having the highest reputation.

With very few exceptions (specially mentioned) every tool in this list is warranted to be of the best material, workmanship and finish, and any faulty article will be readily exchanged if returned within one month from the date of purchase.

My object all through has been to supply best quality at a low price for ready money as is possible; as I am satisfied that best tools are cheapest in the end.

The variety of tools is so great that I cannot include everything in a catalogue of this description. I shall be pleased to quote prices of any other articles required on receipt of specification.

The list is arranged alphabetically, and an index is also given.

This list cancels all previous prices of the goods mentioned herein.

Prices are subject to change without notice.

Earnestly soliciting your orders and enquiries, which shall at all times have my best attention.

I am,

Yours respectfully,

F.T.B. Lawson

Lawsons from that time onwards have always sought to 'solicit orders' and that is why almost one hundred years later, the store with its two branches, one in Tavistock and one in Totnes, thrive.

To return to the history of Lawsons which intrigues me. F.T.B Lawson was the son of a Methodist minister who travelled to the West Indies and he had a brother who also became a Methodist Minister but did not go quite so far afield to find his flock. He settled in Guernsey. Whilst visiting his brother F.T.B. fell in love with a Guernsey girl, daughter of a tool merchant on the island. One side of her family was involved in horticulture and had a business growing tomatoes many of which were exported via Plymouth.

F.T.B. became very interested in the idea of trying to grow tomatoes in Plymouth. One must remember that this was before the days of soil analysis. With a thoroughness which was part of the man's make up, he sent a whole cartload of Elburton soil to Guernsey to see if tomato plants would flourish in Plymouth. The results showed that a tomato crop would be successful and so Guernsey staff came over to start growing in the greenhouses of what is now the Elburton Vinery. By 1910 this experiment was hugely successful and the names over the door in Elburton were 'Dorey and Lawson' recognising the interest of the Guernsey connection. This started the Lawson interest in horticulture which is still carried on today especially in the Tavistock store.

During the bombing of Plymouth, Lawsons was gutted. They moved temporarily to three shops in Pound Street and Saltash Street. When the city centre was rebuilt in 1952 there were no freehold sites available. The Council offered beneficial terms to businesses who were prepared to move back into the centre. The now defunct business of Underhills was going to take the spot where Lawsons are today. At the last moment they changed their minds and Lawsons found themselves able to move back into the same site as their original shop but now renamed New George Street. A happy coincidence.

F.T.B. Lawson died in 1952 and was succeeded by his son Francis who openly admitted that he was far more interested in politics than trade and commerce. He became an Alderman, a magistrate and a member of the National Parks Committee. He was a man with an enormous social conscience and founded the Lawson House for youngsters on probation. John Lawson came into the business in 1961 and learned the trade from the bottom upwards, but it was not until 1971 when a big family meeting was convened that a firm-minded brother-in-law's brother-in-law laid the law down, made decisions with which they all agreed - well almost - and Francis Lawson was persuaded to retire. John Lawson took over running the shop and his brother-in-law ran the horticultural business. It was the best things that ever happened to the firm, and they have grown in size and stature ever since.

John Lawson and his wife, Jennifer's love of the business is evident and married to a shrewd awareness of people's needs and an ability to create around him a staff who still today feel as though they belong to the 'Family Lawson', he has steered the company safely ahead. It was Jennifer who built up the Kitchen and Cake Decorating departments. His children apart from Liz do not work in the business but are directors. They are a talented family and have abilities in all sorts of fields which makes board meetings full of interest, productive of innovative ideas making sure the way ahead is safeguarded but not afraid to make changes. John told me of the new way of purchasing and guidance which has come from their membership of the Associated Independent Stores organisation and Lawsons also use for their hardware business, the retail owned wholesaler Home Hardware (SW) at Braunton, North Devon.. This enables them to buy at the very best prices, gives them a constant insight into what is happening throughout the country and offers them useful advice on a range of matters. AIS also produces for them weekly figures showing how well they are doing. It was through the advice, guidance and buying power of AIS that Lawsons opened their new lighting department.

From John Lawson I also gained knowledge, albeit superficial, of the different manner in which different areas operated when it comes to spending. For example Lawson's Tavistock branch does incredibly well in its Bed Linen Department. Who can tell why! Though why I should be surprised when I remember that Sue Goode of Boots told me that the store at the top of Old Town Street has a totally different clientele than the shop at the bottom of New George Street!

The other thing that John Lawson finds has changed so much is the need to dot the I's and cross the t's in everything one does these days. It is especially important when dealing with staff. Every meeting needs recording. Nothing should be said off the cuff as it were. Not an easy thing to change ones ways when over the years with long standing staff it has always been possible to pat them on the back or give them a sound telling off as required. Both were totally acceptable to staff. However no longer. Watching an episode of the ITV series 'The Bill' the other evening reminded me of the conversation John and I had. On the TV Inspector Conway was telling Sergeant Cryer that in future he must not give any of his relief a bollocking. Everything should be 'Praise and encouragement'!

Lawson's still has some wonderful mementoes and memories of the past. John Lawson tells that in the early 1930's the great Mr Hornby himself came to the shop and sold his famous train sets and Meccano to Lawsons. Since that time Lawson's has always had an account with Meccano or their successors. He showed me some Meccano magazines dated for various months in 1932, carrying small box advertisements for Lawsons.

John Lawson can remember his father remarking that John's grandfather had not done too badly in his first year in 1904. He made £389. John looked at the books and corrected his father, 'No, he made £3pounds 8 shillings and 9d!

It is the Lawson's family's ability to keep the past alive and treasure its artefacts and at the same time be so positive about the future, that ensures their success. Undoubtedly Liz Lawson, as Managing Director, will put all her experience and man management skills into practice and for the good of the business but the sound foundations of the past will not have gone amiss.

The Pannier Market at the bottom of New George Street at one side and Cornwall Street on the other, has had a complete refurbishment. I remember the days before Plymouth was bombed when the old undercover market spilt on to the street outside on certain days a week. The lighting came from oil lamps, plump farm chickens hung on hooks, the subtle fragrance of saffron cake, the smell of cheese pervaded the air around some stalls and over all the strong smell of fresh fish wafted its way around the many fish carts some with awnings some without. It was a colourful scene, always noisy and a fun place to shop. Much of the noise came from the banter between the stallholders allied to the shouts from the traders extolling their wares. High up, the glass roofing was interlaced with green painted wrought iron, which threw strange shadows across the stalls. Sometimes it looked like dragons and my imagination would run riot. It was wonderful. That era has gone for good. Today's market is far more sophisticated with well laid out stalls which are there permanently with just a few 'daily benches' and not just for market days. The hygiene regulations have stopped most of the casual trading but it is still a good place to shop, the fruit and veg stalls sell the ordinary combined with the exotic, the cheese stall is laden with cheese from English to Italian, French to New Zealand. Cheap and cheerful clothes stalls have constantly changing stock and there is still that friendly air accompanied by the chit chat between stallholders.

Plymouth's market has a high reputation throughout the country and is also known to be one of the cheapest, if not the cheapest. The market traders are represented by the Plymouth Market Traders' Association of Express Goldsmith whose busy shop within the market is superbly stocked. The Secretary is another hardworking man, Jon Pope of J&J Hardware from whom you can buy almost anything in this line. The Association has a 10-strong committee who work alongside the City Council always with the aim to improve facilities. Life in the market is a world of its own, but not isolated; every trader is very much part of the community and eager to keep their customers. They are well aware that over the years the out of town supermarkets have lured many people away.

The history of Plymouth Retail Market is interesting. Henry III granted a market charter to the Prior and Convent of Plympton in 1245 and gave them the right to hold a market in what is now the Barbican area of the City. After the incorporation of Plymouth as a municipality by Act of Parliament in 1439, the newly formed Corporation acted quickly to obtain, the following year, a Royal Charter from Henry VI to hold open markets on Mondays and Thursdays.

A covered market was provided in 1565 when a new Guildhall was built on what is believed to have been the site of the original open markets, close to the present day Bretonside Bus Station. The building was raised on granite piers with the space beneath being used for the markets. The entire building was taken down and rebuilt on the same site between July and September 1606 and thereafter remained in use until 1800.

From the 17th century onwards, and probably earlier, the Corporation kept the market clean and in repair but leased the profits to a private person. A Mr Battersbye took 'The Market Standinges' for 99 years on the lives of his wife, son and daughter. He paid a premium of £100 and an annual rent of £5. This system of renting the profits of the market continued until 1892, when the Corporation took the profits and themselves ran the market.

The demolition of the Jacobean Guildhall in 1800 heralded a new beginning for the market, and four years later property was purchased on which a new market hall was erected on a site, between where Marks and Spencers and British Home Stores now stand. The market traded very profitably, was rebuilt in stages between 1885 and 1896 and remained in use as a market until 1959.

Before World War II the Pannier Market was used almost entirely for the sale of farm produce, fruit being sold mostly by street traders from barrows. In addition there was a separate meat market, wholesale meat market, corn exchange and some 40 shops, together with an open air fish market in an adjacent street. The Pannier Market was little used during the week but on Saturdays was packed with about 200 farmers and growers.

Miraculously the market building withstood the onslaught by German Bombers in 1941. Bombed out shopkeepers including Woolworths, Marks and Spencer and many other multiples were given sites in the market hall where concrete stalls were built for them. The normal market traders were moved outside to a succession of corrugated iron stalls arranged each side of one of the adjacent streets. This became known as Tin Pan Alley! It was not the same. The magic had gone but as the City Centre was rebuilt retail traders moved into the new shops and the market traders drifted back into the market. The fruit traders lost their pitches when the old streets in the City Centre disappeared. Many of them came into the market where they rented the stalls built for the shopkeepers. The whole of the premises were demolished in 1959 on the completion of the Plymouth Market complex by which time the character of the old market had completely changed from the pre-war days.

It did not take long for a new market spirit to grow. In the 1960's the Market Trader's Association was formed to protect their interest and to fight increased rents. That fight still continues and it has won the traders better facilities. About 90% of the traders belong to the Association so they have a strong lobby. Meetings between themselves and the City Council are held every six to eight weeks to keep things moving.

The social activities of the Market Traders Association are useful occasions for them all to meet and have some fun. Not the easiest occasions to arrange but they try to do something special at Christmas and perhaps a boat trip up to Calstock during the summer. These outings help their relationship with one another and the friendly attitude that comes across when you shop in the market shows this.

It is probably the atmosphere which strikes you most as you walk in to this different, cheerful world, away from the traffic. It is always buzzing, seldom quiet and you can feel the underlying excitement. Colourful awnings decorate the 'daily benches' which traditionally offer local growers the opportunity to sell their home-grown produce in the market. These days many of the daily benches are used regularly by the same traders, but there was a time when farmers would queue from early in the morning to make sure they secured a bench. They were allocated on a first come, first-served basis. Once in possession of a bench, produce was sold throughout the day and the stock cleared. If there was anything left over at 5pm then the remainder had to be removed. It was a practical and affordable way for locally grown produce to be sold - and still is.

Permanent stalls are much more expensive and are operated on a weekly licence scheme. It is not unknown for stalls and their good-will to be sold for as much as £20,000 when someone leaves. Catering is cared for in the Market by a variety of cafeterias each offering their own specialities.

Perhaps one of the most disappointing buildings in the City is The Armada Centre. It was to have been one of the best trading places in Plymouth, but somehow it has never quite fulfiled its expectations. Nonetheless I for one would not be without the branch of Sainsbury's with its large car park which is part of the complex. For some years it was the only Sainsbury's until the arrival at Marsh Mills of their mega-store. (More of them in Chapter 16). In the heart of the City Centre, next to the Copthorne Hotel, it attracts an enormous number of shoppers who bustle round the well-stocked store every week. I use it because it has just about everything I need under one roof and I am addicted to the buy one get one free syndrome which always seems to be good value here.

I had never thought about the intricate and detailed planning there has to be to make a vast complex, like the Armada Centre, tick. It was originally designed and built for 20 shops and 2 kiosks with an open entrance closed by means of a roller shutter for night-time security. Since those early days when it was opened in February 1986, the shops have become thirty by internal redesigning. More importantly a giant porch was added in the front which keeps out the winds, using the automatic doors as the shield.
The entire centre is computer controlled and takes only ten people to care for the whole building. Cleaners work all day long so they are visible and ready with the mop or dustpan to sort out spillages made by the public. It is very efficient and the staff are friendly; something that the Manager is insistent upon. Because of the efficiency of CCTV and mirrors there is little vandalism even in odd corners or the loos. The physical presence of staff also helps.

Everything is done 'in house' in the Armada Centre, even design and advertising work. Having been given a guided tour I realised that what one sees is only a part of what the building consists of. Behind the scenes there is as much space again as that which is visible; fire alleyways, delivery walkways for example. Underneath, and still accessible from Mayflower Street, is a huge delivery area, able to take several large lorries and a dozen cars all at once. Alongside this is the electrical room with all the SWEB connections, fuse boxes, meters, computer controls, with the primary control in the Manager's office. Yet another room has two large industrial gas heaters to provide warmth to the centre. All these controls are duplicated at the other end of the delivery area for Sainsbury's independent systems.

Above the general shopping area, as well as alongside Sainsbury's, are car parking facilities. These are administered by Sainsbury's during the day and become the responsibility of the Armada Centre overnight.

Up on the roof are two banks of huge extractor fans. These were put in to enable any smoke from a fire perhaps, to be cleared from the whole centre in two minutes. Should a fire ever occur the public are safe because the installation of the automatic front doors, whilst limiting the smoke clearance, has meant that a smoke curtain has been installed where the old roller shutter door was. This creates a smoke-free area low down so that people can escape in the event of a major fire. Running a complex like the Armada Centre is a responsible and very complicated job. It may well be that the new Shopping Malls planned at Drake Circus might learn a lesson or two from the efficient manner in which the Armada Centre is run.

There are many shops in the Armada Centre including Laura Ashley and a myriad of small independent shops. So many have changed ownership since I wrote about

Plymouth eight years ago. I did find The Baggage Centre still there, a member of the group with some 83 outlets all over the country which gives them strong buying power. They are always quick to stock anything new in design whether it is fashion or technological development. It is a comfortable shop with an unashamedly middle-aged staff who are courteous, well informed and well able to understand a customer's needs.

It is an extraordinary shop in which you can buy anything remotely connected with travel from a giant trunk to an electrical ,multi-adaptor for world-wide use, or an electronic mosquito killer! With more and more people travelling, this sort of shop is invaluable, especially when it is so well stocked.

One shop I was not surprised to find had moved. Anthony Horwich, the owner of Healthy Pulses, now in Eastlake Street found trading in the Armada Centre difficult. Largely because people do not like leaving the mainstream unless they have a specific purpose. His business flourishes in Eastlake Street where it is seen daily by thousands of people. He is a man of vision and has created something different from the normal run of Health Food shops. He has a specific range of products all presented by a staff, who like him, are knowledgeable. He works closely with places like the Natural Healing Centre and Unity House in Outlands Road. He lectures when time allows. Healthy Pulses provides everything you need for healthy living whether it is evening primrose oil, garlic or help from Anthony Horwich and his staff.

I have to admit to not going to the centre below Sainsbury's myself, but I do know people who do and enjoy browsing. The shops lead you out into Mayflower Street, itself full of small shops selling a whole variety of goods. If you are looking for clothes that are just that bit different then Francesca's sells beautiful, stylish clothes that are both a delight to the eye and essentially wearable. Francesca's is known for its International designer wear.

For men then Jon Saberton 's cannot be bettered. The man himself opened the shop almost forty years ago when he left Dingles, having worked previously in London for Austin Reed. It was a time when Carnaby Street was all the rage and in order to make sure that Plymouth's menfolk did not lose out on the fashion scene, Jon used to take the sleeper train to London, arrive at 7am and wander round the metropolis to see what was being displayed in the windows. He then brought those fashions to Plymouth. It was a fight to discover the manufacturers, their names and warehouses were closely guarded. He was persistent and eventually found the contacts he needed to supply him with what his fashion conscious customers wanted. He was certainly unique in Plymouth at that time. Many of those early customers still go to him. Times have changed, fashions have altered totally but Jon Saberton has never failed to keep abreast of current trends.

It is difficult to remember Mayflower Street in the early 1960s. It was almost barren land. Jon Saberton was the only shop open on one side and even that did not have a pavement outside on the day he moved in. A tactful but firm word with the council remedied that problem in 24 hours but only outside his shop! It still meant that he and the shop were beset by dirt and grit. Another phone call, another firm word and back the men came to complete the job. Jon Saberton was open for business.

In the succeeding years Jon's philosophy has never changed. He is a man who believes that style and workmanship are more important than designer labels. He looks for the cut, the workmanship and the materials. His service to his customers is second to none and deservedly he has created a regular following in his shops.

He has not always been in Mayflower Street. An increase in business in the 1970's, when flared trousers were all the rage, sent sales rocketing and he moved to a larger unit in Drake Circus. He stayed for eight years but found that Burton's Top Men Shops started eating into his market place and he upped sticks and returned to his original site.

There is more to being a successful retailer than coping with one's own business. The life of the community is very important and Jon Saberton has never shirked making his presence felt. A one time Chairman of the Chamber of Commerce and Industry, he helped to make Plymouth known on the map. It was his efforts that helped towards the formation of the Plymouth Marketing Bureau which to this day works for the promotion of the city. He has travelled widely in America and become an admirer of shopping malls. He will undoubtedly be enthusiastic about the new Drake Circus complex.

Close to Jon Saberton is the well-established Positano Restaurant which is well supported by its many, very satisfied regulars who love the Italian food and atmosphere. The Positano has a new and exciting neighbour Hobbs Coffee and Chocolate House, the brain child of Andy and Helen Hobbs who also own another Hobbs in Eastlake Street. Both establishments are delightful, spacious and very welcoming. I especially like the first floor of the Mayflower Street Hobbs. It is different from anything one finds anywhere in Plymouth. Andy designed and did the work himself. The result is a gentle harmony of soft colours, deep, enticing sofas and armchairs, pine tables and chairs and with space between tables providing comfort and privacy for clients. In both houses the coffee and chocolate are superb and the food is delicious. Once having discovered the virtues of Hobbs Coffee and Chocolate Houses you will become an addict without doubt, and at the same time become incredibly selfish; you will not want to tell your friends in case the venues become too popular as they deserve to be.

Oddbins in Mayflower Street was the first of its kind in Plymouth and I believe did much to encourage wine drinking. It now has many competitors including Bottoms Up in Exeter Street but Oddbins still continues to offer very good bargains and has a staff who are enthusiasts. The philosophy behind employment at Oddbins is to encourage the staff to learn as much as they can about wine and preferably go on to take exams in the subject. The younger of my twin daughters set out from here to become a Wine Master. An ambition not realised because marriage and children intervened. However it has given her a lasting love of wine and an all round knowledge which she enjoys and builds upon.

On a completely different subject I would make a mention of Kenroy Thompson, the suppliers of office stationery and equipment whose shop is on the corner of Mayflower Street and Cobourg Street. It does not pretend to compete with the big boys but the service is second to none. Ideal for the small business and for idiots like myself who need patient understanding! I have much to thank them for.

One of the positive things about the City Centre and one that has arisen in the last eight years from an entirely negative point, is the Shekinah Mission in Bath Street which works ceaselessly for the good of the homeless. Their commonsense approach to this very difficult and painful subject is an enormous benefit to the city. In the years since they became a 'first port of call' they have seen the profile of the users of the mission change from the more traditional 'roadmen' and 'transits'. Nowadays the clients are more likely to be young people, or ex-service personnel who have found it impossible to settle outside the structured life of the army or navy. In the forces they never had to pay bills, they were told what to wear and when to eat. They were used to working hard and playing hard. The life-style they now find themselves part of is an alien world. Then there are the people who are too young to be old and too old to be young. They find it hard to get jobs and absorbing new technology is almost impossible. Housing benefit regulations changed in Plymouth in 1997 and this has meant the almost total collapse of houses in multiple occupation owned by private sector landlords. Youngster, many of whom are not high achievers, find the rules difficult and they rely heavily on the Shekinah Mission.

The positive news in this difficult situation is that Peter Chapman who runs the mission now has two part-time outreach workers and they work closely with a settlement agency to find homes. With money available to provide basic training in English, maths and household management, the mission has been helping an average of one person a week back to work. Despite the opening of a new emergency direct access hostel for the 16-25 age group,Peter does not believe the problem will go away. He fully expects the Shekinah Mission to be serving up free cups of tea, and 12,000 meals a year well into the future.

The Theatre Royal. The City Centre

92

Chapter V

The Media, The Theatre, The Press

Every day, month and year underlines how powerful the Media and the Press are. Nothing is sacrosanct and success of businesses and people power depends largely on how, and if, they are supported by the Press and Television. Sometimes watching events unfold you wonder who is running the country. Equally there is practically no one who does not watch or read avidly news of one kind or another. I have always enjoyed newspapers and they have never been overtaken by television although I have to admit to being an enthusiastic viewer especially as I have got older and more reluctant to go out at night. Plymouth's own newspapers The Western Morning News and Evening Herald together with the Plymouth Extra, a freebie, and the Sunday Independent have supplied us with up to date happenings in the city and beyond for many years, local television has been with us since the sixties and the advent of local radio has given us more than one bite of the cherry in Radio Devon, Plymouth Sound and Pirate FM. But where did it all start?

The seeds of an adventure which was to play an enormous part in the life of Plymouth and the West Country, were germinated in that most sober and elegant of buildings, the Proprietary Library. Built by Foulston, it graced the old Cornwall Street until the German bombs laid it to waste in 1941. The seeds began to bear fruit in 1860 in the capable hands of the planters, William Hunt, Alfred Rooker, William Saunders and Edward Spender, to become the Western Morning News, a paper which with the Evening Herald, has become renowned for the highest standard of journalism and strict political independence. The men were an interesting quartet: Hunt had always had a leaning towards journalism. He lost considerable sums of money when a local paper, the Western Courier failed. He retired from local journalism but continued as Plymouth correspondent for the London Daily News, an appointment made by its editor, Charles Dickens. Alfred Rooker was a respected Tavistock solicitor who was held in such high regard in Plymouth that he was elected to the Council and made an Alderman without having to fight an election. He later became Mayor of Plymouth. William Saunders and Edward Spender were brothers-in-law and successful entrepreneurs who came to Plymouth from Bath seeking new businesses. Instead of going into newspapers these two men could well have invested their money in China Clay or Cornish tin or copper mines. Thankfully they turned all their considerable energies into a truly speculative investment, the Western Morning News.

It is a far cry from the modest offices that the Western Morning News first inhabited in Bedford Street, opposite the old Globe Theatre, to the magnificent and imposing ' Ship of State' at Derriford which they now occupy. For those of us old enough to remember, the original building eventually became Vickerys, an outfitters, which was taken over by Dingles just before World War II whilst the Globe Theatre became the old Prudential building.

The dreams and aspirations of the four men who met under the dome of the Proprietary Library fade into insignificance in what is achieved today with modern technology. The first issue was a little four page paper with six columns to each page. The front page was devoted to advertising and it cost just one penny. Yet for how much we should be grateful to them.

It so happened that this new phenomenon, a daily paper in the West, appeared just two days after Plymouth altered its clocks to conform with Greenwich Mean Time. Like most provincial areas, Plymouth used true solar time, which is about sixteen minutes later than London. It was the arrival of the train and telegraph that made it happen. Compiling timetables otherwise would have been impossible.

In 1860 times were sufficiently exciting for the public to clamour for news, and a real paper bringing news in the morning, some twelve hours before such national newspapers as The Times appeared, was nothing short of a miracle. What an achievement for Hunt who supervised the 'lay-out' and Spender who was the Editor. National news was morse-coded along the new telegraph lines and the Westcountry was almost the first to know what was happening. The times were extraordinary, Napoleon, like Hitler in the 20th century, had been defeated and Plymouth Sound had become a safe anchorage thanks to the building of the Breakwater by John Rennie, aided by Napoleonic prisoners. Isambard Kingdom Brunel had spanned the River Tamar with an enormous Railway Bridge, that opened Cornwall to the whole country and started tourism on a grand scale. Queen Victoria was on the throne encouraging her 'dear Lord Palmerston' to create the coastal defences now known as Palmerston 'follies'.

These follies were the subject of Edward Spender's first attack on the Government just ten days after the paper was launched. His editorial read ' If Plymouth is to maintain her position as capital of the West, if we are to avail ourselves of the advantages offered by the opening of the railways and docks which are now giving us new life and energy, we must keep our town unfettered by these military works that have usually been fatal to every place surrounded by them'.

If the vehemence of that statement rings a bell then it is because with equal ferocity the current editor of The Western Morning News, Barrie Williams and Alan Quatrough the editor of The Evening Herald champion the causes of today. The result of the attack on Palmerston's 'Follies' led to a Royal Commission which, for once, achieved improvements. The message to the current editors is emulate your predecessors, carry on the fight for the well being of Plymouth and its citizens.

Plymouth also had the Plymouth Journal, owned and edited weekly by an ambitious Londoner and friend of Charles Dickens, Isaac Latimer. The growing success of the Western Morning News drove him to set up in opposition and just five months after the birth of this paper, he launched the Western Daily Mercury, strictly adhering to Liberal principles. The two papers were to battle for circulation for many years to come.

It was not many years before William Saunders withdrew from his newspaper venture, and a company, headed by Spender was formed to take over the business. Sadly in 1878 Spender was drowned while bathing with two of his sons at Whitsand Bay. A granite cross still stands at Tregonhawke cliffs above the point where they drowned.

Whilst Spender was Chairman of the company he had recruited a young reporter, Albert Groser, from the Mercury, and he became Editor showing his great gift for organisation and an outstanding knowledge of railway time-tables!!!. As new railway lines came into being he put this knowledge to good use in using a train from one place to catch a train on a rival line to another, to speed delivery.

His son-in-law, Albert Hurd, writing about him, said ' he would have made a good manager for any railway company'. Albert Hurd learned his skills as a naval reporter whilst he was with the Morning News. An expertise for which he was eventually knighted. If the name sounds familiar you should not be surprised. His great-nephew, Douglas Hurd, was at one time Foreign Secretary and remains a writer of some distinction to this day.

The two papers have never lost the spirit of enterprise, nor fearless reporting. Albert Groser added to the paper's laurels continuously. He managed to get dispatches back from various minor wars being fought in Africa long before the London newspapers and sometimes even the Government had got wind of them. With the interest of the armed services close to their hearts, West Country people followed keenly every item of news. The Ashanti War of 1873 and the Zulu War of 1878-9, when the Plymouth man, Major Chard won the VC at Rorke's Drift, were notable instances. Major Chard now lies buried beneath a memorial window in the beautiful 450 year old church at Hatch Beauchamp in Somerset. Major Chard won his VC for his leadership which had given the willpower to 100 men of the South Wales Borderers to withstand the onslaught of 3000 Zulus for 12 hours, suffering fewer than 30 casualties. Plymouth breeds brave men.

Groser made full use of the fact that mail steamers from Africa and many other parts of the world, made their first call at Plymouth - rumour has it that he paid the porters at the Duke of Cornwall Hotel to keep a lookout for these great vessels as they steamed in: the Duke has a wonderful Crow's Nest perched right on top of the building which certainly was used to keep an eye on the liners making sure that the Duke of Cornwall's porters were at Millbay as soon as the tenders brought the passengers ashore, touting for business for the hotel. Groser's scoops were frequently the subject of Parliamentary questions - 'Will the Secretary of State tell us if this report in today's Western Morning News is correct?' This brilliant editor kept the paper ahead right up to the last successful march on Khartoum and when Stanley emerged from Africa after years of silence, it was not only Livingstone who was there - Groser sent a special commissioner to meet him.

Albert Groser's reign as Editor from 1878-1895 coincided with revolutionary changes in printing processes which have been going on ever since. How would he have reacted to the computer controlled printing of today, I wonder.

In 1895 the Mercury started an evening paper, the Western Evening Herald, which was a great success from its first issue. Thomas Owen, Member of Parliament for Launceston, bought the Mercury in 1897, and founded a new company, the Western Newspaper Co Ltd. In 1920 the company was acquired by Sir Leicester Harmsworth, MP for Caithness and Sutherland, who had been closely associated with his elder brothers, Alfred, Harold and Cecil, the future Lords Northcliffe, Rothermere and Harmsworth, in their newspapers and periodical enterprises, which had transformed the face of journalism.

In 1921, after sixty years of intense rivalry, the Western Morning News and the Western Daily Mercury merged and so the Western Evening Herald also came under the control of the Western Morning News Co Ltd, using the premises of the Mercury in Frankfort Street as their headquarters.

Another era began on December 1st 1938 when the building that became so familiar to us over the years, Leicester Harmsworth House in George Street, was opened as the home of the company and its many interests, including the two prestigious newspapers the Western Morning News and the Western Evening Herald. It was built on the same site as the old Mercury offices which had hardly changed since they were built in 1860, 75 years before. It was an astonishing performance because whilst the premises were being rebuilt there was no loss of production. New machinery was installed, more modern equipment, and the editorial staff emerged from their Dickensian cubbyholes into a great open plan floor space with everyone in one room, editors and all. Only the editor-in-chief, James Palmer, had his separate office. They thought the space palatial. When I went there in 1992 at the invitation of the then editor of the Western Morning News, Colin Davison, to sit in on a daily editorial meeting, my immediate reaction was how cramped they all were. What a transformation when I went to Derriford this time, to the stunning and well designed building which is now their home.

No sooner had the new offices, in what is now New George Street, been opened than war broke out in 1939. Paper rationing made the printing of newspapers difficult. James Palmer was removed to Bristol as Chief Regional Information Officer at the Ministry of Information, and W. Owen Mills, the editor of the Western Evening Herald, took over from him, running both the papers. It must be one of their proudest records that in spite of the blitz, which devastated everything around Leicester Harmsworth House, and cut off electricity, water and gas, nonetheless there was never a day that went past without a paper being produced.

It was only the presence of the staff in the building that saved it from certain destruction during the night of March 21st 1941. They literally threw firebombs off the roof, and put out what fires did start. When the All Clear sounded every building around them was either flattened or on fire. The staff collected what copy was in hand and the type that had been set, and piled into their private cars.. Led by Fred Crisp, a sub-editor, who was also a dispatch rider for the Civil Defence services, they weaved their way out of Plymouth around great craters in the road, trying to avoid the debris falling around them from burning buildings, and managed to get to the company's Exeter offices where, with the help of local staff called in, they produced a four page tabloid Morning News which must have looked much like the very first edition in 1860.
Private cars brought the papers back to Plymouth, seeking out remaining newsagents as they went and delivering them with their supply of papers. Wonderful stuff and representative of the way Plymouth withstood this dreadful time.

When power was restored the Herald moved back to Plymouth but it was to be some years before the Western Morning News returned in 1944. That great editor, Noel

Vinson, took over as editor in 1948. He had become assistant editor the previous year and before that news editor of the Herald for a short time. A Plymothian, with a true love for the city, and a great feel for journalism, he was the right man for the job. Always fair, he nonetheless demanded a very high standard from his staff, which he got. The Western Morning News immediately took on a new face. Out went the advertising on the front page to be replaced with headline news. His first front page carried the story of the death of Tommy Handley, an all time favourite comedian, who became famous for the radio show ITMA - It's That Man Again.

Noel Vinson did not have an easy time in those first few years. Industrial disputes disrupted both papers, sometimes just 'working to rule'. Finally in the summer of 1959 a strike stopped printing for five weeks. Rumour has it that Noel Vinson taught his journalists how to play bridge during that time! He certainly was a fine player himself, captaining the Devon bridge team for some years and becoming a founder member of The Plymouth Bridge Club which is still going strong today in Moor View House, just off Mutley Plain by the Fortescue. He partnered my mother, also a bridge fanatic, on many occasions and I still use the silver tankards she won as the winner of the Western Morning News Bridge Cup.

Both the Western Morning News and the Evening Herald have always had editors of stature and this tradition continues today. Barrie Williams edits the Western Morning News and has ensured that it remains one of the most successful morning provincial papers. Now in tabloid format, it covers a wide variety of subjects within the region giving its readers a clear insight as to what is happening within the counties. The articles have a sharpness about them that makes them good reading and frequently bring home controversial points which in turn create constant comment by letter or e-mail from readers. It is fair, non-political, and tackles life from the Mendips to the Isles of Scilly, with different editions for different parts of the territory. It is truly the voice of the West of England.

The Evening Herald which shed its 'Western' title on January 31st 1989 has just acquired a new editor. Rachel Campey, its lively female editor has departed for pastures new as Deputy News Editor of 'The Times' and her successor is Alan Qualtrough from the Daily Express. He is a newcomer to Plymouth and is relishing the opportunity of carrying on, and expanding on, the work of his illustrious predecessors. The role of the Evening Herald, as Rachel Campey pointed out to me, is to highlight the life of Plymouth and the surrounding area and so become its 'meeting point'. It is essentially a Community Newspaper and as such has won prestigious awards. There is no holding back in its columns. It is sharp on news content, friendly and encourages local comment. It is not afraid to print controversial letters on a wide range of issues about which readers feel strongly. These can be City Council decisions or a report in the Evening Herald with which they do not agree. The letters page is a powerful platform for debate. The letters come in by post and these days about 50% are e-mailed. It is a paper eagerly awaited by its readers, and a successful medium for those wanting to advertise, as is witnessed by the endless columns filled with adverts every night offering anything from a cockatoo to a computer. Talk to Plymothians and you will discover that they do feel the Herald is their paper. It reports on what my generation refer to as 'hatched, matched and dispatched' in other words births, marriages and deaths. It supports any number of good causes. St Luke's Hospice for one, where the paper helped to raise £1m for its new extension. Another was the campaign of support for the kidney unit at Derriford hospital which ensured that this unit survived. The Herald also supports an enormous range of community initiatives through financial aid and/or editorial coverage.

Within the building at Derriford which cost somewhere in the region of £33 million, is a power house of industry. Not only does it house the two papers, it is the hub of printing for its own papers, it takes on the printing on its £10 million Goss HT60 machine of other nationals, magazines and contract printing. It is always alive. It is the largest and most influential news gathering, publishing and printing organisation in the South West. Plymouth is proud of its two leading daily papers and its weekly Plymouth Extra. If the original quartet Hunt, Rooker, Saunders and Spender are watching from above, their heads must be too big for their haloes - swollen with justifiable pride.

Slowly but surely Plymouth is beginning to recognise what an asset The Theatre Royal is to the city. I sometimes think it is pride in the success of the theatre that pleases Plymothians most, rather than actually going to the theatre! Their pride is justified but how wrong they are not to revel in all that it offers us. Even today I believe it is true to say that it is not Plymothians who form the giant part of the audience but people from as far away as Bristol who travel by coach, train and car to enjoy the shows that are mounted.

Historically it has never been any different. Before World War II the city supported two major theatres, the old Theatre Royal and the Palace in Union Street as well as some smaller ones including the Repertory Theatre in Princess Street. Amateur theatre has always been very well supported because they have always been of a high standard and really had a ready made audience. It was probably this resistance to things theatrical that prevented the new Theatre Royal from making its appearance. There was a great deal of opposition. Friends of the Palace Theatre felt that it should have been refurbished, and councillors resented the idea of investing vast sums in a theatre of any kind. However one looks at it, to have refurbished the Palace would have been a financial disaster. It does not, nor ever could have, the facilities a theatre of today needs and it is woefully lacking in parking space.

Even so there are many of us who remember with affection this old music hall built in 1898 and many a happy hour have I spent conjuring up visions of all the stars it helped to launch. The long, winding corridor that used to lead to the stalls, had walls covered with old playbills. There was Carrol Levis and his Plymouth and BBC Discoveries, Eddie Gray, Arthur English, Cardew Robinson, Morton Fraser and his Harmonicas, Morecombe and Wise, Dick Emery, Frankie Howard. One poster gave equal billing to Benny Hill and Cherry Lind. There will be few who will not remember Benny Hill but I wonder how many remember Cherry Lind and the fact that she was the daughter of George East who used to conduct his Palm Court Orchestra in Pophams restaurant. Pophams was an upmarket department store which is now occupied by Lloyds TSB and a theme pub. The famous Lily Langtry, Max Miller and Gracie Fields also graced the Palace stage. Gracie was a regular visit to Cawsand where she stayed with her old friend Fred Eteson, the landlord of The Ship Inn. I saw the great Richard Tauber in

'Old Chelsea' in this theatre and over the years many more famous musicals including South Pacific, Oklahoma and Paint Your Wagon. One of the last acts I remember seeing was Jewell and Warris, such fun to watch and yet two men who could not stand the sight of each other. I have no doubt the decision to build the Theatre Royal was the right one, but the memories still flood over me as I drive past the doors of the Palace which is now known as The Dance Academy. Incidentally The Dance Academy now has a new full time promoter, its seasoned and mildly eccentric DJ, Tom Costelloe. In a very short space of time he has regenerated the club. It has gone on-line in a big way with a spanking new web-site. He is bringing 'names' to the Academy and Tom has plans to turn it into Plymouth's version of Cream. He has given himself two years to achieve what he has in mind. He will tell you that the atmosphere is right and the nearest description is of nights on Ibiza. Something that you don't get in other clubs in Britain. He is an all-rounder and in his busy career has found time to work for MTV and IPC magazines, building up expertise in the internet and new technology systems. He is an exciting man and may well be the one to make the old Palace once more a venue - albeit a very different one - that will become famous around the world.

In just over eighteen years the new Theatre Royal has established itself as probably the most prestigious provincial theatre. It is award winning and as I write it has won the most welcoming theatre category in this year's Barclay Theatre Awards. The awards, the only UK-wide awards for excellence in the theatre are presented by the Theatrical Management Associations. Other Plymouth nominations are: Best actor in a supporting role - Guy Henry for the Royal Shakespeare Company's Volpone and Best new play - Silence by Moira Buffini.

The Theatre Royal has been incredibly lucky in its leadership. No one would argue that it was the advent of Roger Redfarn in 1984 which brought the theatre to life. It has always amazed me that such a consummate professional was persuaded to take on the role of artistic director in a theatre which was patently struggling at that time. He told me that me that a council who had the guts to build such a theatre deserved some backing and he had an instinctive feeling that he could do the job. Such modesty is inherent in this talented, internationally acclaimed man. When I first met him I thought he was a touch flamboyant but underneath that protective exterior I discovered there was a man so sensitive that he grieved over the world, bit his finger nails at first nights, and worried about Plymouth.

This was a man who fell in love with Judy Garland when he was seven years old and knew from that moment that the theatre was going to be his career. He told me that when he met his idol some years later, she kissed him and he didn't wash his face for a week! Before he came to the Theatre Royal he had covered a variety of roles within the theatre. Assistant Stage Manager with Penelope Keith amongst others. As a director he spent five years at the Belgrade in Coventry and his work as a freelance director took him all over the globe from America, Japan and Australia to Europe.

His contribution to the ongoing success of the Theatre Royal is something we must never forget. Not only for the various productions which he successfully transferred to the West End but also for his passionate commitment to the City. In his time he directed several of the Theatre Royal's community productions on a gigantic scale. The

Plymouth Blitz was commemorated with a cast of 400 in 'High Heels in the Rubble. He directed the very first 'Music of the Night' in the Citadel - now a treasured bi-annual occasion. Held in the open air, needless to say it rained, but the 4,000 strong audience could not have cared less. Who could resist the excitement of the singing, the dancing, the bands of the Royal Marines and Royal Artillery performing numbers that included a tribute to Andrew Lloyd-Webber, music from Oliver, Me and My Girl, Finlandia, Pomp and Circumstance, Les Miserables and many more? The finale with its spectacular firework display was the best Plymouth had ever seen and no doubt was the basis on which subsequent 'Music of the Night' occasions have striven to outdo each other - and generally succeeded! It might have been the reason why Plymouth has now acquired the annual International Firework Competition which has firework manufacturers competing against each other - a spectacular event over two nights in the summer.

With Roger Redfarn's departure I must admit to wondering how much his loss would be felt. Of course it was but the theatre and the city were lucky enough to acquire the enormously talented and dedicated man, Adrian Vinken, who as Chief Executive of both the Theatre Royal and Plymouth Pavilions, has been both inspirational and commercially brilliant. Under his astute guidance the theatre has developed a close relationship with Cameron Mackintosh, launching the national tours of Les Miserables and the Phantom of the Opera and co-producing the national tour of Oliver. It is nationally recognised as the most accomplished producing theatre for musical theatre in England. It has been proud of its recent world premieres which have included 'The Impostor' by Pete Lawson (based on Moliere's Tartuffe), The Car Man (with the world renowned Adventures in Motion Pictures), 'Silence' by Moira Buffini (with Birmingham Rep) and, by local writers, Meat and Union Street. European premieres have included 'Tiger Tail' by Tennessee Williams and an adaptation of William Wharton's 'Birdy' which went on to the Comedy Theatre, London. 1996 saw six Theatre Royal productions running concurrently in the West End, an achievement unique in regional theatre.

The Royal Shakespeare Company's residence for seasons has caught the imagination of Plymothians and played to largely full houses. One can only hope that the rumours of its departure from the city are unfounded and a way will be found to anchor them here. It is not only the performances which are so important, it is the diverse programme of education and community work which is part of their season.

Musicals have always been one of the strengths of the Theatre Royal and during the summer of 1999 it produced two new musicals - Great Balls of Fire and Spend, Spend, Spend - prior to their West End premieres. Spend, Spend, Spend won the 1999 London Standard/Carlton TV Award for Best Musical and was nominated for 8 Laurence Olivier Awards in 2000.

It is wonderful to have such an alive, thriving theatre which is virtually never dark. Its coffee bar is busy all day with people using it as a meeting place and sometimes just somewhere to sit and look through its massive windows onto the busy Royal Parade outside. When I was there the other day, the grand piano was being played by a man, whose name I do not know. He was not young and obviously had a love of the ivories and a liking for the music of Ivor Novello and Noel Coward. For someone of my age

100

it was delicious nostalgia and all thrown in for the price of a cup of coffee. The upstairs restaurant is delightful and has some interesting and innovative dishes.

Adrian Vinken brought to the Theatre Royal more than just his enormous ability to run and co-ordinate a successful theatre. He also brought with him his dream. A down to earth project which would open up the way to providing the best rehearsal and education facilities of any theatre in the country. He found a piece of land alongside the waters of Cattedown and then began to draw up his plans with sympathetic architects. The dream had just the chance of becoming reality but first he had to find the money! His quest reminded me very much of Dr Geoffrey Potts whose dream of a National Marine Aquarium is now reality and there for the world to see. Geoffrey Potts spent years finding the money for a project that is of enormous benefit to Plymouth. Adrian Vinken had this same passionate belief in the advantage for the city in the realisation of such a project and his tenacity has paid off. He has acquired money from the Lottery, from Heritage, from European Funding and from the Council and so Plymouth is about to profit from one person's belief and determination. Isn't it amazing how often these people and their dreams are not Plymothians but have such a desire to see the city successful?

What will this mean to Plymouth? It means that the existing Education Team will have a base from which to develop audiences and participation in running the largest youth theatre in Britain. It is already doing tremendous work with its 700 strong Young Company and a community theatre with more than 200 members. In January 2000 the Young Company and People's Company worked together for the first time on a production of Spring Awakening by Frank Wedekind.

The Education Team also works with schools throughout the South West to provide curriculum support in the form of skills-based workshops for students and teachers, large scale performance projects and insights into the creative process of theatre production. The 1999 production of Monkey saw more than 150 children from 10 local schools participating in a large-scale musical theatre premiere.

In addition to the best rehearsal facilities, the new buildings will also house the increasingly large Costume Department of the theatre, will allow TRAC to have a base. In fact there is a never ending list of uses which includes the opportunity for the general public to come along and see how shows are developed. It goes without saying that there will be refreshment facilities.

It would have been much easier if this new building had been in operation when the Theatre Royal's terrific Millennium Project was being created. Supported by the Arts Council of England's Millennium Festival Fund, the Union Street Project was an opportunity for people of all ages to celebrate the history of one area of Plymouth.

Known throughout the world Plymouth's Union Street, has for centuries been its watering hole and 'Pleasure Palace'. And so it was appropriate that the story of this famous street should be the inspiration for this remarkable year-long community project led by the people of Plymouth. Building on reminiscence from local people Union Street celebrated the vibrancy and diversity of an area with an international reputation and included original plays, a film reminiscence project, training courses in

writing, acting, dance, music and photography, and a major community theatre production involving 300 local people in August 2000.

The result was an exciting, vibrant theatrical experience, enjoyed by everyone who was fortunate enough to see it.

No one could ever accuse the Theatre Royal of a lack of balance in the programme. You can see theatre at its best across the spectrum from new writers with new approaches to the stage, best loved musicals like West Side Story, Gilbert and Sullivan's HMS Pinafore straight from the Savoy Theatre, London, Opera, Ballet and one must never forget the sensational Pantomime Season.

I have been a devotee of Pantomime ever since I saw my very first one in the old Theatre Royal way back in 1929. I admit to hating any company that dares to go away from pantomime tradition but Plymouth does not allow that, thank heavens. Each year they play to packed houses and each company brings its own stars. In the year 2000 we have Aladdin with Gary Wilmot and John Inman. I wish my favourite pantomime dame was still treading the boards but alas, Plymouth born Jack Tripp has hung up his wigs and costumes and decided at almost eighty years it is time to stop.

Jack talked to me when he was in Plymouth with the inimitable Roy Hudd, June Whitfield and Keith Barron in 'Babes in the Wood'. It was probably one of the best pantomimes I have ever seen in seventy odd years. Much of it came down to the direction, great insight and love of pantomime that Roy Hudd has. This was true pantomime, relying on the time honoured jokes and hisses, Oh yes he will, Oh no he won't. Slick routines which relied on perfect timing. An occasion of magic for children of any age - and I include myself! Jack Tripp had that magic at his finger tips. He knew how to play an audience with an artistry born of natural talent and years of experience. He told me some of the tricks of the trade one of which was that you behave in a totally different way at matinees in the school holidays than you do after the children have gone back to school and matinees are populated with the out-of-town senior citizens who come in droves of coaches to the show. A different gesture, a different intonation will still produce the laughs - absolutely no need for smut.

Jack told me about the weekly visits he used to make to the Palace with his father in his childhood. His father was a baker on the Barbican and the family lived above the shop. His father never missed a Monday night and had his regular seats, and if the young Tripps were well behaved, one of them was allowed to go with Father. Jack remembers all the greats of his childhood including Harry Lauder, Wilson, Keppel and Betty, Gracie Fields and Ella Sheilds of 'Burlington Bertie' fame.

Plymouth is the birthplace of several of our top showbiz names. Sir Donald Sinden lived here as a child and has appeared on the stage of the Theatre Royal. I talked with him when he was appearing with Michael Williams in the Ray Cooney Farce 'Out of Order'. A demanding role if ever there was one. He recalled playing at the Palace. Not the most comfortable of theatres. I first met this fine theatrical knight almost fifty years ago when he and his wife, Diana, were lunching with Nigel Davenport and his first wife Helena, in their flat in Montague Square, London. It was a day he was happy to remember and will never forget. He was almost on the point of abandoning his theatrical career. He only ever got the opportunity to be an understudy. All that changed as a result of one telephone call in the middle of lunch. It was Donald's agent telling him he had a part in the film 'The Cruel Sea'. That role changed his entire life and he has never looked back. Now he is one of the most respected and loved of actors. Apart from his talent who could ever forget his rich, plummy voice!

I saw Nigel Davenport in the Theatre Royal a while later in 'Importance of Being Earnest'. A major star now but at the time of that famous lunch he was a spear carrier in one of Shakespeare's plays in the Aldwych theatre.

Wayne Sleep, Michael Ball, Charles Dance have all graced the stage of the Theatre Royal and have been proud to appear in their home city. New talented Plymouth youngsters are emerging as well and I do not suppose it will be many years before we see three local girls, Ellie Conrad Leigh who is now 18 , Lara Cook 10, and Jodie Falcus 8 in a production in the theatre, They have endeared themselves to us for their performances in the delightful BBC drama series 'Down to Earth' with Warren Clarke and Pauline Quirke.

The advent of Plymouth Pavilions gave the city a new dimension. This modern building standing opposite the Duke of Cornwall Hotel and built on the ground of the old Millbay Railway Station, is a modern building which caters for all needs. £32 million was invested in this multi-purpose leisure, conference and entertainment complex and it is open all year round except for Christmas Day. It has been the topic of many a fiscal argument and the heavy and continual investment is a worry. However having looked at the cost objectively and sounded out several commercial organisations with the thought that they might like to take it on, it has been discovered that the way in which it is run and controlled at present is considerably more cost effective than any outsider could achieve. This is all done in the same way as so much of the city today - in partnership - with the council and the Chief Executive, Adrian Vinken pulling together to make it successful.

The Pavilions provides a great service to the city. It boasts an Arena that is able to cope with such technical diversities as a heavy metal concert, antiques fair, Party Political Conference, or a world class sporting event such as The British Open Snooker. Having been hooked on snooker ever since the talented Steve Davis burst upon our screens, I am always thrilled to see the Snooker Stars arrive in town. The evergreen talent of the Whirlwind, Jimmy White, the amazing dexterity of Ronnie O'Sullivan, and the astounding skills of the up and coming - and frequently arrived - youngsters.

The Arena has played host to an array of top stars including Tom Jones, Stereophonics, Steps, Shirley Bassey, French and Saunders, All Saints, Jim Davidson and Chris Rea. Anyone who has children or grandchildren will have discovered it has some of the best leisure facilities in the South West. No child could be anything but enchanted by The Atlantis pool which has a gentle sloping beach area, shipwrecked galleon, wave machine, waterfalls, jacuzzi and two special flumes.

The Swiss Lake Ice Rink is a busy, popular place where the learners tumble happily and those with greater skills show off! It is decorated on an Alpine Village theme and if you fancy becoming a competent skater, lessons can be arranged by appointment. One of the great things about The Pavilions is that everywhere, including the leisure facilities, is fully accessible for disabled people.

I have spent many an hour waiting for my grandchildren whilst they skated or swam, enjoying coffee and a cake in The Café which is an ideal rendezvous in the centre of the building, from which you can watch the world go by. They provide excellent cakes and scones and a very acceptable light lunch. The Pavilions caterers are known for the proficiency with which they handle outside events like the Lord Mayor's Banquet and preparing dinner for Prime Minister Tony Blair when he last visited the city.

My knowledge of The Barbican Theatre was slight when I visited it eight years ago in my quest for information to include in my book 'Invitation to Plymouth'. I was enormously impressed by the work that was done here but thought it disappointing that such energy and enthusiasm should be kept within such a cramped space. This time I could not believe my eyes when I walked through the doors. I walked up steps into a light, cheerful foyer with space on one side for people to sit and talk and immediately at the top of the steps information on all that is happening in the theatre. It did not take me long to discover that what I saw was nothing to what will be within a short space of time, thanks to further funding. The whole entrance is to be revamped and part of it will become a café bar, open all day to the public, encouraging them to come in and learn for themselves all that this remarkable place has to offer.

It has always been a theatre designed to help the community rather than devoted to performances. It tends to have productions on Thursday, Friday and Saturdays of every week and the productions are a mixture of new plays by new writers, amateur companies, one-man shows and a traditional pantomime, again usually written by a

104

local writer like Hugh Janes who has written Jack and the Beanstalk for the 2000 pantomime. With less than 200 seats in the theatre, it makes for an atmosphere which automatically gathers the audience into the performance. It is an exciting venue and much loved by actors who may well tell you that it is one of their favourite provincial stages in the whole of the country. Throughout the year professional touring companies bring a wide variety of productions to the stage. The work of the theatre today is frequently involved with the Theatre Royal. For example a new play may well be tried out here and then transfer to The Drum.

The Lottery and Heritage funding together with help from Plymouth City Council and the Arts Council of England, the Gulbenkian foundation and others has enabled the theatre to purchase what was Papa Joe's restaurant and the old Bethel Seamen's Mission and in so doing given the theatre all this extra space which now gives them a rehearsal studio as well as the foyer space. More space, better facilities has helped the purpose of the theatre to go forward. With two excellent directors in Sheila Snellgrove and Artistic Director Mark Laville supported by a small, committed team, every day brings something new to their lives. I realised when I was talking to Mark that his role is far more than Artistic Director. It seems to me that he has also to be a business organiser, a fund raiser and many other things that he would never have thought belonged to his role when he first arrived. He thrives on it and like Sheila Snellgrove is totally dedicated and committed.

More and more work is being done in the community. The 'Theatre in Education' service goes out to schools in Devon and Cornwall and has thrown up interesting and innovative ideas. For example, sensitive subjects like drug abuse are dealt with by means of specially written plays for schools which are part performance and part interactive. This has worked very successfully and now through the interest of parents, has been extended to play to audiences of children and parents. It gets the message home in a strong, sympathetic and meaningful way, which straight forward lecturing would never achieve. More importantly it is enabling parents to discuss difficult subjects with their offspring, which would have been almost 'off limits' before. The Barbican is truly a Theatre for the People and proves it by working as much away from the theatre in schools, youth clubs, church halls, village halls and many other almost unexpected venues which have proved suitable.

The Barbican Theatre is alive with activity every day of the week. For example on Mondays Yoga starts the day followed by Belly Dancing. In the afternoon after school there is a drama class 'Strike Lightning' for 5-8 year olds, at 6pm anyone who enjoys singing is invited to join the 'Free Your Voice World Choir' and at 7.30pm there is an Advanced Contemporary Dance Class.

Tuesdays is equally busy with Dance Able from10.30-11.30am, Time to Dance between 2-4pm. Waterfront Writers, a group of established and would-be writers meet at 2pm. Young circus enthusiasts belong to Trapeze at 5pm for beginners and 5.45pm for those who know a little more. The Junior Youth Theatre meets at 5pm - drama for 12-16 year olds. Dancemania takes over at 7.30pm.

On Wednesdays there is Wicked Grin at 1.30pm, an interactive drama and role play class which is designed to develop confidence, self-esteem and discovery for people with learning difficulties, carers and friends. Dramamad at 4.30pm for 8-11 year olds and the Barbican Young Peoples Theatre Company for 16-25 year olds meet at 6pm. The place goes mad at 7pm when Flamenco and Salsa enthusiasts get going.

Dancelink on Thursdays allows 10-16 year olds the chance to work and dance with professionals. This is also the day for the Plymouth Youth Dance Company - you need to attend an audition to join this talented number.

Fridays is devoted to circus. At 6pm for 7-10 year olds there is Junior Youth Circus followed by Senior Youth Circus at 7pm for 10 years old and over.

Saturdays afternoons is for the Barbican Community Theatre Workshop at 2pm. It is described as 'A melting pot for theatre enthusiasts of all ages to develop and explore new skills. No previous experience is necessary, just energy, commitment and willingness to try new experiences. The group forms the backbone of the community pantomime. If you would like to be a performer in the panto or work back-stage in costume design and making, technical stage management just come along any Saturday afternoon and you will be very welcome.' Talk to the actor Colin McIntyre, who is such a favourite in the television series 'Always and Everyone' and you will discover that he started his career here and not so very long ago! Most of these classes and workshops ask for a small fee but the Community Theatre Workshop is free.

I especially liked one of the projects which has come to fruition recently. Plymouth school pupils and others including a group of six people with learning difficulties at St George's Art Group have been involved with designing banners for Union Street. The project was aimed at giving the local community the chance to be involved in designing bold colourful banners to be attached to the new lighting columns in Union Street which are part of the city council's environmental improvement programme for Stonehouse. Inspiration for the designs were hugely varying. The children of Year 6, High Street Primary School, Stonehouse chose the Royal William Yard, Stonehouse Bridge, the marina and Millbay ferryport as their subjects. St George's were inspired by the Australian 'Woga Woga' quilts. They made them by weaving together pictures of clothing, coloured paper and fabrics. The idea of the quilts links with the people who left from Plymouth in the 18th century to go to Australia. Other interesting designs came from a Stonehouse resident, Myra Knowles who created four banners using her own photographic collection as a collage and another lady, Jackie Ball used the fire at Millbay Laundry as her theme for two banners. Yet another great example of the community working together.

The Barbican Theatre also has an Exhibition Space which invites artists and makers to exhibit their work in a new and exciting venue. Artists and makers are encouraged to consider ways in which their exhibition can be extended to directly involve the community and users of the building. This depends entirely on what the artists/makers feel is possible and appropriate. Ideas may include a studio open day, short workshops culminating with a display of work produced alongside the artists work. Just contact Sarah Pym at the theatre and she will give you all the details you require.
Tel:01752 267131

I remember talking to David Oddie, a previous artistic director of the Barbican Theatre. It was his enthusiasm that started this renaissance. In 1980 he formed Rent-a-Role to establish drama as a vital part of learning, therapy and education. It develops approaches, techniques and structures that have made it unique in this field. David's enthusiasm for his project and his determination to acquire the backing he needed led him to pound on the doors of businesses and government until he got what he wanted. Rent-a-Role which has become the present operation, was, and still is, supported by the Arts Council, South West Arts, the Council and many others. Thousands of young people are involved in or watch the programmes that have ensued, year after year and in the safe, imaginative hands of the present team, it is flourishing.

David Oddie's words to me eight years ago are still pertinent and sum up what the Barbican Theatre stands for.

'Art is the process through which we express, share and come to understand our deepest feelings and responses. It belongs to all of us regardless of age, sex, race or class. In these times of division between people art can reach out, unite and remind us of our common heritage'.

The Amateur Theatre in Plymouth is alive and well. Every year a whole variety of productions are staged and will be seen not only by the devoted followers of each company but by Plymothians who know what a high standard is achieved. As I write The Carmenians are in rehearsal for their forthcoming show, My Fair Lady. It has a black and white theme and will star such popular players as Debbie Lawson, Mike Noble, and newcomer Greg Pannell. Directed by John Dane it will be at the Athenaeum Theatre. The Wranglers are about to produce Aladdin as the 50th joint venture directed and written by Barry Sanigar and choreographed by Wendy Holmes over a period of 15 years. The City of Plymouth Operatic Society opted this year for 'Happy as a Sandbag' a wartime musical, as a tribute to the 60th anniversary of the Battle of Britain. Their home is the Devonport Playhouse, once the Devonport Central Methodist Hall. They have the well known and justly respected, Angela Collins as their choreographer. A lady who is also one of the kingpins of 'Music of the Night'.

The Gilbert and Sullivan Fellowship thrive and are always a pleasure to watch and listen to. The Athenaeum is also the home of the Western College Players, The Tamaritans and the local Music Festival.

The Tamaritans who celebrate their 50th birthday this year are to receive a massive funding injection of £100,000 from the South West Regional Development Agency.

The purpose is so that they can redevelop an old warehouse at Manor Gardens to create a community arts, theatre and dance facility that can also be used by other community groups. The Tamaritans is just not an amateur company who perform two or three times a year. They go much further and train their members in stagecraft, lighting, management, sound and performance skills. They are justly proud of their record in sending young people on to drama courses and professional employment in theatre, television and radio.

Estover's Soundhouse Project is another one to receive £100,000 from the South West Regional Development Agency. The project will be housed in a new three-storey community performing arts centre at Estover Community College. The building will provide a 230 seat auditorium, a 170-seat studio, instrument workshop, café, recording studio, music technology suite, music gallery, practice booths, multi-media classroom and a drama/dance suite. One of the main aims is to provide training, business and job opportunities in the field of music and technology.

The main purpose of The Athenaeum is as the home of the members of its Society. Here there are frequently some very fine lectures and it has a very active membership. In recent years I was asked to speak on one evening. Not my most favourite role in life but I need not have become too big-headed. I was informed in no uncertain terms that I was almost a last resort! Their distinguished speaker was unable to come. I duly arrived and was shown into the lecture room and asked to sit in the front row until I was called to the podium. This I duly did and was rewarded by the arrival of a couple who sat directly behind me. The man, quite loudly, told his wife that he could not imagine why he had been dragged there to hear some elderly lady speak about nothing!! It gave me the giggles and inside laughter continued inside me when I stood up to speak and the poor man realised I must have heard every word! He was quite right I am an old f... and I did speak about nothing in particular for over an hour! They seemed to enjoy it - but I haven't been asked back!

In the world of theatre and film one must not forget the Arts Centre in Looe Street, which provides much that is good in the world of film for those who like the unusual and occasionally provides one with the opportunity to see a film that has missed the city or only put in a fleeting appearance.

There are many people who contribute to the entertainment of the people of Plymouth and its far reaching PL postcode. Theatrical Agencies have to be on the ball to survive today and Plymouth is blessed in having two excellent examples. Hartbeat where the owners, Robbie and Liz Hart work their socks off to provide every sort of entertainer for the clubs and hotels, service establishments and any venue that needs cabaret or bands. If you ring them up and ask for their list you will find anything from snake charmers - using live snakes - and street entertainers to comedians, bands, duos, to all that is needed to create a casino for the evening! The Moonlight Agency is the other lively outfit where Kevin and Andre can also offer a fascinating array of musicians, comedians, speciality acts etc. They work with the other agencies within the county including the long established Trevor George Entertainments in Torquay, Vern Allen Management and GB Entertainments in Exeter. Between them all they have a tight control which is beneficial to their acts and to the standard that is now required by even the humblest venue. I have the opportunity to be invited to their Showcases every year where acts available in this part of the country are on show to bookers from around Britain as well as local hoteliers, night clubs and the like.

Theatrical Agents and Managers are always hoping to find a potential star and it does happen. Trevor George and his wife Billie discovered, nurtured and launched Michael Barrymore, even providing him with his name. When he came to them first he was Michael Parker. They also launched Gary Wilmot and the irrepressible Joe Pasquale. Radio Devon's Douglas Mounce was another of their finds.

Since before World War II the BBC has broadcast from Seymour Road. Television became part of the output in the fifties. If you visit the building you will find it set in a pleasant garden and from the outside it is difficult to imagine the vastly busy atmosphere within its walls. Radio Devon broadcasts from here and is so popular that its presenters have almost as big a following as their television counterparts. People like Craig Rich, for example, combine dual roles of broadcasting on air during the day, and presenting the television weather on the Spotlight programme Monday to Friday. His experience as a master mariner as well as his knowledge of the weather allows him to speak with an unassailable authority. His likeable, warmhearted presence comes over to the viewers in the same way as it is appreciated when he opens fetes, bazaars, shops and endless gatherings, which he does willingly, with grace and a great lack of pretension.

Douglas Mounce is another very popular broadcaster. His morning programme is full of chat and good humour and interesting content. I meet him from time to time when we both attend a show of some kind or another, or find ourselves judging in a talent contest. If you have ever seen him as a Pantomime Dame you will appreciate how versatile he is. One of his idols is Jack Tripp, a Plymothian, who before he retired must have been one of the greatest of all Dames. I asked Douglas what makes a good broadcaster. His reply was that in his opinion it is being sincerely interested in people. When he is on air he feels as if he is talking to people he knows. That certainly comes across on the airways and accounts for why he has so many fans.

New technology has given the Radio Devon team, the ability to garner news quickly with a flick of a key on their desktop computers. They can be sure that they are not repeating stories that have already gone out elsewhere in the region, and equally makes them able to link up with other stations in the Westcountry region which extends to Bristol and Gloucester and to the depths of Cornwall. One studio is devoted to links with Broadcasting House in London so that MPs and other guests can speak from London or vice versa.

I was interested to see how the region has been divided up. For example County programmes go out from Plymouth and Exeter, local programmes from Plymouth and a sub-region has been created to include Radio Devon and Radio Cornwall. The Saturday night regional programmes cover Somerset, Bristol and Gloucester as well as Devon and Cornwall.

Spending a little time in Seymour Road always reminds me of my days at the BBC in Broadcasting House in London. It was in the days when everything was recorded on records. Tapes and cassettes were still things of the future. It was quite a difficult business. In this day and age when editing anything is so simple that a child can do it - in fact they are usually more advanced in their technology than their elders - it is hard for anyone to understand that you could erase nothing in those old recordings or even splice together. The height of sophistication was a yellow pencil which we used to mark the places where cuts needed to be made or applause taken out if the programme was over-running. I had responsibility for 'In Town Tonight' which always overran, and also for 'Take it from Here' with Jimmy Edwards and June Whitfield, a great favourite which was recorded weekly. The daily soap 'Mrs Dale's Diary' also came into my care until one dreadful day when I was bringing the disc back from the recording studio in Oxford Street to Broadcasting House for the afternoon programme which went out at 4.15pm. On the way I stopped for a drink in the BBC Club and ran into friends. Mrs Dale was left down beside my chair, completely forgotten. I returned to Broadcasting House oblivious of the fact and it was not until the engineers were screaming for the disc that I realised what I had done. Too late. The programme did not go out and next day the papers carried front page headlines 'BBC Lose Mrs Dale'. I expected the sack but all I got was a polite, if somewhat terse memorandum requesting that anything in transit from Oxford Street, Aeolian Hall in Bond Street, or indeed from any studio, should be directly returned and not the subject of a detour - the gin and tonics were not mentioned!!

Those too were the days when the announcers, the great John Snagge and Alvar Lidell, amongst others, were expected to wear a dinner jacket when they read the news on Saturday evenings. Sounds daft but it upheld the standards of the BBC, never mind that the announcers only obeyed the dictum as far as the jackets and bow ties were concerned!!

The BBC were the sole Television Broadcaster in the Westcountry for some years, until with a fanfare of trumpets Westward Television, with Peter Cadbury at the helm, burst upon the scene in its newly built premises at Derry's Cross, now the home of the solicitors Foot and Bowden. Television was exciting for the broadcasters in those days. Programmes broke down quite regularly, there were no auto cues. The skill of the continuity announcer and the versatility of the 'Anchormen' such as Barry Westward, Reggie Bosanquet and Kenneth Macleod, were called into play almost daily. There was an air of expectancy, too, with local people who suddenly found themselves with 'Television Personalities' doing their shopping in the market, or standing at the bar of a local hostelry enjoying a pint. Plymouth was lucky in that respect; it attracted a number of well known people to its Independent Television Station and spotting the face became a local pastime.

On a more serious note good programmes were made 'in house' on subjects dear to the heart of the Westcountry. Ted Tuckerman became a feature with his fishing spot. His call sign 'Tight Lines' was well known. The gardening programme, the programmes for women, all had a following. Many people would never miss the easy going humour and knowledge of Clive Gunnell as he took us walking around the countryside.

In the course of time internal and boardroom politics caused Westward to lose its franchise to Television South West. A change that the general public hardly noticed except for the Golden Hind that no longer appeared on the screen at the beginning and end of programmes. This was replaced by the new TSW Palm Tree logo. The same faces were one the screen every day, the building was still in use. What viewers did miss was the friendliness of the early days as more and more journalists took over in programmes, and there was less use of the entrepreneurial abilities of performers. Autocues were used. Scripts, which had to be learned before the daily Westward Dairy went on air, were discarded for the Idiot Board that rolled away in front of the speaker but out of sight of the audience, Spontaneity was discouraged. Television was beginning to become part of the furniture and lost its excitement.

Oddly the excitement returned briefly towards the end of TSWs time as franchisees. Long standing staff were going to pastures new or retiring. An air of uncertainty and a certain sadness prevailed, but on that final programme on New Year's Eve 1992, it was one big party. A party full of nostalgia and more than a few tears from almost all the famous and familiar names we had grown used to seeing over the years. Sue King fronted the programme with that doyen of Anchormen, Kenneth Macleod. The construction of the programme was a director's nightmare, but they sailed through the hour long screening with a professionalism that one had come to expect. When the programme finished over five hundred people drank, ate and danced the night away as they waited for midnight to strike. As the chimes of Big Ben sounded the midnight hour, there was an almost uncanny silence. The engineer switched off, the lights went out, TSW was no more, and Westcountry Television sprang into life in its new home in Plympton. For many, apart from those who were retiring, it heralded an unchartered future and for some the opportunity to strike out on their own.

Westcountry Television have since become stalwarts in the business and after several different moves are now part of the vast Carlton network. Their daily Westcountry News programme has a great following and their presenters are part of the Plymouth scene although nowhere near the icons of their predecessors of the early days.

It is interesting to look back on the people who once played so much a part of Independent Television in the Westcountry. The popular actor cum broadcaster Ian Stirling still appears on Westcountry TV and so does Ruth Langsford. The talented director John Bartlett who won many awards over the years with Westward and TSW, is now to be seen heavily engrossed with the Tavistock Festival, Music of the Night and a variety of other interests. A fascinating man with a fund of trivia about the past, he is welcome wherever he goes. He remembers going out one morning at 5am to board the great French liner the Iles de France, as she lay just inside the Breakwater; his quarry Bob Hope. The comedian was preparing to come ashore before going on to London. John says that even at that ungodly hour of the morning Bob Hope was alert, surrounded by his gag men and highly entertaining.

What a wealth of talent Westward and TSW nurtured for Television. David Vine was once the Sports Reporter for Westward. What a revered name he has amongst Sports Commentators and his host of fans. Snooker and Ski Sunday will not be the same without him now he has retired. Angela Rippon is one of Plymouth's own and this able lady endeared herself to us, first of all on the local newspaper before she went to the BBC and then to Westward. She has always acknowledged the debt she owed Westward Television. Her career has soared. Who will forget her dignity and immaculate enunciation when she read the news for the BBC - the first woman to do so. Most of us will probably remember her most when she and her stunning legs appeared with Morecombe and Wise. I thoroughly enjoy her appearances with Richard Whiteley and Carol Vorderman on Countdown.

Jan Leeming, now happily married for the fifth time, followed in Angela's footsteps at the BBC having spent some time at Westward as a reporter and announcer. That is another charming lady. The other female who graces our screens today is the irrepressible Judi Spiers, another Plymouth girl whose family owned the Michael Spiers jewellery Shops in the City.

Good programmes in their thousands have come from Westward and TSW and still do from Westcountry, over the last four decades. There have been some total disasters, the most major of them, and one that has already gone into the television archives, was 'Simply Wonderful' which was the opening programme for TSW. So awful was it that it is destined to be shown time and again in the sort of 'It will be alright on the Night' programmes.

How many people remember the early days when people like Sir Cliff Richard would walk into Studio I to mime his latest record. The studio was used for chat shows, and at one time hired out to the Henson Organisation who wanted to record a series of Mother Goose Stories which eventually won an Emmy award. We know this organisation more for The Muppets. Then there were programmes like Landmark and Treasure Hunt with Kenneth Horne, Keith Fordyce, Kenneth Macleod and David Rogers as Quizmasters.

Few people will know that a tunnel exists connecting the Athanaeum Theatre to the Studios so that equipment could be moved in and out when the theatre was used for programmes in the early days. This very same tunnel provided an escape route for The Beatles one night when they were appearing at the cinema next door.

They were the great days of television which will never be repeated because today's television stations require far less staff, have more sophisticated equipment and location work is now simple. Plymouth and the West Country should always be grateful for this band of people, professionals every one of them, who brought Independent Television to us so many years ago. Forty years on and the West Country is still well served by its Television stations both BBC and Independent.

Fortunately quite a large proportion of film and video footage used by Westward and TSW together with the BBC of the same period, has been saved and is archived. One of the films is of the launch of Westward Television. It shows the special train hired by Westward before the station came into being in April 1961. It was used as part of a publicity drive and travelled all around Devon, Cornwall and Somerset. It depicts the train in London, speeches by the Lord Mayor of London and Peter Cadbury who was the boss of Westward Television.

What is so different in today's world of Television is the advance of various studios and people who accept commissions to produce programmes both for the BBC, Carlton and the other TV companies. It is becoming increasingly accepted in the credits at the end of a programme to read that an outside production company has made it. One of the successful local companies is Denham Productions where the ex BBC presenter, Chris Denham, runs the show. He has just recently made a splendid documentary with Ron Bendell of Westcountry Television which follows the two men driving an old Lagonda in a rally across Europe which ended up in Peking. Great, imaginative and exciting television and something which has brought great pride to Plymouth.

The reason for putting out so many commissioned programmes is no more than one simple word 'Cost'. 'In House' directors, cameramen, researchers and all the many people who are involved in even the smallest programme, have become expensive luxuries. To do it effectively requires a far greater number of permanent staff than any television station wishes to carry. Commission an Independent Production Company to make a programme and there is only a one off payment. The commissioning company agrees a fixed price for a programme or a series. Apart from quality, it is no longer involved in any other expense than writing the cheque when the programme is approved. It is not their responsibility if it pours with rain and filming is held up for days. The Producer can run off with the Director's wife, the cast can go sick, and any number of other interruptions doesn't cost the commissioning company a penny. The company's only concern is that the programme will be available on time and you can bet your bottom dollar that a penalty clause is included in the contract to cover such an eventuality.

The viewer is unaware of what goes on behind TV's closed doors - it would make a fascinating documentary in its own right. However much we moan from time to time about repeats and old films, we still get enormously good value for money and I, for one, would be lost without my daily fix of television.

The National Westminster Bank. City Centre

Chapter VI

Money makes the City go round

Plymouth is no backwater when it comes to financial institutions or financial dealings. It has a plethora but for the general public today the choice of bank or credit card to use becomes totally confusing because of the marriages of so many banks and building societies and the birth of more and more credit cards all promising the most favourable of terms. The acquisition of a mortgage is not much easier and the advent of the Internet is either the last straw or the icing on the cake depending on which way your mind works!. It is a hard world out there and recent years have made it imperative for the man in the street to have a greater understanding and depth of knowledge than in years gone by.

I thought I knew a little about the workings of the financial world but as I set about researching this chapter I soon discovered I was lamentably out of date and needed a thorough re-education. Gone are the days when the 'young ladies of the Bank of England' of whom I was one - and yes it was the Plymouth Branch which many people do not know even existed - went to work every day suitably attired. We were only allowed to wear grey, navy or black. We had to wear a hat and stockings to work. Stockings may sound obvious but believe you me, in the time of war in the forties, stockings were hard to get. The more adventurous of us painted our legs with a repulsive sort of tan coloured paint and then attempted to draw a straight black line up the back of the leg! Nail varnish had to be neutral and the only jewellery apart from a watch, a wedding and engagement ring, had to be a pearl necklace and small stud earrings! Our days were spent dealing with enormous 'Waste Sheets' on which were entered every transaction for the day and at the end of the day, the columns which were added up in your head, had to balance. If we were even a penny out we had to stay in the Bank until it was found. In addition to this we counted, by hand, every note that came into the bank always looking for forgeries. The reward for finding a forgery was a half day's paid leave. This was fine until the Germans flooded the market with forgeries in £5 and £10 notes. At one stage I had piled up a year's leave! Needless to say this system ceased fairly rapidly. Today there is a machine which shows up the forgery immediately. I am also told that the banks would rather make mistakes and pay for them when they are queried rather than have sufficient staff or pay overtime to ensure an accurate balance is made. It is an eye opener to us oldies and makes you realise how important it is to check statements and credit card bills.

One of the perks of being a Bank of England member was that you had the privilege of using its banking facility. It was quite something to have a Bank of England cheque book, something I missed when I left to become the first English woman cashier in Malta for Barclays, Dominion, Colonial and Overseas, as it was then; Barclays International today. We were incredibly well looked after. Lunch was provided for us and for this we used to go over to the Duke of Cornwall Hotel where a special room was set aside. On marriage we were given dowries, the amount varying according to the years of service. I very nearly did not qualify for mine - I eloped one afternoon at the end of working hours, got married in the Registry Office which was then in Thorn Park, and promptly returned to the Bank the next day without telling anyone. It took the Mandarins sitting in Threadneedle Street some time to decide whether this was quite cricket!

The Bank of England did not have a manager it had an Agent. Its three porters wore a livery of black trousers, black tail coats and bright pink waistcoats and always a top hat. I always remember the day I left the Bank. The Agent, a Mr Hopkins, presented me with a leaving gift and adding to it a little speech, summed up with the words that they would miss me, although he was not sure that I had a banking temperament!

From the Bank of England you could see Lloyds Bank across the road. The Bank of England building has gone but Lloyds is now the successful 'Bank' pub, I wonder how many people who drink there would believe that two of Lloyds staff would stack about half a million in used notes, packed in brown paper parcels, each containing £5,000, onto a rickety trolley and just push it across the road to the Bank of England. No one thought about armed robbers in those days. Bank counters were unprotected by bullet proof screens. This reminds me of a splendid print I have with the caption: Bank Clerk to Customer, 'I am sorry, madam, I cannot cash this cheque across the counter'. Reply from customer 'Never mind, I'll just come round the other side'! All that sort of thing has disappeared as we protect ourselves against attacking thugs.

It was not until the American forces arrived in Plymouth and used the Bank of England as their paymaster that the bank's staff realised people, other than themselves, were not quite so sanguine or so trusting. The Americans arrived with an armoured truck escorted by at least two other vehicles from which troops leapt and surrounded the building with rifles at the ready.

One of our jobs in the Bank of England was to escort money and bullion from Plymouth to London or to one of the other Bank of England branches in Liverpool, Southampton or Bristol. This we would do with no other means of protection for the money than two members of staff sitting in a reserved carriage next to the wagon in which the money was stacked. We were paid £5 'Danger Money' for this exercise. So laid back was it that I can remember sitting on a tea chest which housed thousands of pounds, on Platform 7 at North Road Station waiting for the arrival of the train and being asked by a fellow traveller what time the train was due to leave!

What is the future of banking? I have to believe that if the clearing banks and building societies had their choice, we would all do our business via the telephone or through the hole in the wall. As I write yet another Building Society come Bank, The Abbey National looks as though it is reluctantly going to be swallowed up by LloydsTSB. It may be that the consumer outcry will defeat the take over. A conquest by LloydsTSB would mean that more and more financial power and constrictions would come under fewer and fewer financial giants. We are told how good it would be but the question is for whom. Firstly the loss of some 9,000 jobs is forecast and secondly, we, the customers would have even fewer branches to use. LloydsTSB would certainly have no need of the Abbey National branches in Plymouth's City Centre. That is all in the hostile pipeline at the moment. The whole unhappy subject really comes down to cost and how much profit the banks can make. Or at least that what it seems to Joe Public., especially the small business man. I always remember talking to one of Lloyds senior managers, Kevin Waterman, who at one time had been the manager of Lloyds in Stoke village.At the time when I spoke to him he was the manager of Lloyds Bank Area Director's office, Tamar, which covered the Plymouth branches and surrounding branches in both East Cornwall and parts of the South Hams. A man of wide experience he put the bank's side of the story.

The layman forgets the enormous cost the banks incur operating people's personal accounts and this was illustrated when the Dockyard started paying their employees by cheque rather than the traditional cash. Not a popular move but on the face of it great for the banks in the Devonport area. Banks found themselves opening literally thousands of accounts. Good business? Promotion for the Managers? Not a bit of it, mainly a large headache, because for many customers the account was credited with the wage or salary, and the full amount was drawn out the same day. The bank made little, found itself with the cost of administration, printing cheque books, providing paying in books, issuing statements, putting staff under pressure on pay days and all for virtually no gain to the bank. Someone has to cover this cost and obviously it becomes reflected in the charges to every customer. It was an angle I had not considered before. Basically we should look on bank charges much in the same way we do for service charges on water, electricity, gas etc. Not easy to accept because we groan about those too!

Kevin Waterman and I found ourselves looking back on our early banking careers. I was fascinated by his story. He comes from a banking family who had all worked for merchant bankers, the ill-fated Barings, C.Hoare and Co or Coutts, the Queen's bankers, in London - very upmarket private banks.

The pace of life in these banks was totally different from the general run of the mill. Until quite recently frock coated staff served their respected and highly valued clientele. If you go into Hoare's today, you will still find it panelled and gracious, a far cry from the modernistic Lloyds building across the road. By 1969 Kevin realised that he had little hope of promotion at Hoare's other than stepping into dead men's shoes. He made the move to Lloyds. It was quite a traumatic change for him and took him some time to get used to his new role. The transition has obviously been successful. Not only does he have a senior role in the bank, he is also an elected Fellow of the Chartered Institute of Bankers. It is the highest grade of membership, awarded in recognition of his status in the banking profession and for his contribution towards banking education.

Incidentally I was amused to read that Coutt's have set up a new department especially for footballers - the top echelon obviously. They hope to be able to lure the high earners like Beckham to transfer their business to them. How times change and I wonder how Her Majesty feels about that!

But what of the reaction of those who work in the banks today?

I went to see Richard Davis of LloydsTSB who is in fact a Corporate Banker looking after the affairs of some 90 business clients. His sole job is to deal with them. He plays no part in the day to day running of the bank which gives him the opportunity to get to know his client list. His expertise comes in grasping the salient points of his clients business. This does not mean just looking at a balance sheet and seeing what the profit was for the previous year. He takes a far keener look at the affairs, forecasts what the future might be for the company, learns how the business runs and what its needs are. He does not want a client suddenly asking for an extended overdraft, he wants to be able to see where the troughs might fall and be aware of how he can help before the need arises. This is a task that needs Richard to get to know his client, get to understand how he manufactures a widget maybe, where the market place is, how fast is the turn round and how quickly the client's customers settle their bills. One of the great advantages of modern technology, in his case, is On Line banking. He is almost like a hidden director of the company without the responsibilities.

Richard and I talked about the non-business customer who tends to use the over the counter services of the bank less and less.Salaries are paid into the bank, bills are paid by direct debits and cash drawn from a hole in the wall. There is no such thing as the old fashioned branch bank manager who knew all his customers whether they were business or private and had probably dealt with most of them for years. The question why has this breed of manager disappeared, is fairly simply answered. Technology has taken away the primary need. Modern business practices do not really allow for the authority and power that Branch Managers used to have. Most private customers hardly ever need a manager as such; if they want a loan they fill in a form and if the point system works in their favour that loan is forthcoming. The Banks are no longer interested in the personal reasons for such loans and really only need to insure they have protected themselves from a loss situation. The other good reason is that Bank Managers as such cannot advise their customers on mortgages or insurance - that needs to be dealt with by the bank's specialist services. The purchase of shares has the same restrictions.

In a way this has given a far greater opportunity for younger men like Richard Davis to concentrate on his clients. Doing his job well will put him on the promotion rung automatically and probably without leaving the area. His clients are by no means Plymouth based only. He is the sort of modern day banker whom clients would trust and rely upon for sound advice and guidance - and be sure of getting it.

In the curious way of the world I considered changing my household insurance after a telephone conversation with LloydsTSB Insurance arm. Helpful, constructive and simple was how I felt about what they had to offer. I decided to go ahead and make a change only to find that at the end of the day I was offered the same Insurance company I had already been using - the difference, slightly different rates. The financial world is frighteningly small.

Across the road from LloydsTSB in the vast Natwest centre at St Andrew's Cross. I took a lift to the 4th floor and met with Mark Price another, young, highly intelligent and articulate banker, doing almost the same job as his counter part in LloydsTSB but with only 30 corporate clients to care for. We talked much on the same lines but I found the ethos of the merger between Royal Bank of Scotland and Natwest far more sympathetic towards the general public. The most important point was the fact that the marriage between the two banks in this part of the country meant the opening of more branches rather than threatened closures. This is not only good news for customers everywhere but is even better news for staff who have no fear of redundancies. The latter was very much in the mind of managers in particular when I talked to them in 1993 when I was writing my original Plymouth book.

There have been closures of Natwest branches in Plymouth. No longer is there a branch on Mutley Plain nor a small outlet in Stoke village - in fact Stoke village is a prime example of a community deprived of any banking facility other than the Post Office. The loss of a local branch is compensated in a small way by the friendly tellers who man the counters in the main branch in Old Town Street. It is almost always very busy but the atmosphere is pleasant and few people get irate if they have to take their turn. I especially notice the care and consideration that is shown to physically handicapped people particularly those in wheelchairs - staff go out of their way to see to their needs.

I look today with a certain horror and a definite reluctance at the constantly changing face of banking but if I am honest I am sure that in the past small private banks must have felt much the same way. It is quite interesting to look back at some of the old Natwest branches which were almost always privately owned banks before they came under the bigger financial umbrella. One has to remember in doing so that Natwest was once the National Provincial whilst Westminster was a bank on its own. One of the first businesses to be acquired by the National Provincial in Devonport was in Fore Street where I worked for the bank for 6 months in 1941. Previously owned by Husband & Co, the owner, Thomas Husband was forced to sell the bank in 1839 due to the extravagant spending of his sons! I wonder how many customers he rapped over the knuckles for over-spending whilst he was trying to tackle the problems within his own business!

One point came over strongly in the general discussion with Plymouth Bankers. There is a consensus of opinion that it is patently obvious that financial management should become part of the educational curriculum. Fewer young people would get into monetary difficulties if they were taught simple budgeting from an early age and slightly more complex matters as they grow older. In a world which is dominated by the Internet and Mobile phones, money matters should be a priority.

Building Societies are used more and more by customers today. They are there to help in the matter of mortgages and a host of ancillary needs. One Building Society Manager told me that the greatest problem they have is a lack of communication with their customers especially when the customer is in trouble. It seems that the first thing people do if they get into financial hot water for whatever reason, is to stop paying their mortgage and the arrears mount. This Manager told me that if only people would pay a third of the sum due each month and at the same time start a dialogue, half the re-possessions would not happen. I suppose pride, perhaps optimism that things will get better, gets in the way and suddenly it is too late to do anything. Ignoring letters and telephone calls is something else that does not help when there are problems. Facing up to it is the only answer. The problem will not go away of its own accord.

The Building Societies all want to be part of the Plymouth Community. The Halifax for example has a Business Development Officer, part of whose job is to support worthwhile causes in the City.

Enterprise Plymouth Ltd has a business advice centre which was formed in 1984 with the direct involvement of Plymouth City Council. It answers the needs of people who for whatever reason, want to set up their own business. Part of 'Business in the Community' the centre offers assistance and guidance to new and existing small businesses. Within its range of activities it gives practical assistance to innovators who have ideas but lack funds or marketing experience to get their product to the people. That is the simple way of stating their purpose. When you walk into the building in Somerset Place, Stoke, you can just feel the 'get up and go' attitude. Experts in all sorts of fields are there to offer guidance not just in starting a business but on-going. It is somewhere where you can call in for a chat to air views, talk out problems or whatever is needed. Donations from big companies like The Halifax, NatWest, HSBC, Lloyds TSB and Peat Marwick are regularly forthcoming to help the cause.

Plymouth is also blessed by the work of The Prince's Youth Business Trust. This is a charity which helps young people set up in business by offering advice and finance. Their aim is to help you if your circumstances make it especially difficult to get started. It is specifically for people aged between 18 and 25, up to 30 if you are disabled. There are loans of up to £5000 with very reasonable repayments and a bursary of up to £1,500 per person in a business. There is also a grant of £250 which can be used for market research. All you need is a good project, determination and the will to succeed. One of the nicest things about it is that it does not look unfavourably on young offenders who have been daft enough to get into trouble and are looking for a second chance in life.

To find out about the Trust you can write to the Prince's Youth Business Trust 4th Floor. Inter City House, Plymouth Station, Plymouth PL4 6AA or telephone 01752 251051. It seems to me that the only stipulation, other than a good idea, is that you must have tried elsewhere to raise the money. Presumably if your bank has said 'No, that suffices.

What they will want from you is your ideas plus a business plan. A daunting task but this is where the excellent Enterprise Plymouth comes into it. You can go there and they will help you sort out the business plan, the market place and many other things you will need before you are in a position to present your case to the Trust. Having achieved your objective you will find it very encouraging to know that the Trust have a rate of survival of the people it has supported of 66% after 3 years - a much better success rate than the banks. This is really because of the dedication of the people working for the Trust. They are skilled and wise. On the Board is a retired bank manager, a senior accountant, a director of one of the Clearing banks, a well versed solicitor and the manager of a big building firm. It is this board that determines the awards. They try to work fairly swiftly so that an applicant is not left in uncertainty one minute longer than is necessary.

You would be amazed at the breadth of enterprises in which the Trust has invested money. A Graduate set up as a clown, a co-operative graphic and design studio, a maker of children's furniture to name but a few. Everyone who receives financial help from the Trust is allocated a volunteer business adviser who will give free business advice.

The Trust also provides valuable marketing opportunities. It stages an annual trade show and arranges space in exhibitions to enable young people to display their wares to large audiences. Advantageous start up insurance, free legal advice, the opportunity to buy low cost well maintained vans,free membership of a breakdown service, publicity, video training packages on accountancy and computers as well as competition prizes for money, fax and answering machines. It is a scheme that has been admirably thought out.

I had not realised that The Prince's Business Youth Trust and The Prince's Trust were not one and the same thing. Whilst they are complimentary to one another, they act independently and answer different needs. Here a committee makes grants of up to £800 to individual applicants and £2,500 to local organisations and a committee member will visit every applicant. It is a remarkable grant-giving organisation where those responsible meet and talk with potential recipients. If the word 'committee' makes you think of stuffy grey-suited gentlemen who have no notion of the needs of the young, you would be totally out of order in this context. Indeed they are active men and women who keenly relish the task of helping a young person or persons who may have quite unusual requests, perhaps holding on to a dream which seems to have no hope of becoming reality until they talk with a member of the committee. The Prince's Trust can give them a lifeline which may well lead to confidence in themselves, growth and personal freedom. Taking risks in grant-giving is one of the greatest strengths of The Prince's Trust. It does not matter how outlandish or seemingly impossible your request for help might be, The Prince's Trust will look at it sensibly and sympathetically.

The Royal Jubilee Trusts are managed by the Prince's Trust and offer financial help to all sorts of projects. I found it quite hard to grasp how many and varied were the aspects of the work of the Prince's Trust. There were tens of thousands of individuals who contributed to the King George's Jubilee Appeal in 1935 and the Queen's Silver Jubilee Appeal in 1977 and it is their generosity that continues to pay dividends today.

The endowments created at that time are invested by the Prince's Trust and underpin much of the Trust's local and national work, enabling them to launch new ventures or assist in funding existing ones. For example, a grant of £50,000 over three years helped to set up Saneline - a national service which provides telephone counselling in the field of mental illness, giving advice and information during evenings and weekends.
A grant of £35,000 over two years was awarded to help the core costs of Fairbridge, a leading charity working with the most disadvantaged inner city groups. It has a programme involving challenging outdoor activities, with job skills and counselling. The grant has enabled Fairbridge to expand to sixteen centres across the UK.

One project is Volunteers. The idea behind Volunteers is not a new one, but Volunteers is. A great deal is done, and has always been done by voluntary organisations throughout the country. Community Service already exists. People between 16 and 24 years of age are already involved to a greater or lesser degree including Plymothians. But until Volunteers, a large number were just not included. Let's face it, most people get little opportunity to do anything other than their chosen career or their unchosen unemployment. That's what makes Volunteers so interesting and necessary. It is an opportunity to spend some time doing voluntary work. It is not for no-hopers. It is not another source of cheap labour. It is not for do-gooders. It is not for ethnic minorities or ethnic majorities. It is not for the unemployed, the handicapped or young offenders or indeed, anyone in particular. It is for everyone in general. No one is excluded.

Volunteers aims to enable young people to develop their own personal qualities by working in the community as part of a team drawn from widely differing backgrounds. The programme has developed from that pioneered by the Community Venture during the 1980s.

All this takes a tremendous amount of funding. There is a constantly reviewed and developed plan. The support and sponsorship from businesses is unstinting. If you read the annual report of The Prince's Trust you will see that at least 250 familiar names all lend their support in various ways. A charity of this dynamism working closely with others can really achieve a positive difference to a young person's life. We may not always know or hear about the work of The Prince's Trust or be aware of certain individuals in Plymouth benefiting from it but rest assured it is happening every day of every week, thanks to the Prince of Wales' vision and the tremendous team of people who work to fulfil it.

It is the well informed opinion of Dr Ken Hayden, proprietor of Financial Management Services, that everybody, from the most successful business man to the penniless student can benefit greatly from the assistance of an Independent Financial Advisor (IFA)

Dr Hayden came to Plymouth twenty years ago on joining the Navy. At the end of his commission his quick thinking mind led him towards a career in financial services. In 1990 he joined Albany Life and worked there for three years under the supervision of an ex-spitfire pilot, Max, a lively character who had a profound and lasting effect. After Max left the company in 1993 Ken moved on, making the brave decision to go it alone in the shark infested waters of financial advice!

Initially he ran his new enterprise from home, until 1998 when he moved to Garston House and now he works there alongside three other financial consultants and full admin support. Each Independent Financial Advisor at Garston House specialises in their own subject - business mortgages, pensions, investments, tax laws etc, with everybody tackling the area they know most about. There is even a lady in the firm who deals almost exclusively with female clients!

In terms of Information Technology, Financial Management Services are, quite possibly, the best in Plymouth. Not only do they have an extensive networked computer system but they also have the ability to write their own software, design Web Pages and generally do anything within their power to enhance the services they offer. Being a scientist with a degree in theoretical physics, one may wonder how on earth Ken Hayden came to be involved in the world of finance, however his qualifications have given him more than one natural advantage. Firstly his incredible mind; flying around problems, thinking laterally, and sorting them out with minimum turmoil. Secondly his natural curiosity draws him to people, he finds financial problems genuinely interesting and is able to relate to people on a level they can easily understand.

The overall impression I gained from talking with Doctor Hayden is that everyone, regardless of his or her personal situation, can benefit from the help of an IFA. We all have a plan, and sometimes require a little external assistance to make it happen, or just a gentle shove in the right direction. Sound familiar ? Most people are surprised after visiting an IFA by the level of advice they get, how much use it really is, and at the end of the day, how much money they could be saving!

The Royal Navy seems to produce an especial breed of men who, when they leave the Service fit admirably and competently into the business of Financial Services. There can be no better exponent of this than the talented and lively minded David Goodman, who having been a Warfare Officer in ships designed to hunt, find and destroy submarines and second in command of HMS Alacrity, retired and trained as a Financial Adviser. He chose this profession because he thought he could do the job better than some advisers he had come across. Arrogant? No, simply a man who had been taught to use his vision and the clarity of his thinking in the Royal Navy. His last posting in Alacrity was a tour of the West Indies. HMS Alacrity was the West Indies Guard Ship in 1989 and so was on station at the time of Hurricane Hugo which did such tremendous damage and almost destroyed the Island of Montserrat. The main town there was Plymouth and David was flown in with a team to work with the Governor and First Minister to try and get the town back on track after Hugo had done its terrible work. The ship and everyone worked enormously hard to supply water, power and to re-open roads. As a result of all the personal organisation that David Goodman put in he was awarded the M.B.E. by the Queen and received his award from her at Buckingham Palace in 1991 just before he left the Navy.

Having made the decision about his future David went to work with the Robert Fleming Group.. He worked for their Sales Arm, Save and Prosper in Exeter and Plymouth until 1995 gaining experience all the way. At this time he felt more than capable of starting his own business Business and Personal Finances specialising in Investments, Business to Business mainly. His clients come from various Accountants and Solicitors and his office is ideally situated at 19 The Crescent at the rear of the Foot and Bowden Building at Derry's Cross --once the home of Westward and Television South West. He sees all of his clients in his office and if you talk to any of them, you will find that each and every one is made to feel they are the most important client he has. Indeed every client is important and it is the care and attention to detail he gives to everyone and his very real ability to listen to what he is being told, that makes him so successful.

David Goodman has become a name to be reckoned with in Plymouth and as a man who has the present and future of the City very much in his heart. He is Chairman of the Independent Business Group in the Chamber of Commerce, a Member of the Chamber of Commerce Council and also President of Plymouth Mayflower Rotary Club. He is a married man who lives in Mannamead

I have already written at length about PriceWaterhouseCoopers and in this chapter I need only underline the fact that Accountants are the pivot of every business today. No company can do without guide lines, advice and the pros and cons of financial moves laid out before them, nor can any company cope with the endless tax returns and requirements of Companies House. There are many good firms in the city with varying skills and varying charges; in other words the choice is yours.

But a word of warning! Gone are the days when once a year you could take your accounts to your accountant and leave it at that. My happy memory is of a time when David Rice, now an eminent accountant, had just started in his own practice and had an office on Mutley Plain. His instructions to me were 'Put all you have spent in one carrier bag and the receipts in another, and I will do the rest'. Believe me that is not what would be said today. Incidentally you will not find a more understanding accountant if you are a small business. He now practices in The Ridgeway, Plympton.

Solicitors too have changed over the years. Amalgamations swept through the city in the last decade, many of the bigger firms joining with other solicitors in different parts of the country providing clients with expertise on any given facet of the law. Family solicitors are a thing of the past. I can remember the days of Plymouth's leading solicitors Bond Pearce when they were Bond, Pearce, Elliot and Knape. Jimmy Knape and John Elliot were my family's solicitors and both regarded as friends as well as advisors. Today the firm is vast with hundreds of solicitors in the practice. It does make for an impersonal feel and that has been emphasised by their move to Ballard House from their splendid offices in The Crescent which was a bit like a rabbit warren but had a wonderful atmosphere.

Foot and Bowden moved as well a few years ago and now grace the old Westward Television building. Their one time senior partner , Tony Holland used to share his office with Lord Foot in their previous building. He was a great character and one of the most human solicitors I have ever met. He brought honour to Plymouth when he became President of The Law Society. The Foot family have been part of Plymouth's history for a very long time. I remember the late Isaac Foot, who was a friend of my grandfather's. As a child I remember the ferocity of the political debates across the dining table. The next generation of Foots have been equally vociferous in their various fields. Michael Foot, one time Leader of the Labour Party is probably one of the finest orators of our time. Lord Foot himself was no mean advocate.

Even in retirement Tony Holland is a great advocate for Plymouth but perhaps few people know that he is also a great Wagnerian fan and will travel anywhere to hear a Wagner opera. He told me that he considered it his duty to pass on this love of Wagner to his three sons. Whenever Covent Garden staged a Wagnerian performance he would take whichever son was available to hear it. If it interfered with school then they would go to London in the afternoon and return on the night train in time for school the next day. On one occasion, it was a performance of The Ring. Through a technical fault the performance started late and Tony and his son had to leave the theatre before the curtain came down. Son number three was the recipient of this treat and always held it against his father that his musical education had been deprived because he never heard the end of the opera. Many years later the Hollands travelled once more to Covent Garden for The Ring and Tony felt the debt had been repaid. Imagine his chagrin when he found that he had taken the wrong son! He is still teased unmercifully by his family about this omission.

Tony Holland also has another great love, Horatio Hornblower. He was incensed when he found out that the BBC were thinking of using Milford Haven for the series we have seen in recent years, and not Plymouth. Plymouth, as all Hornblower lovers know, is the rightful place. Tony tackled the Council, harried the BBC and would not stay quiet until he got a commitment from the City's Chief executive to fight our corner. The series was filmed and Plymouth was used - The Royal William Yard was the setting.

Carrying on the Foot tradition is the firm of solicitors Nash whose founder was David Foot Nash, related to the Foots and like them a lifelong Methodist. In fact I believe at one time that Nash, Howett, Cocks and Clapp, as they were then known, would not employ anyone who was not a Methodist. David Foot Nash and his partner Cecil Howett attended chapel regularly. Cecil played the organ in the Embankment Methodist Chapel, which is now the Christian Centre. It was not just any organ either but a vast Wurlitzer which once graced a cinema. There will not be many people left who remember this part of going to the cinema. Before the show began, there would be the sound of organ music and slowly from the bowels of the building the organ would rise majestically and be seen in its full glory. The instrument was played by the resident organist who usually had as great a following as local television people today. Dudley Savage was the man in charge of this mighty machine in what was the Royal Cinema at Derry's Cross.

When the Embankment Church closed, Cecil and his Wurlitzer found a new home in Salisbury Road Methodist Chapel.

Nash & Co have their premises in the elegant and gracious Beaumont House in Ebrington Street, a building that they rescued from almost certain destruction and restored wonderfully, adding on a wing that looks as though it has always been part of the main building. It was quite a brave move on the company's part. Their old headquarters in Sussex Street was almost Dickensian in character and inconveniently spread. The contrast in working conditions was an enormous boon to the staff and certainly makes visiting one's solicitor pleasureable. This is a well organised, competent firm, still small enough to give personal attention but providing a comprehensive service which lives up to the tradition and standards set for them by David Foot Nash.

It was good to discover that Plymouth has a female solicitor running her own practice. Nicola Ellis & Co of 5, St Lawrence Road, specialise in Marine Legal Advice.

If you want to discover a firm of solicitors who 'hide their light under a bushel' as the saying goes you will find Curtis at 87-89 Mutley Plain hidden behind the appalling public lavatory hated by every Plymothian. Their offices are well laid out and comfortable but they do look out on this eyesore. In fact one of the partners told me that when they applied for change of use before moving in, they got it quite easily because the Council did not dare to say 'No' because of the ghastly view they have to endure! They are a progressive and aggressive firm who according to one solicitor I spoke to are 'doughty fighters'. Many Plymothians will remember that Wheelers, the old family firm of drapers, and Page, Keen and Page, the jewellers, occupied these premises before the advent of Curtis and before Wheelers were driven out of business by the arrival of this unforgiving monstrosity.

Property Management Services have become the norm in Plymouth in the last few years with more and more properties for letting either furnished or unfurnished.

There are a good many of us who have been tempted into the property market not for somewhere to reside but to own property which can be rented out. It sounds so simple and straightforward but without the help of experts it can be stepping into a minefield. Two people who are very capable of helping the would be, or the existing landlord, are Mike Shally and Lyn Stidwell whose company M&L Associates operates from prestigious offices at 10a Mannamead Road, Mutley Plain.

This intelligent, far seeing pair both worked for several years with other property management companies before they felt they were sufficiently competent to run their own company. Once satisfied that they could operate a successful business, they carried on business from home and then a shop in Laira Road, before setting up in their present offices. One of the reasons for their success is undoubtedly their excellent relationships with both their landlords and tenants. This is because they run their business on a personal and very tight basis. They check references carefully, don't tie landlords into difficult contracts, and Mike collects the rents himself each week, which ensures he is alerted to any potential problems before they arise and before they get out of hand.

Mike's weekly call on tenants also enables him to check that the property is being looked after properly. This is in addition to regular, formal inspections carried out for the landlords' peace of mind. Their motto 'Dedicated to Client Care' really says it all and this is underlined by the fact that they are available day and night, seven days a week to landlords.

M&L Associates have an in-house solicitor and accountant who will advise landlords on all aspects of letting and income - before purchase if necessary. They also hold regular special open days for prospective landlords.

The business is expanding rapidly thanks to Mike and Lynn's innovative ideas, one of which is holding Seminars around the country advising and arranging property investment for new landlords and in so doing removing the minefields. For more information please ring Mike or Lyn on 01752 261596.

It would have been impossible to write about all the excellent firms offering legal and financial advice and opportunities for those brave enough to start their own business. I have taken a cross section and from odd angles trying to illustrate about this side of life in the City. So much changes and so fast in this world, it is a bit like a roller coaster that never seems to stop. Exciting? Yes, if you have the stomach for it!

St Andrew's Church

Mutton Cove - Devonport.

128

Cremyll, near Devonport

Cremyll.

129

The Torpoint Ferry.

The Lawn. Torpoint.

Charles Church.

Chapter VII

Plymouth and the Church

My religious upbringing would have confused anyone. My father came from Methodist stock but was Church of England, my mother's family were firm Wesleyans, yet I was sent, at the age of three and a half, to the Anglo-Catholic convent, St Dunstan's Abbey, then in North Road West. In my school holidays in Cawsand, where we had a house and spent six months of the year, I revelled in the cheerful folk who went to the Congregational Chapel and had the best Sunday School Treats ever. So when I came to look at the various denominations in order to write about them in this book, I was not unnerved by the differences; after all the purpose behind every church, chapel or synagogue is to do the work of God.

The mother church of St Andrew was my first call. A church I know well and which in truth is the city's cathedral in all but name. Many services have I attended there and many times used the sanctuary provided by the ever open door, when I worked in an office just around the corner and needed to escape. It is somewhere that has great strength, it is beautiful, serene and when the magnificent organ is playing, the music reaches out to every corner. For centuries it has been God's house, even when it was destroyed apart from its outer walls, by the German bombers in World War II. I like to think of figures of the past kneeling in prayer. Sir Francis Drake would have done just that and asked for a blessing before he sailed, and he would have knelt again in thanksgiving when he returned from one of his successful voyages.

History tells us that in the middle of the sermon one Sunday morning in 1573, the vicar was in full flight, only realising at the end of his dissertation that he was alone in his church! The congregation had tiptoed out, not from boredom, but because news had filtered into the church that Drake was in harbour having been away for a year on one of his great adventures to the West Indies.

As I sat I could see to my left in the north transept, and cut off from the body of the church by a glass screen, adorned with the crest of the Royal Air Force, the chapel of St Philip and above its altar a memorial to the men of St Andrews who died in the two World Wars. On either side of the altar are memorials to Plymouth policemen and firemen killed between 1939-1945, and outside the chapel are books of remembrance recording the 1178 civilians killed in the blitz.

On the north wall are two modern tablets telling us of the 'hearts' of two great men. Martin Frobisher, commander of one of Drake's divisions in the Armada battles, and Robert Blake, Cromwell's admiral who died as his ship entered Plymouth Sound in 1675. The latter was returning from a successful mission destroying the Spanish treasure fleet in the Canaries.

A lady has lain sleeping in an ancient tomb for some 750 years. She is probably Joan Valletort, whose family were the Norman lords of Plymouth and lived to the west of the church. She was mistress to Richard, Earl of Cornwall, the brother of King Henry III. It was from that line that the Earls of Mount Edgcumbe are descended.

The Piper window at the base of the tower pays glorious tribute to the memory of William Waldorf, the second Viscount Astor who was MP for Sutton from 1910-1919 and Lord Mayor for all the years of the Second World War. He died in 1952.

The window represents the instruments of the passions, with the ladder, the reed and the spear representing a St Andrews cross. Every symbol in the design depicts an event in the Crucifixion, from the thirty pieces of silver to the crowing cock.

The big central monument on the west wall, with a carving of a woman kneeling and her children around her, is to Elizabeth Calmady, wife of Edward Calmady, who died in 1645. The Calmadys used much of their wealth gained from the Newfoundland fishing business, which flourished for centuries, for the benefit of the people of Plymouth.

When I am in St Andrews I always think of Catherine of Aragon who landed in Plymouth before journeying to London to meet her bridegroom, Prince Arthur, brother of Henry, later to become Henry VIII. It was Henry VIII she married after the death of Prince Arthur. She came to this church to pray. The vicar then was the extraordinary Adrian de Castello, secretary to the Borgia Pope who arranged Catherine's marriage. He acquired many high church offices in England and was made a cardinal, yet he never set foot on English soil!. This quiet, shy, valiant lady would have had no idea that her eventual divorce from Henry VIII would lead to the break with Rome and the formation of the Church of England.

St Andrews has a sense of well being. It is well cared for and it is always a pleasure to look at the lovely flowers and especially at the time of the magnificent Flower Festival. It has a fair size congregation at every service which is swollen on special occasions especially at Christmas and Easter. At Midnight Mass on Christmas Eve there is never a seat to be had well before the service starts.

The wonderful atmosphere of the church is particularly poignant when, after the Blitz in 1941, there was nothing left except walls, rubble, charred wood and ash. It says everything about the spirit of the people of Plymouth when you know that the very next morning a board was nailed up over the door and on it was the word 'Resurgam' - I will rise again. That message went through every part of Plymouth reeling under the constant attention of the bombers. Plymouth did not flinch. The shell of St Andrews became a symbol of the determination of Plymothians not to be defeated by the misery of the nightly bombing.

St Andrews did rise again and in 1957, rebuilt, redesigned internally, it was reconsecrated. Yet it was still essentially the church created 500 years earlier.

Listen to the peal of ten bells from the tower. The oldest recorded bell is 1594, the youngest 1874. A carillon plays popular tunes and hymns at 4pm and 8pm. At the top of the tower you get a wonderful panoramic view of the city and as far out to sea as the horizon permits. One unexplained oddity is the name of Sir Francis Chichester carved into the lead of the tower. As far as anyone knows this remarkable solo circumnavigator who sailed into Plymouth at the end of his epic voyage, never set foot in the tower, let alone climbed it although his funeral service was held in the church.

In its history St Andrews has had many vicars, many of whom have become bishops. The present incumbent rector is Nick McKinnel who has endeared himself, not only to the church, but to the people of Plymouth because of his determined involvement in matters stretching way out from the line of duty. He has made people sit up and realise the church is alive, living and is not reserved for Sundays. He is a man of integrity, with a deep feeling for human nature and underneath has a delightful sense of humour. People warm to him and respect that he is not afraid to tackle gritty subjects. He is outspoken, full of energy and has carried on the great team spirit built by his predecessor Prebendary John Watson.

When I went to St Andrews I spotted a light in the vestry window and banged on the door expecting to see Carol Springett, the Church Administrator but instead the door was opened by a smiling priest who welcomed me in to the room which seemed full of young, cheerful clergymen. I was told that I had arrived at the Bishop's door and I realised I was clearly not where I should be. I had stepped inadvertently into a St Andrew's team meeting. The wrong entrance maybe but it was a wonderful introduction to the harmony that prevails amongst those who are responsible for our Mother church. Nick McKinnel has in his team, Martin Bailey who is the team vicar of St Paul's in Stonehouse and two curates, Rob Wilkinson and Joe Dent. Between them they also look after The Royal Chapel of St Katherine upon-the-Hoe which is within the Citadel.

I found the recently appointed administrator Carol Springett a great ambassador for the church. Her task is to ensure that the church runs smoothly. Her role is a mixture of domesticity, estate manager, diplomat, organiser and a hundred other roles. Originally a Maths teacher, the job seemed a strange choice for her but she is revelling in it and I suppose when one considers it, a Maths teacher needs to be numerate and articulate. Carol is both. She told me of the immense work that is carried out in the parish and the city. Because the church is the mother church it is used for much more than ordinary services. Schools come here for commemoration days, the vicar is, in some years, the Lord Mayor's Chaplain. Organisations come for memorial services. The British Legion hold their services in the church. Carol told me a little of the various groups and activities attached to St Andrews. There is something going on somewhere every day including a variety of courses to meet the needs of the congregation and those who are new to it. For example 'Christianity Explained' which is an easy to understand basic explanation of the Christian faith in the context of a relaxed social evening. St Andrew's Night on the first Wednesday of each month is at 8pm in the Lower Abbey Hall and is an informal hour of prayer, praise and fellowship. Homegroups are at the heart of St Andrew's fellowship and provide opportunities for friendship, study and prayer during the week. Andy Bowden the Youth Leader runs Fish Shop for 14-18 years which meets after the Sunday evening service and many times during the week. In fact there is something for every age group providing both pastoral care and the opportunity to enjoy each others company and have fun.

I have no doubt that the next few months - if not years - will be taken up with discussions on how to use the new prayer book 'Common Worship' with its whole collection of services, prayers and resources. Nick McKinnel says in the Church magazine 'The Fisherman'

"A number of reasons have been given for the latest liturgical revision. The increasing informality of much of life in general (and of some church life) has led the authors to offer a wider variety of services and opportunities to meet the demands of different churches. Flexibility is the key word and Common Worship is to be seen less as a book and more as a resource to fit the needs of our multicultural and increasingly secular society.

Some of the new services are not very different from the ASB, and the Sunday 9.30am communion service could remain very much in its present format. However we could also offer a more varied diet week by week, and some services, notably baptism and funeral services have been more radically overhauled.

At least three aspirations underlie our Sunday services (and hopefully a lot more) at St Andrew's. One is excellence, a concern for each service, whatever its form, to be as well-prepared and led as possible, with music of a high standard and a carefully thought-out theme. Another is edification, in other words the desire to build each other up in our faith through the preaching songs, and participation of all of us. The third is evangelism, the priority of being accessible and attractive to those who are interested in and thinking about Jesus Christ. Our desire is to commend him in all that we do."

Whatever form of service is introduced you can be assured of a welcome at St Andrew's and unlike many churches I have attended, you will never be made to feel an outsider. It is a church which is not averse to encompassing new ideas, at least new to this church. In 1997 on the fortieth anniversary of the reconsecration of the church, the Friends of St Andrews was formed on the initiative of Nick McKinnel for the purpose of helping to raise money towards the preservation, maintenance and improvement of the fabric and furnishings of the church and to encourage interest in the precincts and history of St Andrews. The Friends, besides holding a variety of social functions have gone just that bit further. Just before Christmas 2000 the Friends of St Andrew's, as a fund-raising venture and an outreach project, opened their spacious own shop in the back of the church which offers all sorts of merchandise, mainly books and cards and other things which make good presents. The idea is obviously to boost the church's income but unlike most commercial cut throat enterprises, St Andrew's Shop does not set out to clash with gifts on sale elsewhere in the city centre. The Friends of St Andrews had to run the gauntlet of some difficulty before they could start trading. Even English Heritage as well as the church authorities in Exeter had to be persuaded to give the venture their blessing.

The shop is open Monday to Saturday except when services are taking place.

Close by St Andrews in Catherine Street is the Jewish Synagogue, built in 1761 and the oldest in the English Speaking World. It has been treasured by the congregation over the centuries and is about to be refurbished but with a congregation of only 70 families it is suffering, as are all churches, from empty pews and straitened finances. If I had not had dealings with the Jewish community since the days of my childhood I would probably still be unaware of its existence. Thankfully today it is becoming known because of the tremendous time and effort put into it by Mr Greenberg who is the President - they can no longer afford a resident Rabbi. This is a man of remarkable knowledge, energy and as happy to talk to school groups or groups from the various denominations in Plymouth, as he is to his own congregation. He showed me his calendar for the end of this year and the beginning of next and it is full of dates when he will be in the synagogue to show people round or to talk of its history. He was saddened by the fact that most of the wonderful silver that has been acquired over the years seldom sees the light of day and is only taken out of the bank for very special occasions. As I write it is on show with a whole range of items and articles of the Jewish faith, in the Plymouth Museum. The display is superb and illustrates the history not only of the Plymouth Synagogue but many others and tells the story of Judaism graphically, sometimes with tragedy, sometimes joy and most often pathos. It has been agreed quite recently that these inestimably valuable pieces of silver, scrolls and other things will be on permanent loan to Plymouth City Museum. I just hope they will be able to display them frequently enough. If you read my piece on the Museum you will see that they can only display, at any one time, 5% of the wonderful treasures stored by them.

Mr Greenberg laments that it is more often funerals than weddings or Barmitzvahs he is asked to perform. In fact a recent wedding was the first one for fifteen years and to his horror he thought the wedding canopy had been mislaid but fortunately it was found before the wedding day and used for the happy couple. Once upon a time the Jewish cemetery used to be on Plymouth Hoe, but now it is in the ground just to the rear of Gifford Terrace and part of the Ford Park Cemetery. It is odd how things and events link up. My mother was a great bridge player and two of her great friends were Mr and Mrs King-Phillips who owned a chain of tobacconists, one of which was on Mutley Plain. They were Jews and their daughter Mollie, married Colonel Telfer, also a keen bridge player. They all belonged to the Plymouth Bridge Club where Walter Parsons was a member and whose son now carries on the family undertaking business. Through that connection Walter Parsons became virtually the only undertaker to deal with Jewish funerals, a custom which is continued today.

Another interesting connection is the well known Perlmutter family who lived in Plymouth for many years. One of them Billie, married my cousin Trevor George of the famous Trevor George Entertainments, probably the oldest Show business agency in the South West. With yet another curious twist, I have just learned that Colonel Telfer who was on Field Montgomery's personal staff during World War II, gave his medals to the late Tommy Perlmutter, who, in turn, gave them to my cousin Trevor George for safe keeping, where they remain today. It is a very small world. Another oddity is that the Georges were strong Methodists. My maternal grandfather was a friend of that great Methodist, Isaac Foot, father of the one time leader of the Labour Party, Michael Foot. So if my religious upbringing was not complicated enough by being Church of England, attending the High Anglican St Dunstan's Abbey School and spending weekends with Methodist grandparents, I also had to add to that a little touch of Judaism. It is no wonder that my Mother returning home one pouring wet evening from the Bridge Club having been given a lift by Colonel Telfer, said to him as she got out of the car 'Thank you- that was a very Christian Act'. The reply came ' The act may have been kind and my pleasure, but it was not Christian'.!!

I think the very many kind acts that Mr Greenberg carries out for the non-Jewish fraternity in Plymouth should be viewed in the same way. Definitely not Christian - he is a devout Jew, but they are for the community and for the good of the city. It is so important that we all recognise and respect faith in whatever denomination.

As I left Mr Greenberg's house just before Christmas 2000, he said to me with a twinkle in his eye ' I wonder how many of us will have the Hanaka candles lit standing alongside our Christmas trees?' Incidentally I wonder how many Plymothians know that the first Jew recorded in the Plymouth Area was Moses the Navigator who sailed with Sir Francis Drake!'

There is a very happy feeling emanating from the small but lively congregation of the Hope Baptist Church in Peverell. It is essentially a church for people who live locally but that does not mean that they do not give a very warm welcome to anyone who feels like attending a service or dropping in to the Coffee Morning held in the Church Hall every Thursday . It was at this coffee morning that I met the Minister, Andy Saunders. We sat at a table surrounded by people ranging from their eighties to very small people only a few months old. They all seemed to get on so well. I discovered from Andy that the older members of the congregation, some of whom have been there since the church started in the 1920s, genuinely like to see the young ones about them. When it comes to services they are quite prepared to embrace some of the more modern approaches to worship; this is not so in many churches of whatever denomination. The church hall is regularly used for anything from an Ante Natal group to 'Parents and Toddlers, with a special 'Chill Out' sessions and discussion groups on parenting for hard-pressed mums. Incidentally there is a splendid 'Dads and Lads' club run at the YMCA Kitto centre, a special time for fathers and sons to get together with other fathers and sons, have fun, talk and discover what this special sort of relationship can mean. The Devonport Dockyard Players use the hall for their rehearsals and so do many other organisations.

It is always the people who make the church and not the other way round and this fact came across strongly in my talk with Andy Saunders. He is a quiet but very determined man who came into the church having been, like his wife, a school teacher. In the way that one does we chatted about all manner of things amongst which was how he had become a Baptist Minister. He was brought up as a Methodist and his wife was Church of England. It was at University that he embraced Christianity properly for the first time and at that moment the denomination was unimportant; he mixed with students of all faiths. Even when he finished with University and each time he moved when he was teaching, he tended to find a church in which he felt comfortable, rather than a denomination. When he felt GOD call him to the ministry he then sought hard to find the right ology and decided that the Baptist's offered him what he was seeking. He also liked the idea of ministering to a flock small enough to give him the opportunity to know them and this he has certainly found at Hope Baptist. It says much for his ministry that he feels able to take a three month sabbatical to go to a Mission in Nepal with his wife and family. He knows that the church will cope in his absence.with visiting preachers and when necessary provide a leader from their own congregation. I have no doubt he will come back, renewed in everything he does, and the congregation will be the beneficiaries.

The large and very lively Baptist Church on Mutley Plain is always a hive of activity. Every Sunday it has a large congregation and during the week spreads the ministry throughout Plymouth. When I wrote the book 'Invitation to Plymouth' I was lucky enough to spend time with a lifelong Baptist, Hedley Miller, whose love of his church is shown in a book 'The first 100 years' from 1869-1969'. He co-operated in writing this book to celebrate the centenary of the Church. His grandfather used to recall how exciting it had been to look down from the crowded gallery on the opening day. He vividly remembered how, as a boy, he watched the collection plates being carried down the aisles below him, piled high with golden sovereigns.

Externally with its fine style of Palladian architecture, the church has not changed much. Internally a valuable foyer has been incorporated and in 1990, although the solid granite pillars supporting the arch above the organ chamber remain, considerable revamping occurred in order to facilitate modern worship. The pulpit was enlarged to form a rostrum, the platform enlarged to accommodate a music group and the organ replaced with a magnificent three manual Ahlborn Computing organ with seventy stops and combinations.

In the joyful singing of songs and hymns in Mutley Baptist, there is an exuberance which sends sound flying to the lofty ceiling. What is it about nonconformist services that make singing so cheerful and enjoyable? The hymns are not so different from the Church of England but unless you are in a major church, there the similarity ends. Could it be that the Church of England is not willing to adopt modern sound and new approaches to services?

Mutley Baptist reaches out its welcoming arms to newcomers to the city. I have personal experience of this. A few years back I had students living in my house to help me pay the mortgage and one of them was a Baptist from Bristol. During the time of her stay here she was visited regularly by members of the congregation and asked out for Sunday lunch on several occasions. For a youngster on her first adventure away from home this was especially good and one that I hope would be extended to children of mine were they in the same situation.

Active groups participate in the life of the Church. Every member, for instance, is encouraged to join a House Group, usually in their neighbourhood. These serve not only as prayer and study groups but as natural caring groups too. A place where problems can be shared and practical help found. Single parents find help from CLASP (Christian Link Association of Single Parents). The branch at Mutley Baptist provides fellowship, friendship and mutual support to those who find themselves bringing up children alone. There is also a team of people committed to caring for the sick regularly visiting the housebound and helping others with special needs. If ever you feel in need of comfort, or help, or a visit, no matter what your age, or circumstances or religion, please just let them know. Ring the Church on 01752 663784 and a message to the Pastoral team will be passed on.

The Junior Church is strong and very well organised with various departments starting at creche level with children up to 5 years and ending with a bible class for teenagers of fifteen.

Walking through the side door of the Methodist Central Hall I was made aware that the Baptists did not have the monopoly of activity. It was a Tuesday morning and it was like walking into a business - the business of the Lord. It was buzzing with activity. The new café building on the left side, manned by volunteers, had customers enjoying their morning coffee and in the main building the Minister is assisted by a full time staff. Various groups are organised by volunteers, the various groups meet each week and there are many outside activities. The Day Centre has regular meetings for elderly members and provides an opportunity for those who may be almost housebound, to come to the Hall and enjoy the company of others.

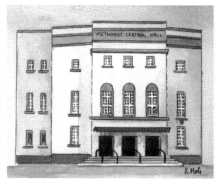

Transport is always readily available for anyone who needs it. Everyone enjoys a lunch prepared by the ever willing kitchen ladies. Afterwards Church members entertain with music, songs, monologues and a gentle time for exercise to music.

The Ladies Circle extends a warm welcome to any lady of whatever age to come and join them for their meetings and outings. They do all sorts of things from playing skittles to going to the theatre.

The Ladies Circle reminded me of the days when I, as a teenager, used to accompany my Grandmother and Aunt to the Tuesday Ladies Meeting in the Wesleyan Chapel in Stuart Road, Stoke. Sadly no longer there; it was destroyed by bombs during the Blitz. My grandfather, William George, was a leading member of the chapel and seemed to rule the roost there in much the same way as he did within the family.

Every Sunday the entire household went to morning service. It was a short walk from my grandparents' home. It was a sort of crocodile that wended its way to the stark chapel and once inside we were seated, in order of seniority, in the three front pews with the servants sitting behind us. Grandfather George, having supervised us settling into the pews, he produced silver coins for us to give to the collection. My child's tithe was sixpence, the servants one shilling, the ladies of the house, a florin and the men a half a crown. This was followed by a ceremonial removal from Grandfather's black and white striped waistcoat, of a gold pocket knife and a stick of black liquorice. A piece for each was cut off and given to us to ensure we kept quiet during the sermon.

Once the preacher - not always the Minister - reached the pulpit to begin the oration, out would come Grandfather's gold Hunter watch. It would be placed on the ledge on the pew in front of him, he would nod his head as a signal for us to start sucking the liquorice. He then leant back and closed his eyes. I never knew whether he had a quick forty winks but I did know that if the unfortunate preacher spoke for one second longer than the allotted twenty minutes, he would be abruptly stopped by a piercing glare from my grandfather and what can only be described as a 'humphing' noise emanating from his mouth which caused his walrus moustache to lift up and down rhythmically. Worse would follow. Sunday lunch was always attended by the resident Minister and his wife or a visiting preacher who was invariably a young man who was patently terrified by the awesome tyrant. The entire conversation during the meal would be dominated by my Grandfather who spoke at length on the subject of people who 'enjoyed the sound of their own voices'!

I always viewed Methodism as a cold and forbidding religion. Perhaps because it lacked the colour and drama of the High Anglican St Peter's Church, Wyndham Square which used to be the parish church for the pupils of St Dunstan's Abbey in my time. Many hours and many services have I attended there. It is only in more recent years that I have discovered the warmth and humanity that is so much a part of today's Methodist approach. The services are full of a different sort of colour, the richness of the choirs, and a true sense of evangelism. John Wesley would be proud of them.

Talking of St Peters, Wyndham Square reminds me of the splendid and frequently joint work which happens between it and the Roman Catholic Cathedral in Wyndham Street. They frequently share services and always work together for the benefit of the young, the elderly and the homeless. The sense of the love of God, the richness of worship, is apparent in both. The music is frequently glorious. I experienced it especially in a funeral service I attended in the Roman Catholic Cathedral. It was both a delight to the ear and a comfort to the heart.

Almost 160 years ago, Father George Prynne and the Sisters of the Community of St Mary the Virgin of Wantage, gave themselves unstintingly to the parish of St Peter's. During their time they had to face two outbreaks of cholera,as well as the various diseases which afflicted the poor people around them. No one could possibly follow better in that tradition, as he has done for almost a quarter of a century, than Father Sam Philpott, a cheerful warm-hearted character.

Father Sam recognises that he has to be just as unstinting in the running of his sprawling inner city parish. He is very much a 'hands on' priest who tackles almost impossible tasks, certain of only one thing; it is God's wish for him to do this work. Over the almost quarter of a century he has produced outstanding results. The derelict, bleak St Peter's Hostel in King Street was his first project. Having transformed that, most of the work being done by himself and his parishioners on a shoestring, he realised that to really get things done he needed to be part of a partnership in action rather than an isolated force competing, albeit unwittingly, against other units. He gathered round him the Stoneham Housing Association, the Probation and Social Services, and from then onwards the action has been almost non-stop.

It might be said to have been divine intervention when a mighty storm on Boxing Day 1979 blew off the roof of the redundant All Saints Church in Harwell Street. The church was demolished and became Annwyl Close, 22 purpose built flats providing temporary accommodation for deprived people who were then helped to cope with an alien world. They were encouraged to polish up whatever skills they had and strike out for independence. The church hall next door, a pathetic, almost derelict eyesore, was transformed into the headquarters of the go-ahead development team under the guiding hand of the Probation Service. It also provides room for a creche run by the city council.

By now the efforts of Father Sam were being recognised everywhere. Grants became available and this human dynamo was joined by other people with a social conscience on other projects. Devonport Guildhall opened its doors to the very successful Rainbow Project which provides a playschool and support for young mothers. You may remember it was one of the projects with which Anneka Rice became involved. The publicity from that programme brought more and more volunteers willing to help make it possible to complete the never ending tasks to achieve success for the project . The Ship Hostel and The Green Bike Scheme, all started through the enthusiasm of Father Sam. A one-to-one counselling service for offenders on probation was begun designed to help them cope with this period. They were encouraged to make good use of their time whether at work or leisure or in community service. In the domestic field the upstairs vestry of St Peters became a haven for couples having marital difficulties. Here trained volunteers act as mediators with a high rate of success.
Father Sam's work and his encouragement to others is what Christianity is all about.

Plymouth has churches or places of worship for all denominations. With the recognition of falling congregations some have closed and their congregations merged with others. Sherwell Congregational Church for example is now used by the University for lectures, seminars and as a concert hall. It has been beautifully converted and has acoustics second to none. The Salvation Army have also closed their Exeter Street meeting place but their work carries on in strength. They have served Plymouth so well for years and are active wherever there is a need. Christmas would not be the same without the sound of their band playing Christmas Carols in the streets and the City Centre. Nor would the homeless find food and warmth without the help of this brave band of men and women assisted by other denominations throughout the city.

The history of the work of Elim in Plymouth is well worth recording. Almost three quarters of a century ago it all began following a series of revival and healing campaigns conducted by the Welsh Evangelists, George and Stephen Jefferies. In the early 1920's revival meetings were held in the Army Drill Hall and the records show that throughout the campaign meeting the evangelists preached to capacity crowds of some 2,600 at each meeting. The religious enthusiasm did not limit itself to the Elims but rubbed off also on churches of all denominations in the city and established the Elim Fellowship in 1925.

For many years the church did not have a proper home; the congregation made do with an old iron foundry in Rendle Street, a dis-used and very run down church in Emma Place and for some 27 years between 1955 and 1982 the old Foot Mission in Notte Street which the congregation acquired from Isaac Foot's family. Nothing prevented them from worshipping together, even the fact that during the years of World War II they had no home at all and were compelled to worship in the foyer of an old cinema in Union Street which was bombed on two occasions, a café on Mutley Plain and in the old Stonehouse Town Hall. Talking to older members of the Church I discovered that those days are remembered with affection and not distress.

I wonder how many people remember the immediate postwar, successful tent campaign that was held on a bomb site at the lower end of what is now Royal Parade. All the evangelical activity produced an ever larger congregation and it was quite obvious that the Notte Street premises were too small and the Elim congregation sought new premises. This difficult task was finally resolved when they purchased the dilapidated premises vacated by the Embankment Road Methodist Church at Cattedown Roundabout.

It needed courage and vision to tackle the project. Both were there in abundance and all the time improvements have been and are being made. The community now consists of the Roundabout Day Nursery, a Luncheon Club for senior citizens, a Residential Nursing Home in Stoke, a Training School for Church Workers and the successful Kings School in Hartley.

The Elim congregation have a commitment to each other and a great concern for the quality of individual and corporate lives. Their worship is joyful and is no doubt why the church is always full.

Active religion for the good of the community is always heartening and this is shown every year by the Pilgrim United Reform Church in Keyham. They work hard for the community throughout the year with the highlight of their work being the Christmas Day lunch party for more than 100 guests at Sylvia's Café in the Wolseley Trust premises in Wolseley Road. Anyone who is faced with spending Christmas on their own is welcome. The traditional Christmas lunch is followed by games and carols and a finally tea. Guests do not even have to get themselves to the party; they get collected by various members of the congregation. Funding for this is always helped by generous gifts from business and especially Plymouth and South West Devon Co-op who provide the money which represents the value of Co-op stamps contributed to the charity box in the Wolseley Road Plymco store. So never waste stamps if you shop at the Co-op.

The services at the Pilgrim United Reformed Church are as warm-hearted as their charitable work. A happy united congregation making Christianity work.

The University of Plymouth.

Chapter VIII

The Importance of Education

Plymouth has become a major centre of learning in recent years with the increased standing of the University and now the addition of the Peninsula Medical School at Derriford Hospital which promises us the first graduates in 2006. Educational establishments at every level are reaching out into the new century with a desire to achieve and stay at the top of the educational ladder.

It was brought home to me how much we have achieved and how much the education available has prompted people to relocate here. It is almost the first thing that people looking to come to Plymouth enquire about. Are the schools good? Of course they are. From Day Nurseries to the University the choice is wide and you do not have to be wealthy to provide a first class grounding for your offspring.

I can only attempt to give you some idea of the scope and range of the educational facilities open to Plymothians or to those who would adopt the city. . No one pretends that there is not still much to do to make education perfect but when I look around I see the enormous advances that have been made. For example when I wrote 'Invitation to Plymouth' in 1993, Parkside Comprehensive was about to open under the headteacher ship of a lady, Balena Jones,who came from Birmingham and took on one of the toughest educational roles in the city. The strides that have been made have been spectacular and the school thrives producing better results every year. Pupils are no longer rebellious, uninterested in learning and determined not to be proud of any uniform. They wear their uniform with pride and the results speak for themselves.

The benefits of good pre-school nursery care and education are firm foundations for life so perhaps that is where my educational journey should start. It is recognised that children of this generation need educational stimulus much earlier than in years gone by. The two and three year olds are no longer happy to play at home all day; more demanding activities are required. Having said that perhaps not all that much has changed! I went to St Dunstan's in 1928 when I was just over three years of age. I spent the next fourteen years there.

I have always had an affection for the Roundabout Day Care Centre in the Christian Centre at Cattedown roundabout. Twelve years ago they came to my rescue when my three years old grandson was left in my care for a month whilst his parents were abroad. He loved it and quite rightly so for it is one of the most welcoming pre-school nurseries I encountered. Angie Curtis has been the manager there for the past 2 1/2 years, and part of the staff for 11 years. It is well established and the organisation is superb. Children are separated into four age groups, each of which has a separate room in the building, specifically equipped to cater for their individual needs. Very young children, from 3 months to 2 years have a one to three staff ratio so no one is lacking in attention at anytime during the day. Grouping the children in this way allows them to enjoy a greater range of activities suited to their particular age. It also provides a close knit family atmosphere, and because the children are only in contact with their own peer group it makes it easier for them to fit in.

145

For the slightly older children, from 3-5 years, the qualified nursery nurse is supported by a primary school teacher in the planning of activities to further their pre-school development and give them a good educational start. The children are given 'lessons' in groups of no more than 8, meaning they have plenty of opportunity for individual stimulation and encouragement. At all times attention is paid to the particular needs of each child, so their education progresses at a suitable individual pace.

The nursery is open from 7.30am to 6pm daily. The younger children are encouraged to take a nap after lunch to break up the activities of their day. Opportunities exist for both indoor and outdoor play, circle time (time to share their news and thoughts) and quiet time when they can relax and unwind. It is Roundabout's policy that all children, and indeed their parents/carers, need a settling in period before they really start - a gentle introduction to nursery life. On the first visit the parent or carer is encouraged to stay with the child, and then gradually start to leave him or her for longer periods of time. As children move from one department to another within the nursery the same level of care is taken, and they will be introduced gently by a familiar member of staff. In fact, the one feature that stands out above all others about the Roundabout Day Care Centre is the level of personal attention and care that each child experiences, gently fostering a happy and balanced attitude.

Caroline Francis owns the Pixieland Day Nurseries and under her watchful eyes a fully qualified manager is employed to run each of the three sites around Plymouth; at Mount Gould Hospital, 17 Hastings Street and 162 Mannamead Road. As we talked in the summer of 2000 a fourth site was due to open at 10 Springfield Drive in Milehouse. The Nurseries all provide for children from birth to five years and have a wonderful caring approach to childcare, inspiring faith from any parent. Caroline Francis told me that 'The Pixieland policy is to offer children a secure and caring environment with maximum opportunity for development of the whole child. It also recognises that as well as any physical needs the most important aspects of a child's development are fostered in play situations..........." of which there are many!

Toddlers and pre-school children will discover the joy of a wet area for sand and water play, a quiet area for books, jigsaws and less exuberant games, a role play/home corner and even a rumpus area for climbing equipment and other fun and exciting activities. Babies have their own separate area for play, into which the older children may be allowed occasionally to encourage interaction and the development of social skills.

Each month of the year sees a new and colourful project for the children to explore; for example March is the time for looking closely at families (including visits from family pets). In August the children are encouraged to find out more about Plymouth and complete a simple project all about the sea. Each month also has a designated colour, shape and number which is concentrated upon and learned, as are the Letterland Letters which give children a good basic grasp of many different aspects of their education by the time they reach schooling age.

In addition to all these fabulous provisions made for the children left in the capable hands of Pixieland staff, these nurseries are also among the most advanced in terms of security and technology. CCTV systems have been installed at every site, and the nursery in Stoke even has a unique entry system which uses finger print recognition to allow parents access. The children also benefit from the addition of new technologies, especially in the Mannamead branch where there is a new 'sensory room' where they can experience a host of new things.

One of the oldest and most respected childcare providers in Plymouth has just celebrated its 75th birthday. The Redwood Family Centre Nursery Unit based at Bretonside, caters for up to 25 children aged two to five throughout the week. The Centre moved from Virginia House to its present site on Looe Street about four years ago having received a grant from the National Lottery of about £250,000. I remember helping in the centre when I was recruited by Lady Astor who was its original instigator. How times have changed and how much better they are for children today.

To get Ofsted praise is rare indeed and was welcomed by the Stuart Road Community Nursery in Stoke. This is a privately run nursery situated in Stuart Road Primary School. It is a bright shining place offering a high standard of nursery education. Children enjoy learning here. The Nursery can take 48 children and its programme has a strong emphasis on social development. For example four year olds become confident, independent learners who behave well, and three-year olds learn routines and boundaries, responding well to the consistent approach, praise and encouragement from staff. The Ofsted report stated that the nursery's programme for languages and literacy was strong, with all children talking articulately, enthusiastically and confidently about their experiences, using a growing vocabulary. The four staff, with Nursery manager Carolyn Thomas in charge, were praised for fostering the children's natural curiosity.

The nursery is open during term-time only and most children transfer to Stuart Road Primary School.

Play should be a major part in any child's formative years and should be complimentary to schooling. One has to admire the ingenuity, the determination and the regenerative spirit of Dave Burgess, a Plymothian born in Whitleigh. He saw the need to provide something for the children of the area. Within the confines of the old Clark's factory at Whitleigh he has built Playzone. It is a perfect example of local democracy -built by the people for the people. It is a first for Plymouth and should be an enormous success. It cost about £500,000 in all and one of the best things is that it has employed local labour and has used locally sourced materials to bring the disused factory back to life in one of Plymouth's less favoured areas.

The Playzone caters for all ages and is a true family entertainment centre, all under cover. It has £15,000 worth of safe but challenging and exciting adventure equipment, slides, cargo nets, ball pools, soft play areas, television rooms, party rooms, a cafeteria, climbing frames, a stage, and an exhilarating 70ft by 25ft high 'death' slide. Parents can be with their children if they wish or they can leave them with the Playzone staff whilst they go and have a quiet drink in the family bar or enjoy a meal.

Small children have their own soft play area from which they cannot wander off, and during the day the main play adventure area is open for children up to 12 years.

The 13-18s have their own evening a bit like a youth club. At night it becomes a family entertainment zone with magicians, kids karaoke, puppets and children's' disco. Pricing throughout is sensible. It costs £3.95 per child for a two hour session. Adults pay £1 which includes a free drink in the café. Twenty six staff are employed here, mainly from Whitleigh, Tamerton and Southway. It is an excellent concept and deserves to be successful.

Plymouth currently has a five year plan to boost the inclusion in mainstream schools of children with special needs. The city has always had a good policy in this regard but like everything else much more needs to be done. It has always been thought imperative to bridge the gulf between mainstream and special schools. But, at the same time,some children need access to highly specialised provision in special schools. The strategic plan means that in future the Education Committee will be able to respond to the growing demand from parents for local mainstream education as well as for high quality specialist facilities. It will undoubtedly benefit all children, both the able-bodied and those with disabilities. Plymouth recognises that this is not a cheap option and is prepared to invest in high quality special provision for the children who need it.

It seems commonsense to me that this scheme opens up opportunities for all special schools to develop partnerships with mainstream schools and other agencies working with children and their families.

It is not only the council who are involved in the pursuit of excellence as far as education is concerned. Plymouth business people as part of the Prince of Wales 'Seeing is Believing' project, have a mission and have formed a group known as BitC Business Support. They are encouraging Plymouth schools to sign up to their scheme which aims to have special reading schemes in place by September 2001. Mount Wise Primary and Parkside Community College were the first targets. The group believe they can make a real difference where it is needed which long term will have an impact on their future employees. It is a humbling thought when one realises that 40% of 11 year olds have a reading average of only eight years. The organisations taking part include Bae, Royal Mail, MoD, CSA, Plymco, Plymouth Hospitals NHS Trust, the RAF, SWEB and Brittany Ferries.

Plymouth's two major independent schools are Plymouth College founded in 1877 and amalgamated with Mannamead School in 1896. Incidentally, Plymouth Historian, Chris Robinson is currently writing the history of the school which should make interesting reading - he is currently up to 1931, I understand! The other is St Dunstan's Abbey for Girls founded at the eastern end of the Royal Naval Burial Ground in 1848 and now in splendid new buildings in the grounds of the old Royal Naval Hospital at Millfields, Stonehouse. This was my school and I first went through its rather forbidding doors in 1928 when I was not quite four.

My visit to the school this time in its new setting provided me with mixed feelings. I mourned the loss of the old school in North Road West which is in the process of being demolished to provide new homes but once in the grounds of the new premises I found a wonderful atmosphere and somehow the lack of the old buildings was totally unimportant. Here the various buildings spread round grassy lawns have an air of well being, friendliness and a sense of purpose with constant movement between one building and another. Before I went in to meet Barbara Brown the headmistress, a charming lady with a keen sense of humour and a decided twinkle in her eye, I sat for a moment or two thinking of the past. All my formative years were spent in this school, albeit in a different place and how things have changed. I remember reading the reminiscences of my first headmistress, Sister Margaret Teresa, the Mother Superior - until the 1950s St Dunstan's was synonymous with the Sisters of the Community of St Mary, Wantage, the Anglican Order whose work included not only teaching but via the Mother House in Wyndham Square, care of the people in the parish of St Peters.

The Millfields. Courtesy of Blackfriars Contracts.

Sister Margaret Teresa wrote
'I may mention another memory that does not fade - that of the many funerals which passed the school from the R.N Hospital. The band and muffled drums, the tramp of feet outside, the girls inside standing silent till the band had passed, then a short prayer for the dead, and work resumed. I wonder how many souls have been speeded by St Dunstan's children's prayers'.

Thinking about this sad little piece as I sat in Millfields, I remembered vividly standing by my desk, bobbed blonde head suitably lowered, black tunic, white shirt, red sash, denoting Downton House, black woollen stockings which did their best to slide down my small legs in their black buttoned shoes. The music was always the Dead March from Saul and I never hear it now without remembering those days which happened with regrettable frequency.

Those days are gone. The days when the Sisters outnumbered the lay teachers and regular attendance in the school chapel and at St Peters was a required part of one's education no matter what your creed, are no more. I have such permanent memories of St Dunstan's. It was a place of happiness, fun, dedication, chocolate cake for tea on Fridays and Saints Days, the annual Ascensiontide picnic for the whole school, myrtle in a bride's bouquet from a bush in the Sisters' Garden - my own sister had her sprig and as she is approaching her golden wedding, I believe she still has it pressed in a book. I never achieved mine - I eloped! There were dark times of course. I remember lunch in the Refectory at the time of Dunkirk, the defeatist attitude of some pupils and the 'up and at them' feeling of the rest of us. No matter how you felt it was an unnerving time and says much for the staff that they kept us all going. I remember too the shame of a girl who had been especially naughty and was deprived of her house girdle and made to wear a black one instead. It would not be allowed to happen today under some Citizen's Rights rule, but to us at that time it brought shame not only to the girl but to her house as well. Times change but thankfully some of the best traditions are continued and I am pleased to report that the myrtle bush survived its transplant from North Road West and now flourishes in Millfields. The school photographs throughout the years have survived and now grace the walls of the reception area - I found one which included me in 1933 and had I spent more time I would have found me again, and my sister as well I expect!

Under the astute and understanding leadership of Barbara Brown St Dunstan's is more than holding its own in Plymouth although Plymouth College becoming co-ed has not helped matters. All sorts of things have been happening in the school bringing the scholastic achievements to an all time high. Part of this is due to the excellence of the staff who come from all over the country, some from public schools. For the first time in some years the Sixth Form will have fifty one girls in September 2000. The school shares some subjects with the Grammar Schools when it is practical so to do and that is reciprocal. There are a whole range of extra curricular activities which keep the school lively out of school hours and recently St Dunstan's has become the home of the Italia Conti Stage School which is proving a great success. The new day nursery for toddlers and babies is another success story. I watched the carers taking their very small charges for a walk round the grounds - a contented group. The preparatory and the junior school is also thriving. Boarders come from far and wide and some from abroad including a girl from Malawi. The girls wear their uniform with pride and that is reflected in their pride and pleasure in the school as a whole. I might mourn the passing of St Dunstan's in North Road West but no one could deny the new school with its grounds is an enormous improvement on the cramped space available in the old Abbey.

Plymouth College used to have the tag 'for Boys' added on to its name. This is no longer the case; it has become co-ed and what started out as an experiment in the Sixth form now starts at Nursery level with Busy Bees in Seymour Road and advances to the preparatory school which has its being in a gracious old house in Mannamead Avenue, Hartley, where, during the war years, the staff of the Royal Naval Engineering College lived and gave early evening parties which started at 4.30pm and ceased before the arrival of the nightly German bombers. Lively tea dances they were too. Here today, the youngsters begin school in earnest and learn how to use education. You might think that an odd remark but it is the epitome of what public schools and grammar schools set out to achieve. Their pupils are taught how to pass exams, how to perform at interviews and generally be prepared for the outside world. I have twin daughters, one of whom had a grammar school education and has gone on to take her Masters degree, her younger twin went to what was then a Secondary Modern School and the difference in the standard of education was marked. This is in no way decrying the State system which is constantly improving and with the excellence of the head teachers and their staff, Plymouth now has a range of first class Comprehensive Schools taking children from 11-18 as well as imaginative Primary Schools. More of them later.

My purpose here is to give you a potted story of Plymouth College - Plymouth Historian and Artist, Chris Robinson is currently writing an in depth history of the school and at the last count had reached 1931! Here is a beloved school known throughout the world wherever there are expatriates who passed through its portals in the early and most informative days of their lives.

I read a book on the history of the school by Charles Robert Serpell, who died in 1949 and had had a longer intimate connection with the school more than any other man. I have drawn on his knowledge, his comments and experiences to add my tribute to this great school.

By profession a lawyer, Charles Serpell was prominent in many directions in the life of Plymouth; but it is safe to say that of all his public work, that which he undertook for the school lay nearest to his heart. His opening paragraph says so much.

" Seventy years in the life of a school is long enough to cover many generations of boys. By the time one of these boys reaches that age he has at most only another decade or so before him. But the school to which he was for a few years contributing for good or ill, consciously or unconsciously, the influence of his personality may well go on making history for centuries. If the school has survived it has anyhow probably got itself well established. It will have created records and acquired traditions such as to justify the hopes of still greater achievement." But how did the school which has reached this so respectable age begin at all?

Plymouth College began in 1877 in the building that is illustrated here. A school that had amalgamated with Mannamead School, its senior by a few years, the classrooms, the well worn floors, the carving of initials on some of the wood still speaks of generations past. This building is still the heart of the school but over the years it has grown tentacles, not in most cases attached so perhaps satellites would be a better word. There is a Sports Hall, a Science Block, new Common rooms, a theatre. Almost the whole of a gracious row of houses alongside the school has been purchased over the years making comfortable quarters for those who board. Whenever another property comes up there is always the hope that funds will be there for the school to acquire it. There may be everything that a school at the beginning of the 21st century requires but no matter what is added, it will never lose its original character. Its staff list under the leadership of the Headmaster, Alan Morsley, speaks of Oxbridge graduates and men of letters from other universities but none the less qualified. They in turn teach the young men and women to a sufficiently high standard to emulate themselves in the ability to obtain university places and to enter professions and industry all over the world.

Famous names have started their days here, the services have always been able to rely on entries from Plymouth College. The law, accountancy and the theatre have all claimed their number. One common bond always holds them together - the School. They meet in London for reunions, they gather in Plymouth for social occasions and it is always with pride that they talk of the past, the present and what they hope will be the future. Many have sons or grandsons currently in school.

Plymouth College. Painted by a pupil of Plymouth College.

152

The Preparatory School operates on a split site. In the Infant Department at Seymour Road life is always hectic, and fun has a skilled habit of becoming educational. The obviously happy children enjoy visits out which are linked to their studies. It could be a visit to the Prickly Ball Hedgehog Hospital or the National Marine Aquarium, a trip up river to Calstock or an insight to farming after a day's visit to Ransom's Farm near St Mellion.. Whatever they do and wherever they go they are a credit to Plymouth College.

Next step is the Junior Department in Hartley Road for the 7-11 years old. The curriculum is all encompassing including extra curricular activities such as Chess, Philately, CDT and Computing. Music plays a large part in the life of the school. There are two choirs and a well established orchestra and individual tuition is available for most instruments. There is a music concert and a drama production every year. Pastoral care plays a major part in the daily lives of the school.

Most children, having reached the required educational standard, go on to the main school in Ford Park Road when they get to the requisite age. The all round academic tuition is accompanied by the very best in sports facilities, an encouragement to take part in the Performing Arts, a chance to join an array of clubs from Chess to Philately, The Bridge Club to the Combined Cadet Force and 'Dukes' - the Duke of Edinburgh Award Scheme. With the highest level of people on the teaching staff, The School seeks to find and develop talent of every kind in academic work, in sports and the arts.

Times change and in 1995 the School admitted girls for the first time. Now they are to be found in every year. In fact a third of the school is female. In all there are some 600 pupils, 60 of whom board in the very comfortable, well equipped houses provided for this purpose.

Common sense and the strain of travelling daily to the school from the outlying reaches of Plymouth finally determined the demise of Saturday morning school. This in no way has affected the sport that occurs every Saturday with teams playing sometimes at home and sometimes away. The familiar playing fields which stretch out before the school to the borders of Devon Terrace and Ford Park Road, are constantly in use. The old Cricket Pavilion has gone and been replaced by a solid stone affair. A new, enlarged swimming pool is just about to open. On summer afternoons the gentle click of a cricket ball as it hits the willow and soars through the air to the boundary brings forth the oohs and ahs according to which eleven you support. It is a sight that please every Plymothian who passes by.

From the outside Plymouth High School for Girls looks quite small but once you walk through its almost unpretentious and Victorian front door you are in a world of academic excellence accompanied by an unexpected warmth of atmosphere. The school has worked its way, building after building around a quadrangle, the most recent addition of which is a new Common Room for sixth formers in a large room distinguished by an old arch.

The school has a proud tradition of providing an excellent education for girls and young women, which is essentially well-rounded. Whilst it demands a high standard from all its pupils it does not ignore the fact that not everyone will be an academic high flyer. Therefore the whole emphasis is on bringing the best out of every girl who attends the school. The Headteacher, Sue Martin, is supported by a staff who are committed and who have a caring attitude toward their students. If you talk to most of the girls who attend Plymouth High you get the feeling that they have a love of learning. In some cases it is the unique talent of a girl that stands out. Equally the school recognises and caters for girls with particular needs and abilities.

One understands having been to the school why the motto is 'For life not school we learn'.
To get a place in Plymouth High is an honour and in return the school not only gives the best education but it demands commitment from its pupils. There are no shirkers here, no truants but at the same time the life of the school produces a very happy environment. The curriculum is designed to ensure that all the girls experience a broad balanced and relevant curriculum which is appropriate to the rapidly changing world in which they will live and work. Self esteem, enquiring minds, thinking skills, creativity and leadership are all ingredients required in taking a girl or young woman into the outside world.

The subjects inside the classroom cover all the needs of education and include besides English, Mathematics, Science, Modern Languages, Geography and History, the essentials for the 21st century, Design and Technology, Information Technology etc.
Art and Music play a large part in the life of the school. Art offers a wide range of processes and techniques from Drawing and Painting to Collage, Printmaking and 3D work. Experimentation is encouraged; the aim is to build confidence through a varied Art experience. The school has a high reputation for its music and for its drama productions. The subject has a broad base from performing to composing, listening to attending concerts.

The school is not lacking either in sporting activities. Pupils are encouraged to be creative and competitive. They are expected to attain a high standard of skills, presentation and self-discipline and to develop a positive attitude towards a healthy lifestyle. Activities include, gymnastics, hockey, netball, volleyball, dance, football, rounders, athletics and tennis.
It seemed to me that it was the marrying of the ideals and principles of the school that impressed me more than anything else. It is a community that treats each other fairly and with respect. The school rules are simple and clear. They are designed to promote courteous and sensible behaviour, respect for each other and the school environment and to ensure the health and safety of all members of the school community - and please do not chew gum in school and place litter in the bins provided.

It is down to earth normality of the last bit of the previous paragraph that underlines that human beings are not perfect and are full of frailties but Plymouth High School for Girls is as near to perfect as its Headteacher, its Staff and its Pupils can make it.

And then we have two excellent schools, Devonport High School for Boys and Devonport High School for Girls. They both have reputations for getting the very best out of their pupils. The two Headteachers have the same aim; to teach a love of learning and life to the pupils in their care.

Devonport High School for Boys has a great site in Millbridge which was formerly Stoke Hospital and buildings which Archibald Ballard bought and wanted to give to the education authorities in the 1920s but was turned down! Its big buildings, dating from 1797, stretch over a wide area and provide a great sense of permanency and tradition. The school was originally in Devonport and moved here in 1945. The ancient walls lend a great character to the school and overlook extensive playing fields. The school has a wide catchment area drawing its 1100 pupils not only from Plymouth but also from West Devon, East Cornwall and the South Hams. Admission is at 11 years but pupils do join in later years and a significant number join the sixth form for 'A' level courses.

In spite of the size of the school, Dr Pettit, the Headteacher, together with his 65 highly qualified staff maintain a strong sense of identity. The school is divided into four houses, Gilbert, Drake, Grenville and Raleigh for both academic and pastoral purposes which ensures that every pupil is well known and well looked after. It also has another and very important purpose. Each house has a House Captain who urges his house to greater efforts. These efforts are rewarded with house points and it has become a matter of pride to be the highest scoring house. Dr Pettit, incidentally, is only the 8th Headteacher in the 104 year history of the school. He has a son in school and I wondered if this was difficult for him or his son. The answer was a firm 'No'. In fact it helped them both. His son is a well-rounded young man and father gains knowledge of the school from an insider - his son. Not in a tale -telling way but just reactions from time to time.

Strong links are kept with parents, both through individual meetings and in formal consultation evenings. These precede the taking of all-important decisions about a boy's curriculum or career. Experience has shown that it is perfectly possible for a boy gaining entry to the school to go on to university, get a flying scholarship or whatever, if that is the boy's wish. Some, of course, enter employment at sixteen or after 'A' levels, and the school has maintained its traditional capacity for preparing young men for entry into the Royal Navy. Academic and industrial awards help many pupils to support their courses in higher education.

Dr Pettit believes passionately that every boy needs to be encouraged to fulfil his ambitions and these do not always have to be academic. Naturally boys coming here have already achieved a certain level of ability to learn which helps but in this day and age the ways of successfully earning a living do not always come from acquiring degrees. He feels that getting to know his pupils is all important and for that reason he is not averse to joining in some of their outdoor activities.

It is certainly not all study at Devonport High School for Boys. Physical development and participation in sport is an important element in school life. Rugby, soccer and basketball are the main winter sports, with strong interest in badminton, squash, hockey and cross-country running; in summer the main emphasis is on athletics and cricket. That the school is as successful in sport as it is in academic studies is undoubted. In recent years they have won county or area titles in 11 different sports, represented the county in 19, and competing in no fewer than 11 different sports at schools' national level. When I visited the school in June 2000 a new Sports Hall was being built for use by the summer of 2001, Playing fields were being given all weather surfaces and a new Canteen was in the pipeline.

A strong musical tradition is sustained by many boys learning one of a range of fourteen instruments, which coupled with the enthusiasm for drama, enables the school to mount major musical or dramatic productions every year. They are joined in productions with the girls from Devonport High School for Girls. The more accomplished musicians play for the county orchestras, while a large number forming the school's 'Big Band' undertake annual visits to international musical events abroad.

The school has strong links with industry, especially BAE SYSTEMS through the Sainsbury Trusts' engineering scheme and through a number of practising engineers directly supporting the work of various subject departments. The school also makes good use of industry and the City's institutions of higher education, for assistance with technological and design project work.

One of the most exciting projects of the last few years has been the schools alliance with the village of Uzel in Brittany. The school has a house here which gives pupils regular opportunities to stay and study in France. By living in a small community, using the resources of the area, and through associating with local schools, pupils are gaining an invaluable insight into the French way of life and so are better prepared to play a full part in Europe.

Dr Pettit will tell you that the Parent Teacher Association to which all parents and members of staff automatically belong, has been invaluable in bringing about improvements in the school facilities. Guided by a large committee drawn from parents with children at every stage in the school, parents have become increasingly involved in raising funds for practical projects and in developing social activities to bring parents closer together, and in serving as Governors of the School.

Devonport High School for Girls has the air of a well-run, well-oiled ship with a Captain who knows exactly how to get the best out of her officers and crew! Mrs Dunball, the Headteacher for many years, and whom many girls will remember gratefully, has retired and Mrs Smith is her successor. She is ably assisted by two Deputy Headteachers and a highly qualified staff of fifty. The school was founded in 1911 and moved to its present, purpose built site in 1937. It is situated on a pleasant site overlooking Central Park. It is a selective girls' grammar school with approximately 700 girls with four forms of entry and about one hundred and eighty sixth formers.

Places here are fought for keenly both by parents and would-be pupils. The work ethic is very strong, though fun and relaxation are essential ingredients of its success. The staff manage to retain a strong sense of humour and keep firmly in touch with the world outside, believing that students do not thrive in a rarefied atmosphere. Most of the girls go on to academic success at the very highest levels and staff are deeply committed to their teaching. The innovative and traditional methods of teaching are finely balanced providing the very best for the girls in a professionally stimulating and personally supportive environment.

There are many excellent aspects at the school and one picked up by the Inspection Report in January 2000 pointed out the good support for those with special educational needs and for those whose achievements are relatively weaker. It is so important for those children to have the right backing and be in the right environment. The sort of schooling they get here prepares them for the rigours of life in the big world and provides them with the confidence they need. There is no doubt that there is a high level of care and support through the pastoral system and by subject teachers, Staff and the girls work well together to overcome any academic or personal problems that arise. The school is also named in the forthcoming Annual Report by the Chief Inspector of Ofsted because it received an outstanding report and has performed well in national tests and examinations. Ofsted have asked the school to feature on their Website celebrating effective practice. The area where the school is adjudged most effective is 'teaching'.

In addition to its comprehensive academic curriculum there are cultural and sporting opportunities. These range from a well equipped music department providing scope for choral, instrumental and composition work, to aerobics and technology clubs. The Local Education Authority provides a peripatetic service for instrumental music. The orchestras, choirs and band give regular concerts at the school and perform at the School Speech Day in the Guildhall. Several pupils are members of County orchestras and choirs. Drama productions are put on by the English department, the Drama Society and the Sixth form. Often these productions draw on the talent of the whole age range. The girls also take part in productions with Devonport High School for Boys and St Boniface College for Boys.

Throughout the school the syllabus recognises both the position of Christianity and other faiths in Britain. In accordance with the 1988 Education Reform Act the school will, wherever possible, hold a daily act of collective worship, which will be of a 'mainly broadly Christian character'. Some pupils and staff support an active Christian Union, and together produce several assemblies for the school. Sixth formers and representatives from each form make up the school Council and present a forum whereby pupils can exchange ideas and influence school life.

Schools today rely heavily on Parent Teacher Associations. At Devonport High School for Girls the P.T.A is an invaluable part of the school. Its Committee meets regularly and raises funds to support the education of pupils by providing 'extras' and facilities the school could not afford otherwise. The school's library and music centre are evidence of P.T.A generosity. There are a variety of fund raising occasions throughout the year and no parents' meeting would be complete without the P.T.A. Time is also set aside for social functions which enable parents to get to know each other, and to relax socially. Without the P.T.A the community of the school would be much poorer.

European school Exchanges take place every year with pupils visiting Quimper and Toulon in France, Santander in Spain, Hanover in Germany, or Verona in Italy. There are clubs and societies including a popular mathematics club, badminton and many other sporting activities.

With such an excellent educational opportunity across the whole spectrum, Plymouth is privileged. I have a great affection for one of the best state primary and junior schools, Hyde Park Infant and Juniors. The slightly uncompromising building has a warmth inside with classrooms that have been brought to life by the dedicated staff and pupils who respond to the desire to learn with an enthusiasm that is infectious.

I was asked to speak to two classes a few years ago. They listened with polite attention but it was not until I had finished talking and asked them a question about Plymouth and how they thought it ought to be that I fully understood what an intelligent, lively bunch they were. The environment was one of the main things that caused them concern. They wanted more trees in the parks, less litter and greater safety. I had forgotten how perceptive the very young could be. It says much for the quality of their teachers that these young minds were being given the opportunity to learn quickly about their home city.

One poignant memory I have of Hyde Park School is during the intense bombing of Plymouth. I lived, with my parents, just up the road from the school. One night my father and I were out patrolling in case incendiary bombs came hurtling down and needed extinguishing. We looked up towards the sky and there was a new phenomenon floating down on a parachute - a land mine. It was coming directly towards us and in the stupid way one behaves in moments of high tension, my father and I shook hands and wished each other goodbye! I am still here and my father lived for many more years. The land mine landed on the roof of the school.

One of Plymouth's remarkable schools is King's School in Hartley. Remarkable because it opened its doors as a direct request from the parents of the children at the Roundabout Nursery. When children left the Nursery School parents had to look for suitable schools in which to place their children. They approached Mary Smyth who was then head of nursery to provide such a school.

After discussing the matter with the leadership of the Christian Centre, it was decided to open a reception class for rising fives in one spare room, near the nursery complex. The venture soon showed every indication of success and a search for a building in which the proposed school could be housed, commenced. After a time the Hartley Road building became available. It was purchased and now King's School caters for 3-11 year olds and is co-educational. There is a nursery for those aged 0-3 on site.

Educationally it offers a broad challenge in a Christian based co-educational environment teaching the National Curriculum. There are small classes, an emphasis on developing confidence, self-discipline and social skills.

The building is gracious, with a large playground/hard sports pitch. Parental involvement is encouraged. It also offers holiday and aftercare for working parents. King's School is a remarkable establishment, offering an excellent education at moderate fees.

One needs to say a bit more about this school because if ever you have doubted the power of prayer, this is a story which underlines how much we are all dependent on the Supreme Power.

When King's School was about to commence it did not have a qualified teacher. Pressure was put on Mary Smyth to advertise for a suitably trained person. This she resisted because she wanted a committed Christian. She remembers sitting in her office and banging her desk in sheer frustration saying 'Lord, you started all this! You must know who my teacher is - now I need to know'.

Later that day a face came into her mind. A woman she had met two years previously. She knew her parents but did not know if the girl was a teacher. Mary rang up the parents and was told that yes, the daughter was a teacher but was only working on a part-time basis. Theresa was the girl's name and she was married. Neither Theresa or her husband were too keen on what Mary was offering but once Mary's vision had been explained they prayed together and Theresa joined the school.

The following year the church spent £12,000 on another classroom and equipment and now had a total of 32 children. New premises were becoming essential. Everything they looked at that was suitable they could not afford. Everything they could afford was refused planning consent unless they could undertake prohibitive conversions.

Suddenly, out of the blue, after a lot of prayer, someone appeared at the Christian Centre saying that they had a school which had now closed and would the premises be of any use to them? They moved at Easter 1991, and now have 176 3-11year olds and a 0-3 unit of about 45.. The staff are all committed Christians. Their salaries are a little low at the moment but they feel they are fulfilling their role as teachers.

When the school was visited by HM Inspector of Schools he was amazed at the calibre of staff and wanted to know Mary Smyth's recruiting methods. He was more than a little startled to be told 'By prayer'. His reply 'Keep doing it, it works'.

The school continues to receive excellent Ofsted reports for their provision of four year olds.

The Ridgeway School in Plympton is another excellent school. It was opened in 1983 and is a mixed comprehensive catering for 880 pupils aged 11-18. The headteacher is intensely proud of the record that the school has achieved in less than twenty years. The GSCE pass rate is one of the highest in West Devon and the A level results improve significantly every year.

Coombe Dean School at Plymstock is a fine educational establishment with a visionary headteacher, Peter Reid. His school is an excellent example of the comprehensive system which looks beyond the conventional curriculum to see what can be done to prepare pupils for the outside world.

Several schools in Plymouth have Governors who are part of the commerce and industry sector. In the case of Coombe Dean, interest in the school has been taken by one of the earliest American companies to come to Plymouth,Gleasons. The Vice President of the Company is Robert Ball who is Plymouth born and bred. He believed the Coombe Dean project would greatly benefit future education in the locality and asked Peter Reiod how Gleasons could help.

Peter Reid explained his vision and concept of a business centre within the school with state-of-the-art equipment, running courses in finance, business management and secretarial skills. The centre was to be available to members of the community and available throughout the day, in the evenings and at the weekends.

Peter Reid asked for £20,000 for the building and £27,000 for the equipment. After studying the proposals and costings, the Gleason Memorial Fund presented the school with a cheque for £47.000.

The well-equipped building allows 16-17 year old students the opportunity to follow vocational courses without leaving the school site. The facilities are also available to pupils from other years and to adults. Courses are run in the evenings and in the holidays.

Bob Ball was thrilled with the outcome and said at the time of the opening 'Our company needs highly trained young people and many of our best apprentices have come from Coombe Dean'.

To have chosen only a handful of comprehensive schools to write about when there are so many good ones, must seem inexcusable to those who have been omitted, but please believe that every one of them has high standards and offers good opportunities to the children who attend. Plymouth's change of status from a Polytechnic to the University of Plymouth has not changed its desire to be the best or to quote the old Polytechnic and use their motto 'The Quest to be the Best'. The University has a fine reputation which is growing steadily even though it is only in its first decade. I am sufficiently old to remember it as a Technical School in Drake Circus and even then it worked to a very high standard. After the war new buildings were added and still continue to be, bringing it first to Polytechnic status and then the final accolade of University.

A place in the University is highly regarded by students whether full or part-time, whether taking degree courses or released by their companies. The range of subjects is vast and increasing. The University also runs courses at partner colleges in Plymouth and across the region while always looking to Industry for substantial help which is willingly given. It is interesting though that there are two schools of thought. Some resent the fact that it is comparatively easy to get a place here and others see the number of places giving opportunity to those who might not reach the required A level standards. I have listened to both arguments and I appreciate that to keep the University financially viable one must have numbers and I also appreciate that one might not get some of the high fliers here but outweighing it all, in my eyes, is the opportunity Plymouth gives to those who really want to learn and perhaps would not get a chance elsewhere.

One of the things that appeals to me most about the University of Plymouth is its willingness to support anyone if they have a good idea, whether student, graduate or lecturer. Of course you must have a good plan and preferably not one which has been copied from someone else's initiative. Through the University there are various supportive agencies who will assist any young entrepreneur to start up and continue to do so until the fledgling enterprise is established. Of course some plans are entirely unsuitable, some have already been done successfully elsewhere and some simply have not been thought out.

When three members of the University of Plymouth staff came up with a proposal to set up a company providing a 'Web-Based Business for Web-Minded Businesses', the idea was welcomed and Mark Stone, Teaching Fellow, Neil Witt, Senior Lecturer and David Gadd, Research and Project Manager, were provided with an office and help to get off the ground. The idea especially pleased because for £99 per year plus the dreaded VAT they will set up a live, professional six page Web Site, providing a unique co.uk Domain name, obtain 5Mb space on a high speed commercial server, and promote the site. They also send a daily e-mail report on how effective that promotion is proving and create one advanced feature for the site - like a game, search facility, animation, quiz, feedback form or shopping cart system. The business is successful for several reasons. Firstly they do care about their clients and are not averse to turning people down if they believe they cannot help. Secondly their pricing policy is totally transparent. It is honest and does not ask ridiculous sums for a simple job unlike many web-site companies. I have had some experience of the sharks in the business and thoroughly appreciate what these three men are offering. The odd thing is that they are frequently rejected when they quote for a job because they are considered to be too cheap!

David Gadd, the Project Manager of Internet Co-op - the name of their company, says that their aim is to provide cost effective Internet Solutions for small businesses. The three men have worked with more than one thousand companies on web-based work through the European-funded ADAPT CUCOL project and it is that experience and expertise that enables them to offer a service they believe will be of huge benefit to anyone wanting to use the Web for marketing purposes. Having listened to their enthusiastic and competent assessment of their business I am sure they are right.

If you would like advice on a web-site do ring David Gadd on 01752 233722 or visit the Web Site at http://www.internetco-op.co.uk

When talking to David and Mark I was made aware of the enormous use the facilities available to them throughout the University have been and continue to be. When I thought about it afterwards I realised that within the umbrella of the University they have access to the best brains in almost any field. They can look for legal advice, European rules and regulations and a hundred and one other minefields they might run into whilst getting a new web-site up and running. It also made me realise how running a University is not just academic, it is as much a business as any other corporation in Plymouth with the added problem of the mental and physical welfare of thousands of students.

The Internet Co-op is a business unit of Plymouth Enterprise Partnerships Ltd (PEP). PEP is a subsidiary company of the University of Plymouth with the remit of managing the University's commercial activities, protecting its intellectual property and providing a technology transfer service.

Apart from the Internet Co-op, The Business School is also of enormous help to small businesses. They will tell you that 'In Love there is said to be the seven-year ITCH. For small businesses the hazard is the three year HITCH! But Plymouth Business School is there to help. Small to medium sized enterprises represent a major component of the economy of the South West which is why the Business School has been heavily involved in research, consultancy and training initiatives to assist the growth of smaller firms in Devon and Cornwall.

The University of Plymouth contributes so much more than just education. As I write a graduate from the University, Conrad Humphreys and his crew are currently leading in the BT Global Challenge race, often described as the world's toughest yacht race. Designed by Sir Chay Blythe the BT Global Challenge is a 30,000-mile circum navigation of the globe going the 'wrong way' - against prevailing winds and currents More seriously the University is also a place of research much of which ranks high in national and international league tables.

Marine Biologists work closely with the National Marine Aquarium and the Marine Biological Association. A computerised system that has led to a more effective use of foetal monitoring, saving patient stress and Health service money through a reduction in unnecessary Caesarean births, has been developed in the faculty of Technology's School of Electronic, Communication and Electrical Engineering. The Analytical Chemistry Unit of the Department of Environmental Sciences, using its fast and incredibly accurate inductively coupled plasma mass-spectrometer has been used to monitor contaminated milk, confirm that arsenic in fish is not harmful to human beings and investigate trace element levels in supplements eaten by vegetarians and vegans. There are scientists testing gases that could help win the ozone layer are - a subject close to our hearts and minds at this time.

One of the most exciting additions to the University is the Peninsula School of Medicine, headquarters Tamar Science Park which in conjunction with Derriford Hospital will allow us to train doctors in the City; something that has been needed for so long. It is expected to attract around 120 students each year. Starting in October 2002. The government will fund its annual running costs of around £20 million. It is one of two being set up in the UK - the other will be in East Anglia - the first new ones in Britain for almost 30 years. It is expected to attract top forward-looking specialists

Music matters to almost everyone and the University is never lacking in applicants to join the University of Plymouth Choral Society and Orchestra. They perform regularly and give considerable pleasure to both the performers and their audiences.

The College of Further Education is continually extending its courses to more and more students and in more and more subjects. Their range of courses encourages even old fogies like myself to take up something new. The fact that you can take part-time courses or those in which you can go to the CFE whenever you have time, as well as the full time excellent courses that are on offer, makes the curriculum possible for many who would not normally be able to take up further education. It is a very busy place, international in its students, and fascinating in the array of subjects.

There is even a brewery, one of only two beer-making plants in Britain on an education campus. It is in the charge of a beer-loving ex-policeman Roger Pengelly who has always been a beer enthusiast and built up an interest over 30 years with the real-ale organisation Camra. When he was offered the job he really thought he had gone to heaven!!

The brewery means he and his staff can teach people how to brew, provide training for breweries, do testing and even production for local breweries. For example a commercial brewery might not want to tie up all its 10 barrel (360 gallons) capacity producing a special ale, say a porter for Christmas, and then only be able to sell half.
The CFE Brewery can do the quantity the commercial brewery needs in their five-barrel micro-brewery, leaving them free.

Added to this remarkable innovation in education Plymouth College of Further Education has set up a Summerlands project in which South West farmers and fish traders join together to produce and market food at a price that is kind to producers and consumers. Summerlands cuts out the supermarket giants and helps producers use raw ingredients, to prepare, package and market foods, helping them to boost profit.

Richard Davies of CFE says that a farmer or a farmer's wife might have a great idea to boost profits by selling their own salami or special pies, but they might not have the expertise in perfecting the recipe, dealing with the environmental health issues of food production, and packaging and marketing. Summerlands can provide that experience.

The CFE has two new kitchens and expert staff who can do everything from perfecting recipes to providing business support. The concept and the project, partly backed by European Union grants, should be an enormous success. It does not intend to try and create a food processing giant like Heinz but merely to act as a catalyst to help producers develop, perfect and market the foods.

All sorts of people are taking advantage of Summerlands from a small farmer who is using their expertise to create delicatessen-style and ready to cook foods for shops, hotels and restaurants to Ann and Lloyd Down of Plymouth's Pannier Market who want the help to perfect recipes for the Greek-style fish dip taramasalata and salmon paste which they sell alongside their fresh fish.

Education has certainly changed since my day!!

Students come to Plymouth for education from all over the world and the country, as well as a very large contingent from the city itself. Whatever their subject they find life fulfilling, the work demanding but the sports, the social life, the accommodation available in the city and above all the surrounding sea and countryside, is among the very best in England and Wales.

Away from the University one must recommend the Swarthmore Adult Education Centre on Mutley Plain. Here you can opt for anything from Spanish for Beginners to the Dynamics of Art Therapy. There are several language classes at different levels. Keep Fit, 'So you think you can't sing?' Drawing and Painting, Life Classes, Archaeology. There must be well over 100 classes available in the morning, afternoon and evening. It is a remarkable place with an interesting background. Sometimes it is the unexpected benefits from paying your £3 to become a member of the Swarthmore that shine through. One such benefit I discovered in conversation with one of my neighbours. Ted Luxon has been retired some years but has always been keen on walking. By joining the Swarthmore he was able to take part in the organised walks that set out most Saturday afternoons to introduce, discover and enjoy a whole host of places that might possibly get missed by the uninformed. The original purpose was to give pleasure to students but has since grown to give endless hours of enjoyment to a wider number of people. Ted frequently finds himself doing a recce to plan out a new walk. He told me that even in the heart of the city there is a wealth of unknown treasures. Not of material value, but along Durnford Street and Millbay Road going towards the Hoe, there are plaques set in paving stones and on walls commemorating historic events and famous people. There are new places to walk along river banks and a splendid leaflet describes the now completed South Coastal Path.

The Swarthmore was founded in 1920 by the Society of Friends (Quakers) but it is now run democratically by representatives of all groups involved in the centre. Courses are organised under the auspices of Devon County Council and Exeter University and are available to all those over school age who wish to take advantage of them at whatever stage of their lives suits them best.

I remember the Swarthmore from my young days when I was taught First Aid by St John Ambulance. I remember the friendly coffee bar and I also remember when various small repertory companies used the stage and auditorium for productions. The great actress Joan Plowright, widow of Lord Olivier, trod the boards here on more than one occasion. We went there for the sheer pleasure of seeing live theatre, the seats were hard, the auditorium frequently cold, but nothing would have kept us away.

The West Devon Outdoor Education Centre now has its base in the Mountbatten Sailing and Watersport Centre. It provides outdoor activity for West Devon - football, rugby and cricket are not included. It is largely self-financing but it is subsidised by Devon. The basis of the activities is 50% teaching the skill itself and 50% developing the persons themselves. For example teaching sailing to workers in industry does not just teach them the skill of sailing but also develops judgemental abilities to cope with varying conditions and options.

The range of activities covers sailing, caving, climbing, canoeing, kyaking, cycling and a series of tasks based on encouraging, problem-solving and personal development. I wondered who the end users would be at the centre. I rapidly discovered that companies send managers, supervisors and employment trainees. Then there are school children and Social Services referrals.

It is a busy place, run by Martin Northcott for the last 25 years. He has a secretary and a staff of six full time people as well as himself. This number is added to in the summer when it almost doubles.

Martin is dedicated and instills the same feeling in his staff. The job they have is onerous and they deserve both recognition and support. One ambition Martin had in 1993 when I last wrote about the West Devon Centre was that people needing special help could be included in the activities. With the combined efforts of West Devon and the Mountbatten Sailing and Water Sports Centre this has recently come about and it is hoped that it will be enlarged.

Suzanne Sparrow Plymouth Language School in North Road East is respected throughout Europe and beyond. Started by the redoubtable lady herself, a one time boating Wren during the war, Chairman of the Chamber of Commerce at one stage, the school began quite modestly, when Suzanne saw the need for the teaching of languages outside schools and for the adult population.

In 1987 it became apparent that she was running out of space for her classes and if she was to expand and meet the needs of pupils clamouring at her doors, a new building was needed. Nothing was suitable until she found an hotel in North Road East which the owners wanted to sell. For a very short time she not only became the owner of the premises but a hotelier as well. Gradually she got rid of her guests and on Boxing Day 1987 she and her right hand man, Peter Clarke, with some willing volunteers started tearing the building apart. They re-wired, knocked down walls, tore off endless layers of ugly wallpaper, plastered, papered and painted and by the first day of term on January 4th 1988, there was a complete transformation. The Suzanne Sparrow Plymouth Language School opened its doors with more classrooms, more space and more pupils.

There are few languages that are not taught. Certainly those of the Western World with Russian, Chinese and Japanese adding to them but it is English that is being taught to foreigners in the main rather than the other way round. The tuition is taken very seriously although the element of fun is always there in anything that Suzanne Sparrow undertakes. Pupils come from foreign parts for a few weeks, a term or maybe a very short time. Part of the purpose of the school is to find suitable accommodation for these visitors and preferably in homes where they will be encouraged to speak English and at the same time not feel too homesick.

It has taken some years to acquire the number of families prepared to offer this accommodation but now it falls into a regular pattern. The families have become Suzanne's friends and the pupils invariably invite their hosts and frequently Suzanne and Peter, to visit them in their homes. Suzanne has more invitations in any one year than she can possibly accept.

The quality of the work done in the school is recognised by the British Council who carry out spot checks every three years. Their praise is high. Business men send employees for lessons when it is necessary for them to work abroad. This is becoming more and more important as we strengthen our links with Europe.

It is odd how much fate plays a part in our lives. Peter was firmly settled permanently in France and teaching there, or at least he thought he was, when he first met Suzanne Sparrow. He will tell you that he found it impossible to refuse Suzanne when she offered him the post in the school as her number two. He returned to England and to the Suzanne Sparrow Plymouth Language School and has never regretted it for one moment.

We should always remember that teachers and even headteachers need teaching. The College of St Mark and St John as a training college for teachers, has become a successful and much respected educational centre in the city. They take part in virtually everything that goes on and the students are given a well-rounded teacher training which enables them to set out on a distinguished career. The buildings are excellent, the grounds well cared for and out of the academic year they provide a base for many seminars and summer schools. They have an excellent catering organisation which enables them to offer the premises for functions including weddings. Most recently they have become the base for The Centre for School Leadership and Management. The purpose is to support heads and senior staff from across the South West. To give them the opportunity to improve their leadership skills. The centre is only one of four in the country and some headteachers from as far afield as Bulgaria and Nigeria have been helped by the courses.

The centre works with heads and deputies, councils and the private sector to develop its programmes. Senior staff can study at the college or through distance learning for a recognised qualification. Hopefully 30-40 people a year will be able to undertake the 300 hour learning programme. A demanding course but with great rewards.

There is not only help for Headteachers. A new resource centre for school governors, based at the Central Library, has a range of support materials which governors can use to keep up-to-date with developments in education.
No one doubts that educational opportunities are the future of Plymouth's young people and anyway that can be found to help students from non-privileged backgrounds is welcome. The Sutton Trust offers these students an opportunity to attend summer courses which are designed to help them get to a top-ranked university.

The courses allow students aged 16-17 years to spend a taster week in July attending lectures and sampling the social life at Bristol, Cambridge, Nottingham or Oxford universities. The scheme is aimed at students from non-professional or managerial backgrounds whose parents did not themselves go to university. The week's course is designed by each university to 'level' the playing fields for university entrance.

The scheme was dreamt up by Peter Lampi, who is now chairman of the trust. Having lived in the USA and made a fortune, he was shocked at how poor the opportunities were for bright students from non-privileged backgrounds and by the waste of talent.

When he went back to his old college at Oxford, he found so much had changed. At one time students used to come from all over the country but they no longer applied. Mr Lampi looked more deeply into the problem and found it was not only Oxford and Cambridge but other top universities as well. Bright A level students from non-privileged backgrounds believed they would not get in nor fit in if they did succeed. The Sutton Trust plan is there to blow away the 'myths' and encourage bright, talented students to see that they can apply and they can fit in.

Students or parents/carers/teachers can apply for further information to The Sutton Trust Summer School Freepost WD2983/1, The Mere, Upton Park, Slough SL1 2BR or call 0208 788 3223.

One might call this a fleeting look at what Plymouth has to offer in terms of education. I have had to leave out far more than I have included but I hope the reader will gather from the chapter how rich Plymouth is in terms of learning.

The Royal Western Yacht Club – Queen Anne's Battery.

Chapter IX

Sport for All

The first part of this chapter is dedicated to my very dear friend Spud Spedding, a direct descendant of Sir Francis Drake, who died at the end of August from a distressing brain tumour. His personality and ability to spread his friendship world wide amongst the yachting fraternity and others is a loss that has left everyone bereft.

So many people today find that their sport is to be found messing about in boats whether it is the gracious, sleek lines of some of the superb motor launches that are to be found in the various Marinas around Plymouth, the sailing boats which are to be seen everywhere, racing in Plymouth Sound from April to October or laid up during the winter months or the racing gigs manned by enthusiastic oarsmen in local regattas. Whatever the craft, sailing and yachting have become one of the major industries in Plymouth and it is nothing short of a delight to watch the small boats bobbing about in the Sound, their multi coloured sails lighting up the scenery. Equally pleasureable is it to admire the bigger boats and frequently envy their owners as one dreams of foreign ports, Mediterranean waters or small French inlets where the harbours are lined with delightful wine bars and cafes. Financially one becomes aware of the enormous international success of the magnificent launches built by Marine Projects, the increasingly busy boatyards like Mashfords but more of them later. My interest in this chapter is the growth of the Marinas and the life style that has grown around them.

Taking the major Marinas first, I have to say I do have a preference for the Mayflower International Marina at Ocean Quay, to be found at the end of Richmond Walk, just over the old Halfpenny Bridge at Stonehouse. It has a friendly family atmosphere about it which quietly hides its efficient management and the many international activities which range from collecting together boats for a big race or as in August sending world famous yachtsman Tony Bullimore on his voyage to the Caribbean with comedian Lenny Henry - who had never sailed before. A voyage which Lenny found excruciating terrifying and enthralling. In return the two men provided us with excellent television viewing. The Marina has a quiet setting in a creek close to the entrance to the River Tamar looking over the water to the Royal William Yard and the other way towards Mount Edgcumbe. It appeals to the many who berth here because it is secure and they feel well cared for. It is totally lacking in pretension and with berth holders as shareholders the interests of those who bring their craft alongside, know their wishes are always guaranteed a hearing. Whilst I was waiting to talk to Robin Page, the Managing Director, I stood in what is effectively the control tower of the Marina, listening to incoming calls from craft wanting a berth or needing to find out about something relevant. Every call was dealt with courteously and in many cases you knew the girls were talking to old friends. It just felt a happy place to be and I must say the view over the water made it a super place to work in the most therapeutic surroundings. I know it is not always so calm especially when sailors are in trouble, then every stop is pulled out to do whatever they can.

Accessible at all states of the tide, Mayflower International Marina richly deserves the industry's highest 'Five Gold Anchor' accolade. Visitors are welcome at any time of the year and are welcome to join in the many social events such as an annual beach barbecue and end of season dance as well as many weekend events. The facilities are excellent including first class Showers and toilets as well as a launderette. The ample car parking is free. Electricity and water supplies, Calor Gas, Camping Gas and Paraffin Supplies are all available. Yacht Charter and Management is another service on offer as well as a towing and delivery service. There is Shore Storage for the winter months and Boat Yard Storage in the short term for summer months.

Robin Page and his staff, without any thought of recognition, lend their support and that of the Marina to one of the most worthwhile of Plymouth Charities, Horizon. This is a charity designed to bring excitement, knowledge of the sea and Plymouth from the Waterfront into the lives of less advantaged children in Plymouth. To achieve its aim it started in a small way with a boat lent to it by the then Vicar of St Matthews. The boat could only take two handlers and three children which was not enough but then word got around and the number of boats has grown every year. The charity owns a Princess, amongst others, and now takes children to sea regularly combining pleasure with education and working with the schools in Devonport. Mayflower Marina's role in all of this has been to house and maintain some of the boats. To find out more about the charity read Chapter 13, The Time, The Place and The People.

You are only fifteen minutes walk from Plymouth's city centre and in the high season a courtesy bus runs between the marina and the city centre. Mayflower Marina is completely self-contained with a grocery, bar, restaurant, off licence, chandlery and club house all on-site.

What never fails to surprise me is that more non-sailing Plymouth folk have not discovered the pleasure of eating at the The Brasserie on the Marina. Here Chris and Eileen Hadlington have established a restaurant renowned for the quality of its fish dishes. Their scallops are to die for! All the fish comes directly from a trawler so it is always fresh and what is in the catch of the day depends on what appears on the menu. If you hate fish then succulent steak or tender lamb will delight the palate. Probably the nicest thing about The Brasserie is its relaxed, informal atmosphere, warm in winter and with the added pleasure in warmer weather of being able to dine al fresco on the patio.The Hadlingtons have made many friends here over the decade in which they have been in situ. Their ability to remember people even if they haven't seen them for a year or more makes diners feel special. You do not have to dine or lunch if you would prefer to settle for a sandwich or a snack of some kind with a drink. I love it - what could be better than a well filled prawn sandwich, an aromatic dish of coffee, a seat in the sun and the sound of the sea and the boats for company.

The Hadlingtons also run a very successful outdoor catering company Cuisine Elite which caters as happily for two people as it does for nine hundred. Meticulous planning and organisation go into everything they do and they are as much at home in a village hall as they are in a stately home. Eileen Hadlington admits that outdoor catering is incredibly hard work and very tiring. Its not the occasion or the preparation of the food that is the hardest part but the carting of food, equipment and all the ancilliary bits and pieces that a caterer needs when working away from base. One can well understand that it is a fallacy to suppose that the cost of employing outdoor caterers is cheaper than using a recognised venue

The Hadlingtons took over the running of The Orangery in Mount Edgcumbe Park a couple of years ago. The cream teas and home-made cakes there are memorable. Just the thing after a walk in the park. It is also becoming a popular venue for wedding receptions. What an idyllic setting.

Queen Anne's Battery would consider itself to be the premier marina in Plymouth, with just cause if you take a look at the type of boat clientele it attracts. When you look at the yachts tied up and laid up on shore, they shout money! The original managing director of QAB, is the intrepid yachtsman, Mark Gatehouse, who in 1992 was named as the Yachtsman of the Year by the Port of Plymouth Sailing Association and became the first person to receive a new trophy at the Association's first prize giving ceremony. As a regular transatlantic sailor his love of the sport combined with his business acumen set the standard for the Marina which has been built upon ever since. Mark now owns and runs the busy Victoria Wharf at Cattedown.

Queen Anne's Battery was purpose built and is not only home to yachts but to a host of other businesses, not all associated with yachts and sailing. It is the home of the annual boat show which creates business for many people. It is also a time when inventions are on display. Not so many years ago Prince Charles' Business Youth Award was the source from which the inventor of a car trailer that converts to a boat, was financed..The inventor, Trevor Thompson who was only 24 at the time had been made redundant and this new enterprise has set him up.

It is the ability of Queen Anne's Battery to act as a gathering point for yachts that has enabled Plymouth to attract major sailing events. That the Royal Western Yacht Club has premises at the Marina makes it that much easier to attract events and acquire sponsors. One of the things I have never understood is why Plymouth City Council, whatever the politics of the ruling party, never appears to back any of the major sailing events. They are allowed to be poached by other ports like Portsmouth, which seems to me to be just plain ridiculous, when any event of this nature brings visitors to the city from all over the world, all with money to spend. You would suppose that a Maritime City with such a wealth of history and such super facilities would be constantly backing the initiatives that exist and constantly looking for more.

When yachts are arriving at Queen Anne's Battery for big races, they provide a colourful and wonderful sight. The boats of all shapes and sizes rock gently alongside, their halyards tinkling. All these boats will have brought business to the city with their need of engineering, chandlery, sailmaking and much more. When they put to sea for the start of a race, Plymouth Sound is the scene of a flurry of activity with the yachts making for the starting line followed by a bevy of small boats, all anxious to speed them on their way. Most of the crews and passengers in these small boats secretly wish they were off to take part in a great adventure as well. The whole thing creates a great atmosphere and the bar of the Royal Western, the natural meeting place, buzzes with different languages and the sounds of reunion. Many of these sailors know each other well from other races.

It is not only the big yachts who take pride of place in the marina. Through the year local yachtsmen keep their boats berthed here. It is safe, protected and friendly, and with every facility a yachtsman could wish for.

171

Plymouth has seen many great moments of triumph and sadness when boats return after memorable voyages. No one will ever forget the arrival of Sir Francis Chichester in Gyspy Moth. That was in the days when The Royal Western was based in its old quarters, now occupied by The Waterfront, a friendly eating and drinking establishment on The Hoe. Stunning photographs of this occasion and many others can be seen as you climb the stairs in the current premises of the venerable Royal Western Yacht Club at Queen Anne's Battery. It was in 1989 that the Club moved to these new, purpose built premises overlooking Plymouth Sound. The new headquarters was officially opened by HRH The Princess Royal who at the same time accepted honorary life membership of the Club. Now approaching its 175th year - it was founded in 1827, few organising bodies in international sport can claim a bigger role on the world stage. It is quite difficult to imagine our ancestors visiting a yacht club in the early 19th century but that is what they did. Plymouth for centuries has been inseparable from every kind of maritime venture and so it should not be a surprise that it gave birth to one of the very first yacht clubs.

It was not originally called the Royal Western but answered to the name of the Port of Plymouth Royal Clarence Regatta Club. Its purpose was to organise an annual regatta, to provide an interesting and informative social programme, and through racing, to stimulate improvements in naval architecture. If you talk to the Commodore, Professor Tim Whitten, or to the Secretary, Major John Lewis, Royal Marines, you will find the aims are much the same today. Certainly the principles are upheld. One principle is paramount in the mind of the Royal Western today and that is the need to encourage youngsters to take part in both the sailing and in suitable club functions. The Cadet policy is eagerly pursued, as encouraging the interest of the young ensures that a sailing interest, among the many other activities is maintained. Carefully nurtured this programme is bearing fruit.

In the early days the club showed its strength in long distance cruising. Members' yachts wearing the blue ensign for which the royal patron, Queen Victoria, had granted a warrant, were received in the farthest corners of the globe from Brazil to Russia, Capetown and Ceylon.

Even at the very beginning the club did more than run an annual regatta. Each year it organised a series of races for J-class yachts. This continued right up until 1934.

Yachts competing in such races never ventured too far offshore. With Plymouth as its base, the starting point for the voyages of Anson, Drake and Cook, it was natural that the world's first ocean race should be sailed under the burgee of the Royal Western Yacht Club. The course was round the Fastnet rock, and the year was the year of my birth, 1925. It was at dinner in the club afterwards that the Ocean Racing Club, later to become the Royal Ocean Racing Club, was conceived.

The Fastnet Race remains one of the ocean racing classics for fully-crewed yachts. The Royal Western has been instrumental in organising the arrangements ever since.

Perhaps the unique claim to recognition the Royal Western has in the world of yachting today is for the short-handed ocean racing. For almost forty years, since the inception of the first single handed ocean race, the club has been at the forefront of short-handed racing. In addition to those which it organises directly, there are others which it has inspired.

Probably the most exciting race and the one that thrills even those who are not nautically minded, is the Single-Handed Transatlantic Race which all began in 1959 when Blondie Haslar, an ex-Royal Marine Cockleshell war hero, made a name for himself all over again as an innovator in sailing. He wrote to the Royal Western to ask if the club would organise a single-handed race across the Atlantic in which he and Francis Chichester would take part. The Club agreed, and the first race was sailed in 1960 with sponsorship from the Observer newspaper. There were four entries and the race was won by Francis Chichester in forty and a half days.

What has marked out the Single-Handed Transatlantic Race as an event of far reaching importance is not, as one might expect, simply that competitors are single-handed. Nor that it launched Sir Francis Chichester's remarkable sailing career. Nor even that yachting in France can be directly attributed to it. It was, in fact, the far sighted approach of the Royal Western Yacht Club which ran, and still runs, the race under its own liberal rules, allowing lines of development which would have been strangled at birth in conventional yacht racing. The club allowed multihulls, indeed yachts of all types to race together. It permitted sponsorship, and introduced rules to guide and control its growth. The club encouraged invention and experimentation: self-steering systems for example, would not have reached the current state of the art without the incentive provided by the race.

All this development has had a measurable influence on sailing boats today. Compare the time of the first winner (401/2 days) with the recent ten days.

Another suggestion of Blondie Hasler's taken up by the Royal Western was the Round Britain and Ireland Race - two-handed in recognition of the demands of long distance racing close to land. There are four compulsory stops of 48 hours each. I remember well the return of my late friend 'Spud Spedding' returning to Plymouth after the race with Mervyn somewhat low down in the pecking order but never to be outdone, they sailed in from the Breakwater in their own inimitable style with the music of The Pirates of Penzance echoing around the waters of the Sound. He lived up to the fact that he was a direct descendant of Sir Francis Drake. He is missed by everyone who ever met him.

The Royal Western is not just about major international races. Throughout its history the Club has followed the aims of the Victorian founders, Its busy events programme includes summer, autumn and winter race series as well as offshore races to France, Spain and other Channel ports. It also plays host to national and international championships, particularly for classes like the Sigma 33 and J24. The cadet section is strongly encouraged and has regular weekly training sessions throughout the summer season. In 1996 it introduced a new keelboat class to Plymouth, the ever popular Squib.

There is no question that as one of the world's leading yacht clubs, The Royal Western Yacht Club of England enjoys an enviable reputation. Internationally recognised in the sailing world for its major contribution to the development of short-handed ocean racing, the Club is widely acknowledged as one of the finest sports clubs in Southern England.

The Club has a lively, well supported social programme, popular with its sailing and non-sailing members. The traditional laying up and fitting out parties are complemented by dances, discos and formal dinner parties, throughout the year. During the winter months a series of films and lectures are held. The Club hosts a variety of charity functions and children's parties. It is known for its superb service and stylish handling of wedding receptions, and other special occasions.

Membership of The Royal Western Yacht Club of England extends beyond the use of the Club's own excellent facilities. Its members also benefit from the reciprocal arrangements made by the Club to enable its members to enjoy the amenities of a wide range of other prestigious clubs both in the UK and abroad.

It is a long time sine the original members in the time of Queen Victoria looked out over the waterfront in Plymouth and planned the first regatta. If they could see what the club has achieved, what kind of mark it has made on the world of sailing, and how it has lived up to those early ideals, they would probably be astounded. They would certainly be proud.

The Sea Chest Nautical Bookshop is one of the thriving businesses within the marina. You will find it in the Dolphin Building. Owned and run by Robert Dearn, an ex air sea rescue man stationed at RAF Mount Batten, and a Yachtmaster Examiner with the Island Sailing Club at Salcombe. He specialises in charts and tide tables as well as a whole library of nautical books from knots, ropes and canvaswork to voyages, narratives and biography, radio, radar and electronics and world cruising and passage planning. He is one of about fourteen Admiralty chart agents in the country: charts which have to be corrected daily. He has pilotage information for all round the world, a secondhand section on maritime affairs, particularly useful for finding an out of print book, and a hundred other interests. Mail order is quite a significant part of his business.

I had no idea that the correction and updating of Admiralty charts was carried out on such a daily basis. Each day the postman delivers a package from the Hydrographics Department at Taunton. In the package will be any alterations, for example a buoy or lightship being re-positioned. Bob Dearn then has to alter the appropriate charts in stock. It genuinely is a daily routine for him; I was amazed that there could possibly be so many changes. I love bookshops anyway and the Sea Chest was a new and fascinating experience.

The Royal Corinthian Yacht Club has its premises tucked away below Madeira Road on Plymouth Hoe providing it with the most superb views of Plymouth Sound that anyone could wish for and giving the members the best grandstand view of anything happening on the water. The first recorded use of the site was in 1688 when it was closely associated with the construction of the Royal Citadel which is immediately behind it. However it was not until 1753 that two batteries were built to protect the foreshore to the mouth of the Tamar at Devil's Point and the mouth of the River Plym. The first was Ligonier's Battery which was demolished to make way for the construction of Madeira Road and the second, Fredericks, was decommissioned in 1850 and forms the basis for the Club's premises today. The remains of the tunnel connecting these two batteries can still be found at the North West corner of the harbour.

It was 1877 before the Royal Plymouth Corinthian Yacht Club was founded and rented premises at West Hoe and on Plymouth Pier from which to conduct the Club's sailing programme. Its objective was to promote local sailing rather than the grander events of the Royal Western. It was so successful that in 1886 it was granted the status of a Royal Yacht Club and seven years later given permission to fly a defaced blue ensign. The Club kept on growing in popularity and needed bigger premises so in 1896 the present Clubhouse was acquired and after three years of renovation and alterations which included accommodation for a live-in steward, the Club's activities were transferred in their entirety.

The move did not meet with universal approval from its members and some broke into splinter groups one of which remained at the West Hoe premises and formed the Royal South Western Yacht Club which no longer exists and the other group became the Minima Yacht Club using Plymouth Pier as their premises. They also did not survive.

Originally the Royal Corinthian gave races to three classes of yachts and then in 1902 pioneered dinghy racing in Plymouth Sound. This grew in numbers and in stature until sailing was stopped by the First World War. The Club itself remained active for social purposes and had its membership enhanced by members of the Royal Flying Corps who were stationed at Mount Batten.

When sailing resumed in 1920 more and more classes were catered for on the water including the prestigious 'J'Class followed by the 12 metres, but then had to stop because of World War II which also disrupted the social side as the premises were used by the Ministry of Defence for a varied assortment of wartime activities.

In 1947 the members re-emerged and the Club began to operate a full sailing programme. Various dinghy championships were promoted, National, European and World events were staged from the Snipes European Championships in which only one boat from each country was allowed, to Firefly Nationals with 231 starters. About 100 starters are now commonplace proving to be an excellent number for good racing. Weekly evening races are held with 40/50 boats competing. The Club promotes the annual Morlaix Race for yachts, the bi-annual Brest Race and various offshore races for yachts and power boat racing.

The last fifty years have seen constant improvements to the Clubhouse. In the 50's and 60's the slipway and dinghy park were constructed. There is no longer a live-in steward making more space for clubrooms. New changing rooms and better facilities have been added. In October 1997 HRH The Princess Royal formally opened the newly refurbished premises.

A great day for this old and prestigious club which has a wonderful atmosphere. It is the most friendly place to visit and if you are not a keen sailor you are still very welcome. I know several people who are members and simply enjoy the social side of the club. One lady in her sixties moved, as a widow, to Plymouth where she knew no one. She joined the Club and has found many new friends there. It is the sort of place where women can go on their own and feel welcome and comfortable. The members are a cross-section of the community with widely diverse interests but drawn together for the benefit of the club which is ultimately their own benefit as well.

Just after I was there in October 2000, the Club acquired a licence to hold weddings. The room used for weddings has spectacular views; it could not be a better place in which to have wedding photographs taken. The price is right and the food is imaginative and good. The added bonus for the bride and groom is that two car parking spaces are reserved just outside the club - what a blessing in summer when the Hoe is packed.

The Royal Corinthian runs a varied programme of social events from theme nights to concerts. A great club to belong to. Before I finish this piece I must say thank-you to Club Member, Les Haines who provided me with the information and made me very welcome when I called there.

One of the most exciting happenings for decades has been the creation of the Mount Batten Centre for Sailing and Watersports. Don't imagine for one moment that you are being invited to join a snooty Yacht Club where you might have to wait five years for membership. Here is a down to earth - or should one say down to the water establishment built for fun and learning. It is somewhere to gain sailing and watersports experience, to do business if needs be,or simply to entertain and have fun. Above all it offers you one of the most spectacular, waterfront venues in the South West of England. It is open all the year round to the public. Although the public do not need to be members to use the facilities at the MBC, there are in fact many advantages to becoming a member. Enquire from Jackie and you will find out all the details The wide range of facilities include comfortable low-priced accommodation and waterside bars with excellent food. All sorts of special services cater for groups, businesses and private functions who enjoy the superb purpose built facilities.

If you ask Mike Gilbert, the Chief Executive, an ex-submariner and dedicated diver, and his expert staff what they feel is the role of the Centre, they will give you the facts but what they will not tell you, for modesty's sake, is all the extra things that happen which make the place so exciting and special. It exists basically to promote access to a range of water based and other activities and provide the necessary facilities for enjoyable, safe and affordable participation. This is achieved in association with a number of activity providers and affiliated organisations who are based at the centre.

Where else would you find such an opportunity for outdoor activities, including Sailing, Windsurfing, Canoeing, Kayaking, Powerboating, Gig Racing, Diving, Angling, Climbing, Caving, Orienteering and Rambling. All with expert tuition if it is required.

Just look at the facilities. There is substantial boat and car parking. Easy launching with beach master facilities. A 100 metre pontoon. Access to race support and rescue craft. A Dedicated Race Management Office which includes rooms for results, briefing, protests and meetings. There are hot showers and changing rooms, an extensive range of catering facilities, wet and dry bars. Excellent value accommodation on-site, with reasonable facilities within reasonable travelling distance. On-site facilities for a limited number of campervans. Function, entertainment and corporate hospitality facilities. Easy access to chandleries and other support services. Internal and external public address systems. Access to additional rescue and support craft.

The Port of Plymouth Sailing Association which represents all the major sailing clubs in the area, co-ordinates all race events in and around Plymouth. Organisations and dinghy class associations who require a Club to host an event should contact the PPSA through the Centre. Advice on race management and race support is available through the Centre and the Royal Yachting Association with whom they work closely to develop the range of race facilities available at the Centre.

No one would argue about the exceptional nature of the waters of Plymouth which has provided its maritime history for centuries. This is why the Centre exists. Whilst Plymouth is the Country's largest naval port and a centre for considerable maritime commerce there is ample space for recreational activities. The breakwater protecting Plymouth Sound provides a huge area of sheltered water with the option for open sea activities, still relatively close to the Centre itself. The Cattewater, Tamar, Plym and Lynher Rivers open up yet more miles of sheltered water to explore and enjoy.

On Dry Land the Centre is an ideal place to stay. It is within minutes by water taxi from the historic centre of Plymouth and only 20 minutes by road from the Dartmoor National Park.

The world famous yachtsman, Sir Robin Knox-Johnston wrote to Mike Gilbert in September 2000 and I quote:

'If ever you wished to demonstrate the capabilities of the Centre and its team, I think the visit of the Clipper fleet gave you an opportunity and you took full advantage. The crews thoroughly enjoyed the competition you arranged, it was fun and competitive and has done a great deal to pull them further into teams for the race.

Personally, having been slightly involved in the project stage of the centre, I am always pleased to see it so active. It has brought a very valuable facility to the City and greatly enhanced its ability to host major events, both national and international.

The fleet won't be able to visit Plymouth again before the race starts, but you left everyone with an excellent impression, and gave the Plymouth crew something more to be proud about.'

For anyone reading this who does not know about the Clipper boats, let me briefly tell you. A few years ago Sir Robin conceived the idea of building a number of boats, all identical, which would allow young people the opportunity to crew a boat around the world, racing against each other. It has been a highly successful concept and boats are now sponsored by various cities throughout the country, Plymouth is one of them and intensely proud to have its own boat.

Plymouth City Council has also taken the boats under its wing and before they set sail this time there was a superb Barbecue evening for everyone down at the Mayflower Centre.

If I had any doubt about the enthusiasm for The Mount Batten Centre that exists within the management and staff, it would have immediately dismissed when I met Jackie Littlejohn, a mature lady who has all the zest of a youngster but brings to her demanding job a wealth of experience and commonsense. She is the PR lady, the organiser of events and much more. From her I learned of the exciting fact that the Centre is now developing its capabilities for Disabled Diving. There are only five centres in the whole of Great Britain who have achieved this level of provision for the Disabled. Working with the disabled is part of the ethos of Mount Batten. Frequently they have people on work placement and if they enjoy the job then whenever possible they will be taken on full time. You sense that here no one is disadvantage - they are all part of a very special team. Jackie organises all sorts of special days for disadvantaged children in particular. It may be canoeing or sailing, with a buffet and a talk after by someone well known like Alex Bennett who is the youngest member of Pete Goss's crew. In addition to Alex the Centre is to have Olympic Gold Medallist in Sailing, Iain Persey, who will give a talk in January 2001.

Anything about the water does not scare me having been brought up to mess about in boats but it has always engendered in me a healthy regard for the sea and for the inherent dangers therein. At least I thought I could make that statement honestly until I learned from MBC about the world of Freedive who now operate from the Centre. The members dive without the assistance of any of the recognised equipment. Freediving or maybe one should call it breath-hold diving is a growing sport and is now competitive. One hears such terms as static apnea, dynamic apnea and constant ballast. To translate, static apnea is a practice that involves the participant to hold their breath while the airway is submerged below the water. With dynamic apnea a person will swim a horizontal distance in a pool on one breath. Constant ballast is the most respected of the six recognised disciplines and in a competition the competitors dive down in only a mask, fins, snorkel, wetsuit and weight belt. They have to retrieve a tag at a specified depth by swimming down and back unassisted on one breath! It sounds horrendous and terrifying to me but I am told it is one of the most exciting things one can ever do. I think I will simply stand and stare!

I also learned that the Mount Batten Centre is now licensed for weddings. What a perfect spot. The scenery is outstanding, parking is no problem, food and drink are sensibly priced and the function rooms are of a size which can deal with a wedding reception for 150 buffet style or a little as ten or twenty guests. The same thing applies for other special occasions like reunions, birthdays, christenings.

On the day I met Jackie Littlejohn, I was to go on to the Plymouth Yacht Haven on the Mount Batten peninsula. Having got carried away in conversation I was running very late but when I told Jackie where I was going, she assured me that my being late would not matter a jot - the director of Plymouth Yacht Haven is her sister. When I met Bobbie Blackler I discovered a lady with the same enthusiasm for her role, the same commitment and the same great skill of communication. Needless to say I stayed much longer than I should have.

The history of Plymouth Yacht Haven is a story in its own right. Formerly the Clovelly Bay Marina it is located at the mouth of the Cattewater and is sheltered from the prevailing South Westerly winds unlike its neighbour across the way Queen Annes Battery. These days it can boast of berths for 450 vessels with a mixture of finger and alongside berths. It is possible to cater for vessels up to 150ft in length and 24ft in draft. All berths offer electricity and water services.

Security is all important and the friendly and helpful staff provide cover for the marina 24 hours a day. A regular check is kept on vessels afloat and a patrol is mounted more frequently in bad weather. In spite of the excellence of the facilities which include vast hangars in which repair work can be done undercover, Plymouth Yacht Haven is still the cheapest marina option in Plymouth and the largest. What it does not have is the restaurant and bar facilities that QAB and The Mayflower Marina can offer but that really does not matter when just next door the Mount Batten Centre has such excellent food and a good bar.

Bobbie will tell you that the most demanding months of her life were spent whilst the new office and control block was being built. They had only a portacabin from which to work and berth holders had to make do with the uncertainty of loos in portacabins which did not make for the most harmonious of relationships. Last Christmas the decision was made that the haven would not be open on Christmas Day - the only day in the year when reception facilities were not available. Come Christmas Eve the weather began to deteriorate and by the time the staff were hoping to go home, the wind was blowing at 100mph from the West, every boat was swinging uneasily and then to the horror of everyone some poles failed, allowing the pontoons, boats still attached, to drift up the river. and pulled the pontoons away from the retaining poles. No matter what the staff did they could not stop the boats moving, funnily enough in a slow and quite orderly fashion, up towards Turnchapel, where eventually the pontoons and the boats came to rest. The staff gave up the struggle at 2am of trying to do any form of rescue work but by 6am on Christmas Day, unasked, every member of staff turned in to see what they could do. Not a chandler open, not a DIY store, in fact nowhere from which they could get the rope and other things they needed to effect a rescue, however basic. Eventually with a little help from their friends they found rope and slowly but surely tied every pontoon, every boat up securely. To their amazement, there was little damage to the boats but the pontoons were precarious without piles to hold them in place. It took until April before the Haven was fully restored. It shows the faith their berth holders have in Bobbie Blackler and her staff that today there is not one free berth available.

You might think that Plymouth Yacht Haven was a bit separated from the city. It is not. Yacht Haven's Water Taxi will take berth holders to a multitude of shops, restaurants, bars and nightlife. There are wonderful coastal walks, a golf course and a fitness centre with a heated swimming pool, all close to the marina.

In the last few years the whole of the country has become more and more aware of the benefits of exercise. For years there have been enthusiastic joggers, squash players, swimmers but gradually it has become more and more apparent that families who joined together to enjoy sport or exercise of some kind became happier, healthier and much more aware of the benefits that came with it. For that reason clubs have sprung up all over the place, hotels of any stature have their own leisure centres and swimming pools, golf clubs have added other leisure facilities wherever possible and now Plymouth has just acquired The Devonshire Health and Racquet Club in Plymbridge Lane. Tel: 01752 796222 which has to be the epitome of all anyone could want in a Leisure Club. It is part of Invicta Leisure Clubs which are steadily growing in number throughout the country. Andrew Robinson is the General Manager. He has adopted Plymouth and both he and his wife and family find the city a splendid place in which to live. He was interesting to talk to and was quite forthright in his views on why Invicta Leisure had made such an enormous investment in the city. The fact that since the decline in the size of the Dockyard and the armed forces in Plymouth, had forced the city to look for outside businesses in different industries to fill the gap, the changing face and incomes of the people who now live here means that there are those who enjoy a higher life style and consequently will appreciate and be able to afford all the The Devonshire has to offer. It was especially important to the company to find a big enough site on the right side of the city to create somewhere with such terrific facilities. Luckily for them the site at Derriford was available which also gives them a catchment area taking in Tavistock and other places. The club is looking for a membership of about 4,000 people.

The Devonshire has 80,000 sq feet designed to encompass everything any member could possibly require. There are eight indoor tennis courts, squash courts, indoor and outdoor swimming pools , a sports hall, aerobics, fitness suite, activities, treatment rooms, sauna, spa, steam room, sunbeds. There is an excellent Brasserie, a bar, a creche, play area plus a children's soft play area. It is leisure at its very best and designed to be as much a social venue as somewhere for a workout.

You might ask the question why exercise here? The Devonshire will tell you - something you probably already know - that an exercise programme is difficult to start and even harder to keep going. This club offers a complete quality fitness package; trained staff, understanding, high levels of service and a programme which is adaptable to everyone with contrasting fitness aspirations.

The Health and Fitness Department has been developed by Rob Shannon the Group Development Manager. He brings to The Devonshire Health and Racquet Club a wealth of experience having been responsible for fitness departments at all Invicta Leisure sites. Rob has a Masters Degree in Exercise and Health Behaviour. A degree in psychology and is a visiting lecturer at London's City University, where he talks on physical and psychological aspects of eating, exercises and bodyweight and health behaviour change. He is a regular presenter at conferences for the health and fitness industry and his articles often appear in magazines and the national press.

The 6,000sq ft air-conditioned Fitness Room has a comprehensive range of the latest exercise equipment designed to accommodate every possible requirement and it is supervised constantly by Fitness Leaders who have been selected on the basis of their friendly, empathic and enthusiastic personalities. Before you start in the Fitness Room you will have a free personalised session that is designed to help an appropriate exercise plan for you which will accommodate your aspirations, likes and dislikes, time available and consider any barriers or concerns you may have. You will then be shown how to use all the equipment necessary for your programme. You will be encouraged to keep regular contact with staff experienced in helping people. They are there to give you support and preempt any problems you may experience.

For people like myself who have great difficulty in controlling their weight, the Learn programme addresses how you think about food, weight and your body. The key objective is to help you change your lifestyle and focuses on permanent weight loss. The magical phrase 'permanent weight loss' is something all of us want to hear.

The Racquet facilities are superb and once again directed by people who know! The club is confident that the programme of events, drill sessions and mix-in's will provide just about everything you will need to play the game, whether it is tennis, squash or badminton. The Group Tennis Director is Robin Drysdale, once ranked in the top 60 in the world. He has been responsible for setting up the tennis programme with the Group Tennis Manager, Gary Stewart. A former ATP Tour player and member of the county championship winning Devon team, Gary is positive the weekly timetable offered at the Club will be the best found anywhere.

The delight of playing tennis and improving ones technique is something everyone can experience. The Devonshire Club believes in looking after the advanced player and the first timer and also that you are never too young or too old to stop. Tennis is a game for life and no matter who you are, there will always be someone at the Club of your own level to play with.

The badminton and squash clubs meet on a regular basis with mix-in's, coaching and beginner's classes. Both will run their own ladders, league and teams.

For Juniors there is a wide spectrum of activities in the weekly timetable. There are sessions for Soccer, Cricket and Basketball in their respective Schools of Excellence. Swimming lessons, fencing, ballet/stage/countryline/disco, badminton, racquetball,tennis, judo and karate. Even the 1-2 year olds have their own Tumble Tots session in the Sports Hall on a Tuesday morning. The activities cover all ages from 3-16 years.

Victa's Café-Bar is a stylish and welcoming place.where members can relax, talk, have a meal and read the papers. It is also the venue for social events which will be developed to suit all ages and tastes. Members are asked to help in putting together an exciting and varied social calendar. The large terrace extending from the Café-bar and overlooking the outdoor tennis courts, provides a perfect setting for the summer months and here barbecues will be a common evening feature.

The Devonshire Health and Racquet Club offers Plymothians a great opportunity for family health and fitness and the chance for youngsters to start sport at an early age. It is another great addition to forward thinking Plymouth.

Not everyone is entirely happy with a big establishment like Devonshire Racquets and Health and for those there is a first class option. Cannons Health Club in the Barbican Leisure Park is excellent. Its advantages are numerous but lets start with the fact that parking is easy! Then once inside the doors of this compact, friendly health club, you have every facility you want. The thing that struck me when I went to see the General Manager Linda O'Dell, was the relaxed, easy going atmosphere that prevailed everywhere. We sat at one of the tables in the small, comfortable club lounge and bar. The coffee was piping hot, aromatic and delicious and everyone seemed to know everyone else. I even met a couple of people I know who without prompting told me they were regulars and wouldn't go anywhere else.

So what can Cannons Health Club offer its members? It is a great place for beginners and experts to get more out of life. No one would argue that in today's world we all need to have a healthy life style and Cannons will certainly endeavour to assist you to achieve the results you want and enjoy it on the way. The club understands that for most people time is precious and so whether you have a near-impossible schedule or hours to fill, they will help you make the most of it. The opening hours, seven days a week, are designed to suit the early birds and the late leavers. Even though the club is for adults without children rather than families, the young ones are allowed at certain times and they can be kept occupied in a creche by a trained staff.

Your choice of activity comes from a well thought out plan which includes a 20m swimming pool, a gymnasium, an exercise studio, sauna, steam and spa and beauty treatment rooms. There really is no better environment in which to relax and exercise. You can book a treatment, join a class, meet a friend or simply drop in for a work out. The qualified instructors and therapists are always on hand to help you get the most out of your membership.

In addition to the convenience of Cannons situation - it is almost in the city centre - Cannons Adventures and Golf are free additions to your Cannons Health Club membership. There are all sorts of exciting possibilities. For example as the summer nights draw in, you can work up that winter fitness for the fast approaching Ski & Boarding season. You could find yourself on the slopes at Tignes, Meribel, St Anton, Les Deux Alpes, Andorra and Sauze d'Ouix.

Cannons Golf continues to be a great success with over 3,000 golfers now registered and playing regularly with the club. Beginners are especially delighted that they can at last meet Golfers of a similar standard, and enjoy playing, inconspicuously, on un-intimidating courses! Cannons offers a '3 Stepes to the Fairways' programme.

Step 1   The Cannons Golf Academy which is ideal for the total beginner.
Step 2   The 9 hole Club for those who have progressed just beyond the basics and want to meet up with fellow beginners for small group get-togethers on carefully selected 9 hole courses.
Step 3   The Cannons Golf Society is for golfers of a reasonable standard upwards.

It is all good fun, well organised and all you have to do is ask at the reception desk for more information.

Cannons is for anyone who enjoys a great atmosphere combined with all the facilities the modern day healthy lifestyle seeker could wish for.

Plymouth Argyle may fight for survival in the league but they do a lot to encourage Plymouth youngsters to play football. I read very recently of an initiative between themselves and the radio station Pirate FM102 in which Argyle will run a series of soccer schools. The Club's Community Officer, Geoff Cruddingtl will organise the schools with the aim of encouraging six to 14-year olds to develop their skills as well as having fun and making friends. You never know Argyle might discover another Alan Shearer along the way. Certainly it is only this sort of initiative that will prevent England from becoming a has been in the world of soccer. Stoke Damerel Community College was the first school to have a to day course for boys and a one day course for girls, the latter staffed by qualified female coaches.

John Nike Leisuresport Plymouth Ski and Snowboard Centre has gone from strength to strength since its start up over ten years ago. It is recognised as the South West's Premier Winter Sport facility and is open all the year round. People go there now not just to learn how to ski, or to get themselves in shape for their next trip to the European Ski slopes, but also to enjoy the sheer exhilaration and comradeship at anytime. The annual open day is a prime example of its popularity. About 200 people attended this year and they were able to enjoy a whole host of equipment as part of a Mission Adventure sport exhibition at the Marshmills site as well as receive expert advice from the centre's instructors. The price of lessons was cut from £7 per hour to £3 to encourage more people to attend.

The Plymouth Ski Kids, a charity organisation set up by local people to offer skiing lessons to children whose parents are on low incomes, supported the day and thoroughly enjoyed the series of demonstrations organised at various stages throughout the day.

Andy Rushton, the manager of Plymouth Ski Centre believes these open days are a way of breaking down the barriers that surround the sport and help get the message across to as many people as possible to persuade them to give the sport a go. Both he and the graduate manager, Suzanna May, believe that many people think they are too old or that they just won't be able to ski and they are almost always surprised to find that they can when they try.

Snowboarding and skiing is accessible to all ages and the Plymouth Ski Centre make it both educational and fun as they teach people from the young to the old, skills and techniques. Just think of the fun you could have tobogganing down the Cresta Run which at 520m in length is the longest run of its type in the South West. It is very worthwhile going to take a look, hear what the instructors say and trying it out for yourself.

A piece of good news for anyone who is interested in sport is that the Royal Navy have gifted Plymouth the sportsfield at Brickfields recreation ground. As a result the city council is making ambitious plans to turn the grounds into one of the best sporting facilities in the South West. Their plan, providing they can get the funding, is to turn Brickfields into an arena attracting national and international sporting events.

It is a great opportunity because Plymouth has lagged behind many other major cities with poor facilities forcing many clubs and teams out of the area. It would be wonderful to see new athletic facilities. If the council achieve their purpose and Home Park gets its ambitious redevelopment facilities, Plymouth will be firmly on the sporting map.

One of the great sporting revivals has been at Plymouth Albion Rugby Football Club with success on the pitch and great improvements in the facilities. When dockyard apprentices originated the Albion Club in 1876 they could not have foreseen that their enthusiasm would lead to the club still being in existence 125 years later. Times have been good and bad for them but the present season is one of the best they have had. Their spirit and feeling of togetherness comes across when you meet members of this highly respected club. They are a credit to the game and to the city in their behaviour when they play away and always in their sportsmanship.

One of the problems they face every season is Plymouth's geographical situation which makes away games frequently played at considerable distances. Many of their players also live away from the city which makes heavy demands on them when it comes to training. What must be very irksome too is that the emergence of a shining star makes the club immediately liable to lose the player to bigger and more prestigious clubs. However phlegmatically Plymouth Albion takes the rough with the smooth and sets out always to entertain their supporters and in so doing thoroughly enjoy their own game. When you watch a game at Beacon

Park you are left in no doubt about the enthusiasm of the spectators and the gathering in the clubhouse afterwards is in the true fashion of rugby union.

Not many people know that at one time Plymouth Albion shared Home Park with Plymouth Argyle Football Club. This was not a good marriage and lasted only a short while. Neither was comfortable in the other's presence. Few grounds in the country can be situated in such a beautiful setting. Surrounded by the tree filled Central Park it has almost the feel of being in a rural area. Parking facilities are excellent and little crowd violence is witnessed, with the result that Home Park is a football venue for the family. I only wish I could say that the team were successful. They are not in spite of the Chairman, Dan Macauley's millions. They have steadily slipped down the divisions and now languish only just outside the relegation zone of the Third Division - next stop The Conference League. Difficult to say why this has happened. They have had splendid moments when promotion from the Second to the First Division seemed possible but it all comes to nothing. Without doubt small clubs do suffer today with the enormous cost of running the club and paying its players.

Add to this the cost of buying good players and one can understand how billions rather than millions invested is probably the only answer.

We are promised a new stadium, new facilities, an international size swimming pool, other activities as well as football all combined in a new, state of the art complex. I do hope it happens.

Mention the name Archibald Ballard to older Plymothians and you get a mixed reaction. His name remains important in the city for his legacy of the Ballard Centre, just off Union Street. It has all sorts of uses and is where many Plymouth children learned to swim; mine certainly did.

If you read some of the old newspaper cuttings about Archibald Ballard you will discover that he was considered to be a man of taciturn nature, one of the city's most mysterious and controversial figures between the wars and reputed to be a millionaire. What he did do was to give devoted but erratic service to the boys in the neighbourhood. He formed clubs for them and it was his habit to give threepenny bits to the boys who came to his clubs, and promise ten shillings in cash or kind to every boy, when the attendance at the Sunday morning service at the Ballard Institute reached 5,000. This did not go down too well with the public. The boys however loved him for himself and his eccentricities. They never knew what to expect. They could turn up at the club and find they were sent to the cinema or local theatre. On one famous occasion, a certain number of boys found themselves presented with dinner jackets!

The churches objected to Mr Ballard. He was robbing them of their Sunday School membership, and in calculating the wrong principles, - that of receiving instead of giving. The Ballard Boys were all out to get their ten shillings and got it when one Sunday the attendance reached 5,800. Their benefactor defended himself by saying that he only gave to those who needed his help.

In 1930 Mr Ballard handed over his Institute for Boys in Millbay Road to the local education authority, insisting however that the name remained intact. He had grown tired of criticism. Today we would recognise what he was trying to do but in the 1920s he was probably the only man in Plymouth who understood the needs of youth and realised that they had problems. Yet here was a man who was not even a Plymothian. When he was asked why he came to the city from London, he replied 'I noticed on a visit in 1923 how unruly the youngsters were.' Before he took on the lavish Millbay site - where Bond Pearce are now - he had two boys clubs in Treville Street and Athenaeum Lane. He was determined that boys from underprivileged families should be well educated but in a typically Victorian manner, he deemed education for girls unnecessary.

The Ballard Institute was overseen by 12 Trustees. The Plymouth Education Authority was given the right to nominate 7 of the Trustees. The Chairman of the Plymouth Education Authority was automatically the chair of the Trustees, and the Director of Education the Secretary. There are still 12 Trustees but they are all Plymothians who have an interest in Youth work.

Archibald Ballard might have become frustrated with the council, but his philanthropy continued. In 1933 he bought the former Stoke Military Hospital and offered it to the University College of the South West and Plymouth Education Committee with the idea it should be used to establish an extension of the University College in Plymouth. The offer was not well received and eventually Mr Ballard withdrew it and sold the building to the local authority for use in primary education. Today it is Devonport High School for Boys.

The original Ballard Institute was bombed in 1943 much at the same time as Archibald Casanova Ballard died in a home in Teignmouth - an undeservedly lonely old man.

Temporary premises were used for Ballards until 1963 when the present premises were designed and built. Ballards gained recognition for being the best Youth Club in Great Britain. It has its own theatre seating 400,a Games Room, Gym, Television, Swimming Pool and Coffee Bar. When it first started some 7000 people a week used its facilities but with the advent of TV, clubs, videos and other venues, the numbers declined to such an extent that in the 1980s it nearly had to close down. The Trustees managed to change the original Trust Charter and became self supporting. This has been very successful and it has become more of a Community Centre. A whole range of activities takes place from Aerobics and Weight Watchers to serious Martial Art practice. It is of great benefit to the community.

The swimming pool only has limited access for the general public and is mainly used for classes for learners and for teaching swimming to primary schools. Under water hockey is popular and the pool is also used for the Sub-Aqua diving club. The public can swim between 7-8am and noon to 1.40pm. About 3000 people use the pool every week.

With everyone more fitness and diet conscious today and senior citizens more active, the centre endeavours to cater for everyone from 3-83 years in a socio/leisure way. I think Archibald Casanova Ballard would be pleased although he would probably find it hard to understand the way of life today. He certainly would be more delighted with the continuity of the Ballard Centre than he was of the gift of a silver tea and coffee service presented to him in 1939 by the City Council in 'deep appreciation of his work'.

Brian Hearn, the dynamic owner of the Matchroom Snooker Centre in Plympton, is a cousin of the boxing, snooker and now football supremo, Barry Hearn. They vie with each other to see who can work the longest day! Brian claims he is the winner with a 16 hour day. When he set about establishing the Matchroom, he was told Plymouth did not need another Snooker Club. He has proved the cynics wrong. The Matchroom was planned to incorporate every need of snooker players and has been a sought after and popular venue ever since it opened its doors. Brian Hearn apart from being dedicated to the success of his club, is also a man who will work for any charity, in particular the Lifeboat Appeal and Cancer Research. What is a must for him is that all the money goes to charity and is not siphoned off for unnecessary expenses.

The main function room, situated in a separate building, has been designed with care ensuring that everyone can see the stage. The seats are built in tiers. Brian has made the rooms interesting and full of character. For example he went to Warrington in Lancashire to get the curtains and a pelmet for the stage, from an old theatre. His aim has always been to provide a first class venue in which working-class people can enjoy themselves at prices that are less than restaurants and pubs. He comes from a working class Plymouth background himself and feels very strongly about it. There is only individual membership - no family membership. It really is a super place and certainly an example of everything that is good in the sporting world and a great asset for Plymouth.

Golf players have a variety of courses within easy reach of the city. The nearest is probably Staddon Heights and then Yelverton Golf Club, on Dartmoor. The championship course   St Mellion   with its Country Club is very popular. Designed by Jack Nicklaus, it is regarded as one of the finest in Europe. It also has a second course designed by J. Hamilton Stutt which is just under 600 yards and provides the perfect complement to the Nicklaus Course. It offers both testing and pleasant golf in the midst of some of Cornwall's most beautiful countryside. For those who like playing by the sea, the course at the Whitsand Bay Hotel, Crafthole, is spectacular.

Outdoor activity is also the name of the game at Newnham Park, Plympton. This fine old estate lends itself perfectly for the many activities on offer from Clay Shooting, Off road karting, Archery, Fly Casting, Air Pistol Shooting, 4x4 Driving, Mountain Biking, Orienteering to Target Golf. It hosts and specialises in major events during the course of the year and in offering Corporate Hospitality immaculately run to any number of major companies.

How did Newnham Park become part of the sporting scene? When I met Michael Cobbold in 1992 the estate was a victim of the European Common Agricultural Policy. He told me that it was difficult to know what to do with redundant farmland that is no longer viable but is part of an estate which has been in his wife's family for over 900 years and which was entailed to her in 1950 - the third time in 200 years that it passed through the female line. Since that time the Cobbolds have broken the entail and will only pass the house on to their children if they want it. Michael Cobbold described the house and estate, beautiful as it undoubtedly is, as a 'Millstone in the Making' for future generations. One hopes it will never come to this because the early Georgian '5 window square' house is so gracious.

By 1970 the Cobbolds decided that being absentee landlords was not a good idea and so they moved into the house. Like all big houses, it is expensive to run and necessity spawned the idea for using the land and the house for private and corporate days out Clay Pigeon shooting. More often than not the days are corporate ones because of the difficulty of getting enough individuals together.

David Cobbold, Michael's son has taken on the reins of running all the varied activities with the help of a team of dedicated people. He is a down to earth man with a love of the land and an awareness that success from events must not be allowed to irreparably damage the land. From experience which was learned the hard way, the Cobbold team understands the needs of up to 20,000 spectators or equally caring for a handful of participants. They are probably unique in the way they manage the various events. Certainly they are respected by everyone they deal with. They have standard events but they are never averse to turning their imaginative and innovative minds into creating an event that will fit more specific needs and requirements than the norm - if anything in this adventurous world could be called the norm.

This charming country estate nestles between the outskirts of Plymouth and the foothills of Dartmoor National Park. The setting is superb overlooking a natural valley with a free flowing stream and only 5 miles from the centre of Plymouth, its airport and railway station which makes it an idyllic location for all kinds of outdoor activities from the Major sporting events to the corporate days out.

What can you expect if you come here? The Newnham estate continues to host prestigious sporting events such as the UCI Mountain Bike World Cup, ARC National Land Rover Rally, National Carriage Driving Trials and the Devon Clay Shooting Championships. If you want corporate entertaining then you can choose Clay Shooting. I like their motto 'good shooting is no accident'. This shows that they place equal importance on the need for safety alongside the desire to ensure all participants have a successful day out. It is the Cobbold's experience of staging National Championship shooting events that the Newnham Park shooting ground is able to provide a range of targets that are suitable for beginners and the more experienced shooter. All guests need to do is arrive prepared for the vagaries of the English weather and be ready to enjoy the challenge this activity offers.

Providing you are not fainthearted a group of 10 or more can enjoy a thrilling day Off road karting. You are well briefed and issued with smart red racing overalls and helmets - naturally you will want your photograph taken! After a safety briefing and a practice session to familiarise yourself with the karts performance on the grass track, it is time for a time trial, driving skills, slalom challenge and a Le Mans style relay to finish. You can be competitive or just have fun.

Newnham Park.

Archery with a minimum group of six can be staged in or outdoors, making it an ideal all year round option. The equipment is modern and the coaching expert. Fly Casting poses a great problem for some and at Newnham in a group of not less than 10 you can take the opportunity to experience this difficult skill with coaching supplied by an ex- England International. This is ideal as an accompaniment to a multi-activity day.

Another indoor or outdoor sport is Air Pistol Shooting with a group of not less than 6. The indoor range is located adjacent to the indoor archery so it is an ideal partner for an all year round session of two target based activities.

4x4 Driving is an opportunity to drive over terrain you would not attempt in a normal car. Driving through water and rough terrain will test your driving skills to the limit. If you are either very brave or slightly mad you can also drive blindfolded!

Then there is a Fun Day for 8 or more which is perfect for a stag/hen party. It offers a blend of off-road karting and clay shooting joined together with a pint 'n' pasty. The Multi-Activity Day is exactly what it says and Newnham prides itself on the ability to suit most budgets and group sizes. Up to 50 people can be accommodated.

Catering options are also available. You can enjoy an informal snack served in the shooting ground, a hot buffet in the Newnham Undercroft or a truly gourmet meal in the elegant licensed dining room of Newnham House.

David Cobbold's busy office with a constant ringing telephone, confirms how popular the events are. The estate looks good, the house well-loved and one hopes that the Cobbold family will at least achieve 1000 years at Newnham Park if not many more.

The War Memorial. The Hoe

The Citadel Gate.

Chapter X

The Armed Services, The Dockyard, the Garrison City

Not so many years ago the name 'Garrison City' would have fitted Plymouth like a glove. Those days are gone and as the effect of the demise slowly crept amongst us, Plymouth was made to realise it would have to, in modern day parlance 'Get a life'. You have only to look at the exciting emergence of the city today to know that we took heed of that phrase and Plymouth definitely has a new life. But, living amongst us still are a smaller number of servicemen, ships, establishments and a dockyard, which have all been trimmed to meet with modern requirements. Now Plymouth has a happy balance and is still proud to call itself a naval port, the home of the Royal Navy, the Royal Marines and of the Army. The RAF, never strong here since World War II has virtually upped sticks and flown away. Gone are Seaton Barracks, Plumer Barracks, Mount Batten and very soon HMS Cambridge, the gunnery school will have closed its doors.

What have we got left? You have only got to read the local papers to see how busy the Royal Navy is. The comings and goings of all the ships are listed. You read of the departure of HMS Montrose, the arrival of HMS Monmouth, the return of an RFA, the homecoming of a ship that has been away on patrol for months and so it continues but what fascinates me is the happenings behind the almost endless stone walls of the Dockyard as they stretch from Mutton Cove to Camels Head. Inside these walls is a world that is almost unknown to Plymothians except for those who work within it. What an extraordinary world it is and one I felt privileged to learn about from two highly knowledgeable men. Reg Shield of DML for the Dockyard and Commander Charles Crichton for the Naval Base. One might call it a world of romance and reality. The romance comes from the history and current life of the Naval Base, the reality from the practicality of repairing and refitting ships of the Navy and others, repairing and reconditioning rolling stock for the railways and building and refitting luxury vessels for people like Sir Donald Gosling whose autocratic motor vessel even boasts a helicopter pad!

Lets start with the Dockyard. It is the largest marine engineering complex in Europe and with 4,200 workers is Plymouth's largest employer. It generates over 12% of the city's income which proves how important it is for our welfare. DML was created in 1987 to operate and bring commercial business to the Dockyard and then ten years later DML bought the dockyard from the Ministry of Defence and it has forged successfully ahead and now has a turnover of £340 million per annum.

Those are the cold facts but the story is so much warmer and more exciting. You have only to be taken on a tour round the yards to sense the history and smell the present. All around you is a world of its own with the waters of the Hamoaze on one side and all around it the walls which keep the everyday world apart. I love the boat trips which one can take up the river on one of the pleasure boats from The Hoe. It gives one a more vivid impression than entering one of the Dockyard Gates where inevitably the glamour dies a bit when visitors are, quite rightly, subjected to security checks and on passing, issued with a pass which allows you to enter providing you are met and escorted by someone in authority. There are ships in for refitting - a destroyer here, a submarine there. There are ships tied up along side being revictualled and made ready to sail. There are ships just returned to port, looking slightly worse for wear having been a long time at sea. There are two destroyers, tied up alongside, decommissioned, abandoned and waiting for some third world foreign power to buy them. Then there are two submarines which no one seems to want and which will lie in an inner basin waiting for a decision to be made about scrapping them. Way across the basin tied up against the wall, is a very odd looking vessel. It looks, at a distance, a bit like one of those cut out cardboard models, but I was told by my guide, Reg Shield that this ugly duckling holds the Blue Riband for the fastest crossing of the Atlantic. It was built as a research ship to show that a conventional single-hulled vessel could, with careful detail design, be made to go just as fast and with as great a fuel-efficiency as a twin-hulled catamaran. Now DML's brief is to cut the vessel in half, add another section to it to make it longer and fit additional engines to make her go even faster. The cost of this odd exercise runs into millions! Strange how some people choose to use their money.

Everywhere you go in the Dockyard you come, in spite of the damage German bombers did during World War II, to old buildings which have been there for centuries and have been maintained meticulously by the Admiralty originally and now by DML. More recently DML has been concerned with the sort of buildings and equipment required for their operational tasks.

One needs to look at the background of this efficient and streamlined concern which as a Dockyard began its life in December 1690 at the behest of William of Orange. Parliament even then, was never happy with the effectiveness of running an engineering establishment as part of the Civil Service. As early as fifty years after the yard opened, Samuel Pepys, then Secretary to the Navy, was recording in his diaries Parliament's dissatisfaction with the cost of the operation. You never know he might have even discussed it with his friend William Castle, the originator of what is now Plymouth's Castle Kitchens. (see the story of Castle Kitchens in Chapter 16)

Whilst the Dockyard was run by the Civil Service it was in many ways overstaffed but the reason behind this was sound. It had to be prepared for any contingency that might occur. Wars of varying sizes kept rearing their ugly heads and the demands on the services of the Dockyard were heavy. I am just young enough not to remember World War I when the Dockyard worked full out but I do remember World War II and the heroic effort made by the Dockyard to turn ships around fast and get them to sea quickly. In those days the ships were not powered by diesel or nuclear power with the result that they had to return to port for what was known as a boiler clean. A time for the ship's company to relax a bit, go ashore and have some fun. I remember it especially when the bombing was so apallingly heavy that Lord Mountbatten led his Destroyer flotilla out to sea in the hope that the German Bombers would pursue them rather than rain their bombs on the Dockyard. The ruse did not work and much was destroyed. Virtually all the houses in South Yard were reduced to rubble, Storehouses were hit and ships damaged by blast but nothing stopped the work of the men. They risked life and limb, as much as any fighting man, to patch, repair, revictual, re-arm and send to sea again, every ship that came into their hands. Sleepless nights whilst the Germans kept up their nightly visits, did not deter them. They frequently had to walk to work climbing over craters, boulders, burnt out vehicles, the result of the previous night's attack. They had amazing stamina and a cheerfulness that was a tonic for everyone.

There is an amusing story told to me by one of the Dockyard Police Force who used to guard the gates. It was after a particularly bad night and my father, a retired Colonel who had been seconded, because of his age and much to his disgust, to command the Plymouth Battalion of the Home Guard, based at Crownhill Fort. He with his adjutant, Captain Tom Hussey, a Cavalry Officer, visited the Dockyard on this particular morning, duly showed their passes and were signed in. They drove further into the Yard in their camouflaged Beetle, a tiny car for two men, both well over six feet. On their way out they encountered the mid-day exodus of workers on their lunch break streaming through Albert Gate. The Police on duty recognised my father and the car and simply waved them on. This was not good enough for Tom Hussey who was driving. He stopped the car and unperturbed by the volume of men leaving the yard, he reversed the car back to where the policemen stood. The car was brought to a halt and he unwound his 6ft 5inches from the interior of this small, low vehicle. He walked over to the Police and in a somewhat haughty voice, and looking down at the much smaller policeman said in loud tones ' My good man, how dare you fail to stop us. You are putting National Security in jeopardy. For all you know we might have a destroyer in the boot of this car!'

I remember also the phenomenal work rate in the Dockyard during the Falkland conflict when the need to get ships ready for sea and the conflict was crucial. Strangely enough people living in the Midlands and in the North away from ports had almost no idea of what was happening. They watched the news but whereas the whole of Plymouth waited for the bulletins with anxiety and frequently pride, the rest of the country, apart from other service ports, like Portsmouth and Southampton, seemed to take it as just another world problem. I suppose we are all hardened to disasters as we see them on the news and do not react strongly unless we are in someway involved.

The work done by DML is immensely important to the well-being of our Royal Navy and its attendants like the RFA. No one can emphasise too much the need for safety and security and no one is more aware of that than DML who are responsible for the refitting of frigates and submarines. The latter excite media and press interest every time they move and as I write we are in the midst of the problems caused by the crack in a reactor in HMS Tireless, now in Gibraltar awaiting repairs much against the wish of Gibraltarians who are convinced that they are in mortal danger. This is certainly scaremongering and definitely not true. Unfortunately the anxiety has been increased by the recall of all the Trident submarines in service for the purpose of checking what may turn out to be a design fault. At this moment of writing no one knows the whole truth but one thing I am absolutely sure about is that it poses no danger to the people of Plymouth anymore than it does to Gibraltarians. It is a far greater problem for our Service chiefs who are woefully short now of submarine power around the world.

Why am I so sure? Let me tell you what I have discovered and what I know to be fact and not fiction or unnecessary hysteria. If you ever had any doubt of how much DML care for our safety and how much is demanded of them by the various agencies, you would not worry.

DML is the only dockyard dealing with our submarines and in order to be able to undertake the work, especially where nuclear power is concerned they have had to carry out the most stringent demands. First of all they have had to build new facilities. The key to the campaign has been the development of a new 'low level' approach to refuelling nuclear submarines for the Vanguard class. In the past, one of the main features at Devonport has been a massive earthquake-qualified crane which lifts reactor elements out of the submarine and transfers them into the core pond to await disposal. Every foot of height of the lift, and every foot of the height of the crane making the lift, makes it much more difficult - and expensive   to meet the earthquake-resistant requirements of the Nuclear Installations Inspectorate - known as NII. DML's low level system is designed to reduce all heights to a minimum. The submarine is docked only just below ground level - the dock floor is being raised to achieve this - and the remote handling Reactor Access House sits on beams which span the dock at ground level. The submarine docks stern first so the beams do not have to pass over the conning tower, they are low down over the hull itself. Individual fuel elements are lifted the short distance from the reactor into the Reactor Access House and then all subsequent movements are at ground level. The nuclear fuel flasks are not lifted at all. They are removed horizontally from the Reactor Access House at ground level and are then transferred using a dedicated rail system to a new Low Lever Refuelling Facility where they are loaded for trans-shipment out of the dockyard by rail.

This low level approach to reactor refuelling is the key which enabled DML, to meet the NII earthquake requirements with improved safety standards at substantially below the cost of conventional refuelling methods.

The new Vanguard class submarines are much larger than any other current class of British submarine. DML's Submarine Refit Complex has two dry docks, 14 and 15 Docks. The new Vanguard class of submarine is too large to fit in these docks so No 9 Dock is being converted specially for the purpose. Because of the advantages of DML's new low level refuelling system it is also being introduced to 14 and 15 docks at the same time.

So much has been done in DML's Redevelopment Scheme since I was there in 1993. The D151 project was completed in February 1998 which upgraded and extended the facilities for storing intermediate level radioactive waste material, and effectively makes DML independent of any national intermediate level waste storage site. The level of radioactivity of the waste drops as time goes by. DML now has the capacity to store on site all the intermediate level nuclear waste we generate until the level of radioactivity drops to the point where the waste is reclassified as low level waste. It is then disposed of using the low level waste route.

196

The next project is the 10 Dock. DML needed to retain the ability to dock attack submarines while 14 and 15 docks are being redeveloped to meet the new NII safety standards and to install the low level refuelling system, and so Number 10 has been brought up to the latest nuclear standards for use as an interim non-refuelling dock for Swiftsure and Trafalgar class submarines whilst the Submarine Refitting Complex docks are out of commission.

No 10 dock was originally built about 1900 for the dreadnoughts of the day and was huge and formed one of the three large ship docks. The conversion was designed to render the dock earthquake proof up to seismic shocks of 0.25g plus a 40% overload.

Incidentally the last earthquake to hit Plymouth or the area was something like 270 million years ago! That tells us how far reaching are the required safety standards. Such an earthquake happening now would destroy Plymouth and miles around but would leave No 10 dock untouched!

The dock structure of granite and mass concrete sits on bedrock but to enhance stability during seismic shock the west wall was physically tied into the bedrock by 70 metre deep rock anchors set at one metre intervals. The old welded steel dock gate was discarded and replaced by a multi-cellular 7500 tonne reinforced concrete leviathan. This seals on a flat sliding face rather than being wedged in a slot so relative movement between the dock gate and dock structure under seismic shock does not result in crushing of the gate. New concrete 'arrestor' cradles were built in the dock bottom round the dock blocks on which the submarine rests. These ensure that in the event of a catastrophic failure leading to a massive inrush of water the submarine will be held safely in place. A steel safety grillage was built on the dockside to prevent the crane there from being able to topple over onto the submarine below.

It cost DML £25 million to complete this project in October 1997.

That £25 million fades into insignificance when you look at the D154 project. £350 million is to be invested in the upgrade of the existing Submarine Refitting Complex facilities used for refitting and refuelling the attack submarine fleet and create the new facilities required to meet the sophisticated and technologically advance requirements of refitting and refuelling the new Vanguard class of nuclear powered submarines in No 9 dock.

The constant attention to safety really has been underlined by the thirty years since the Submarine Refitting Complex was built in the north west corner of 5 Basin. We all used to watch its progress as we crossed the Hamoaze on the Torpoint Ferry. Constant discussions were had everywhere by people concerned about having such a facility in our midst. Surely time has proved that we did not need to have any fears.

197

The complex was designed and constructed specifically for the task of maintaining, refitting and refuelling nuclear powered submarines in two dry docks, 14 and 15, built specifically for the purpose on either side of a central promontory which houses, offices, plant and workshop facilities.

The D154 Project will see the two docks upgraded to the same seismic standard as No 10 dock with wall strengthening, the addition of massive concrete caisson dock gates and arrestor cradles fastened to the dock bottom. This work will be undertaken in phases to allow planned refuelling operations to proceed in parallel with the upgrading work. The massive refuelling crane, which is a prominent feature of the Devonport skyline, will be removed and the seven story central office block will be reduced in height to reduce the risk of the building collapsing during an earthquake. The new design of low level refuelling equipment will be installed, allowing attack submarines to be refitted and refuelled in the future to the latest legislative standards and also at lower cost.

D154 also includes the most important task of all, converting to No 9 Dock for use in refitting and refuelling Vanguard class nuclear-powered submarines. Like 10 Dock, 9 Dock built circa 1900 for the dreadnoughts and until recently has been in regular use as one of DML's large ship docks. Like 10 Dock it will be rendered earthquake proof using the same techniques and systems. The new design of low level refuelling equipment will be installed and a complex of stores, workshops, plant rooms and offices will be built to create a complete refitting and refuelling facility.

No one can deny that Devonport Royal Dockyard's nuclear facilities are of vital national importance. With the upgrading DML are providing, without disrupting the existing flow of submarine support work, the means to support not only the UK's attack submarine fleet, but also the nuclear deterrent fleet.

It is a tremendous undertaking and Plymouth should be proud to recognise that its Royal Dockyard is not only efficient, it is profitable and at no cost to the tax or ratepayer.

With all this activity I wondered what and how DML did to deal with surface warships. The answer was simple ' Competition'. They have to fight for every contract in a commercial manner and then the MOD decide what suits them best. To my mind and reading what the papers have to say, it seems that a lot of the decisions are political rather than commercial. I read only this week that a contract which should have gone to the Appledore shipyard in North Devon, upon which that yard had been counting, is now to go to Govan in Scotland. Being slightly cynical I cannot help wondering if that move is to conjure up Scottish votes in the next General Election!

Mark you DML does holds it own in the competitive battle and they recently won the competition which will bring HMS Lancaster to DML for refitting. Also with the new Devonport based large ships coming into the Royal Navy - Ocean and Scott now with Albion and Bulwark to follow, this should act to DML's advantage. It will also help the economy of the city.

With all the future submarine refitting and refuelling work in DML's hands there is not all that much room for expanding their traditional business. In looking for defence sector growth DML has turned its attention to the white collar area. The company has always provided a range of design office services - updating and archiving ship's drawing 'datum packs' and providing design input to refit planning. Recently the company has been trying to expand the range of design and management led services it provides. A company 'first' in this area was the winning in June 95, of a £20 million contract to design, develop and supply a new chilled water system for Trafalgar class submarines. Working closely with York International, this project has been successful and the first production system is currently being installed on HMS Torbay. More attention grabbing was the winning of the £20 million five year submarine in-service support contract, covering all the classes of British submarines. This project really moves DML up a notch in the management services stakes and provides a springboard for other advances.

Whilst most of DML's business comes from the Royal Navy, their vigorous approach to finding work in the outside commercial world has brought its rewards and now something like 20% of their business is won commercially. They get orders as well from Overseas Navies and in the last few years have refitted ten frigates for India, Pakistan and Brazil. The company also offers various support activities ranging from technical assistance and supply of spares to consultancy on warship upgrades.

I was astounded to find that DML has made steady inroads into the rail support industry. Although not obvious at first sight, the synergy between a ship and a train is quite remarkable. OK, a ship is sharper at the front and a train doesn't float as well but apart from that..... They both have power generation and propulsion systems. They both have life support systems, safety critical sensor and control systems. Both rely on mechanical engineering allied with hydraulics, pneumatics, electric and electronics. Both are subject to the jurisdiction of regulatory authorities and both undergo prescribed formal test programmes on a regular basis before being put to work.

DML Rail Support is the major overhaul contractor for IC125 diesel electric power units for the UK rail companies, rebuilding nearly fifty engines last year. DML has also broken into bogie overhaul and now has a regular production line of bogies. The company also does railway coach work - DML was one of three companies which fitted the new door locking systems to Intercity coaches and they plan to expand more into this market.
DML has never been afraid of striking out into new fields and has developed new applications for advanced composite engineering.

Except for in aerospace, industry is still, very cautious about the use of advanced composites. DML tackled this caution by proposing a series of industry-funded joint R&D programmes, based on the development of a system for bonding carbon fibre composite material to metal structures. Getting industry buy-in at this early stage helped to reduce the investment risk, but more importantly, it served to make their target markets much more receptive to composite solutions.

A composite solution to an engineering problem is generally more expensive than traditional methods, per se. However, it is possible to make substantial savings in the associated costs. For example, a weld repair is simple and cheap, but before a weld can be made on an offshore oil and gas platform, production has to be shut down. A platform can be generating £1 million a day in revenue, so shutting down makes it a pretty expensive weld. A cold-blooded composite allows production to be maintained.

Several offshore oil and gas platforms have now been supplied with blast protection systems and structural strengthening systems, and DML's first subsea application has been manufactured.

Then there is roof beam strengthening work being done for London Underground. The benefit lies in the fact that the very thin layers of composite required do not intrude into the tunnel's 'loading gauge' and in DML's ability to undertake the work using only the four silent hours each night.

Experimental work is in hand on warship structural repair techniques. The benefit is that there is no need to dismantle heat-sensitive equipment on the other side of a panel as would be required for a weld repair. If the equipment happens to be a major run of sensor cables, one can imagine the time and cost involved.

DML holds patents on its technology and as market appreciation of the benefits of this process grows, they believe that this business is capable of significant expansion.

I knew that DML built and refitted large yachts but in my uninformed layman's mind, it had not occurred to me how different the characteristics of naval upkeep and commercial work were. When it was explained it made sense, even to this bear of little brain. A commercial ship's crew are busiest when loading and unloading rather than in transit between ports. During the voyage crew are available to undertake maintenance tasks which on a warship are done in port, because at sea a warship's crew are occupied.

For a commercial ship minimising downtime is crucial so when she is docked, it is for the minimum time. A warship refit might take a year, whereas a cruise ship's four year docking, for example, might take two weeks. Getting through the work list in such a short time requires the assembly of an army of subcontractors and short-term contract staff. Warship work provides full-time employment for many more men per dock per hour than commercial ship work and this results in an operating philosophy and overhead structure which makes it difficult to mix the two types of work.

Oddly enough within the marine industry, yacht work is the only area which is like warship work. The owner does not want upkeep tasks going on around him while he or she is on board, so upkeep is undertaken in port. There is not the imperative need to minimise downtime because yachting is a seasonal activity, so the yachts are docked and maintained out of season.

DML had its first experience of the large yacht market in 1987 by giving the ex-Royal Yacht HMY Brittania her last major refit. They have built, rebuilt, converted and refitted many other large yachts since then. DML's FRP hulled motor yacht Lady Tiffany won the 'Showboats 'Most innovative yacht of 1995' trophy and this was capped when it was voted as one of the best motor yachts launched in 1995, by the Superyacht Society.

Devonport Yachts has worked on most of the world's major yachts. In the last few years they have stretched the 64 metre Southern Cross III, refitting the 40 metre sailing yacht Twirlybird, refitting the 64 meter motor yacht Virginian, building the 74 metre motor yacht Salem and adding 5 metres to the aft deck of the 75 metre Leander. They have also built a 50 metre aluminium-hulled motor yacht.

Racing Yachts have also come under their baileywick. The whole of the Challenge fleet of sixteen 67 foot steel hulled yachts were built by them. They have also supplied eleven 73 foot Challenge 2000 steel racing yachts for the BT Global Challenge round-the-world yacht race being held to mark the Millennium.

Built on the centuries old Dockyard and its fine reputation, DML have entered the Millennium with one of the most admired companys in the world. They take pride in the long tradition of service. Their aim is to deliver quality at the right price and on time. The staff are impeccably trained. Each project has its own manager. One might almost say they take as their motto 'Get it right, first time, every time.'

Now for Devonport Naval Base and the exciting, growing Naval Base Museum. HMS Drake has long been synonymous for shore based sailors carrying out the business of the big Naval Base. I heard it described not so long ago as a 'One-stop' shop for the Fleet. A pretty apt description. Devonport is the biggest naval base in Western Europe, covering 622 acres with 25 tidal berths, five basins and 44 alongside berths. If you look around you can see that there are 12 dry docks of various sizes which will accommodate any ship from an aircraft carrier to a submarine.

Statistics can be boring but it is quite fascinating to consider what economic value is brought to the city by the 13,500 men and women who serve in the Plymouth area. The Naval Base directly employs over 1,000 Service personnel and 1,450 civilians, while the dockyard operators DML have 4,000 staff. Budgets for the Naval Base Commander, DML and Flag Officer Sea Training total almost £400 million. The Naval Base directly/indirectly generates 10% of Plymouth's income. Business is conducted with some 400 local firms. It conducts over 5000 ship movements every year as well as 45+ Assisted Maintenance Periods on ships and submarines.

Apart from the well-being of ships the importance of caring for personnel has been given great consideration. The Lowdon Facilities are satellites of the main Fleet Accommodation Centre and provide alongside offices, galleys and crew accommodation, strategically sited close to ships undergoing refit. The Fleet Accommodation Centre apart from providing over 2,000 beds has impressive leisure facilities, including a gymnasium, swimming pool, sports pitches, bars and a skittle alley. There is also a 20-bed sick bay and a dental centre.

It took years to bring together all the disparate organisations responsible for providing specialist services to the Fleet. On arrival in Devonport ships used to encounter an alarming array of Service and civilian authorities to meet their alongside requirements. Since 1994 all the elements have been amalgamated to form an integrated Naval Base dedicated to providing seamless, one-stop support. The name for this amalgamation is HMS Drake perpetuating the title of the Naval Barracks and named after one of Britain's greatest seafarers.

From an architectural point of view the Naval Base has a number of old imposing buildings married to new ones providing up to date accommodation for personnel. It has the appeal that centuries of occupation brings to a place, a sense of stability and continuity. Within its walls lies the church of St Nicholas, filled with a quiet beauty and much loved and cared for by its congregation. This integrated concept is a highly successful platform from which to manage Naval Base business and has yielded dividends through increased efficiency, quality of service and a sense of purpose.

The Devonport Naval Base involves itself in outside activities such as Ten Tors when a team of six assist by camping at specific Tors to provide a checkpoint for the youngsters taking part to track their progress and provide medical and moral support. From April 2000 the base has its own Naval Base Nature Conservation Office whose first job has been to produce a nature conservation management plan for conservation sites within the Naval Base and identifying any sensitive sites. John has completed the annual MoD Bird Count and during 2001 will be monitoring the area of Bullpoint where RAFT is to be built, to provide a base line survey of the waders using the mud flats, and also a similar survey of bird breeding populations using the buildings for nesting. This will be an on-going five-year study into the birds in the area and to quantify what charges, if any, the RAFT development has on them.

For many serving officers, men and their families, Plymouth is home. It is one of the most popular postings in the Royal Navy because of the friendliness of the city and for the facilities that Plymouth offers. No-one seeing the faces of wives, girl-friends, children as they watch the ships sail out can fail to recognise the lonely time ahead for them. It is one of the penalties of marrying into the service. The compensation comes from the knowledge that, on the whole, the ships are not away for more than six months at a time, and even if they remain on station longer in some far distant sea, then their menfolk are flown home when their tour of duty finishes. Gone are the days when a ship's company could be away from the home base for years.

There will be many past and present service wives who have stood at Devil's Point watching the ships go and return and, when a commission finishes, seeing the ship sail proudly in with the white pennant streaming from its mast - the longer the ship had been away, the longer the paying off pennant. Those moments of reunion are never forgotten; all the loneliness, the worries, the heartaches, disappear as the ship draws alongside and families are reunited.

We are used to seeing the daily activity in Plymouth Sound as ships come and go but sometimes we forget the floating supermarkets - the ships of the Royal Fleet Auxiliary. These are the ships that carry everything to restock the Royal Navy at sea. The captain of such a ship might well describe it as an extension of Devonport Naval Base in that they take all the supplies away with them for the benefit of other ships as the need arises. An RFA can supply the fleet with everything from diesel generators to chocolate bars, ammunition to soap. It can carry enough food to supply 15,000 men for a month. Without these hard working ships the Royal Navy could not stay at sea.

It is the gathering together of Naval memorabilia, artefacts and many other factors together with the superb old buildings in South Yard, that has inspired the instigators of the Naval Base Museum to explore the means of making it a place of National importance . The idea, in a smaller way, is not new. In the late 1960's a small museum was opened in Devonport Royal Dockyard. This constituted the third attempt to assemble naval memorabilia and historic artefacts in Devonport. Previous collections had been destroyed either in the Great Fire of 1840 or in the bombing of the Second World War. A large collection of artefacts in the Royal William Victualling Yard survived the war and continued to be added to and displayed in the Victualling Yard until it closed in 1992. This collection, together with the remains of the original dockyard museum, is now housed in the 19th century Police and Cashier's Office and the Old Fire Station in the historic South Yard of HMS Drake, HM Naval Base, Devonport, Plymouth and is the catalyst for the exciting, large and international Naval Base Museum that is envisaged and is quietly being worked on by Commander Charles Crichton OBE and a band of 50 volunteers who will have welcomed over 20,000 by the end of this millennium year.

The site is wonderful with exciting old buildings that are to be developed like the Ropery, now devoid of machinery but ideal for the display of artefacts. The West and East Ropehouses, each 1,200 feet long were constructed in 1773, as a laying house and spinning house respectively. Built at the same time were four associated buildings, a white yarn store, a tarring and wheel house (the motive power centre for the tarring process) and two tarred yarn houses. The east ropehouse was destroyed by fire in 1808 and rebuilt to a fireproof design in 1815, making it one of the largest fireproof buildings of its time. A gibbet, used to execute condemned men, remains intact in the tarring and

The Naval Base Museum

wheel house and is one of the sights on view to visitors. It is grisly and I have to admit to preferring the elegance of the Gazebo! Then there is Number One Covered Slip built between 1814 and 1821 which is the sole surviving eighteenth century covered slip in a Royal Dockyard. Visitors will be able to see it together with seven   splendid figure heads which have found their way into the slip from all over the Naval Base.

In 2000 for the first time all the memorabilia and artefacts belonging to the Royal Navy Field Gun Crews has been put on display complete with photographs of the teams throughout the years. It is well displayed and will provide much interest for visitors. It is so important for everyone to see that the history of the Field Gun Crews is recorded for posterity. So many people have been involved with the competition over many year. Devonport has a proud record in the competition and when the final curtain came down on their final run at the Royal Tournament in August 1999 strong men were seen to weep. It brought to an end nearly a century of blood, sweat and tears. Had you been in Earls Court on that memorable night you would have seen the 90 men of the Devonport team proud at their win but grieving for the passing of a tradition. Some shook hands with colleagues, some just sat with their heads in their hands as they struggled with their emotions. Neither support staff nor visitors, families or friends could find words that would bring any form of comfort to the field gunners in their loss.

The tournament has come to an end because the increasingly stretched armed services have found it ever more difficult to provide personnel. It is an enormous loss and even more reason why the opening of a display of the memorabilia in the Naval Base Museum is so important.

Incidentally Plymouth artist, Richard Clark was commissioned by the Devonport Field Gun Crew to produce a painting to commemorate the Ladysmith Centenary. It is a powerful painting and prints from the limited run signed by the artist, are available from the Armada Gallery in Southside Street.

What excites me is that new things to see are being developed all the time and there will be full public access as part of a wider celebration of Plymouth's maritime heritage. The aim of the Plymouth Naval Base Museum will be to tell the story of

'Support to the Fleet at Plymouth since the days of Edward I'. There will be an emphasis on the history of the growth of Devonport Dockyard, the local community and great engineering achievements. The museum will also celebrate the significant advances in the provision of engineering, education and training, victualling, medical care, armament supply and ship and submarine support facilities.

With its excellent visitor centre, its catering facilities and the glorious views of the rivers, the feeling of being wrapped in history, this has to be one of the most exciting adventures for Plymothians and for visitors for a very long time. Imagine you will have the opportunity to see the largest Naval Base in Western Europe where almost half the ships and submarines of the Royal Navy are supported. You will be able to hear about the past, the present and future of the United Kingdom's premier Naval Base. Want to know more - and there will be much more, contact the Museum Visitors Office Tel: 01752 554200.

Across the River Tamar H.M.S Raleigh is a unique and complex Establishment with many diverse and important tasks, running almost 100 different courses per year with a throughput of some 44,000 people. One of the most significant safeguards of the future capability of the Royal Navy is the achievement of very high standards of training here. It is the New Entry training establishment for all ratings joining the Royal Navy, Women's Royal Naval Service, RNR, WRNR and the Queen Alexandra Royal Navy Nursing Service. Officers' initial training is not conducted here but at Britannia Royal Naval College in Dartmouth. In addition to basic general training the establishment is also home to the Royal Naval Supply School, Royal Naval Seamanship School, and the latest addition the RN Submarine School. HMS Raleigh also has the Command Schools which include the Trevol Range, the Firefighting School, the Damage Control School, the First Aid School and the Nuclear Biological Chemical Defence School. These schools provide training facilities for ships and establishments in the Plymouth Command area.

HMS Raleigh is perfectly situated in the South East corner of Cornwall on the outskirts of the small town of Torpoint. It is an area of outstanding natural beauty. The close proximity of the Cornish coast, sheltered inlets and the open spaces of Dartmoor make it an ideal natural training environment afloat and for adventurous training of all kinds.

There is a ship's company of some 524 Servicemen and women and 380 civilians here. Together with the trainees there are, on a daily basis, about 2,500 people working in the Establishment. A New Entry of up to 100 ratings join almost every week, 40 weeks of the year.

It is quite intriguing to consider what the ship's company of the first Raleigh would make of a sailor's life aboard today. He would have known that his ship was a prize captured in 1778 and subsequently registered in the Navy List. In 1780 she took part in the blockade of Charleston and was sold on in 1841. The second Raleigh was a 16 gun 'brig sloop; of 382 tons built in 1806 and saw service in the China Seas. She also was sold in 1841. The third was a 50 gun ship which foundered on entering Macao when she struck an unchartered rock. The fourth was a 22 gun iron built screw frigate and the fifth a light cruiser launched in 1919 and wrecked in the Strait of Belle Isle on

8th August 1922. Today's HMS Raleigh was commissioned as a shore establishment for Naval Training of men called up under the Military Training Act of 1938. She was commissioned on January 9th 1940 as a Training Establishment for Ordinary Seamen. New entries were accepted direct from shore at a rate of 300 a week for a course lasting 11 weeks. In 1944 Naval forces of the USA took over the entire camp as an embarkation centre for the D-Day attack on the French coast. HMS Raleigh was returned to the Royal Navy on July 29th 1944 to continue the task of training New Entry Seamen.

In 1958 came the integration of Seamen and Marine Engineers during Part I training. In 1959 this was further developed so that Raleigh became the Royal Navy's New Entry/Part I Training Establishment.

HMS Raleigh was completely modernised between 1971 and 1978 and is much larger, but more compact than before. In September 1981 WRNA Part I Training commenced at Raleigh following the closure of Dauntless. In September 1983 the Royal Navy Supply School, previously based at HMS Pembroke, became part of HMS Raleigh and the New Entry Training of Artificer Apprentices was transferred from HMS Fisgard.

In September 1990 WRNS training was integrated with that of male trainees. In April 1991 the Royal Navy School of Seamanship moved to Raleigh and the Seamanship Training Squadron was disbanded. The RN Cookery School moved from Army Catering Corps headquarters at Aldershot to Raleigh in November 1994 and the last major re-location process to take place was that of the RN Submarine School moving from HMS Dolphin in Gosport to Raleigh in January 2000.

The facilities at HMS Raleigh are second to none. The parade ground, where all will finally pass out on completion of their courses, still provides one of the most effective ways of instilling teamwork, pride, co-ordination and discipline into those who have recently joined the Service. Jupiter Point, the Sail Training Centre, is on the River Lynher. It has over 91 various craft for water borne training and recreation. The Physical and Recreational Training Centre has excellent sporting facilities, including two gymnasiums, three squash courts, a swimming pool, sauna, solarium and numerous sports pitches. The complex is also used extensively by a wide variety of civilian clubs, organisations and Service personnel generally, as indeed are a number of Raleigh's other facilities.

HMS Raleigh is fortunate to have the Royal Marine Band based there. The band is in demand all over the country but by careful management it is present for the majority of the weekly passing out parades. The band's presence adds depth to the occasion and never fails to delight the 600 or so relatives and friends who visit each week. Each Friday you will see many proud parents crossing the Torpoint Ferry en route to HMS Raleigh for the passing out parade. They discover that their young sons and daughters who left home as young adults to join the Service have suddenly grown up and gained confidence.

Plymouth is shortly to lose HMS Cambridge which is a sad loss. It is a name that goes back 321 years , when in 1664 King Charles II gave this name to one of the 4 new men-of-war ordered in view of the expected hostilities with Holland. The King selected the name in honour of the baby Prince James, Duke of Cambridge, second son of the Duke of York, being created a Royal Duke and Knight of the Garter. Cambridge, a 70 gun, 3-decker of 860 tons was launched in the spring of 1666. Since then there have been many ships of the name: the last was a paddle-boat hired for use as a minesweeper by the Royal Navy in 1914.

Today's HMS Cambridge is a shore establishment occupying one of the most beautiful sites in the South Hams at Wembury looking out over glorious views of the sea and the coastline. I visited there one morning when the wind was howling and the seas rolling in, white crested, against the cliffs. I could barely stand up as I was taken by a courteous young sailor from my car to the main building.

I had a particular interest in looking through some of the records and photographs: my brother-in-law, Freddie Buckler, was at one time the Captain. The site was acquired by the Admiralty in 1940 and used as a firing range for training in practical gunnery of the large numbers of men required to man the expanded wartime fleet. It was then known as HM Gunnery Range, Wembury. In 1956 the Gunnery School in HMS Drake closed and the Wembury range was commissioned as the seventh HMS Cambridge exactly one hundred years to the day after the commissioning of the fourth HMS Cambridge. When the Establishment closes it will be a sad loss.

Another great loss to the City is HMS Thunderer, the Royal Naval Engineering College which was considered too expensive to run and closed down. Its buildings have all gone and in its place there is an upmarket housing estate.

The Royal Naval Engineering College had been part of life in Plymouth since the late 19th century. It was not always housed at Manadon. My early remembrance of it is an old, grey stoned building at Keyham just above the dockyard's St Levan's Gate. It was the war years that started the move to Manadon. Nissen huts were built there as classrooms and at night the students returned to their quarters in Hartley Road, now used by Plymouth College Preparatory School.

The value of RNEC Manadon to the navies of the world has been proven time and time again. Together with Shrivenham in Wiltshire which is the Army's equivalent and now used for the Combined Services, it enabled them to take an internationally respected degree and go on to different roles in the services.

While the workload at Manadon was demanding, it did encourage its officers to take part in the community and social life of the city. I can remember the days when the height of my social ambition was to go to a tea-dance at the college - we could not dance at night because of the German bombers. These tea dances were held in the Officers Mess in Hartley Road and we would dance to the band of the late and much loved Frank Fuge.

These were the days when young officers were expected to sign in at night and before midnight unless they had a late pass. I remember an occasion when one young man asked a colleague to sign in for him. The miscreant's name was Middleditch and when the signature was checked in the morning it read, Middleditch! Be sure your sins will find you out.

Those were the days when Admiral Louis le Bailly whom I knew as a Lieutenant Commander at Keyham. Later in his career he was second in command at Manadon and with the support of his Captain, the late Admiral Sir John Walsham, planted a number of trees. Not just any tree but one from the country of each foreign student. It resulted in a thriving and fascinating collection of trees indigenous to all sorts of places in the world. The white handkerchief tree was probably the most unusual. Whether they have survived the builders bulldozers, I do not know.

Manadon has many happy memories for me over the years. Not the least because it was there we held the reception for my daughter's wedding to a young lieutenant returned from the Falklands conflict. There is a nice story attached to this wedding and shows how one should always go to the top if you want something done!

About six weeks before my daughter's wedding for which the Great Hall at Manadon had been booked for the reception, my future son-in-law arrived at our house looking decidedly unhappy. He broke the news that a mistake had been made and we could not have the Great Hall for the reception because the Queen was coming and the only time it was possible to do the spring cleaning, painting, polishing etc of the hall for the Royal visit was at the time planned for the wedding. My daughter was horrified and in tears. It was a big wedding and Plymouth could not produce another venue big enough. The Navy courteously offered us the Wardroom at HMS Drake but it was too small, or HMS Britannia at Dartmouth which was too far away. I did my best to comfort my daughter and told her not to worry; I would sort it out! I have never been one to give up easily and so taking a notepad to the hairdressers with me, I composed a letter to the Queen whilst I was under the dryer. I told her of the problem and having been fortunate to have known her in Malta in my younger days, I knew she hated fuss and would not like anyone to be put out because she was coming. The letter was duly posted and I heard nothing at all from the Palace. But within a week or so there was a great deal of activity. Manadon was asking who was this woman who had not hesitated to go above the Captain, above the Admirals and cause a stir! I was quietly amused and waited to see what would happen. I got a phone call from the Captain's secretary asking if I would go and have a drink with the Captain. A car was sent to fetch me and over a drink I was told that whilst the Great Hall could not be used for the reception, all the rooms of the Wardroom were available to us. No mention was made of any letter to HM. I accepted the offer and so the day of the wedding dawned. I went downstairs to pick up the post and there on the mat was a letter from Windsor Castle from Her Majesty wishing my daughter and her bridegroom every happiness and hoping that their wedding day would be everything they wished for. I thought it was wonderful and a perfect example of Public Relations.

Two wells link the past with the present when I think about the Royal Marines. Sounds ridiculous doesn't it but quite by chance on the day that I was to see Lieutenant Commander Gordon Crocker who is the Property Manager for the Royal Marines at Stonehouse Barracks, I had a chance meeting with a Padre, Scott Anderson I think was his name, who rescued me as I tried to find my way about the barracks enroute to the Property Management Department. He and I strolled across the parade ground together and I discovered he had been back just one day from Kosovo where 42 Commando are currently serving. We talked of the Balkan problems and the fact that we must accept

208

their culture is totally different to ours. Our democratic ways just did not fit into their way of life. His remark that 'Their wells and family are more important to them than creed, race or country' proving how vital things like water are, tied in with Gordon Crocker's description of why in 1780, the Royal Marine Barracks was situated on the Stonehouse Peninsula with natural well water available at the chosen site. How often in our ultra civilised existence do we just take water for granted?

In the last two decades much of the work of the Royal Marines or The Corps as it is more regularly called, has been guarding people's rights to their own cultures, protecting them sometimes from almost unseen enemies. A tour of duty in Northern Ireland, in spite of the so called 'Peace' is still a peace keeping role in which for six months at a time they run the gauntlet of possible attack by Terrorists in places like County Fermanagh, which borders the Irish Republic. They live in base camps and border outposts scattered across the unfriendly terrain. There is little social life for them. A visit to the local village pub is out of the question. They are too vulnerable and could, by their presence, also endanger the lives of other people. The majority of these, a mixed population of Catholic and Protestants, offer friendship. Even those with the desire to see unification loathe and denounce the violent methods used by the IRA or any other terrorist organisation. It is not a popular posting but accepted phlegmatically.

Probably action in the Falklands made Plymouth even prouder of the Royal Marines than it already was. A sense of pride in all their achievements, all over the world, in different theatres and different situations, was underlined for me when they came back to the city from the Falklands conflict. I happened to be travelling on the A38 from Exeter to Plymouth on one of the days when these magnificent men were returning having disembarked at Southampton. The memory of the welcome they received from crowds along the route will remain with me always. Every road that crossed the highway was lined with cheering people. The closer we got to Plymouth, the deeper the crowds. Private cars drove in to the inner lanes to let the coaches bearing the men go by. Every window of every car was open, the occupants clapping and  waving. The Royal Marines were bemused! They had not expected anything like it. Tough men were reduced to tears. I certainly had seen nothing like it since the end of World War II.

It is sometimes harder for the civilian mind to register the fact that conflicts, whether it be the Falklands or the Gulf War, are easier for fighting men to handle than peace keeping or mercy missions. I remember being told that Operation Haven, an errand of mercy in Kurdistan produced more cases of trauma than any battle, however fierce.

The sight of the thousands of helpless people with small children wandering the hillsides, afraid of the vengeance of Saddam Hussein, pierced their hearts. Homeless, almost without food, without shelter and for most of them, little hope for the future, the Marines wanted to do anything they could to help them. In spite of their training, their experience and their willingness there was little they could do except provide some degree of safety from the Iraqis. It angered them far more than the attack by the Argentinians in the Falklands or the Iraqi's on the neighbouring barren wastes of Kuwait.

Kosovo, Sierra Leone, Northern Ireland, or wherever they are sent has taught this supremely well trained force that patience is a necessity. The rules of peace keeping are strict and toeing the line extremely difficult especially when they see horrific acts taking place before them. One can do nothing but admire their ability to help wherever possible, defend where necessary, face great discomfort and frequently danger and at the same time try and live a life that is in keeping with their long tradition.

I always remember many years ago being entertained to dinner by the Argyll and Sutherland Highlanders two days before they were leaving for Aden to take part in yet another conflict. The table was singularly devoid of their treasured mess silver. Apologies were profuse for this lack but it was explained it had been packed ready for its journey to the mess tent in Aden. It is this keeping up of standards and traditions that is so important and I was happy to discover that Royal Marine silver appears on the dinner table in Kosovo. Perhaps to the layman such things seem out of place in this modern age but to the Royal Marines, the Royal Navy and the Army it is pride in their units, their ships, their colours, their battle honours which engenders the terrific spirit which is still alive and well throughout the Services.

As one walks along Durnford Street, Stonehouse, it is quite hard to conjure up a picture of how it must have looked in 1780. At this time although there were a number of military barracks in and around Plymouth, Marines were billeted in private accommodation and local inns mainly in the Barbican area. Daily parades were held on the square in front of the Customs House, which is still known as The Parade, whilst Manoeuvres, Drill and Ceremonial parades were held on the open expanse of The Hoe. This was not efficient and it was decided to give the Marines their own barracks. A number of sites were considered but eventually, no doubt because of its natural wells, the site on the Stonehouse peninsula was chosen. That same barracks is what we see today, many of the buildings are original and still lived in. Gradually houses appeared around the barracks and the busy community which still exists began to grow.

Inside the barracks there is the delightful, small Globe Theatre which has been beautifully restored and I am told it can be made available for public use. I remember producing a play there in 1946 - Terence Rattigan's 'French Without Tears'. It was a sell out but we got the most awful reviews and so ended my aims in this direction. Later I can remember going there where my twin daughters aged about 6 or 7 took part in their schools entertainment. I hope it will become a popular venue again.

Perhaps my funniest memory of the Royal Marine Barracks was in the height of the Blitz. It was a Sunday morning after a hefty air raid during the night. I had been invited by a then boyfriend to attend Church Parade and drinks in the Mess afterwards. The young man in question was in charge of the Parade. When it came to the moment when he had to march up to the Colonel and report the 'Parade Correct Sir', his highly polished boot caught in one of the many shrapnel holes on the ground, relics of the previous night. He fell but managed to hang on to his sword as he slithered along the ground arriving almost at the Colonel's feet. Without showing any discomfort he got to his feet, saluted and reported. The Colonel, equally unphased, returned the salute and the Parade was dismissed. In the Mess, the Colonel bought Ian a drink and said 'Well done. A memorable morning!'

For anyone who wants a fascinating tour of Stonehouse Barracks, the only actual purpose built Royal Marine barracks remaining in the country, do get hold of Commander Crocker. He is a keen historian in his spare time and provides groups with a memorable and very interesting tour, pointing out all the historical points.

In 1984 the Royal Marines formed 539 Assault Squadron. It came about because of the successful manner in which 3 Commando Brigade made maximum use of waterborne transport before and during landing phases. The concept of being able to operate efficiently in waterborne operations was developed over many years in northern Norway and put to the test, at very short notice during the Falklands War in 1982. Its role now is to provide integral amphibious support to the Commando Brigade. The squadron has a strength of 104, including 11 RN engineering specialists. It is equipped with a variety of boats, from the 90ft Landing Craft Utility Mk 9R - capable of carrying a 60 ton tank up to 100 men - to smaller landing craft which can carry 30 men or a one-tonne Land Rover and 104mm light gun.

Then there are inflatable Raiding Craft or Rigid Raiders that can accommodate up to 8 fully equipped commandos. In 1994 the squadron acquired four hovercraft that are well suited to river and estuary operations - and these were used with Rigid Raiders when 539 deployed to the River Congo to stand by to protect Britons caught up in the region's civil war. The Plymouth based squadron also provided humanitarian relief in the wake of Hurricane Mitch which hit Central America two years ago.

The Army presence in the city is provided by 29 Commando Regiment Royal Artillery who as part of 3 Commando Brigade with the Royal Marines are garrisoned in The Citadel on Plymouth Hoe. It has a commanding position looking both out to sea and over Plymouth. Charles II had it built when he regained his throne and because Plymouth favoured Parliamentarians in the time of the Civil War, the cannons were ordered to face the town and not the French coastline. His Majesty was not inclined to trust Plymothians. Having seen his father's head chopped off, he was not in the market to suffer the same fate himself.

My visit to the Citadel was not to enjoy an excellent conducted tour which is available to visitors throughout the summer, and conducted by Blue Badge Guides who have its history at their fingertips. I wanted to discover a bit about the lives of the men wherever they happen to be in the world.

Living in a Garrison Town - even though it is now diminished in numbers by the various cuts and amalgamations, one is still very much aware of their presence , and all that the soldiers' ability to fight in any corner of the earth under the most severe conditions, must entail. No one wants to go to war but if you join the armed services this is something that you agree to do. It has been so long before World War II, Korea, Borneo, Vietnam, The Falklands and The Gulf. Nowadays there are many soldiers who have never seen any action apart from Northern Ireland and the various peace-keeping roles.

Being nosey I wanted to know how the army catered for itself wherever it might be in the world. The Royal Logistic Corp are in charge and my hosts were Major Francis, the Quartermaster, Corporal Rob, an experienced and award winning chef and WO2 Neal Barnes. Once they had ascertained that I really did want to know and that I was not on some odd PR operation, they could not have been more welcoming and frequently more amusing.

'How' I asked 'do you cope if you are miles from base, in the jungle somewhere?' The reply came quickly, without hesitation and with a straight face, 'Squeeze the shit out of worms and they taste quite good!' Read more about the SAS in the SAS Survival Handbook written by Lottie Wiseman and you will learn much, much more - a complete eye opener.

I cannot say that this was what I really had in mind. My lack of modern military procedure made me ignorant of the workings of a battalion or any other unit in today's army. I was rapidly educated.

There is no question that Breakfast is regarded as the most important meal of the day, wherever the troops may be. In Barracks the meal is a traditional one of cereals, eggs, bacon, baked beans and all the trimmings. Once away on exercises things are different. Supposing it is a survival exercise in the UK.? That's simple because there is a bountiful supply of edible produce everywhere from fish in the streams to the pick of the hedgerows. In the Arctic, where there are no bacteria, everything is safe to eat. The men tend to construct for themselves a sort of Indian tepee to keep them from the cold and then feed themselves from their ration packs which contain 5000 calories. Beef jerky is a favourite and because the temperature is 20 degrees, stores will last for four weeks. In the jungle things are different. Packs remain much the same but have the addition of extra salt and the instruction to drink more to combat the heat. Every squaddie carries curry powder, rice and pasta to boost his rations. Frequently they pool their supplies in order to make a tasty concoction. Not perhaps something one would see on a restaurant menu, but in the wilds and away from base, anything that varies the daily diet is acceptable - almost! I was told that Porridge Oats added to a chocolate drink, make a splendid dessert!

I have often thought about how supplies are brought to front line troops especially under fire. The answer is that there are various lines of catering and if one fails, the next one takes up the strain. Where do they get their supplies? In the first instance everything comes from Bookers Cash and Carry in the UK with the exception of fresh produce and vegetables. For these the Corp sends out a recce party to get what they need. If one thinks back two centuries to Wellington's men, not much has changed. Then they would have scoured the countryside for food to keep the army going. They were not too scrupulous in the manner in which it was taken either. That certainly has changed. Not for them the supplies flown in to be loaded onto fourwheel drive vehicles able to contend with almost any kind of terrain. It is a whole new ball game today. The degree of efficiency is impressive and made especially so by the tight budget within which the Royal Logistic Corp has to cater.

Imagine feeding tough men who have such a strenuous existence, three times a day for £1.66 per man! A housewife on a strict housekeeping allowance would be hard put to feed a family of four on £7 a day. The fact that the army buys in bulk does enable them to get the very best of prices but it still needs good housekeeping to keep the troops well fed.

The more glamorous side of the job is catering for social occasions; Regimental dinners in the Officers Mess, complete with the Regimental silver, and food that would be acceptable in a five star hotel. Every chef and caterer in the army is highly trained and when they join, their first posting is to the Army School of Catering where they are taught all they need to know in practical terms. Some of the end products such as butter or ice carvings are sensational. However no amount of 'in house' training can take the place of field training, cooking under canvas in the most difficult temperatures and circumstances.

The complexity of what the Royal Logistic Corp achieves would daunt most people. In addition to their catering and supply skills, they are also trained soldiers, capable of using weaponry as well as the next man.

I had no idea my visit to the historic Citadel would be so fascinating and provide me with a totally new image of life in the Army or the Royal Marines. To me they are unsung heroes who could well do with a little PR.

The Citadel Commandos 2000

213

The Royal Naval Hospital

Chapter XI

A Spoonful of Medicine

Throughout the whole of Britain there is much anguish over the well-being of the National Health Service. Quite rightly, but perhaps we should stop, count our blessings for what we have got and then try to remember the vision of those who set up the service in 1948. No one could have foreseen the giant steps that have been taken since then. No one could have forecast the escalating costs. Everything has changed. Advances have been made in every single department of healthcare. You have only to watch the television, listen to the radio or read the newspapers every day, to find out that a miracle operation has been performed, a new drug has been produced that will alleviate some area of pain. There are less deaths in childbirth and people live much longer. Infectious diseases like Scarlet Fever and Diphtheria no longer become of epidemic proportions, closing schools down with regularity, as they did in my young days.

In 1948 there were no transplant operations, no highly expensive treatments, drugs had not advanced much beyond antibiotics and paracetamol. The shortage of money today in the National Health Service is directly due to the advances and to longer life. I thank God for that and for the National Health Service. I thank God for the life saving operations and treatments that are nothing short of miracles, but miracles do not come cheap. I am equally thankful that I live in Plymouth where treatment for patients in the National Health Service is as good as anywhere, and frequently much better.

If you think that Pigeon Post had little to do with the latter part of the last century, you may be amused - and amazed - to learn that, as reported in the Evening Herald on November 11th 1982

'Plymouth hospitals' pigeon post service is being closed down because new, larger blood sample containers, will be too big for the birds' air-lift......'

The service was started several years ago to speed blood samples from Devonport Hospital to the central blood bank at Freedom Fields. (Neither hospitals exists anymore). The complete service took only six minutes from Devonport Hospital to the special loft built on the roof of the Dieticians Department at Freedom Fields.

Derriford Hospital is enormous and continually stretching out further. Inevitably when something grows to this size it is not all going to be perfect and from time to time will have shortcomings. The skill of its surgeons, the diagnostic ability of its doctors and the quality of its nurses is undoubted. Shortage of staff at the moment is one of the greatest anxieties. In spite of big recruitment drives, the bevy of nurses the hospital hoped would emerge, has not done so, but this is something that is endemic throughout the hospitals in this country. It does seem ridiculous to me that our nurses leave in droves to get jobs abroad because they are so much better paid and we, in turn, look to recruit nurses from foreign countries.

The Plymouth Postgraduate Medical School which was set up as part of the University of Plymouth, is now well established. Towards the end of the century it outgrew its space at Derriford and the University and relocated adjacent to the hospital at the The Tamar Science Park. Plymouth Hospitals NHS Trust has developed plans for a dedicated academic/research centre. From its research Plymouth doctors made national news for a discovery about new variant CJD - the human version of 'mad cow disease'. Dr David Hilton, Dr John Zajicek and Dr Edward Father discovered that a Devon man who died of new variant CJD had been carrying the 'rogue' protein associated with the disease in his appendix, which had been removed several years earlier. At the time of his appendix operation, the man was showing no symptoms of the disease. Thanks to the discovery, Plymouth is taking part in a prestigious national research programme into the disease, along with centres in London and Edinburgh. Dr Hillton was subsequently awarded £200,000 of government funding to look for the 'rogue' protein in tonsils and appendix biopsies taken from people in Devon and Cornwall since 1986.

As there is no treatment or cure yet for nvCJD, the research will be anonymous - neither the tissue nor the research results will be traceable to individuals. It is this sort of research that will help to profile the incubation of nvCJD.

The advent of the Peninsula Medical School is another great advance for Plymouth and the South West. The school will take up to 120 students providing them with a flexible foundation course followed by three years of clinical training in placements across the region. This will bring more resources, more expertise and more doctors to the South West. We already have The South West School of Anaesthesia which was established in 1998 to provide high quality registrar training in anaesthesia and intensive care medicine. Trainees rotate through the school's hospitals in Plymouth, Exeter, Truro and Taunton, with the opportunity to gain specialist experience in recognised centres abroad.

Sometimes to those who have never had reason to visit Derriford Hospital, it seems strange to see attractive, immaculately dressed nurses in crisp, slightly old fashioned uniforms with frilled and highly starched caps, moving about the hospital. These are Naval Nurses who since the closure of the Royal Naval Hospital in Stonehouse, have become part of the Military Unit in Derriford Hospital caring for personnel from all three services, There are 140 members of staff working alongside their civilian colleagues. This unit was established in 1995 and is now a model for the rest of the country.

For most Plymothians, the closure of the old Royal Naval Hospital in Stonehouse, left a definite gap in their lives. We all benefited from the opening of its doors to civilians and its departure was greeted with a deal of sadness. It was not unexpected when you consider the diminishing number of personnel serving in the armed forces. There was really no need for a hospital of this size or for the number of skilled surgeons, physicians and nurses who worked there. It is now playing a totally different role with the dominant factor being housing and the home of St Dunstan's Abbey School. Its history is fascinating and for that reason I have included it in this chapter. The construction of the Royal Naval Hospital was revolutionary in 1758. It was built on the block system and was the earliest specimen of a hospital in this country with a limited number of patients in each block building. The reason was the desire to cut down the spreading of infection. I have taken the liberty of quoting the description of the hospital written by Doctor Farr, the first physician appointed - the staff then consisted of himself, his junior, Dr Walker, and two surgeons, Mr Geach and his junior Mr Fuge. In addition they had the services of two assistants and a dispenser.

'The Royal Hospital for the reception of sick and hurt seamen and marines is situated at Stonehouse, nearly equidistant from the two towns of Plymouth and Plymouth Dock; a small arm of the sea which passes by Stonehouse, under the hospital wall, admitting boats to land at the outer gate, by the time of half-flood tide.

It consists of eleven large buildings, and four lesser, the whole forming a square but detached from each other, for the purpose of admitting freer circulation of air, as also of classing disorders, in such manner, as may best prevent the spread of contagion.

The buildings are rough marble, raised in the neighbourhood, with Purbeck rusticated coyns, and in front is a handsome colonnade, supported by more stone pillars, with a flat roof covered with lead, which serves as an airing ground for the convalescents in bad weather.

Ten buildings (exclusive of the centre or chapel building) each containing six wards, in all 60; each ward will conveniently hold 20 cradles, and in the recovery wards, if required 25; so that four underground wards, 1500 patients may on emergency be accommodated.

The ground floor of the centre or chapel building, contains the dispensary, laboratory, surgery and dispensers apartments; the first floor, the chapel, council room, with apartments in that and the attic storey for the matrons, assistant surgeons, assistant dispensers, etc. The area in the middle of the hospital is handsomely laid out with grass plots intersected by gravel walks, which are kept in very good order; besides which there is a large airing ground, surrounding the whole, containing in all about 12 acres.

At the higher end of the airing ground to the north is a large reservoir of water, which by means of a chain pump, throws the water into a leaden cistern, which being higher, conveys the water by means of leaden pipes, into every ward, for use of the patients, cleansing the water closets, filling the baths etc, every building being furnished with a bath and copper for heating the water to the temperature required.

Patients on admission are washed and supplied with hospital dresses, and their own clothes are carried to the fumigating house. A nurse is allowed for every ten men; the greatest attention is paid to cleanliness, and keeping the ward always well ventilated.

Dr Farr did not prescribe a very exciting menu. Today's menus at Derriford would seem like ambrosia in comparison! The menu read something like this;-

1st Low Diet - Water gruel, panado, rice gruel, milk pottage or broth and bread and butter if necessary. For drink, toast and water, tisane or white concoction.

2nd Half Diet - For breakfast, milk pottage, for dinner, half a pound of mutton, some light bread pudding, or in lieu of it, some greens; a pint of broth one pound of bread, one quart of small beer; the men upon this diet to dine in their own wards.

3rd Full Diet - Breakfast as above; dinner one pound of meat, one pint of broth, one pound of bread, three pints of small beer; supper in the last two named diets to be of broth, left at dinner; or if thought necessary, to be of milk pottage. Rice milk, orange whey, orange and lemon water, tamarind whey and water, vinegar whey, balm tea, sage tea. These to be discretionally ordered by the Physicians and Surgeons.

St. Luke's Hospice

Plymouth has been sad to lose the Royal Naval Hospital but delighted to find that it has become a home for St Dunstan's Abbey, a lot of contented residents and many varied small businesses. We are very fortunate that so much of its history is recorded.

Probably the most important event in the long history of the hospital was the arrival on the evening of August 27th 1795, of Captain Richard Creyke. He was appointed Governor of the Royal Hospital at Plymouth. The importance of this appointment was endorsed at a Levee when he was presented to King George III. He knew nothing of medicine but his diligence in getting himself briefed for the task ahead, and the tremendous vigour with which he attacked the job, guided the hospital through the difficult years of the Napoleonic Wars and beyond that. He was still in charge when he died at the age of eighty. He left to posterity a priceless document, his daily journal. It embraced every detail of administration covering a period of just over four years to 1799. Why he stopped then we will never know, but the entries he made give a remarkable insight into the life of Plymouth at that time. What you discover on reading it, is that during those four years he did not take a single day's leave and only missed Sunday Divine Service in the Hospital Chapel twice. Once when he was in attendance on His Royal Highness, the Duke of York, on a visit to Maker Camp, and once when he was ill. I had no idea that a camp even existed at Maker in those days.

There are some very sad entries in the journal. In 1797 on December 11th the record reads, 'On the request of the Port Admiral gave directions that 2 coffins shall be sent tomorrow morning to receive the bodies of the two mutineers of the Saturn, who are ordered to be executed on board the Marlborough in Plymouth Sound'.

That year was notable for the mutinies at Spithead and the Nore but also shows that Plymouth was affected. Governor Creyke did report that ; No symptoms of mutiny appeared among the patients in the Hospital.

The dedicated care of the staff of this hospital has continued through the centuries. Throughout World War I and World War II, it worked to capacity and beyond. In the years that have followed casualties have come from Korea, Suez, Aden, Malaysia, Northern Ireland and the Falklands.

Plymouth NHS Trust is constantly looking for new ways of working which will deliver better care and reduce costs. One innovation is that children requiring tonsillectomies who have to come from a distance from the hospital, can have their operations done in a day without needing to stay a night in hospital. However they do need for 12-18 hours after the operation to be within easy travelling distance of the hospital. Now the Trust has a scheme whereby the child and a parent can stay overnight in a local hotel, rather than keeping them in hospital. This provides a better environment for Mum or Dad and their child, and means that hospital beds can be kept for children who are more seriously ill.

Since the possible but very remote suggestion that surgical instruments used for tonsillectomies could possibly carry the CJD virus, Derriford Hospital now uses disposable surgical instruments - one of the first hospitals in the country to do so.

Waiting lists are always a nightmare for any hospital and Derriford has had its fair share of concerns. However the matter is slowly but surely improving and I, for one, have total faith in Derriford Hospital. The current outcry about hospitals being dirty places, should never apply to Derriford. The Trust sets high standards and with its cleaning contractors ISS Mediclean they came through stiff competition to win a national Golden Service Award for the best-cleaned health care premises.

As a patient I have experienced the very best of care in some instances from Derriford and at others been appalled by what has been happening around me. However at the end of the day, I have recovered from Breast cancer, been treated for heart problems and various other bits and pieces. In fact my GP said not so long ago 'You have had a full MOT and passed it well'. So Derriford has done me proud.

To write about every department in the hospital would take forever and be boring, but the two departments I know well seem to provide a good picture of the ability of the hospital to cope not only with Plymothians but from those in the catchment area for miles around.

When my son was a youngster my visits to the Casualty Department, in those days at Freedom Fields, were of such regularity that the Casualty Sister knew us well and on one occasion threatened to provide me with a cap and apron so I could help, if I brought him there anymore! Years later and with my son, now well into his thirties, I had to take him to Derriford A&E to deal with a damaged hand. Sister was still there, recognised us, and treated us as though it might have been yesterday that we had put in our last appearance. It is that friendly warmth that makes the busy A&E a less frightening place to be when something unfortunate has happened to you or your family. On my last visit to Casualty I had to sit and wait for a considerable time until my son was ready to be taken home, this gave me the opportunity to watch the amazingly calm and resourceful way the team worked. They were not phased by a noisy entourage accompanying an injured footballer, they were kind and considerate to an elderly couple who were very anxious, they worked quickly and efficiently and seemingly without stress although the number of casualties arriving though the door seemed endless.

My brush with breast cancer has meant regular visits to the Oncology department whose praises I cannot shout about loudly enough. From the first day of diagnosis, having been told by my GP that it was probably just a cist, only to discover that the lump was malignant, I was cared for superbly. John Broadrib, the surgeon, had me admitted within two weeks, the operation was successful, and in a very short time I was home again, lopsided, but with a good prognosis. I hated the ward I was on, I hated the fact that three of us were housed in a room that was otherwise being used for every piece of furniture and junk that could not be found a home elsewhere. It was intensely depressing, we felt cut off from everyone else and became definite end of the line patients when it came to any form of attention. However once I left there, that was in the past, and from that moment on I have had the greatest care and treatment throughout my time in Radiotherapy. It was here I came to realise how lucky I was when I saw those so much worse off than me arriving for their daily treatment. The staff were super, friendly and efficient and always encouraging. There will be no one who has been through Radiotherapy treatment who has not experienced that terrible sense of isolation when you lie under the wretched machine and everyone else disappears behind closed doors for safety!

After the six weeks treatment, I went for monthly checkups which whittled down to three months, six months and now annually. I was one of the lucky ones and given the all clear. But one of the continuing pleasing factors is that when I walk into the reception at the Oncology Department, even after a year, I know I am going to be welcomed by the two smiling faces of Tricia and Myra the receptionists, who greet everyone like long lost friends. Very good for ones ego and very comforting.

One of the strange things about cancer is the difficulty one has in discussing it with your family and close friends. It is almost as if it is more frightening for them than it is for you. At least that is how I felt and the subject became almost taboo. That is why I was so delighted to learn about the success of The Mustard Tree Macmillan Centre which you will find on Level Three above the Oncology Centre in the hospital. It started in a small way in Freedom Fields before it was moved to Derriford. The instigator was Dr Sheila Cassidy to whom Plymouth must be truly thankful, firstly for her work at St Luke's Hospice and now this highly successful project. Its whole purpose is to support people with cancer, their families and carers. You walk into a restful, warmly decorated room full of deep armchairs and sofas covered in rich apricot, yellows and blues. It is so welcoming and it is here you can sit, have a cup of tea and talk with the professional staff and trained volunteers, many of whom have personal experience of cancer. Beyond the main room there are smaller offshoots where one to one consultations take place, providing privacy if that is what you need. To me it is the ideal place to find strength and purpose on your illness and how to cope. Nobody minds talking to you and nobody is filled with negativity. It is a totally positive place to be, but sympathetic at the same time. I wish I had had the opportunity to use it when I had cancer. My questions would have been answered and I would not have bottled so much up inside of me. Stupid things get to you. For example I put on a lot of weight when I started taking Tamoxofen - nobody told me this would happen. I just knew I had to take a pill every day for five years and it would help prevent cancer attacking any other part of my body - and it did. Specialist nurses are available to you who will provide information which is specific to your individual needs.

The diagnosis of cancer is a devastating experience and our natural instinct is to protect those we love, especially our children. Often children are quick to pick up something is wrong and draw their own conclusion, which may be quite inaccurate. Children need to know and if they are not told a parent is ill they will feel shut out and may well become angry and depressed. This is where The Mustard Tree can help with support or advice on how to talk to your children.

The Palliative Care team offer support to you, your family and friends by providing advice on pain and symptom management, and meeting your needs in situations where your disease may no longer be curable. There is also a team of Macmillan Nurses who are able to see you at home.

A confidential counselling service operates within the Support Centre. You are welcome, whether you are a patient, family or carer, to make an appointment which will last about an hour. They are there if you are experiencing stress, anxiety or depression. Two Chaplains are available as well who are good listeners and try to answer the sort of question that we all ask, 'Why me?'

I think it is super that Complementary Therapies are available at The Mustard Tree Macmillan Centre. Massage is there for patients and carers and so is Reflexology, which is a gentle treatment of the reflexes of the foot that can be restful and relaxing. Relaxation classes take place every Monday afternoon between 3-4pm. Classes are run in small groups and both patients and carers are welcome. A variety of types of relaxation are available and classes vary so that clients can find the form of relaxation that suits them best. Healing is another option. The sessions are not offered as an alternative to conventional treatment, but may be helpful for those looking for emotional peace of mind.

The Head and Neck Support Group offer patients receiving treatment to the head and neck, access to a wide variety of health care professionals, and this is where patients have the opportunity to meet with others in a similar situation and also talk to a Dental Hygienist, Dietition, Mould Room Technician, Head and Neck Specialist Nurse, Therapy Radiologist and a Cancer Support Centre representative. Sessions are held every month on a Tuesday afternoon.

Sometimes cancer makes you feel helpless and out of control. If this is so you can learn more about how to cope with your illness, its treatment and the role of complementary therapies through 'Fighting Spirit'. This is a psycho-educational group where women with breast cancer meet up to receive support, share experiences and learn more about their illness. The groups are small (6-8 people) and meetings last 2 hours. They are held weekly for eight weeks on a Wednesday morning usually between 10am-12 noon.

Any woman who has had cancer always feels a bit of a frump and longs to look good again. This is where 'Look Good...Feel Better' comes in. The Mustard Tree Macmillan Centre can offer its patients, a free service, providing advice on skin care and make up application, together with a gift of products - and this is no small box of samples, it is products for real.

The programme, developed and provided through the Cosmetic, Toiletry and Perfumery Foundation, a charity, aims to help patients care for, and make the most of their appearance whilst they are undergoing treatment for cancer. It has been shown through clinical research that such a therapy can help build up confidence and self esteem. The sessions last for two hours and are run by specially trained Beauticians who provide advice and information. In addition to their skills as beauticians, they also attend The Mustard Tree to be taught how to deal with the problems cancer patients can experience. Incidentally, patients who are having radiotherapy to their face or neck are advised to wait until six weeks after their radiotherapy is complete, in order to gain the full benefit from the session. Approximately 12 ladies can be accommodated at each session which takes place every three weeks on a Tuesday afternoon. What is so nice about this is that the beauticians come from places like Dingles, Debenhams and Boots, who give the girls paid time off to fulfil this role.

The Body Shop also helps in the beauty field. They have adopted The Mustard Tree Macmillan Centre as their community project. The Body Shop Staff attend the Centre every other Thursday afternoon to provide a service of FREE makeovers, facials and manicures for oncology patients and their carers. You also get a 10% discount card to use at The Body Shop in the Hospital.

Whilst The Mustard Tree Macmillan Centre is within the hospital, the building was paid for and equipped by Macmillan.. Its staff, its running costs, are all paid for by the charity which is always in need of funds!

Within the Centre is another project, Jeremiah's Journey. This is a grief support programme for children and their parents who have lost someone precious to them through death. It is made up of a team of professionals experienced in working with bereaved children and parents, and they in turn are assisted by volunteers. The meetings are held at the Mustard Tree Macmillan Centre and after an initial visit at home from one of the team, children and their parents are invited to attend a group. The group meets weekly after school, for six sessions.

The funding comes from all sorts of activities arranged by a dedicated and active team of volunteers. That they succeed and The Centre succeeds is entirely down to the willingness of the staff and volunteers. Plymouth has the biggest Centre in the country and is held up as an example to other hospitals who want to emulate the success here. If you have a mind to raise funds or become a volunteer, you will be welcomed with open arms by The Mustard Tree team. Sue Morton-Smith leads the team and her quiet, thorough, professionalism sets an example which the others are only too willing to follow.

Plymouth patients with mental illnesses are now treated in a superb new unit away from the forbidding walls of Moorhaven, which for so long housed patients in a situation that leant itself to stigma and prejudice. The Glenbourne Unit resembles an upmarket motel. Moorhaven nurses worked alongside architects to provide a pretty, relaxing colour scheme. The bright floral curtains hang against primrose walls, the floors are carpeted. Inside the facilities include a modern gym, beauty therapy and art therapy rooms, a woodwork room and a therapy kitchen. In the three wards, christened Harford, Bridford and Dunsford after villages in Devon, the emphasis is on privacy and comfort. There are four four-bed rooms, two twin-bedded rooms and five single rooms on each ward. Each room is partitioned from the next and has its own desk.

Thought has been given to mentally ill mothers with babies and toddlers. Cots are provided on one of the wards so that mother and child need not be separated.

The new unit will provide assessments and diagnosis for a wide range of mental illnesses, from severe post-natal depression to schizophrenia. With all the new facilities and treatments, the desire is to make it possible for most patients to go home within a few days. Glenbourne is the central piece in the highly complex business of mental care.

One of the things that impressed me especially about Derriford is the handling of what I call taboo illnesses. For example, the indignity and stigma that colostomy, ileostomy and urostomy patients feel. Each and every one has to come to terms with coping for the rest of their lives with a stoma - an artificial opening that enables the body to discharge waste. Imagine the fear and the dread. What will people say, how will one's partner react? All this anguish is dealt with by a lot of caring and understanding people at Derriford. People from all walks of life and all ages suffer in this way. Every month there are some 20 new patients in Plymouth alone, and they seem to be getting younger.

It is perhaps comforting to know that you are not alone and that there are people out there who do cope and realise that you can still feel good, look good and lead a perfectly normal life. Before surgery a patient has a stoma 'sited' to find out where it will be most comfortable. The patient is asked to sit and stand, bend and stretch to see how it will feel when the patient is in a normal relaxed position. I discovered that there are many former patients who ski, swim, sail, abseil, hang-glide and climb mountains; so horrid as a stoma may be, it is something one can learn to live with.

No one is going to claim it is easy, particularly in the beginning. Education and understanding are paramount at the time, just as love and support are vital in relationships. All of these Derriford helps you to find. Part of this excellent hospital's caring service.

Derriford gets support for its work from all sorts of sources including a number of charities. For example, seven years ago, a cardiac nurse, Val Fryer, suggested that a lot more could be done for much-needed care and support for cardiac patients and their carers, and so Plymouth Heartbeat was formed. The charity is a support organisation and not to be confused with Heartswell whose main purpose is fund raising to build a lodge to accommodate carers or relatives of cardiac patients receiving treatment at Derriford. Heartbeat looks to provide comforts for cardiac patients and carers both in and out of hospital. It also acts as a pressure group to provide extra facilities for cardiac patients and carers, and helps with the cost of travelling and accommodation for carers of patients receiving treatment in London. For the last three years an exercise centre has been established at the Wolseley Trust Centre. This is available on Fridays between 10am and noon, at a nominal charge of £1 per session.

Currently Heartbeat is seeking with the help of the Wolseley Trust, to secure funding to provide permanent accommodation at the North Prospect Healthy Living Centre at Scott Hospital. This will enable the group to provide an improved service, including permanent exercise facilities, help, advice and information, and a place where people can meet and talk informally with others who have similar problems. If you would like further information contact Barbara Luckham, the Chairperson on 01752 789508

As I write there is confirmation of funds for a brand new £100 million hospital to be built on a site close to Derriford. The new facility which will run alongside the current hospital will be a huge boost for the area, creating scores of new jobs for doctors and nurses. Plymouth Hospital NHS Trust wants a new unit where 'elective' cases such as hip operations and cataract operations, could be dealt with. Substantial funding will come from the Government and the rest will be secured from the health authority and private finance. It will be wonderful for Plymouth but there must be some anxiety over the question of staffing. For example it is only a short while ago that a unit had to be closed in the Glenbourne Unit, because of a shortage of 27 registered mental nurses. There is no doubt Plymouth needs a new hospital. As one doctor put it 'Derriford has outgrown its site, and cannot provide all the required services. It is like trying to put a quart into a pint pot.'

The Royal Eye Infirmary close to Plymouth Station has been providing the city with first class treatment for over a century. It still has an old fashioned air about it but that belies the excellent treatment received from its more than competent doctors and nursing staff. The latter have worked hard to become able casualty nurses. After following a special training scheme, the nurses diagnose, treat and dispense drugs to patients with conditions such as scratched cornea, conjunctivitis and foreign bodies in the eye. People are always asked if they would prefer to see a doctor, but most are happy to see a nurse, especially if they are treated more quickly. Before this scheme came into operation only 36% of patients were discharged within two hours - now it is up to 82%.

It is a depressing sign of the times that four years ago the hospital together with Derriford, had to address violence against staff. Most patients understand they have to wait if an emergency comes in - but some can get very aggressive, particularly if they are under the influence of drugs or drink. Personal alarms have been made available to all staff, closed circuit television installed. There are electronic door locks and screw-down seating which all helps to make the staff safer. Some staff have also been taught control and restraint and breakaway techniques.

It is always worth remembering if you have to wait at Derriford or the Eye Infirmary, that they see not far short of 100,000 patients a year who all deserve the best possible treatment in safe surroundings.

As in so many hospitals The League of Friends plays a major role. In The Royal Eye Infirmary they helped the hospital to acquire a second operating theatre giving them £35,000 for equipment, £23,000 of which was spent on a hi-tech microscope. Public donations paid for some of the smaller items in the new theatre and its adjoining waiting room. The theatre allows surgeons to treat many disorders, such as cataracts and squints, within a day. Patients arrive in the morning for their operation and recover in the purpose-built five-bed day care area. Plymouth as a result, can boast the best equipped eye treatment centre west of Bristol.

Just for the record more than 50,000 outpatients a year are seen at The Royal Eye Infirmary, and pressure on the hospital is increasing as the number of elderly people in the area continues to rise.

Mount Gould Hospital has had a considerable facelift in recent years and has a good reputation for its care and consideration of its mainly elderly or orthopaedic patients. More recently it has become the centre for acute mental illness. I was more than somewhat impressed by the treatment of an elderly friend of mine who dislocated her replacement hip and had to spend Christmas and New Year in the hospital. Her 87 years old husband with their daughter and her husband were invited to have

225

Christmas lunch in the ward. On New Year's Eve her husband was given a bed there by her side, so that they could see the New Year in together, as they had done in over fifty years of marriage. The care she was given, the patient understanding of her sometimes demanding manner, was far and away beyond the call of duty. She was well fed. Albeit not always on her favourite foods!

Across the road from Derriford Hospital is the Nuffield Hospital, offering first class private patient care for those of us able to afford it, and it is easier to afford than you might think. You do not need private medical insurance to use the services of The Nuffield. More and more patients are saving and paying their own bills for anything from an £80.00 X-ray to £7,000 for a total hip replacement operation

Nuffield's Fixed Price Direct plan is a way in which people who don't have private medical insurance, or those who find that their insurance doesn't cover a particular condition, can enjoy the benefit of private care, whilst knowing exactly how much it is going to cost. You simply pay for all your treatment, whatever it might be, in one go. The Hospital agrees the price of everything your consultant and the hospital think you will need in advance, provide you with an all inclusive price and guarantee that it won't change. So if you have to be in hospital for any longer than was first considered, you won't have to pay another penny. This frees you from the financial uncertainties that coming into a private hospital can sometimes bring. You could say the price is fixed until you are fixed!

In many ways The Nuffield compliments the expertise available at Derriford. Many of its consultants also work at Derriford. There are even times when Derriford under stress, will send a patient to The Nuffield for an operation. Nuffield also has a resident doctor on duty 24 hours a day. I learned much of this in conversation with Bryn Jones, a quiet man who conveys strength. It is his job to make sure the Nuffield runs smoothly and provides everything its patients need and does it extremely well.

What of The Nuffield in its own right? It is a first class hospital with a brilliant, efficient and caring nursing staff . The doctors and surgeons are excellent. Become a patient here and you will be given a charming en-suite bedroom, furnished comfortably and tastefully and complete with television. Every day you are offered a comprehensive menu from which to choose your meals, accompanied by the wine of your choice, if it is permitted. It is being ill in the best possible comfort and attended by professionals. Much to be recommended.

My feeling has always been that if you can afford it, you should have private medical insurance. This is not so much for your own convenience, but to alleviate the waiting time for National Health patients who have no other choice.

One of the services that Plymouth's Nuffield Hospital offers is something which would benefit all of us; a health assessment. Good health is an asset we all need to cultivate.

We would none of us dream about not getting our car serviced. It is something that is costed into your budget, but what about a service for your body? Isn't it equally important to make sure there is nothing wrong with your body? Such a 'service' enables everyone to discover what is happening to them and if anything needs attention. The Nuffield offers assessments designed to help the early identification of health risks. Confirmation that you are fit, as two thirds of people are, will bring peace of mind and renewed confidence. Alternately it identifies areas of concern. Early detection is vital for successful treatment.

The CBI will tell you that 360 million working days are lost annually through illness, at a cost of £8 billion to UK companies. An awful lot of money!

There is no guarantee that an assessment will stop an employee becoming ill but what it can do is to detect symptoms at an early stage. I always remember hearing about Graeme Souness, an ex-football player and now Manager at Blackburn Rovers,a very fit man who never shirked a check up. It was on one of these check ups that it was discovered he needed triple bypass heart surgery. Had it not been detected he could have dropped dead at any moment. It is a fact that one in four men and one in five women start developing coronary heart disease at a time when they are entering the most productive period of their working lives. It pays every employer to make sure his people get regular, thorough check ups. What better place to go than The Nuffield.

Women have slightly differing health concerns from men and Nuffield tests take this into account. For both sexes a full examination with tests and results is on offer. Women in addition have the benefit of well-woman screening.

It is worth remembering your car is replaceable you are not! Surely two and a half hours invested in a Nuffield check has to be a worthwhile investment, whatever your age.

Most of us do not even want to consider that a member of our family could be hooked on drugs and alcohol, but sadly it is the case today that many parents, husbands and wives find it is something they have to deal with. I probably would never have known of the enormous and far reaching work of Broadreach House who run Treatment Centres for Alcohol and Drug Dependence, had I not been told about it by my daughter who, as a University Lecturer and Counsellor, works in this field. This is a quietly run charitable organisation founded in 1982, offering help both to the sufferers and their families. It is a not for profit charity, based on the outskirts of Plymouth, close to Dartmoor National Park. The charity owns and manages three residential homes; Broadreach, which has 36 beds for men and women who are in need of the intensive 6-8 week treatment programme. Clients often undergoing a medically supervised detoxification during their stay at Broadreach. Closereach, the 17 bed second stage house, opened in 1987, and provides support and rehabilitation for men as they work towards returning to the community. This may take between 3 and 6 months. Longreach, for women, opened in 1996 with 15 beds but due to huge demand expanded to 20 beds in 1998. Many of the women have child care issues as well as their addiction problems, therefore much time is spent helping families to be reunited once the mother is better able to cope. This may take between 3-12 months.

The treatment approach to all three of the houses is based on the understanding that alcohol and drug dependency can best be treated if the complexity of the condition is acknowledged This means taking into consideration the interactive nature of cultural, social, psychological and physiological factors. Abstinence is the cornerstone of people's recovery at Broadreach House, particularly in the light of the severity of the dependence they have. It must be an accepted goal for recovery to be achieved. The staff's role is to help clients achieve a substance free state, not simply as an end in itself, but as a means of improving the quality of their lives. These objectives are best achieved by supporting a shift in client's behaviour, whilst emphasising the need for attitudinal change. This is achieved by active participation in the integrated , research-supported intervention employed, which provides ongoing support and encouragement for each client, enabling control of his or her life to be gained through individual programmes.

Broadreach House is also able to offer ongoing support once clients return to the community. This may take the form of follow up after care or access to the resettlement co-ordinator who can guide people through the maze of difficulties they may meet. These on-going support services are largely funded charitably by Broadreach.

Funding is probably the thing that exercises Broadreach's Chief Executive, Dick Ward, more than anything else. When I talked to this shrewd, quick thinking man, I began to understand what it means to be an unglamorous charity! Frequently the mere mention of alcohol or drug dependency will dampen the enthusiasm of any contributor. It is not something they want to talk about. This means that Broadreach has to rely on a hardcore of benefactors who repeatedly turn up to funding events, thank heavens. Dick constantly looks for grants that may be available, he reaches out to anyone who can possibly contribute. Funding the operation is always difficult. Clients rely heavily on overstretched and insufficient budgets of Health and Local Authorities. Some clients pay for themselves but Broadreach House is always aware of its charitable, founding ethos and strives, whenever possible, to assist those who need help regardless of their financial situation. Broadreach really is a very worthwhile charity and stretches way out beyond Plymouth. Dick Ward heads a European council looking at ways and means to combat drug and alcohol dependency. The success of Broadreach is a shining example of what can be done to tackle this very difficult subject.

Everything in Government today seems to relate to League Tables. Sometimes they are helpful and sometimes not. I was delighted to read that Plymouth has emerged as one of the few councils in England to meet tough Government targets for monitoring children on its 'at risk' register.

The council has been ranked at the top of the Government league tables charting the work of 150 social services departments providing for children in care - and was one of just 29 councils found to have reviewed all child protection cases during 2000.

Another recipient of a standard of excellence has been awarded to Plymouth Mencap Society. It has become one of the latest winners of the 'Investors in People' accolade for its staff development programmes. The society based in

Outland Road, employs 17 full and part-time staff and runs a range of services for people with learning disabilities. Among its recent achievements is a visiting support service for people with learning disabilities, set up in response to calls from parents and families and a three day conference on self-advocacy held at Plymouth Pavilions. It has also started a Community Enabling Service that helps users access services such as further education and cinema visits.

In addition to its hospitals Plymouth has an excellent reputation for its General Practitioners. In the years since I returned to Plymouth in 1963 I have only ever been on the list of two practices. The first was the Mannamead Surgery where my family and I could not have had better treatment. The only reason I changed was a move to a different part of the city where I was lucky enough to become a patient at Stoke Surgery who are equally caring.

Modern purpose built surgeries seem to be almost the norm today and gone are the rather, dreary, brown-painted, hard-seated waiting rooms. I have met many doctors over the years and at one time did market research for a pharmaceutical company. We had many a good evening in the Moat House, discussing new drugs and accompanying the conversation with some food and more than a glass or two of wine. These were times when I got to know quite a lot about the doctors themselves and how they spent their precious free time. Rugby, fishing and cricket seemed to be the most favourite pastimes. I learned also that doctors are not persuaded to favour any pharmaceutical company by such evenings or by any promise of free tickets for Twickenham or a day out at Lords, or even a fishing weekend. When asked to try out new drugs, they took the lead from the consultants in hospitals, rather than from any form of advertising or promotion.

Most of us are worried about, or by our teeth. Access to a dentist unless you can afford to go privately, is very difficult. At present only three dentists in Plymouth accept NHS patients on to their lists compared to 118 a few years ago. As I write a staggering 54% of people in Plymouth are no longer registered with a dentist.

The new Dental Access Centre could well help many people. It is run by the Plymouth Community Trust and staffed by NHS dentists.

The service is available on the NHS but is restricted to people not registered at a dental practice. Here patients can get any course of treatment necessary to give them healthy teeth again but are then expected to sign on with a local dentist for any future treatment.

It is run mainly as a drop in centre for initial consultations but some treatments require booked appointments. Open five days a week from 8-15-8pm it has four full time dentists.

There are many people in Plymouth who need the care of either Nursing or Residential Homes. There are many of them and all well run. Cost varies but even those having to rely entirely on help from the Social Services can find comfortable homes. One of the greatest problems for these dedicated Residential and Nursing Home owners, is making ends meet. There have been rumblings recently that many of them will not be able to carry on without Government support. It is a difficult quandary but it is one that has to be addressed with so many of us living longer and longer and frequently without families able to care for us.

It would be invidious really to pick any home out out but from personal knowledge I can say one that is run excellently by Doctor Pepper and his wife, is Vicarage House Residential Home, 1 Honicknowle Lane. Silly things count; they allow one elderly gentleman a small patch of garden which he, at almost a hundred, loves to tend. His sight is bad, so much so that he frequently puts bulbs in upside down, but there is always someone to rescue the situation and both he and his fellow residents, watch the results keenly. It makes a talking point.

Age Concern play a great part in the welfare of senior citizens in Plymouth. Their premises in Hoegate Street are busy every day providing a day centre and all that entails. Coaches bring people to the centre and return them to their homes. Good food at reasonable prices and companionship provide the elderly with something to look forward to. The staff are thoughtful and kind and unfailingly willing to listen to problems. Various entertainments and outings are also arranged.

Another building, the four storey centre on the site of the former Astor Institute at Mount Gould owes its being to the generosity of the widow of a Barbican boy, William Venton, who became a noted architect and one who retained his love of Plymouth generally, all his life. The gift, £3.5 million to Plymouth Age Concern was the biggest single donation ever made to any organisation in the city.

The building, overlooking the River Plym, provides residential care for 25 active people over 60, giving them their much cherished independence. Each resident has a comfortably furnished bed-sitting room with kitchen facilities, separate bathroom and toilet. For companionship and meals there is a private dining room, a large restaurant or a coffee lounge where anyone is welcome to drop in. This one gesture will benefit Plymothians for many generations to come and is not the first time Plymouth has been on the receiving end from the generosity of the Ventons. In 1988 Mrs Venton gave £55,000 towards the building of the Plymstock Age Concern Centre which was named after her.

William Venton spent the first fifteen years of his life on the Barbican where the fishing boats 'adopted' him and he spent many, never to be forgotten times aboard with the crews. In spite of living firstly in London and then in Durban, South Africa, he never forgot the happiness of those early years.

This is a moment to give thanks and praise for the efficiency of The Ambulance Service. I hate the sound of their sirens and flashing blue lights mainly because I don't want to think of the reason behind the noise. Yet for people involved in an accident inside or outside the home, sudden heart attacks, strokes and other illnesses, the sound of the approaching paramedics is the most welcome sound they could wish to hear. Quiet, calm professional care takes over the moment they arrive. Something we should all be thankful for. Their skills have saved so many lives and comforted so many distressed people.

A different kind of caring in the community is at Astor Hall, Devonport Road, Stoke, where the Plymouth and District Disabled Fellowship has been providing support and care for disabled people in the community for over 40 years. It enjoys a membership of approximately ninety disabled people who live in their own homes in the city and its outlying districts. These members find the support of the Fellowship's Welfare Officer to be of particular benefit. They and their carers draw extra peace of mind from the knowledge that they will be visited regularly by someone who can provide positive assistance.

Astor Hall is also a residential home for 28 disabled people, from 18 years of age upwards, mainly from Plymouth, but some from other parts of the country. The home is a member of the Residential Care Homes Trust and is registered with Devon County Council. It is fully accredited by them as a provider of care. The high level of support given to residents is supervised 24 hours a day by qualified nursing staff.

A full programme of daytime and evening entertainment and occupational activity is provided for the benefit of both residents and community members, who are transported by means of the Fellowship's specially adapted vehicles. Astor Hall is a cheerful, friendly place to visit.

St Luke's Hospice from the day it first opened in a small house in Plymstock and now at its bigger, better equipped premises at Mount Batten, is one of the best things that ever happened to Plymouth. Its warmth, its sense of calm and purpose makes you realise that it is about living and not about dying at all. It is a place of true holistic nursing within a family atmosphere. No one could possibly doubt the genuine care, the laughter, the coping with stress. Nor would anyone want to pretend that people do not go there without problems and some will result in death, but when you have been part of this enriching experience in this community, death will never be quite such a grim reaper, nor so frightening for those at the end of their life or their relatives who have to rebuild their own lives.

Financially St Luke's struggles. It is a charity and relies on public funding. We need St Luke's Hospice and in turn they desperately need our support.

One of the most painful features of bereavement and one of constant reminder, is where the remains of one's loved ones are laid. The scattering of ashes after cremations has become the norm but there are many who still have burial plots and it is the care of these plots that has caused so much anguish in recent years at Ford Park Cemetery. The cemetery became almost derelict as a result of the failure of the private company who owned it. Now, after a tremendous campaign to save the cemetery, spearheaded by Jean Northey and Ted Northmore, a new headquarters for the site is open in the grounds of the cemetery and is the base for volunteer workers. The cemetery is well maintained and an investment of £5,000 was made available to create a computerised database of names, grave locations and transcriptions. Already people are starting to use the office to get information about graves. The new office was opened by the Lord Mayor who thanked the volunteers, on behalf of the city, for their hard work. He said 'Plymouth's history is recorded here, but most of all it is the place of rest for our loved ones. What happened to the cemetery in recent years was an absolute disgrace and I am delighted that Plymothians have now got together to restore Ford Park.'

The new office is just part of a massive project to restore the 19th century cemetery to its former glory. The trust, now managing the site, was set up following a campaign by The Evening Herald to save the cemetery after the private company running it was forced into liquidation.

Going back in time and adding just a touch more history, if you happen to drive along North Road West passing the old St Dunstan's Abbey building on your right, you will see an opening which reveals a small war memorial and a number of polished headstones, all of which relate back to the time when this was part of a Naval burial ground. It has been beautifully constructed and has a quiet dignity. A mark of respect to the many officers and men who were buried here.

Mt. Batten, site of R.A.F. Mt. Batten.

Brittany Ferries

Chapter XII

By Land, Sea, Air, Train & Bus

Without its spectacular waterfront Plymouth would be little different from many another city and so in this chapter Plymouth, the port, takes prime position. Millbay Docks owned and operated by Associated British Ports, has been the major player in the waterfront for centuries. There are times when I look at the growth of the docks at Southampton and then at what is happening in Plymouth, I wonder if ABT regard Plymouth as the poor relation. Plymouth deserves every bit as much investment as Southampton; something that perhaps Plymothians should shout about. Though I hasten to add that this is not in any way a criticism of the present manager of Millbay Docks, Ray Escrig.

In the early days Millbay existed before Plymouth became Plymouth because from the 12th century north, eastward of the present site, was a creek called Sourpole, which spread over the low lying land now occupied by the Octagon, Union Street Phoenix Street and Rendle Street. It was here that Ralph of Valletort, an early member of the well known Plymouth family, granted to God and the Priors of Plympton a convenient place upon which to erect a mill. It was in early times that the inlet on the west side of the Hoe became known as Mill Bay.

At one time ships were accommodated as far inland as the Octagon, a fact confirmed by the fact that anchors have been discovered there. However, the first attempt at dock formation at Millbay appears in a map prepared in the late1830's where the Union Dock is shown between Martin and Phoenix Streets. This dock was the property of three Plymothians, Richard Derry, David Derry and James Meadows-Rendel. James Meadows-Rendel was a distinguished engineer, David Derry was Mayor of Plymouth from 1850-1851 and Derry's Clock in the centre of the city was given to the Corporation by a different member of the same family. Derry and Company were Cartage Contractors and Railway Agents, the company later being absorbed in the next century by the Great Western Railway.

The quarries, which can still be seen at West Hoe, were in full swing in 1840, steadily removing the famous Hoe in the recovery of limestone. The only other dock in the vicinity was the small West Hoe Dock situated in the quarries and here the excavated stone and lime from the adjacent kilns was loaded into small vessels which passed to and from the dock through a small channel located to the south east of the root portion of Trinity Pier.

Thomas Gill was Mayor of Plymouth in 1836 and the first person to hold that office under the Municipal Reform Act. He was the owner of the West Hoe estate and proprietor of the quarries, and it was he who realised the potential that existed within the Mill Bay for development. In 1840 he obtained an Act of Parliament which gave him powers to deepen the bed at Mill Bay and to erect at his own expense a pier and other works. This was the same year that the 'penny post' was introduced.

Several well known engineers were engaged in the construction of the docks at Mill Bay and the first of these was Mr Meadows-Rendel, also part owner of the Union Dock. He was ingenious and inventive. He designed Laira Bridge for Lord Morley, the first in England to be built of cast iron.

In 1840 the developers were given powers to take tolls in respect of the facilities they provided. Thomas Gill, as owner of the West Hoe Estate, was allowed to continue receiving tolls during the time of war in respect of prisoners landed at the new pier and passing through the estate to Mill prison, which accommodated thousands of prisoners during the Napoleonic Wars and earlier. At this time the Royal Marine Barracks had a landing place for boats on the beach at the rear of Caroline Place. On the East Quay adjacent to the present Trinity Pier, there was a drawbridge to enable vessels to pass to and fro from the West Hoe Quarry owned by Thomas Gill.

Thomas Gill was a wealthy man but he could not sustain the cost of developing Mill Bay. An Act of Parliament, called the Great Western Docks Act, in August 1846, authorised the expenditure of £980,000 to be subscribed in £20 shares and permit borrowing powers to a further £30,000. It empowered the new company to buy the existing works from Thomas Gill who became one of its directors. The building of the inner basin, and the provision of a dry dock, was part of the new programme. It was perhaps a prophetic inspiration for this dock company to be named Great Western because at the time the Great Western Railway had only reached Bristol. The directors could have had no idea that 32 years later the dock would become part of that railway's undertakings.

Isambard Kingdom Brunel was appointed Engineer to the new Great Western Dock Company in 1846 and he used to travel to Plymouth in a first class GWR carriage which had the wheels coming up under the seats, a door between the two halves of the compartment and the luggage on the roof. He oversaw a great deal of work at this time. The inner basin and the dry dock were completed by the end of 1856.

An unexpected source of revenue came into the company via the dry dock; large quantities of fish became trapped in it and a record catch of mullet on the 16th October 1875 was sold for a considerable amount of money.

When Millbay Docks were taken over by the Great Western Railway in 1875, a rock stood off the end of Trinity Pier. This was called Brunel's Rock because the great man had been compelled to leave it there when the pier was constructed; funds were not available to remove it. As a consequence vessels entering the inner basin had to pass through a narrow channel. This led to trouble. In 1880 the Company was faced with a law suit following damages to a grain vessel which struck the rock and defied the efforts of four tugs to move her. The company was required to compensate the owners not only for the cost of repairs but for the 45 days the ship was out of commission.

Today's environmentalists would have been horrified at what followed. The rock was too expensive to retain and was blown up by explosives killing or stunning thousands of fish. The seagulls had a field day!

In those days the docks were free from labour disputes although a labour agitator, Bill Sprow, demonstrated his annoyance by pulling the Dock Inspector's beard violently in 1890. He was fined £2.10s 0d!

Over the years the docks were improved and further building carried out. For some time Plymouth had been the depot for Government emigrants, and the ocean passenger traffic following in its steps began in 1850 with the introduction of the Cape Mail Union Line. Though the emigration traffic did not pass through the Great Western Docks, its development helped to show the shipping lines the value of Plymouth as a passenger port. In 1876 twenty five vessels left Plymouth with 10,194 emigrants for Australia and New Zealand. These were three vessels for Sydney with 1,118 passengers, two vessels for Queensland with 428 passengers; one vessel for Canterbury with 283 passengers; and nineteen vessels for Adelaide with 8,303 passengers. This figure did not include the large number of passengers who sailed regularly for America.

Emigrants, many of whom arrived by steamer from Ireland, would spend weeks in Plymouth waiting for the sailing ships to arrive. They were accommodated at the Emigrants Depot at Baltic Wharf where every adult was awarded a sum of money by the government to cover his travelling expenses to Plymouth.

With few exceptions, ocean liners never came alongside. Plymouth was only used as a port of call because a great saving of time could be achieved by the steamers anchoring in the Sound or in Cawsand Bay and tenders bringing the passengers, baggage and mail ashore.

The busy tenders serviced all sorts of passenger ships and they themselves were a motley crew. Over the years there were paddle steamers, twin screw steamers, and occasionally a purpose built one like the 'Sir Francis Drake' built in 1873, and worked until 1903.

At a very early stage in the development of Millbay Docks it was realised the saving of time for overseas passengers and mail was a worthwhile benefit to be obtained. A Government decision in 1849 to award mail contracts to steamship companies in open competition, thereby replacing the Admiralty Packet Services, led to the promotion of Plymouth as an overseas mail port. This was not altogether successful, with some disappointing times set on the runs, and eventually the Post Office cancelled the contract. Peninsula and Orient began calling at Plymouth in 1874 and this was the beginning of a regular service. In 1877 every passenger landing at Millbay Docks was charged 6d which covered his baggage. Believe it or not, some passengers thought this exorbitant and local newspapers received letters of complaint; passengers believed there should be no landing fee at all.

From 1879 onwards Plymouth became more and more dominant as a passenger port. By 1930 many famous ocean liners were using Millbay Docks: the 'Mauretania', 'Bremen'. Lusitania' and 'Ile de France' were calling here. The 'Normandie' called on her maiden voyage in 1935 and the following year the 'Queen Mary'. My memories of these great ships are still firmly imprinted on my mind. As a youngster I used to sail my dinghy out of Cawsand where I lived and became used to being hailed by the crews especially the Dutch Fleet, 'Vollendam' and 'Rotterdam' who came regularly. The crew would throw gifts down to me - not always sensibly! On one occasion my head was the recipient of a' whole, round, red Edam cheese which almost knocked me unconscious. They were exciting years which came to an abrupt end with the advent of World War II.

War had an immediate effect on Millbay Docks. In September 1939 fourteen survivors from the 'SS Kensington Court' were landed after being rescued off the Scilly Isles by seaplane - probably the first recorded case of a ship's crew being rescued by a seaplane. On October 15th 1939, four hundred and forty four survivors were landed from a number of different ships. In January 1940, the 'SS Pacific Shipper' arrived in Millbay Docks in a damaged condition and was berthed at West Wharf. She had 8,000 tons of general cargo including fresh fruit, canned goods, timber and pig lead. This was the first of a steady flow of damaged ships arriving throughout the war.

From June 1st to the 28th 1940, not a single day passed without a contribution to the war effort. It is impossible now to imagine how the work force coped in those days with the pressure of work, anxiety over members of their own families fighting on the Continent and the injuries, exhaustion that they must have seen that summer when refugees and troops streamed through the docks.

Between June 11th and July 7th, 1940, over 67,000 members of the British and Allied troops disembarked from France. 45,000 were British and the rest a mixture of French, Belgium, Polish and Czechoslovakian. Between the 22nd and 28th June almost 3,800 refugees from France were disembarked. France capitulated on July 15th 1940, and the 'SS Penchateau' on passage between two ports in France was diverted to Millbay Docks with her cargo of military stores, bread, oats, hay and wine.

Plymothians gave each Plymouth air raid a number and Number 61 occurred on the 27th August 1940 destroying a car, doing extensive damage to the tender Sir John Hawkins, and holing the pontoon and buildings on Millbay and Trinity Piers. By the 15th December the tender, 'Sir William Raleigh', anchored in the Sound was hit and a number of the crew injured. By the 13th January 1941, Plymouth was experiencing air raid No 273 between 6.30pm and 9.35pm. At least 200 incendiary bombs fell in the docks area, and so it went on relentlessly. On the 19th February a high explosive shell fell on number six shed on North Quay close to where the digital readout weighbridge is now located. The most sustained damage occurred just after King George VI and Queen Elizabeth had left the city on the 20th March. In the docks, Jewson's timber yard, Sheds 76 and 81 were burnt out. Clyde Sheds badly damaged by a high explosive bomb and two cranes at Clyde Quay badly damaged. A high explosive bomb felled the operating gear of West Outer Gate. The SS Marie II and two naval tugs were sunk at West Wharf plus two crabbers which burnt and sank in an inner basin. Worse was to follow. Even greater damage was done on the following night.

The heavy bombardment of Millbay Docks was repeated on the 22nd and 23rd April, 1941 when the estimated cost of the damage was £143,400. These two nights wreaked havoc on the buildings in the dock area and it demanded a very special kind of courage to report for work and endure bombing night after night, sometimes for hours at a time.

I can vouch personally for the uncertainty and anxiety we all felt. When you left home in the morning you had no idea whether your home or your workplace would be in evidence by the evening. Yet we got through it and smiled for most of the time. I could write on for pages listing all the damage but suffice it to say it was considerable. It did not stop work being carried out every day.

In 1943 the Admiralty started building the grid in the corner of the outer basin which is still visible from the corner of East Quay near the present workshop. The silo which still dominates the Plymouth skyline, was first used in February 1943 and camouflaged the following month.

On the 17th January 1944, the Prime Minister landed at Millbay Docks at 11.18pm accompanied by Mrs Churchill and their daughter Sarah, who was in the W.A.A.F's. They were returning from the Teheran Conference during which time Winston had been severely ill with pneumonia.

The intensive preparations for D-Day brought untold work to Millbay Docks. There were many rehearsals and once again the docks were in use for the return of wounded men and women, or the landing of prisoners of war. Even the Nazi flag was seen at West Wharf when a captured German hospital ship was berthed on September 20th 1944. A week later the 'SS General Black' also berthed at West Wharf to embark 1,000 German prisoners of war for shipment to America.

In October a French trawler lay alongside East Quay with 10,000 bottles of wine on board which three French wine merchants wished to exchange with the British Government for arms to be used by the Free French - the offer was declined!

With the war nearing its end it was a time for counting the cost. For most Plymothians it was a time of hardship but I suspect for those who had worked in and around the docks throughout the war years, the horror of war would remain for ever deeply engrained. Casualties passed through in large number in very short periods of time and the cost of life and human suffering was very apparent. In January and February 1945, there were over three thousand casualties.

The first Ocean Mail and Passenger liner returned to Plymouth on the 19th June 1945, after a period of almost six years. In August 1945, the King arrived at Millbay Docks in the royal train, on his way to welcome President Truman on board the battleship HMS Renown, which was anchored in the Sound.

In June 1946, all the tenders were returned to their peace time occupations with civilian crews, and the enormous contribution of Millbay Docks and its staff to the war effort, came to an end.

Times had changed by the end of the war. Air travel was becoming a faster means of moving around the world, and in 1958 the 'Ile de France' made her last voyage calling at Plymouth, as she had on her maiden voyage 31 years earlier. P & O who, through companies which it had absorbed, could trace its links back as far as 1850,was persuaded to resume calls with its Australian vessels in 1962. This lasted just a year when they too stopped.

The fact that Millbay Docks remains successful in spite of the chequered career is almost entirely down to the skills of Associated British Ports and their dedicated local staff whose aims are totally directed at making the docks the most sought after in the world. They have had to be flexible, forward thinking and at the same time cautious in their use of the land and water available to them. This adaptability was highlighted at the beginning of the 1970's when Breton producers decided to alter their transport arrangements to the United Kingdom by introducing a Roll-on Roll-off operation to ensure goods were not repeatedly handled. As Breton produce formed a large part of the business of the docks, it was imperative A.B.P. made Millbay Docks capable of handling the traffic by the revised method. Facilities were constructed during 1972 and brought into use in January 1973, coinciding with Britain's entry into the European Economic Community.

At first there were only three sailings per week but it eventually increased to one a day. For part of the year vessels arrived during the evening so produce could be delivered to fruit and vegetable markets ready for sale the next morning.

In the beginning only freight facilities were provided, but interest from the general public was so strong that during 1973 limited opportunities were made available for passenger movements and almost 14,000 passengers were carried in that first year. It became obvious that substantial growth could result from obtaining passenger vessels and providing shore based passenger facilities. This part of the activity at Millbay Docks has grown significantly and services for both passengers and freight have been extended to cover Northern Spain.

Before 1978 when the Spanish route was introduced, the then British Transport Docks Board (later to become Associated British Ports) had identified the possibility of linking Plymouth with Northern Spain. The savings on steaming times, and utilisation of hauliers' vehicles, was to prove attractive and the service came into existence in 1978 with two sailings each week predominantly for passengers. Limited amounts of freight were carried until in June 1980, an additional ferry was obtained by Brittany Ferries to provide extra accommodation for freight vehicles.

Brittany Ferries has become very much a part of the life of Plymouth just as Millbay Docks has been since it was a creek called Sourpole in the 12th century. I have no doubt they will continue to grow and prosper as Plymouth does.

I visited the offices of A.B.P. on Millbay Docks to chat with the current Manager. An interesting man, Ray Escrig, is a Plymothian and I found in him the same desire to see Plymouth succeed as I have. His vision for the Docks is comprehensive but shows just that bit of caution which tells him not to allow too much in the way of residential building in the remaining part of Millbay which needs developing. He recognises that houses can be built almost anywhere but waterfront is scarce and should be carefully used. One of the things I discovered, which really has nothing to do with what I am currently writing, is that on a wall in what is now the Millbay Marina Village, complete with moorings for residents, is a plaque which informs us that here survivors of the crew of the Titanic were landed.

The work that has been done in Millbay over the last decade is tremendous. At one time it had a run down derelict look, now it is smart, well maintained and every inch that has been developed has been used to good advantage. Customs areas, car parking for passenger traffic and freight. A vast building which houses Brittany Ferries and provides passengers with excellent facilities stands at one end. The road leading in is new and pristine. As I write this virtually all the ugly and almost derelict buildings just outside the gates of the port have been demolished and new buildings are rapidly rising. Renwicks, the VW dealers in the city are to have their new headquarters here. The area needs imaginative development and quickly. What about knocking a road right through to join on to Western Approach, picking its way from the Dock Gates along in front of the Duke of Cornwall, running behind the Pavilions and the Continental and coming out by the traffic lights in Union Street? Crazy idea? Not so. It would enable us to say that once leaving the docks one could drive straight up the road, all the way to Glasgow!!

Ray Escrig is a keen exponent of the ever growing cruise business in Plymouth. Several Cruise liners call in regularly now whether they are from Festive Cruises, Travelscope, or one of the many cruise operators. The Sound is a marvellous berth, some of the smaller ones can berth alongside. It brings business to the city and certainly adds kudos around the world. The cruise operators will tell you how much they appreciate the efficiency and co-operation of Associated British Ports.

In my enthusiasm for the history and current activities of Millbay Docks, I must not forget the importance to Plymouth of Cattewater Harbour. Today the main activities centre on Cattedown Wharves, chiefly involved in the import of petroleum products, and Victoria Wharves, specialising in dry bulk. Between them more than a million tonnes of cargo is handled in a 175 hectare stretch of sheltered water which includes the original port of Plymouth, where the Phoenecians were among the early traders,

Incidentally it is said that we can attribute clotted cream to the Phoenecians. Over 3000 years ago, Devon, Cornwall and part of Somerset were known as Dunmonia, and tin was mined on Dartmoor and Bodmin Moor. At that time the Phoenecians were great travellers and traders, and it is thought that they came to these far off shores to trade for tin and other metals. Because of the long sea journeys, the Phoenecians 'cooked' their milk to preserve it for the journey, and make it last longer. Their milk was usually that of goats, but when they came to our shores they found cows were more readily available than goats. The breed of cow is very important for the butter content, and today we know that the rich traditional cream we receive comes from the Jersey, Guernsey and South Devon cows. So it is presumed that the breed used all those years ago was the South Devon, and the cooked milk produced what we know today as Clotted Cream. This is not quite the end of the story - the tin and other metals purchased by the Phoenecians, had to be brought to their ships which we believe anchored in Plymouth Sound and the argument is, that the metal was transported down the rivers by barge and landed on what we now call Drake's Island. The awaiting Phoenecians would load their ships with the metals, and with supplies for the long journey home. Now it is quite possible that this is where they would cook the milk, because it made good sense to leave it as late as possible, to lessen the chance of it 'going off'. So if this theory is correct then Clotted Cream was actually invented on Drake's Island! Fascinating isn't it?

Another interesting part of that story is the link between Drake's Island and the Cornish shore. To most sailors in this part of the world there is an area in the Sound known as 'The Bridges', which is a line of submerged rocks between the island and the shore, and which could prove dangerous if you were not aware they were there. Again, the theory is, that these were once covered in silt which has been washed away over the decades, but that at low tide they once formed a causeway which could be walked upon, right out to the island. This also lends credence to the theory of the Phoenecians anchoring at the island, and trading with the locals for their produce.

The vast area of dockside occupied by Brittany Ferries as offices, landing and boarding areas plus substantial parking , buzz with hectic life when the ferries are in waiting to embark or disembark their passengers and vehicles. You can sense the excitement of the holidaymakers and the earnestness of those who are here to attend their business and overall the supremely competent Brittany Ferries staff oversee the whole with an iron hand in a velvet glove. Sometimes it is all very straightforward but by no means always. There are days of disruption caused by bad weather and road congestion - a difficult situation to contend with. Then, because of Plymouth's situation there are those who risk their freedom for the money to be had from the trafficking of drugs. The Customs Officers, with the aid of International intelligence, are adept at winkling out offenders. Brittany Ferries runs a highly professional and well organised service to the Continent which has enabled them to combat the competition posed by the Channel Tunnel, at one time a possible threat.

In the last few years the Company has done much to consolidate its position in the City, developing its business and making it even more efficient. It has invested heavily in refurbishing what many people will remember as the 'old Ferry Terminal Building' in Millbay Docks. Whilst the shell remains, the building is otherwise barely recognisable as it has been totally remodelled and furnished to high standards to accommodate the Brittany Ferries 'IT and Corporate Training' functions. The building is now known as Kerisnel House' in memory of the first ship that made the crossing from Roscoff to Plymouth back in 1972.

Since 1997 the Company has invested heavily in updating its computer systems to handle reservations and port operations. The Reservations 'Call Centre' in Plymouth has grown substantially underpinning the Company's commitment to the City. Its Corporate Training Centre hosts courses for its employees from all 3 UK sites and occasionally, from France.

All this adds to the excellence of the wide range of holidays, short breaks and ferry services. It is also right up to the minute in offering internet access and on line quotations and reservations for its services.

People come from all over the country to enjoy crossings in the comfortable ships. There are daily services to France. The Val de Loire is the flagship and operates the Plymouth to Santander service twice a week. Whilst on board it is very much like enjoying a cruise. The cabins are comfortable, the food is excellent and the entertainment provided is lively, colourful and good fun. Needless to say the bars are well stocked. The Normandie, the Barfleur and the Bretagne are equally comfortable and the service is first class. There is no doubt that these large cruiseferries persuade many holiday makers to steer clear of the Channel Tunnel, largely because it makes sense. Brittany Ferries serves the western channel and so more than two out of three of the firm's current passengers would have to make a detour to get to the tunnel. Little time or money would be saved anyway because they would have to drive further in France, paying for petrol, tolls, meals and even overnight accommodation.

For many it is the fun of the crossing, the entertainment provided, which also includes games for children, that makes a great start to any holiday.

Plymouth itself benefits from the presence of Brittany Ferries. Passengers frequently stay overnight - indeed there are hotels and guest houses on Plymouth Hoe which are specially geared for Ferry Passengers. In addition both the Theatre Royal, the Cinemas and the City Centre shops gain from the willingness of travellers to be entertained and to enjoy different shops.

Brittany Ferries is a fine example of working together with the community to make Plymouth commercially successful.

Proving that small is beautiful is probably the best way of introducing the water taxis, little passenger ferries and pleasure cruisers which are so much a part of Plymouth life. Tamar Cruising operates the ferry that crosses the river from Admiral's Hard in Stonehouse to Cremyll and Mount Edgcumbe on the other side. As a family we use it regularly and I have done so all my life. Plymouth people tend to use it as an easy way of reaching the glory of Mt Edgcumbe Park, generously given to the city by the Earl of Mt Edgcumbe just after World War II.

All day and every day the little ferry chugs its way to and from taking people who live on the other side to and from work and to link up with the buses that regularly leave from Cremyll for Cawsand, Whitsand Bay, Millbrook and Torpoint. I used the ferry as a child on my way home from school to Cawsand. That was almost 70 years ago, and I believe one of the ferries, the old Armadillo is still in service.

Nothing has changed really except there is now a car park on the Plymouth side where visitors can leave their vehicles and on the Cremyll side gone are the rickety old Skinner buses that used to run to Cawsand; they have been replaced by more modern versions. On a fine day it is a beautiful, peaceful crossing with the elegant, handsome Royal William Yard on one side and the busy Mayflower Marina on the other. It is still a slippery landing on the Plymouth side at low tide and the gangway which is run out for landing on either side is just as rickety! The ferry still has the same marine smell, makes the same noises and the crew are friendly and caring.

The owners of Tamar Cruising gave me an account of a journey in 1698 which enchanted me and I thought you might enjoy reading it as well.

The Journey of Celia Fieans to Cornwall
Her Account of Crossing Cremyll Ferry

'From Plymouth I went one mile to Cribly (Cremyll) Ferry which is a very
hazardous passage by reason of three tydes meeting; had I known the danger
before, I should not have been very willing to have gone it, not but that it is
the constant way all people go, and saved several miles, riding; I was at least
an hour going over, it was about a mile but indeed in some places notwithstanding
there was five men rowed and I set my own men to row also, I do believe we made
not a step of the way for a quarter of an hour, but blessed by God I came
safely over; but those ferry boats are so wet and then the sea and wind is always
cold to be upon, that I never faile to catch cold in a ferry-boate as I did this day, having
2 more ferrys to cross tho' none so bad or half so long as this; thence Millbrooke 2
miles and went along by water and had full view of the Dockyards.'

Not much has changed. The tides still meet but are counteracted by the power of the
engines and the crossing takes but a bare ten minutes. It can certainly be cold and wet
but there is a cabin and it certainly saves many miles if you want to get to Cawsand or
Millbrook.

Judging from the several yarns about the Tamar crossing which appeared in the
Evening Herald before 1946 things were not too different then either. I thank the
Evening Herald for the permission to quote one.

The Cremyll Ferry

244

'To Cawsand folk who sail the seas
From Cremyll to the Hard
To me seem very hard to please
And apt to disregard
The vast amount of fun they get
When sailing to and fro
They always have a chance to bet
On 'will it stop or go?'
But when they have to cross in fog
That's when the fun begins,
And every soul is all agog
And thinking of past sins.
Up in the bow like sheep they crowd
The skipper to advise
Although this should not be allowed
This right they exercise
Some tell him he should go to port
Whilst others favour starboard
And ancient mariners have sought
That he should steer to larboard
In spite of this we oft arrive
Right at the spot we aimed for
And if we don't the rest contrive
The skipper all to blame for.

And having reached the other side
We bravely breast the slope
And put on speed with every stride
To catch the bus we hope
But as we get to Durnford Street
It dashes past like smoke
These busmen have no boat to meet
And love this little joke
And then we have the Turnstile Stakes
For those who're homeward bound
Each one in hand his life he takes
As up the ramp we pound
The leaders wildly storm the bus
They proudly sit in state
The panting losers stop and cuss
They have to walk or wait.

And when the ferry plies no more
And all of us are fliers
Our wretched offspring we will bore
(Tis said 'All men are liars')
With gruesome tales no man could crown
No tall yarn being barred
Of how we ran the Armadillo down
From Cremyll to the Hard.

245

In the year 2000 we are not fliers, our children's children enjoy the ferry which still serves us faithfully - and long may it do so.

In addition to running the Cremyll Ferry, Tamar Cruising operate regular cruises up and down the Hamoaze to see the warships and on to Calstock, a supremely beautiful trip which gives you a totally different view of Plymouth. The Hamoaze will give you a quick look at what is destined to become the finest Naval and Maritime Museum and Visitor Centre in the whole of Europe. At the moment it is in embryo but I predict that within five years every cruise boat and water taxi will stop at the pontoons on the edge of what is now the South Yard of the Naval Base, to allow visitors to disembark and find themselves enveloped in one of the most exciting experiences they will ever have. You can read more about this and in greater depth elsewhere in the book.

From the departure points on Plymouth Hoe you can also cruise up towards Newton Ferrers and the River Yealm. Going either way, it is something that visitors to Plymouth and indeed Plymothians, too, need to be reminded by such a gentle voyage like this, how beautiful is our heritage. We all need reminding from time to time.

If Plymothians have one fault, it is that they are too complacent of the endless beauty around them.

Special occasions and evening trips are part of the itinerary with Tamar Cruising. Throughout the season there are all sorts of different trips with supper or a barbecue as part of the fun. The boats are licensed, the fares not too expensive and it is a great evening out.

Torpoint Ferries have been the backbone of Tamar crossings for a very long time. The advent of the Tamar Bridge in 1960 eased their burden but without the crossing regularly from Devonport to Torpoint, many miles would be put on people's journeys. For the visitor the short crossing is an interesting experience. You can abandon your car and climb to the top deck which gives you a splendid view of the activity of the  Hamoaze, a clear appreciation of the number of Royal Naval ships tied up alongside the Dockyard wall, the enclosed Submarine and Frigate complexes where ships undergo repairs and refits.

Plymouth has one of the best public transport systems in the country. It is plentiful, covers the city thoroughly and while it is not cheap, it is not as steep as many places.

The Bus Station at Bretonside is an eye opener. If you sit there long enough you will see buses and coaches departing at regular intervals for destinations as far away as Scotland and as close as Plympton. It is also the starting point and the destination of many tour companies who whisk you away to magical places for a package holiday in Europe or an afternoon's mystery tour somewhere quite near to the City. The booking service is efficient and when I did a sort of mini market - research with coach and bus users I found that 90% had no complaints whatsoever, and of those who had, I found that in general their problem had been resolved amicably.

One small instance I can quote is of two elderly ladies waiting for a bus in Looe to take them back to Plymouth. It was the last bus of the day on that particular route. The ladies waited but no bus appeared. The ladies maintained that the bus must have left early leaving them stranded. They had to get a taxi back to Plymouth at a cost of £20. Not good for pensioners. The company concerned was The Western National. When they were telephoned and told what had happened, they sent two inspectors to see the ladies, courteously took statements and went away to investigate. The ladies were convinced that they would hear no more but before very long the inspectors were back with an apology, a refund of the £20 and two return tickets from Plymouth to Looe to be used whenever the ladies wished.

When I talked to Western National about this incident they told me that not only was it very important to maintain good customer relationships but it was equally important to ensure that their drivers did not leave even half a minute before the scheduled time. I was impressed by their courtesy and efficiency and I would add that they had no idea I was writing a book.

In June 1892 Plymouth Corporation bought the Plymouth Tramways Company and so began the history of what is one of the most go ahead and efficient bus companies in the country Plymouth Citybus. Jonathan Bayliss is now the Managing Director of the company and his description of himself 'I am essentially a bus man' comes across strongly in his conversation. His knowledge and love of this form of transport is evident. He came to Plymouth from Yorkshire, having worked in Bristol and The Midlands before that and en route, so to speak. acquired a vast knowledge of what is required to keep a company like Citybus running smoothly, effectively and financially viable. I think we are all impressed by the number of sleek, low entry buses now in service. Designed to help the young mother with a pushchair, shoppers with their bags and the elderly; they are comfortable, quiet and pleasant to ride in. Seldom are the unwieldy double deckers to be seen in general use. They are now almost entirely devoted to school runs, a service which has become a large part of the company's business. I live opposite the College of Further Education and regularly watch the endless stream of double deckers disgorging their passengers. Multiply that number by all the schools in the city and you realise just how many buses are in service especially for that role. Talking of school buses inevitably, in this day and age, led me to ask Jonathan about the amount of vandalism encountered on these runs. I was reassured when he told me that the percentage was small and where it did occur was soon rectified by the Head Teachers being informed and the threat of a removal of the service! Today's young people are not enthusiastic walkers!

How much do the new slimline buses cost?' Over £100,000 a bus was the reply and in any given financial year Citybus invest £1.3 million in new vehicles. A horrendous amount to justify was my immediate reaction, but then I was told that in having constant new intakes, the cost of maintenance comes down and therefore less people need to be employed to service and repair vehicles. From a domestic point of view, the removal of double deckers from the bus routes means that cleaners have a quicker job in turning buses around after cleaning them out. It also gives the driver greater control of the passengers who cannot disappear upstairs and resort to mischief of some kind or another.

Looking at the ease with which the sleek new buses traverse the city, it is difficult to imagine the days, only just over a hundred years ago when trams were drawn by horses. There was almost a carnival atmosphere in 1899 when the tramlines were electrified! The last horse drawn tram ran on June 21st 1907. By 1915 Plymouth Corporation had acquired the Devonport and District tramways and the Plymouth, Stonehouse and Devonport Tramways Company. It was not until 1922 when all three systems came under the one ownership that work began to properly co-ordinate the network. By 1928, with a total of 127 trams it was at its height. The first bus service began in 1932 with 20 vehicles covering four routes. The first double deckers arrived in 1930 by which time the trams were fighting a losing battle and in 1934 only two circular routes were left. The last route from Old Town Street to Peverell via Mutley Plain was abandoned in 1945.

Milehouse has always been the headquarters of Citybus and over the years it has been modernised and one very special new feature in 1985 was the engineering complex which is one of the most modern facilities in the South West.

In that same year the Transport Act changed the way the company operated. From being a department of Plymouth City Council, Plymouth Citybus emerged as a commercial company with the Council as its shareholder.

The Act also de-regulated bus services, which led to a major overhaul of routes. In October 1986 Citybus put 85 minibuses onto the streets of Plymouth. These were very successful but are slowly being replaced by the new larger slimline buses. Co-ordinating all the routes is a major operation which is undertaken with the sort of skill which makes it all look so simple! It makes you stop and think when you realise that the weekly fleet mileage is close to 100,000 miles.

The bulk of Citybus routes are run on a strictly commercial basis but a number of routes are subsidised by Plymouth City Council where the social need has to be considered. Plymouth Citybus is essentially a caring company with a great understanding of people's needs. Their drivers are well trained, generally extremely courteous - although I have to admit having come across one or two who seem to dislike humanity! Maybe they were having an off day.

Community involvement also includes charity work. The drivers nominate charities, and money is raised by all sorts of means. I can remember a special Mufti Day in a Christmas period when drivers wore fancy dress and management dressed as drivers.

Together they raised £1500 in one day for one of their nominated charities. These occasions have a great deal of value both for the charities who benefit and for the team work required which in turn rubs off on the daily routine. Citybus Social Club is a members club for everyone who works for Citybus past and present. It is a happy club which is there for fun but they use it too to raise money for special causes like Derriford Hospital's Breastcare Unit for which they recently held an Abba night which raised £324 for the charity. Another one coming up is for the Alzheimer's Disease Society.

Jonathan Bayliss has the required touch when it comes to motivating his workforce. He is a great communicator and believes, like his predecessor, that an open door policy is the best option in which to provide staff with easy access to managers at all convenient times.

The increasing Citycoach operation which takes people all over Europe, is one of Plymouth Citybus's great successes. The fleet has luxury coaches smartly painted with the company livery. For smaller parties there are nippy 21-seater mini-coaches. You can go out to potential customers without waiting for them to find you!

Most laymen will appreciate the work that is done by the car and commercial division. They do repair work of all kinds and their sights are firmly set on winning new business. Their capabilities cover anything from the private motorist to heavy commercial vehicles and fleet operators to the light van section. It is an impressive array of skills in the fields of repair and maintenance, electrics and electronics, spraying and signwriting, in body work and specialist engineering services.

The Citybus Driving School has professionally trained instructors who have an excellent pass rate. In addition to the on-road training, the company's classroom tuition covers such vital areas as the Highway Code, Drivers' Hours Regulations and Tachograph Training. They offer courses of up to three weeks duration as well as pay-as-you learn lessons on most type of training.

PSV training for Class I and Class 3 public service vehicle licences are available, using Leyland PD2 or PD3 and Renault Dodge minibuses respectively. Semi-automatic vehicles can also be dealt with.

The school operates Plymouth City Council's Taxi Driving Assessment which is something all new and prospective taxi drivers must pass before they can be licensed. There is PGV training and Fork Lift training. In fact a fully comprehensive driving school.

For me one of the best things that Plymouth Citybus does is the guided tour on their open-topped double decker which goes round the city. The bus is comfortable and the commentary excellent. I learned all sorts of interesting things. For example, did you know that in 1797 three United Irishmen were executed on the Hoe by firing squad for treason. Or that on the front of the Hoe there is an area where bulls were deliberately baited in the belief that it would ensure their meat was tender? I learned that Friese-Greene, a pioneer of the motion pictures, had a shop in Union Street where the Two Trees pub now stands. I had forgotten too that Stanley Gibbons, whose name is synonymous with stamp collecting,had a shop in Treville Street on Bretonside opposite the bus station where the taxi rank is today. For a time he also had a shop on North Hill just above the reservoir.

The open topped bus is a perfect way to see the city and I would recommend it to all Plymothians as well as to visitors. You can pick it up at various stops one of which is in the centre of Royal Parade.

The City Council's joint venture with Plymouth Citybus on 'Park and Ride' from the car park at Home Park and Coypool has been very successful. The park and ride scheme operates from 7.30am to 6.15pm Monday to Friday with buses running every ten minutes during peak periods. Specially marked 'Park and Ride' bus stops are at Western Approach, Union Street, Royal Parade, Exeter Street, Charles Cross and Coburg Street

Vospers has been synonymous with cars and service since it was founded in 1946 in Russell Street by Frank Vosper, father of the present Chairman, Peter Vosper. In a very short space of time the motor business expanded and in the mid fifties they held 7 agencies for new cars. In 1960 Vospers were appointed Ford Main Dealers and acquired their first premises in Millbay Road. In 1970, with the closure of Reeds, Vospers became sole Ford Main Dealers in the City.

This family business continued to grow and today is one of the leading Ford Dealers in the UK. The interest was not only in cars but in other areas. In 1966 they became truck dealers for a large part of Devon and East Cornwall and today are Iveco Ford Main Dealer for that area. Motorcycles were an obvious market and again Vospers became a main dealer, this time for Honda Motorcycles.

Vospers Rental and Contract hire has become an important part of the business. It runs over 2,500 vehicles throughout Britain from its Plymouth base. Like everything Vospers does, it is an efficient and courteous service using a great understanding of the client's needs.

Today the premises at Millbay have been demolished and Vospers have super new premises at Marsh Mills which are spacious and provide both the company and its customers with every facility.

Is buying a car via the Internet going to be the way of the future? How can you possibly tell whether the car will be right for you without actually sitting in the driving seat, testing the steering and all the myriad things one needs to do before deciding on what make, what colour, what size the car should be. I put these questions to Brian Dwelly, C D Bramall Dealership Director at Coxside, Plymouth who has been with them for over twenty five years and certainly knows just about everything there is to know about Vauxhalls - the company's main distributorship . No one could ever accuse him of being anything but forward thinking and he has already accepted that buying on the Internet has arrived and is probably here to stay. He does not believe, however, that it will take over from the traditional way of buying a vehicle. He has had a couple of instances where a potential client has seen what they want on the Internet and then asked for the car to be brought to their home to be test driven and generally assessed. In each case, the client bought the car, but not straight away. So would it not have been better to have visited C D Bramall's showroom and seen what the company has on offer? As a shopper I am incredibly lazy but even I would want to take a look and see what choices I had before making a decision with which I would probably have to live for several years.

Apart from any other reason, I think I would miss out on the excitement of seeing the other vehicles on offer, listening to the well-trained sales staff going through their paces. I would also be deprived of the opportunity of seeing the extent of the company's operation which includes the servicing and repairing of all their vehicles. I would miss the chance of being nosey, in fact!

So apart from new cars C D Bramall have an excellent reputation for their secondhand car division and are well known for the courtesy and efficiency of their engineers. I have had no experience of their engineering efficiency but I found great courtesy from one man who helped me park my car in a very full parking area, That was much appreciated.

It interested me to find out that C D Bramall were no longer part of an enormous international company for whom the Motor business was almost an insignificant part. They are now part of a specialist motor group who know the Motor trade inside out. This makes for quicker and smarter decision making better profitability and provides improved working conditions and customer service from top to bottom. Certainly there is a sense of well-being when you visit their showroom, everyone appears to be busy but everyone has time to deal with customers.

Plymouth Station is one of the busiest in Devon and Cornwall and certainly the highest revenue earning. It can best be described today as a tight knit community with an extended family. You may think this is a curious description but it is apt if you look at the incredibly involved relationship between all the various entities that make up today's railway. At Plymouth Station the cool, level headed Michael Robinson is the head of the family. As the Station Manager he has a complex organisation to run and does it with a friendly, open door policy - his office is on Platform 1 and he has a cheery greeting for everyone as they pass his office. With the busy noise of the station all around us, I listened, fascinated as he endeavoured to unravel the complexities of his role. Take the station itself, that is the property of Railtrack but is leased to First Great Western. They in turn are responsible for the general upkeep of the Concourse, and must actively encourage Railtrack to resolve any major task, for which First Great Western are not accountable For example after much infighting and determination, £65,000 has now been allotted for the modernisation and refurbishment of the station lavatories - something which every traveller using the station will welcome.

Plymouth is a clean, bright station and is seen as an important part of the first impression visitors have of the city. The Concourse is light and airy, the automatic doors work efficiently and keep the place comparatively warm in winter - something else that Mike Robinson had to fight for. Shopping has become easier with the enlargement of the Spar Shop, W.H. Smith has a bright and well stocked site and the Refreshment Room sets out its stall to make its customers comfortable and well fed. Most importantly the ticket counters are manned by staff who have consideration for travellers, are helpful and seem to have abundant knowledge.

Staff training has been one of Mike Robinson's main concerns since his arrival. Firmly, politely and objectively he has instilled in the people under his control that working for the Station is not to be thought of as a sinecure and a job for life. You have to be good at your job, shirkers are not welcome. Patient retraining of people has become a priority allowing a number of staff who in the past might have found themselves as square pegs in round holes, to have the training to alter their roles and frequently their way of life. Judging from the mainly smiling faces I saw on the station, the task has been successful. First Great Western are revamping their passenger service, with multi-skilled staff on trains, free newspapers and refreshments in First Class and better train announcements. This move will prove how valuable the retraining has been.

The most difficult thing the station has to handle is the turn round of trains which belong to other companies like Virgin and Wales and West. Mike's staff are responsible for the cleaning and fast turn round of these trains as they finish their journey in Plymouth including the revictualling. If a train is late in then the cleaning time is short and it maybe, for example, that Virgin Railways control room in Birmingham wants the immediate turn round of the train and does not always consider the need for cleaning the train. This, naturally leads to complaints from travellers who level those complaints on Plymouth Station operatives rather than the Virgin, Birmingham. It seemed to me that Mike Robinson's hands were frequently tied and not always happily.

Trains for London leave almost every hour and there are excellent services throughout Britain. The Golden Hind Pullman leaves at 7am and takes only three hours to reach London. Every First Class Pullman offers unrivalled levels of welcome and service with a choice of light refreshment or full breakfast, lunch, afternoon tea and dinner, beautifully presented at your seat. Recently restored is the Car Service from London to Penzance - saves all that driving and allows you to enjoy a comfortable rail journey instead.

It was through the eyes of my grandson who has a great passion for trains and stations that I discovered just how many sorts of trains, locomotives and engines, come and go from Plymouth Station during the course of the day. Local services abound, goods trains trundle through and the regular long distance trains pull in and out more often than not on time - sometimes they even arrive early!

Mike told me also about the vastly improved parking facilities which are run by an outside operator. Safety for both cars, their drivers and passengers has become one of the most important aspects. Security cameras keep a watchful eye all the time, the car park is well lit and gone is the creepy feeling I always had if I returned to Plymouth late at night and had to go into the cavernous, dark, and slightly spooky area. Plymouth still has small satellite stations and halts, but these belong to Wales and West and are not Mike's responsibility. Totnes Station has been added to Mike's portfolio and is slowly but surely benefiting from the disciplines which have to be employed by a 21st century Station Manager.

Outside the Station the rows of black cabs are a credit to the city. The company and the drivers belong to the 'Welcome Host' scheme whose purpose is to ensure that visitors arriving in Plymouth by train, feel welcome, safe and cared for. Every driver has been part of a training course, has not only 'The Knowledge' that all black cab drivers are required to have, but also has a working knowledge of what is happening in the city. I was very thrilled when I wrote 'Invitation to Plymouth' to find that copies of the book were available in the cabs for visitors. The company has sole rights to the very valuable taxi concession at the station which makes them very conscious of the need to give the utmost service to their passengers. Every cab is spotless, the drivers seem to be of what one would call 'the old school' although many are quite young men.

A city without an airport would be worse than Easter without an egg or Christmas without Santa Claus. In reality this could have happened in 1975 when property developers did their utmost to prevent Brymon Airways from taking over Plymouth Airport. Fortunately Brymon won and were able to acquire a lengthy lease which then secured its future. Today a quarter of a century later, Sutton Harbour Holdings plc owns the airport and much has changed - most of it to the advantage of travellers. Brymon fly out of here on regular scheduled flights. Their Cork flight has become so successful that they are extending it to a daily flight instead of four days a week. Their London service is quick and efficient .In fact they consistently introduce new routes. They should be thanked for bringing much needed business to Plymouth. Celtic Airlines are the new kids on the block and they plan to begin scheduled flights to Brussells from March 2001 and to introduce daily flights into London. The sadness is that the size of the airport cannot be increased. One day we might have another airport but the question is where?

The history of Roborough Airport is interesting. Way before the 1939-45 war the City Fathers had been brave enough to look at the question of air transport out of Plymouth. As far back as 1923 the Chamber of Commerce had the concept in mind to fly mail which had crossed the Atlantic by ship, from Plymouth to London. From there it would be transferred to a regular air service to Europe within seven hours of arriving by sea. It sounds very tame now but then it was almost an unimaginable feat.

From a small grass plot at Chelson Meadows - now the refuse tip for the city - Alan Cobham, who became one of the best known airmen ever, took off on a proving flight to Croydon. This was successful and the city council started looking for a suitable site. Roborough appeared to be the ideal spot and from then onwards the airport has grown.

After the war it was used by small airlines and had resident planes belonging to the Britannia Royal Naval College. Dennis Teague, an aviation historian with many books to his credit on our local aerodromes, told me one day when we met in The Dome, 'It might be fair to say that Roborough played a more important part in the Falklands conflict than it did in World War II, because every Naval Sea Harrier and helicopter pilot received their basic training in the Chipmunks at Plymouth Airport'. Not many people know that!

With travel uppermost in my mind throughout this chapter, I needed to find the best possible travel agent in the city, excluding the giants, Thomas Cook etc. In Peter Goord Travel I found the epitome of what a small independent company should be. This is a family business in which Anthony Goord and his brother are now full partners with their father, Peter. They are successful, helpful, courteous and very knowledgeable.

Those who wish to take specially built holidays are as well catered for as those who want the normal package holiday. At Goords you will find many brochures not seen in other travel agencies. The company personally checks out as many destinations and as much accommodation as possible.

You will find the company based at West Park which is a convenient geographical situation for anyone in Plymouth and parking is easy!. Peter Goord himself is a Plymothian and his first business, which is still in existence, was insurance. That was almost forty years ago and this ex-Devonport High School boy is proud to have his sons as partners. Peter has become equally well known for his work on Radio Devon as the travel consultant giving his listeners the benefit of the vast knowledge about travel around the world; a knowledge that is of inestimable value to his listeners and to his clients.

For Plymothians flying from Exeter has become a boon although it does not always present the best option. I understand why people like Exeter. It is small and easy to understand rather than the vast Heathrow or Gatwick. All sorts of destinations can be reached from Exeter including Cyprus and Turkey. Peter will tell you that many more people look for unusual places today. Spain is no longer the prime favourite. Cruises have become major players. Whatever you want, you will find Goords have the answer and the ability to make sure your holiday is thoroughly catered for.

I have no doubt that Peter Goord Travel will continue to be successful largely because of their courtesy, their understanding and their commonsense.

The Torpoint Ferry today.

Brian Whipp. 'Sir Francis Drake'
Note; Drake's hand on the shoulder.

256

Chapter XIII

The Time, The Place and The People

I have to admit to being a 'people person'. Nothing gives me greater pleasure than meeting and getting to know men, women and children from every walk of life and no age limit. Sometimes the conversations end in my wishing I was forty years younger, sometimes I am grateful for my age but invariably I am stimulated by what I learn.

Plymouth has such a diversity of talented people. People who make things happen, people who somehow have the knack of pulling the rabbit out of the hat when no one else can, people who quietly go about their daily work unobtrusively doing good. It is this portrait I want to paint for you in this chapter. The sketches do not come in any specific order of importance but they are of people who have all given me pleasure to meet and in my opinion add to the rich tapestry of the city.

Some six years ago I needed radio therapy after an operation for breast cancer. It is a terrifying thought for anyone having to face it but for those of us lucky enough to attend the Oncology Outpatient Department at Derriford, the whole experience is made pleasant - no one could make it pleasureable - by the two receptionists Tricia and Myra who have been there over all the years I have been attending. At first I went every day for six weeks and every day these two ladies would welcome me, have a little chat and I would go into the treatment feeling I was among friends. Since those days I have been on a gradually reducing number of visits every year until now it is annual but however long it has been, these two women never forget my name, never fail to make one welcome and seem genuinely delighted when the news of the check up is good. Whilst I waited to be called on my last visit I watched them leave their desks to give a big hug to one patient who had, at last, been given the all clear.

No-one can know, except those of us who have attended the Oncology Out Patient clinic, how much it means to us. If only the rest of the NHS was as understanding, efficient and genuinely interested as Myra and Tricia, it would become a pleasure to be there - well almost!

One fascinating encounter was with the elegant lady, Diana Hurst, who is a Blue Badge Guide working within the city and the south west generally. Apart from enjoying her lively conversation I also learned about the work of Blue Badge Guides. Before this meeting I had no idea how they came about, where they learned their craft and once having learned how they operated. To achieve the accolade of 'Blue Badge Guide' courses are generally run within establishments such as Colleges of Further Education/Universities with the Blue Badge awarded by Tourist Boards once the candidates have successfully completed the training. Whilst there is no such thing as a Blue Badge Guide Organisation once trained Blue Badge Guides can join regional Associations or a national body like The Guild of Registered Tourist Guides. There are approximately 1600 members of The Guild at present, of which about half will be London based and the other half made up by guides based in regions across the country. The Blue Badge is an internationally recognised benchmark of excellence both in site and heritage interpretation and communication skills. There is so much a Blue Badge

Guide needs to know, and this is acquired through experience and the willingness to find the knowledge about their own area, then how to impart that knowledge in a friendly, easy to understand manner, how to be courteous at all time whatever the provocation might be to lose ones cool! Not the least is to have an understanding of people of all nationalities and the ability to cope with their foibles!

The success of each individual guide depends on his or her ability to market their talents. Every effort is made to nurture contacts made with hotels, tour operators, cruise ships, tourist boards, etc, as well as those whose 'fingers are on the pulse' such as in Plymouth, the highly successful Marketing Bureau and Chamber of Commerce. Business can emanate from a number of directions, whether leisure, education or commerce. However these efforts have to be made on an on-going basis and, as ever, it is often a question of being in the right place at the right time to get the plum jobs. It is essentially a job for someone with a positive approach to life, who can smile in adversity and has a keen, if controlled sense of humour. Diana Hurst has all the qualities that are needed for this onerous job - and some extra ones as well. She is an excellent ambassador for Plymouth and her praises are sung by any one who has used her services as a guide. She now sits on several influential committees and her thoughts and opinions are both welcomed and respected.

No one does more to keep the spirit of the Elizabethan Plymouth and especially Sir Francis Drake alive than the remarkable Brian Whipp who with his lady has dedicated their lives to bringing home to adults and children the wonderful heritage of this country, especially Plymouth and Sir Francis Drake, proving to people that history is not a dead subject. They are to be seen regularly on the Barbican in period costumes that are both sumptuous and authentic. They attend all manner of functions wearing raiment , boots and gloves together with the right kind of weapons. Husband and wife design the costumes together and then Mrs Whipp skilfully makes them. The results are stunning and they have a wardrobe which must be worth thousands of pounds. It all started in 1978 when Brian was the Chairman of a Fayre and Pageant committee. Since that date the couple have appeared at a myriad of functions from a re-enactment of the Drake-Mary Newman wedding in St Budeaux Parish Church to Royal Navy events, days at Buckland Abbey to helping Plymouth companies at exhibitions.

When Sir Francis appears on The Barbican during the season, he has the same effect as the Pied Piper of Hamelin; he is followed wherever he goes. This is good business for Barbican traders, although as one lady put it to me, 'You have to watch out for his sword as he swings around, it can be lethal!' One of Brian's greatest moments was during the visit of Her Majesty The Queen to HMS Drake in 1999 when he had the honour to be presented to Her Majesty. Dressed perfectly as Sir Francis, Brian greeted her with the words 'Ma'am, I bring thee greetings from Elizabeth Regina and compliments on how you represent this land of ours' The Queen responded with delight and asked him why he did this. He explained and said ' Ma'am with a Queen Elizabeth on the throne, we must have a Sir Francis Drake, must we not?' Her Majesty came closer to him, waggled her finger at him and replied 'Yes, we must, mustn't we?'
If you ask Brian to sum up his reasons for the time, the dedication, the work that he has put into his Sir Francis Drake over a quarter of a century he says:

A Picture says a thousand words - we, my good lady and I, are the picture and we bring to life Sir Francis Drake and Plymouth. Drake would say ;

'There must be a beginning to any event, but the continuation unto the end until it be finished, yields the true glory'

One hopes then end will be a long time coming. Brian Whipp's colourful presence, his booming voice and ebullient personality personify The Elizabethans and the city is richer for it.

'Do Fools rush in where Angels fear to tread' ? I had to ponder this thought when I heard that Plymouth businessman Paul Kirsten of The Kitchen Factory had committed himself to producing a three day Air Show on Plymouth Hoe to commemorate the 60th anniversary of the Battle of Britain. This would be his third Air Show but the previous events were small, one day affairs. The sheer size of this undertaking would have frightened most people off but not so Paul. His passion in life is aeroplanes of any kind and any sort belonging to any country. Over the years he has developed an extraordinary relationship not only with civil display teams but seemingly with most Air Forces around the world and certainly the Europeans and Americans. He has an uncanny knack of cutting through red tape to get directly to the people he wants and so neither being an angel or a fool, he had no hesitation in telling all of us who know him that AirAid 2000 would be the biggest and best regional air show anywhere in Europe. Back in September 1999 one might have had doubts that he could bring it off but slowly the scenario grew, he gathered his cast of aircraft and by the first day of the Air Show on September 15th 2000 he had persuaded, by means which perhaps we should not question, some 200 aircraft to take place in this three day event. How ? Heaven alone knows. What we do know is that the airways were full of telephone calls to his mobile phone from all around the world. The hour of day was immaterial and frequently at night when all sensible Englishmen were sound asleep but other countries were just starting their day. Even the weather rose to the occasion. The three days were blessed with sunshine and clear skies. The setting over Plymouth Sound with the spectators massed on the broad plain of Plymouth Hoe and Foreshore, Mountbatten and Mount Edgcumbe, was perfect. Nine planes of The Red Arrow team were the icing on this spectacular cake. Their leader said that nowhere in the world that they performed ever had a better setting, He described it as 'the perfect natural amphitheatre for his team's acrobatic wizardry'. They swept in over the sea, weaving the magic of their immaculate display and left the arena making for the National Memorial Day at Biggin Hill where bigger crowds and crowded runways awaited them but the scenic backdrop was not a patch on Plymouth Sound. Incidentally The Red Arrows had near enough 200 requests for their attendance at various places for the Anniversary weekend but only two were chosen - Biggin Hill and Plymouth. Certainly a feather in Paul Kirsten's cap. There were Russians and Poles, Danes and the French, displays from old aircraft, parachute drops by the RAF display team. The air was alive and magical and on the ground the famous Naval Gun Crews fought hard and long over a three day competition. Police Dogs showed their skills aided by their handlers, stalls selling everything from sweets to hot dogs, chairs to souvenirs, double glazing to the AA were kept busy by the visitors to the Hoe. In the background the Fair buzzed with life. In the major Marquee a ball was held on the Saturday night with dancing to the music of the 1940s and cabaret in the hilarious hands of Frank Carson.. On all three days the

Marquee was used to raise money for Charity including lunches and an auction . Civic and Service dignitaries attended, wreaths were laid on the Hoe Memorial. For the spectators it was three days of immense enjoyment but perhaps now we should look behind the scenes and see what Paul Kirsten and his small team had to deal with.

Paul has immense stamina and courage and combined with his passionate interest in aircraft he achieved his aim virtually against all odds. Putting on an Air Show is not just about aircraft. Paul set up his 'office' together with the veteran, ex RAF and ex Distribution Director for the Daily Mirror Group, Archie Roberts in a quiet corner of the Marina Snooker Club on Sutton Harbour. Nobody in their right minds would attempt planning such a mammoth event in such surroundings apart from these two intrepid warriors. Most of us would have needed an office with every kind of modern facility from Fax to E-mail, Secretaries to the Internet. A battery of telephones and God knows how many assistants. This sort of happening is about meticulous organisation down to the sort of mundane details like where the rubbish bins are sited. For starters most venues have the luxury of being able to charge an entrance fee to help cover the cost but Plymouth Hoe is open to the public and no fee is possible.

This meant that money had to be raised from other sources to cover even the basic cost of fuel for the planes, insurance etc. Paul, complete with his mobile phone went to every other Air Show he could find and at every one he looked for stall holders who were prepared to come to Plymouth for three days and pay for their stands. He found people who offered help with the catering - just think, the Gun Crews alone needed no less than 840 well filled sandwiches to keep them going. How do you cater for high-powered guests in a marquee away from kitchen facilities? Licences for bars, insurance for Public Liability and Aircraft, Rescue divers in Plymouth Sound in case of a plane ditching, Police to control the crowds, Paramedics, Generators for power, and so the list grew day by day, the telephone calls increased, tempers frayed, but each and every day achieved something. It all began to look good and really the only uncertainty was the weather but nothing ever does run to plan. The Navy had to pull out of its catering assistance because of military duties so now 80 waiting staff had to be found - and paid! The Russian plane could not come unless cash was set up in advance to pay for fuel. And then, something totally unexpected occurred - the rising against the cost of fuel by farmers and truckers. Just a week before the show and the telephone never stopped ringing. The Navy could not supply its Harriers because of fuel. The firm putting up the Marquee doubted if they would be able to make the trip from London, various stands pulled out because they could not get to Plymouth. The shortage of food in the Superstores meant that the promise of supplies from them had to be cancelled - their customers came first. Throughout all of this Paul Kirsten somehow kept his calm, refused to even consider cancelling the Show and D-Day crept nearer and nearer but using the old adage 'The Show Must Go On' he cajoled and berated his volunteer helpers, the marquee appeared a bit late in the day, stall holders turned up, and the morning of September 15th started darkly but by half way through the morning the sun was shining, Plymouth Hoe was filling up with people and AirAid 2000 was on its way. By the evening of September 17th when the curtain came down and the last plane had flown on its way, an exhausted Paul and his team knew they had brought off the impossible - but at what cost?

260

The aftermath is a bit like clearing up after a flood. The bills come pouring in, the money trickles in, the collecting boxes are being gathered in and money counted. The Show was a great success but the high hopes of several charities for whom the Show had been run, are doomed to disappointment. Much of the loss comes from the Fuel shortage but it does bring home the fact that really only professionals can take on a show like this. Perhaps Paul should take a leaf out of the organisers of Plymouth Navy Days who had to learn the lesson of making something pay. They bowed to what modern day events require and now run one of the most successful, financially viable and enjoyable events in the bi-annual calendar.

We all hope Plymouth will have another Air Show but lets support the incredible effort and tenacity of people like Paul Kirsten who just need the help of the professionals and the backing of Plymouth Council, who in the words of the Lord Mayor, should go all out to make such an event the most prestigious Air Show in the country.

What does a hero look like? The mind plays funny games with images but Sam Swabey would be the first person to laugh if you called him a hero and to look at the man he certainly does not have the romantic looks that go with one's dreams! Nonetheless to the people who live in the Granby area of the city, this large man with his long hair swept back into a pony tail and frequently a couple of day's growth of beard on his well lived- in-face, four heavy silver chains round his neck, the longest finger nails, is a hero. It took a severe fright when he thought he was having a heart attack, followed by several very boring days in Derriford to make Sam see what it was he really wanted out of life. He was tired of making and spending money as fast as it came in, he was tired of living what seemed a pretty fruitless existence. The final decision was made for him by his wife who decided he should not even attempt to cope anymore with his video business and whilst he was ill, she sold it. When he left hospital he spent sometime convalescing and from the balcony of his flat watched the local kids playing football. He knew that the chance of these youngsters getting into mischief because they had nothing really to do and nowhere to go, was highly likely - he had done that very thing in his childhood.

As soon as he was able Sam asked a community worker if there was anything he could do with and for these kids. He was given the task, with the lads, of doing up a vandalised and burnt-out portable building. They all entered into the spirit of the job and at the end of the week the kids were so thrilled with the building that they refused to give it up. So Sam helped set up a youth club which has grown and grown in stature and is now a base for adventure activities with canoeing and camping high on the list of popular adventures. Whilst the older ones are away on these trips the younger ones have their own club. By this time Sam was well and truly hooked on the idea of caring for his local community. He bothered and badgered people for help. A summer play scheme was instigated but with no equipment and typically English wet weather, ingenuity had to be the name of the game. With eight adult helpers and forty children between 3 and 13 years success was achieved from necessity. Sam and his helpers simply turned the lights out and told stories to an enthralled audience. He remembers it as being one of the best days of his life. DML having heard of Sam's activities presented the community with a new portable building. Everyone in the Granby area was now getting involved in what was going on. Support grew and Sam and his team got grants of around £150,000 to convert and restore an old NAAFI building which became the Granby Island Community Centre. The project supported by Lottery money and £250,000 of Government education money, is now a thriving place of play and learning. Sam is the Manager and the Centre provides jobs for 15 people. There is also an excellent creche and the successful 'Computers-in-the-Community' project.

Sam has put pride back into the Granby estate. In so doing he has met Tony Blair and Government minister Lord Falconer. To his community Sam is a hero. It is not as he sees himself. He will tell you that he is only the front man who pulls it altogether. Everything else comes from the help he has received from Community workers, Volunteers, The College of Further Education staff, DML and not the least from his wife.

Another man who is a hero to many youngsters and who has gained the respect of a host of people in Plymouth is the unassuming Cos Cosway who with the aid of some like minded people developed the charity Horizon. Its purpose in life is to provide deprived children with some fun in life that is both stimulating and educational, and it is all done in boats! It started with the gift of a boat from a parishioner of a Devonport vicar, who suggested that it could be used to take less fortunate children out on the water. The boat could only take three children plus the two crew, which was fun but not really satisfactory. This germinated an idea which was to result in a fleet of boats now being what makes up Horizon. These are not just common or garden sailing boats but speed boats which provide the children with an exhilaration that they have never had in their young lives. For many,when the boats set sail from Devonport and round the bend near Plymouth Hoe, the sight is something they have never seen before and somewhere frequently they did not even know existed! Hard to believe but true. Where did this motley fleet of boats come from? One of the first was a gift from David Owen, others have been purchased when funds have permitted and some have been outright gifts. There is a Princess motor vessel built by Marine Products, several smaller power boats, a big launch that was purchased from Spain and several others in the process of being converted for the use of these children.

When Horizon first started it was a sort of hit and miss operation and not geared specifically to any one purpose other than providing pleasure for these children who had never been on the water before. Just imagine their excitement when they were allowed to steer a fast motor boat across the Sound. As the charity developed so did the thinking about its objectives. Now the trips are for pleasure but also have other purposes. The boats are available to schools so that frequently children go afloat to learn as well as have fun - a sort of floating schoolroom. The ongoing planning will see NVQ's become available for youngsters to learn boat maintenance and building. It is hoped to buy a permanent base, perhaps like Potters Quay, where workshops can be built, the boats housed and maintained. At this present moment there are boats stored all over the city anywhere from DML to private garages. Church Urban funds have been allotted to help the cause; recently £28,000 and the Lottery has just given the charity £158,000.

All this work just doesn't happen by itself and that is why Cos Cosway is a hero to so many. Every day he is busy planning schedules for boat trips, seeing to maintenance, sorting out clothing and filling in forms which he hopes will bring Horizon grant funds. Did you know that it takes 52 working hours to put together a request for a grant from the National Lottery? He has given over his life to nurturing this cause, he has travelled Europe to find boats, he has tapped every source he can think of for money. For example Sonia Donovan of the Armada Gallery, one of his many supporters, had an exhibition for the charity and raised £300. His determination, his likeable personality and his total belief in what he is doing, has made sure he has a lot of support from many people for this worthwhile cause. He is very funny about the number of times he has had to make himself redundant from the cause because the funds have run out, but one knows that even if there were no sizeable funds, he would somehow create a way in which to carry this project forward. If you would like to know more about Horizon, offer your services or funding please ring Cos Cosway on 01752 216823

It is said that charity begins at home but sometimes it is necessary to reach out thousands of miles from home to help. This is what Jim and Maureen Elliot have done with their Safecare organisation. Since 1990 Jim and Maureen have been making trips to the impoverished and needy people of Romania offering help to orphans and disabled children. They have made endless  trips in support of hospitals and last year built a home for disabled youngsters in Oradea. At last they are beginning to see improvement in the children every time they go. They were thrilled to see that two of the children they were once told were brain dead were walking and talking and even feeding themselves.

This last trip completed in February 2001 highlighted another need. They met a Romanian businessman who wants to build a home for the homeless elderly. He came to Maureen and Jim for advice and they were appalled at how many elderly there were wandering the streets without any form of shelter and frequently starving. Whilst Maureen and Jim's main purpose will always be the children whilst the need is there, they were both moved and now are appealing for sponsors for this latest project. If you can help or know anyone who will, please do ring them on 01752 778985.

When, in 1992, I met Commander Charles Howeson for the first time, I was immediately impressed by the enthusiasm, the excitement and the professionalism he brought to his role as Executive Director of the Groundwork Trust. He had recently retired from the Royal Navy with an exemplary record and many prestigious postings, to explore the commercial world, but I do not think that even he had any idea how deeply he was to become involved in the affairs of Plymouth. He was one of the architects of the local plan for the Plymouth City Challenge bid (1992) which we lost to Nottingham. Oddly enough its loss started the winning streak that has developed into the 'partnership' that has developed all over the city since then and is currently producing very thrilling and satisfying results.

Charles' career allowed him the opportunity to pursue various interests which now make impressive reading; Fellow of the Institute of Directors, Fellow of the Royal

Society of Arts, Fellow of the British Institute of Management, RYA Yachtmaster, Younger Brother of Trinity House and a Liveryman of the Worshipful Company of Shipwrights and Freeman of the City of London amongst others. From 1991 onwards after his retirement from the Navy the list of directorships is enough to make one dizzy and includes such varied appointments as Chairman of the Fairbridge (SW) Charity, Chairman of the Sail Training Association (Plymouth) Charity, Chairman of the Independent Legal Practitioners (UK) Ltd, Vice Chairman Plymouth Chamber of Commerce, Member of the 2020 Plymouth Partnership Board, Director The Mayflower Marina Plymouth. Governor of St Dunstan's Abbey School. Director of Development of The Plymouth Theatre Royal and Member of the Regional Flood Defence Committee of the NRA. More recently his involvement in the Voluntary and Community Sector has included appointments as Vice Chairman Millfields Community Economic Development Trust (a flagship regeneration project), Chairman of Plymouth Employment Action Zone, and Chairman of the new (lottery funded) Mount Batten Water Sports and Sailing Centre.

The list seems endless and would make someone who does not know the man, believe they were dealing with someone superhuman who could not possibly be a normal, contented family man. And yet that is just what he is, with a delightful and very pretty wife and three excellent children plus a Dalmatian! His home is warm and large like the man himself. He fascinates me because whenever you talk to him about almost anything he is like the AA advertisement 'He knows a man who does'! He is never too busy to provide a helping hand for anyone and is not averse to literally having a hands on approach to any task. I am told that when he took over the board of the £5M lottery funded Regional Water Sports and Sailing Centre at Mount Batten, which he was asked to chair by the consortium of waterfront organisations who had originally put the proposal together, that to the great satisfaction of everyone involved, he almost single-handedly cleared the log-jam of difficulties both financial and physical which had been holding up progress. He had the same approach when he was dealing with the highly complicated situation in Millfields - formerly the Royal Naval Hospital. Much of the enormous success of this development is down to his tenacity which, if rumour is correct, also meant risking his own financial neck to achieve the end result. He got involved with Plymouth's 60-60-60 Taxi firm (an apolitical co-operative) and for the benefit of the City helped them to turn themselves into a very customer orientated and responsive organisation through the medium of formal passenger handling training - wrongly, in his view, called the 'charm school'! This innovative approach was designed to provide the City with over 100 mobile 'black cab' ambassadors who would be able to help to market the City and brief visitors. One result of this is that Plymouth Taxis Limited now look after all the customers at Plymouth Station for Railtrack and First Great Western trains.

With all these various interests one might suppose he was a jack of all trades and master of none. That is entirely untrue and anyone who has any dealings with him will know that the depth of his knowledge about anything he deals with, is profound and has been acquired by a genuine wish to do his very best for any project or organisation with which he gets involved.

Charles, like Chris Freegard in the Civic Centre, John Ingham whose knowledge and love of the city has proved inspirational to a lot of people, Charles Crichton of the

Naval Base Museum. Steve Lobb of Chesterton and Mike Pallot of Pricewaterhouse Coopers are among a breed of men and women who see clearly what a successful city Plymouth can be. One of the factors in his approach to anything he does is that he insists on a completely apolitical approach to running his business interests and his community voluntary sector participation. He is an active 'regionalist' dedicated to championing the improvement of the prosperity of the West Country and its economy as well as the environment and quality of life across the Plymouth area. This is what makes him so acceptable to politicians at both national and local level and he is not only able to, but also thoroughly enjoys, working closely with all sectors of the community.

In spite of all his vast number of business activities he is still a keen cruising yachtsman, tennis player, jazz piano player, fish farmer and R/C boat collector.

Is it the name Charles or does the rank of Commander produce someone special. I haven't the slightest idea but another achiever, in a different way, is the softly spoken, Northern Irishman Commander Charles Crichton OBE. Here is a man who in his own quiet way is providing Plymouth with an amazing opportunity in the shape of the Naval Base Museum. It was when he was in command of HMS Illustrious for a major refit some years ago that he first took an interest in the history of the Naval Base and thought to himself that it really should be on a par with Portsmouth and have its own story told in a living Museum. As a serving officer you need to be disciplined and organised but marketing and other skills could not really be included in the job description. With a growing desire to have something to do with preservation of this country's heritage and with his retirement looming ahead, Charles took the unusual step of studying to get the letters M SocSc after his name. A degree that would allow him to take on something like running LANHYDROCK or SALTRAM. Never in his wildest dreams can he have imagined how this degree would eventually prove useful. First of all after retirement he was back to the Navy, still with the rank of Commander. His role was to develop the concept of a Naval Base Visitor Centre and to organise Navy Days which are held in Devonport one year and Portsmouth the next. Running Navy Days is a tough job and made even tougher by the need to create a highly attractive and enjoyable public event. This is where Charles' ability and determination come into play. He gathered around him a team who clearly understood his objective. He drew up a blue print which would be used for Navy Days in 1995 and be able to be used as the basis for subsequent events at Devonport. The result was an enormous and very profitable success. Everything went with a swing. There was something to occupy visitors all day and many returned for a second day as there was so much to see. Navy Days in 1999 proved to be the best ever and even the portable loos were of the right sort!

All the while this was going on Charles, with the blessing of the Naval Base Commander, was quietly working away on the vision of a Visitor Centre starting with the enlargement of the small Naval Base Museum. The historic South Yard was the right place for the Museum which in Charles' mind was already a major international attraction. There are many buildings steeped in history and dated back to the 17th and 18th century. First came the use of the Officers Houses built in 1694 - the only two survivors from the days of the German Blitz of World War II when the Admiral Superintendent's home and other splendid officers' houses were destroyed in one dreadful night.

Operating from the Officers House, things began to happen. Various pieces of land in South Yard and other buildings were taken on for use by the Naval Base Museum, more and more artefacts were being discovered, a Trust was set up to operate the Museum and Charles' dream did not seem so unreal. He was kind enough to take me round South Yard one day, pointing out the buildings he wanted to use, showing me the Old Police Station and the Fire Station, the Ropery and the Covered Slip. By the time we had finished our tour I could hear, in my mind, the arrival of a constant stream of coaches bringing visitors, I could see the water taxis tying up at the pontoons and visitors having embarked at the Barbican, stepping off to see all the attractions ending up in the restaurant where a cream tea was waiting. I could see the Naval Base Museum as just part of a substantial Visitor Centre being a world wide attraction. A dream activated. More on the Naval Museum is in Chapter Ten.

But Charles Crichton does not stop there. Meet Drum Major Charles Crichton who assists Pipe Major Eddie Campbell to lead the City of Plymouth Pipe Band. Formed in 1975 by a former member of the Argyll and Sutherland Highlanders changing its name in 1985 from The Argyll and Sutherland Highlanders Regimental Association Pipes and Drums to its present name by permission of the City Council. Charles dressed for the part in his kilt, leads them out with pride to the many displays and carnivals all over the west country including Plymouth's Lord Mayor's Parade, and various shows in Plymouth theatres including the Plymouth Pavilions. The band has strong links with the Royal Navy and is proud to have,as Patron, the Naval Base Commander, HM Naval Base, Devonport. The band has also performed at Navy Days, Field Gun runs and social functions in the Naval Base and featured in the highly successful Navy Days Tattoo in 1999. They are regular performers at the ever growing American Thanksgiving Week in November each year. The band has played at pipe band competitions throughout the country and has appeared on both local and national television. Their last performance in 2000 will be on Plymouth Hoe to celebrate the incoming 2001.

In recent years the band has made a number of successful trips to Germany and France. In 2000 it represented Plymouth at Europe's largest maritime event Brest 2000 in July. The Band also joined 10,000 pipers and drummers for a millennium piping festival in Edinburgh on August 5th 2000 in aid of the Marie Curie Cancer Care raising, I believe some £500,000.

If you are interested in joining the band they are delighted to hear from new or experienced drummers, male or female of all ages and would also like to hear from new or experienced pipers. Tuition on the latest Premier drums is free. Equipment and uniform is provided. The Band meets on Monday evenings. Interested? Ring Charles Crichton on 01752 552593.

If you want to make something happen you need 'to make the jelly wobble'! At least that is what John Redwood, the Minister for the Environment in the last Conservative Government told John Ingham the Leader of the Labour led Council in Plymouth until quite recently. The Minister really had no need to say this to a man for whom I have the highest regard and respect. Known today as 'The Father of the Plymouth Partnership', he is one of the rocks of Plymouth Politics and in his time from 1992 until he retired, he made jellies of every conceivable colour and flavour wobble until he got the results he wanted. He inherited a dysfunctional council who seemed to have no particular idea where Plymouth ought to go. This was an era when the services and the dockyard were scaling down. It was a time for decisions, and once John had come to terms with the situation both financial and commercial, he set about to breathe new life in the City. It was a time when the thought of partnership with manufacturers, retailers and other businesses in the city was unheard of. It was this partnership that was so vital and with a lot of blood, sweat and tears John, helped by the then Chief Executive, Mike Boxall, the Chamber of Commerce, The Institute of Directors, Mike Lees of DML, Admiral Newman and countless others including Charles Howeson whom I have just told you about, a partnership was put together to produce a plan for the City Challenge, a competition between cities to get for themselves a lot of funding. Under John's persistent leadership, politics went out of the window - well almost - and everyone set about achieving projects for the advancement of the city and its people.

Its odd how sometimes failure can result in success. This is what happened as the result of the failure of the City Challenge bid which then gave rise to a more wide ranging partnership. It involved the public, private, community and voluntary sectors represented in a democratic system coming together to agree the strategic way forward for the city. To make the most of any opportunity that surfaced particularly for community development in areas of deprivation. This is the only model nationally covering all sectors which satisfied the then government so much that they allowed Plymouth to monitor its own progress on project completions. This has now become the 2020 Partnership and hopefully still looks for any opportunity to advance the City.

One innovative decision John made in the recruitment policy of the Civic Centre, has given more genuine Equal Opportunity to women at all levels. He did away with any information about race, colour, creed, age etc on the forms of application so that when people were short listed for jobs no one knew whether they were male or female, black or white, young or mature. This meant that many more women and more mature people have been promoted into more important jobs which otherwise they might have never been considered for.

Now when I talked to John Ingham, I found an assured man, entirely comfortable with his own persona and willing to share his vast experience with anyone, whatever political colour and as such, is of inestimable value. He firmly believes that politics can be a handicap when you are dealing with the needs of Plymouth. In his opinion everything that is done should be, not for the party, but for the good of everyone. He is more than willing to help the new Conservative led council, in the hands of the young and determined Patrick Nicholson and his able deputy Kevin Wigens. He is delighted when he sees councillors, whatever their persuasion, taking a keen interest in what happens in their wards. He has great admiration for people like Councillor Connie Pascoe who never fails to rise to any challenge presented to her. He is none too sure that our Labour MP's have exploited their strong position within a Labour Government to advance Plymouth's case and its special needs, but that seems to apply to almost all the MPs we have in the last decade. I remember Alan Clarke telling me that he could not be bothered with 'parochial matters'! He was of the opinion that never the twain should meet, and would go out of his way to avoid getting sucked in to local politics.

He did not even have a house in his constituency, preferring to stay in the Post House if he had to, but generally staying in his house in North Devon, well out of reach! We are lucky today in our three MP's who all live in Plymouth.

John Ingham has achieved so much and still has so many roles. It was John who first mooted the idea for an Science Park which now flourishes on a site almost next door to Derriford Hospital. He envisaged it as a place for research and development and discovered, after he had set about achieving his aim, that it was more needed than he thought. Apparently when the Derriford Trust were trying to recruit consultants and surgeons for the hospital, they failed to get the people they wanted because the hospital had no facility for each man to carry out research into his own project. All top notch men pursue a project that is close to their clinical hearts. Now they have some of the best facilities in the country. John is currently a Governor of the Hospital Trust amongst many other interests. He is still keenly involved with the Pavilions and the Theatre Royal. His interests stretch out to education and leisure. In fact his interest and love for Plymouth is comprehensive and his life's work.

For me, meeting up with John after eight years was an absolute eye opener and after talking with him for two hours which flew past, I left wishing I had more time to spare to take on board all that he had to talk about.

Whilst I still have John Ingham in mind it is a good moment to write about our Parliamentary Members past and present. Plymouth has a remarkable history in its selection of Members of Parliament. The city seldom seems to have been without a leading parliamentarian and frequently has had one or more holding high office.

It was John Ingham who took me to have tea in the drawing room of 3 Elliot Terrace, once the home of Lord and Lady Astor, who bequeathed it to the City. On that occasion we started talking about strong women who dominated politics in the City for some time. Nancy Astor being the most outstanding. What a woman! Not even English but an American from the South. Virginia to be precise. She married Waldorf Astor and when he inherited his title and was no longer eligible to sit in the House of Commons, Nancy stood in his place. The ensuing twenty five years were good for Plymouth. With Waldorf increasingly involved in local politics and Nancy championing the City at national level, I doubt if we have ever been so prominently represented.

Lady Astor was never backwards in coming forwards! A strict teetotaller and a Christian Scientist, she did her best to correct the drinking habits of the armed services in the City. A hopeless task but she was never daunted. With her husband, Lord Astor, they became Lord Mayor and Lady Mayoress throughout the war years with the consent of all political parties. Both worked tirelessly in their efforts to assist the population during the stress of the endless bombing. Later they worked equally forcefully and successfully to help Plymouth rise from the ashes. On Lady Astor becoming an Honorary Freeman in 1959, Plymouth was gifted with their home, 3 Elliot Terrace, right on The Hoe, and with it some wonderful silver, many fine pictures and a mountain of memorabilia, much of which can now be seen if you get the opportunity to visit the house. Incidentally if you would like to be taken round, there are opportunities and the dates and times can be found at Plymouth Dome. The other wonderful gift Nancy Astor gave the city was a diamond and sapphire necklace that she literally used to wrap round her neck. On the day she was made an Honorary Freeman of the City of Plymouth, an honour which had been bestowed on her husband in 1936, she took the necklace off and placed it around the neck of the then Lady Mayoress, Mrs Washbourne, saying that in future it was for the Lady Mayoresses to wear during their term of office. The present Lady Mayoress may only wear it six times a year, to satisfy the insurers. It has been modernised and can be worn at any length with wrist bands and earrings to match. It is stunning and I imagine every Lady Mayoress must get great pleasure in wearing it during its six outings a year.

The Victorian house, No 3 Elliot Terrace looks right out across Plymouth Sound. It is gracious and elegant but essentially a home. Visiting it one wonders how the council could ever have thought of turning down this generous bequest to the City. Lady Astor thought it should be used as a Lord Mayor's residence during his term of office. This was totally impractical and possibly was the reason that the gift was only accepted by a narrow margin. Thirty six councillors voted for it and thirty four against. Has it been a drain on the civic purse? Of course it has because the upkeep is horrendous and will continue to be so. Does it matter? The answer to that is an emphatic, No. One has to recognise that this is a house used for occasions that the general populace know nothing about and from which millions of pounds are acquired for the City.

Let me just give you two examples. The first is the annual visit made to Plymouth by Mr and Mrs Gleason, the Presidents of the American Gleason Corporation which has a factory out at Estover where Plymothian Bob Ball is in charge, and who is also now a Vice President of the Corporation. Together with the Lord Mayor and other dignitaries, they always have dinner at 3 Elliot Terrace when they are in Plymouth, and not only do they continue to invest in their Estover plant, the Gleasons also make substantial gifts to many worthwhile causes in Plymouth including quite a lot of money which goes into Combe Dean Comprehensive School.

Elliott Terrace and The Grand Hotel.

Graham Stirling of the Barden Corporation will tell you that a few years back when the Plymouth operation of this American company needed more funding to allow for expansion, it looked a shade doubtful as to whether they would get what they wanted. The American parent company could not see the advantage of investing more in a city so far away from London, and almost unheard of. Eventually they were persuaded to pay a fleeting visit to Plymouth next time they were in the UK.

How to entertain them and how to make them realise just what we had to offer became all important. It was suggested to Graham Stirling by the Leader of the Council that perhaps the city might entertain them to dinner in Elliot Terrace. This was agreed and the Americans were entranced with the view, the house, the meal and the company. Before the end of the meal the senior director informed Graham Stirling that they would be delighted to invest further in the Plymouth factory. This brought not only millions to the city but also more jobs and therefore more spending power down the line. That one dinner virtually paid for the cost of running the house for at least a year. An example of co-operation between business and the city fathers and what can be done by pulling together.

There can be no doubt that the purchase by the Astors of 3 Elliot Terrace and the Astor's position as leading lights in both political and social life at national level, brought enormous benefits to Plymouth. They brought so many politicians and other influential people to enjoy their hospitality and see what Plymouth had to offer. Not all of us today are particularly happy in the way in which the plan for Plymouth after the Blitz was conceived by Professor Abercrombie but he was a personal friend and a frequent and welcome visitor. Winston Churchill came on more than one occasion. Field Marshal Montgomery on another. Then there was George Bernard Shaw, Lawrence of Arabia, Charlie Chaplin, Queen Marie of Romania, King Peter of Yugoslavia, General Eisenhower and John F. Kennedy. King George VI and Queen Elizabeth honoured them with their presence for a typically wartime meal after which they went upstairs to the first floor drawing room to enjoy the spectacular view from the balcony across the Hoe and Plymouth Sound. It was only a matter of hours after that visit that the Plymouth Blitz began. Plymouth as we knew it was about to crumble before our eyes.

A retired Royal Marine Colour Sergeant, known as Les, acts as butler amongst other duties at 3 Elliot Terrace. He has a love of the house and keeps it perfectly, spending much of his time seeking out some of the hidden treasures of the house which have been buried away in the basement or elsewhere in the house for a long time. Every find is carefully cleaned and polished and lovingly placed in a suitable setting. He has become an expert on the lives of the Astors and either through looking around the house or getting into conversation with him you will learn that in the 1800's the Astors were one of the richest families in the world. In 1905 Waldorf and Nancy met on a liner crossing the Atlantic and fell in love. Waldorf's father did not attend the wedding in 1906; he was annoyed with his son because he was marrying a divorcee. Nancy had been through a disastrous marriage with Robert Shaw, a drunkard and womaniser by whom she had a son, Bobby. Waldorf owned the great Cliveden estate. When in 1908 he decided to become an MP, he did not choose a safe seat but the anti-Conservative Plymouth Sutton. It took him two attempts to succeed. In 1917 his father was created a Viscount and died in 1919 forcing Waldorf to become the second Lord Astor and to sit in the Lords. He tried to disinherit the title but could not and so Plymouth Sutton became vacant. Nancy, however, could sit in the House of Commons. On the 28th November 1919 after one of the most dazzling election performances, she was duly elected MP for Sutton and became the first lady to be an MP although not the first lady to be elected. Baroness Markiewicz of the Sein Fein Party had that honour. She, with thirty five others from that party refused to swear allegiance to the Crown and so they did not become MPs.

Plymothians should feel proud of this house, get to know a little more about it and realise what an enormous asset it is to the City.

Not in the same mould as Nancy Astor, Baroness Vickers, formerly Joan Vickers, became MP for Devonport in the 1955 General Election, amazing everyone when she toppled Michael Foot. Not only did she gain the seat then but she held on to it for the next 19 years. This stylish, blue-rinsed lady, always wore a hat which matched her smart, business-like but feminine suits. She always believed her success came because she so badly wanted to be an MP but those of us who knew her were aware it was much more than that. Joan Vickers did not drive a car and so, because she wanted to get to know Plymothians, she walked or got on a bus to her destination which gave her the chance to meet all sorts of people. She got to know Dockyard men, bus crews, and many others who were won over by her straightforward, no nonsense attitude. She did not harangue those of a different persuasion. When she called at houses within the constituency, she explained that if she was going to ask for their vote, the least she could do was visit them personally. Seldom did she experience a door shut in her face. Her victory was sweet and especially for the Conservatives in Devonport having fought such a hopeless campaign in the previous election with Randolph Churchill, Winston's son, as the candidate. I do not think I ever met a ruder or more arrogant man than him, and it is no wonder he did not win the seat.

There was a very definite dislike between Joan Vickers and Nancy Astor, born largely because of Lady Astor's extraordinary treatment of her successor. She did her best to make a fool of Joan Vickers, made catty remarks in public and never failed to make some derogatory remark about Joan Vicker's hats. This was very unlike Nancy Astor and one wonders if there was not a little jealousy there. Certainly no one was more annoyed and disappointed than Lady Astor when she was persuaded by her family, not to stand in the election immediately after the war. They recognised that the country was ready for a change and that she might well lose her seat. They were right. Labour got in by a landslide.

The Baroness was none too fond of David Owen either. He defeated her by 437 votes in the 1974 election. She saw it as a cold calculation on his part, when he decided to drop Sutton when the boundary changes were made, which would have made it harder for him to win Sutton. He moved over to Devonport which looked to be the safer seat.

Following her defeat, Joan Vickers might well have become a European MP but Lady Thatcher persuaded her to take a seat in the House of Lords instead. In her remarkable career she espoused many and varied causes. Giving Falklanders the right to British Citizenship, effective ways to deal with kerb-crawlers and prostitution, the threatened closure of the Royal Marines band, support for fish farm and the continuing development of Devonport Dockyard.

271

When she was made a Freeman of the City of Plymouth with her one time political foe Michael Foot, I wonder if she thought of Nancy Astor and said ' What kind of fool am I?'

When I wrote 'Invitation to Plymouth' in 1993 I said 'If I were a betting person I would lay odds on Plymouth born David Owen or more correctly the Rt Hon Lord Owen CH, being the next person to be made a Freeman of the City'. I was out by 8 years because I understand that both he and Baroness Janet Fookes, are both about to become Freemen as I write in November 2000. Lord Owen of Plymouth is an extraordinary and larger than life man in many ways. A great servant of the people and a master of diplomacy as we have seen when he was our youngest Foreign Secretary and more recently when he had the impossible task of trying to get the Serbs, the Bosnians , Croats and all the other former members of Yugoslavia to reach agreement.

It is not often that such a character is thrown up on the political arena. He is a bit like Nancy Astor, inasmuch as he fears no one and is his own man. Incidentally as MP for Devonport, he sat in the House just a few days longer than that great lady. Like her, he has always had the ability to be extremely controversial. Few people would have chosen to move their political position as he did when he joined the gang of four and formed the SDP. What a pity it is that rigid party adherence makes it impossible, without a coalition government, for men of David Owen's stature to be in the Cabinet. We need people of his outstanding ability. I would like to see him as Ambassador to the United Nations or a similar role. His qualifications are impeccable.

Underneath the ruthless determination that marks him out as a cut about most, there is a gentle, family man with a love of poetry and the sea. He has loved the water and boats since childhood. His love of the sea made him particularly sensitive to the needs of the charity Horizon, which provides deprived children with the opportunity of taking to the waters around Plymouth in boats crewed by volunteers and providing children with the chance to see Plymouth from another viewpoint, and give them the excitement so sadly lacking in their daily lives. David Owen gave the charity a boat which helped start the considerable fleet of boats now in use for this purpose and about which I have already written. He is a restless creature who always needs to be doing something. How much Plymouth could benefit from this energy. I can see him in a leading role in the running of Derriford Hospital or perhaps in the University. Sadly I do not think that would be demanding enough for him. Whatever he does will be well done and he richly deserves the Freedom of the City.

I was reminded by John Ingham that the renowned Lucy Middleton was another woman who had stood successfully for Plymouth - until Linda Gilroy, the only woman Labour member for the City, I think. Then there was the remarkable Albert Medland who, firstly was a revered councillor and then late in life became an MP and very influential. His knowledge of Plymouth, its post war problems, and rebuilding projects, made him a respected authority in the eyes of the Government of the day. There were few members in the House of Commons who had been through the experiences, trauma and tragedy that Plymouth had suffered during the years of the war.

Further back also Devonport had Leslie Hore Belisha MP. Today's generation will have no idea who he was but others will remember him for the Belisha Beacons which flashed on and off at road crossings. The first acknowledgment of the dangers that the increasing motor traffic was causing pedestrians. The Belisha Beacons have disappeared but they were the forerunners of the present traffic light crossings.

Isaac Foot and his sons will always be remembered by Plymouth. Isaac was almost as good an orator as his son Michael Foot once leader of the Labour Party. Isaac was a staunch Liberal and a staunch Methodist. A great friend of my maternal grandfather, William George, I can remember, as a child, listening to the magnificent battle of words these two dominant men had. They were both Liberals, both Methodists, but that did not stop the verbal sparks flying. Isaac also spawned three other famous sons; Lord Foot of Foot and Bowden, the diplomat Lord Caradon and the MP Sir Dingle Foot QC.

Janet Fookes, now Baroness Fookes achieved great things for Plymouth when she sat in the House of Commons. Eventually she became Deputy Speaker, a role she was honoured to accept. But I wonder if Plymothians realised quite what restrictions this put on this redoubtable lady. It meant that she could not voice any public opinion on such issues as the Dockyard and Defence. She had to remain neutral. It used to gall me when I saw letters in the Press from uninformed people who thought she was doing nothing. Little did they know how much she had to wheel and deal in the corridors of power for the benefit of Plymouth. Without doubt her influence behind the scenes helped Devonport win the battle of the Dockyards, Devonport v Rosyth. We know now just how successful her efforts were and why, quite rightly, she is to become a Freeman of the City of Plymouth.

The Baroness tells a lovely story about coming to Plymouth. It was Joan Vickers who suggested that Janet Fookes might care to stand for Plymouth Drake. She was gratified naturally but did not think for one moment that the selection committee would choose her. However after several meetings she came for her final visit to the selection committee. Never one for travelling light generally, on this occasion she decided to be different. It was just for one night and for one appointment. She chose her outfit with care, a suitable pair of shoes and just packed an overnight bag. The train arrived in Plymouth on time at 5.20pm and as she stepped off the train, briefcase and overnight bag in hand, she caught the heel of her elegant court shoe on something unseen and the heel broke off. Flashing through her mind was the time of the day and that she did not have another pair of shoes in her luggage. The thought of appearing either barefoot or with one leg shorter than the other before the selection committee and Joan Vickers disapproval, filled her with horror. She cursed travelling light - and has never again done so. She rushed, hopping, to the taxi rank and directed the driver to find the nearest shoe shop with the utmost speed. Bemused, the poor man drove fast against the rush hour traffic and arrived in the then unpedestrianised New George Street outside one of the many shoe shops just as the clock was reaching the half hour. Dashing into a shop which was just closing its doors, Janet purchased the first pair of likely shoes she saw. Whether the selection committee noticed them history does not relate. They would certainly have been surprised if she had been sufficiently unconservative to arrive barefoot! Anyway the outcome was that Plymouth Drake acquired another first class Member of Parliament.

It seems strange even now that the aura of Alan Clark still shines in the political world. He has been dead sometime but there are constant references to him for all sorts of reasons. What an extraordinary man. I found him fascinating but having met him once or twice I was none too sure that I liked him. This was a man who represented Plymouth for years. Wealthy, privileged, highly educated and a Minister of Defence, yet he seemed to be without any real depth of feeling for this city. We talked about many things and I enjoyed his rapier mind but what I did not like was his declared policy of not getting himself involved with local matters. Plymouth as a place, seemed almost a mystery to him. He had no idea about the geography of the city and was the only member at that time who did not have a residence in the city. I wondered how you could truly represent people if you did nothing to get to know them or have their interests at heart.

In his favour I have to say that he worked hard at the Ministry of Defence, even though, like Janet Fookes as Deputy Speaker, his position took away the right to fight openly for Plymouth as a Naval Base and for the Dockyard. Now that he is dead I am aware that the country has lost another strong, exciting personality whose political presence could not be ignored. His personal life is better ignored!

Currently we have three hard working Members, each with very different personalities and ways of tackling things. The interesting factor is that they are all Plymothians if only by adoption, and all three have homes in the city. Linda Gilroy, the Labour and Co-operative Member for Plymouth Sutton is one of those people one warms to the more you know her. She is essentially down to earth and in the true spirit of the Co-operative Movement, in her mind her role is to help the people of Plymouth in whatever way she can. She has the same evangelical approach to the future of Plymouth that I have come across so many times since I started writing this book and which was nowhere near as apparent eight years ago when I wrote 'Invitation to Plymouth'.

When I said to her that I thought she had a refreshing outlook on politics and the House of Commons, her reply amused me. 'The House of Commons is a world of unreality, full of teachers and lawyers who are not averse o speaking out, making it difficult sometimes for the rest of us to get a word in. I love it but I need to spend a lot of time in Plymouth to make sure that I belong to the real world'!

She certainly belongs to the real world and whilst she supports her party, she is in many ways apolitical in her thinking and in her actions. She represents all the people in her constituency irrespective of party, colour, class or creed. A nice touch is the competition she promoted to find a young Plymouth artist to design her Christmas Card this year. The result has been a stunning exhibition in the Theatre Royal displaying the work of these talented youngsters. Linda's work load is heavy, her office a corner in a Union Office in Exeter Street. When it was first suggested that she should stand for Parliament she was slightly shocked. No member of her family was especially political and she herself had been working for some years for Age Concern in Scotland. However it was time for a change and she wanted to come to Devon where she had spent many happy holidays in her childhood. Before taking on the mantle of politics she looked for another post, something different from Age Concern and found herself short listed for a job with the Gas Consumer Council. It was this job that brought her to Plymouth and finally gave her the chance to take up the suggestion that she should stand for Parliament. A well run election campaign, the ability to get to know her constituents and for them to trust her, resulted in her election in 1997, and on her way to join Blair's Babes! Many people in Plymouth Sutton have reason to be grateful for the care in which she has handled all sorts of problems both large and small since that momentous day in her life..

Her maiden speech in the House was on Defence Policy. One might almost say 'What else' in Plymouth? It was a masterly speech and if you read some of the points she made then, you realise how much has been achieved in the last almost four years. Drawing skilfully on matters historical in politics and talking as the fifth woman representing the city, she pointed out the need to increase the number of women in The House. 'There still have not been many more than 200 women Members since Lady Astor took her seat in 1919. In the same time there have been more than 4,000 male members of Parliament.'

That Plymouth in 1997 had 11 people unemployed for every job vacancy shows a dramatic change in the fortunes of the City. Today we have something like 3.2% unemployment and that is likely to improve with the tremendous work that has been put in to bring new business to the City. You have only to look at the number of Call Centres we have let alone the expansion of other businesses.

Linda went on to say ' I stress the importance of the Royal Naval Dockyard. Again and again, Devonport Management Ltd and its workers have been able to report completion of work ahead of schedule. The efficiency of the docking and essential defects programme on the type 23 frigate HMS Montrose resulted in its being undocked four days ahead of schedule.'

And so her speech continued underlining much that I have already written about at length where the Dockyard is concerned. It was a well constructed Maiden Speech and ended by stating something which Plymouth should never forget. 'Cradle of the Commonwealth, springboard for the New World, Defender of the Peace in this new Millennium - the city of Plymouth has a proud, heritage, and a challenging future.'

All that Linda Gilroy MP said in that speech is happening. Plymouth is surging ahead.

David Jamieson never wastes time in his efforts to strive for the good of Plymothians whilst he is in the House of Commons and equally when he returns to his home beat. It was David Owen's old seat he captured; a seat that was traditionally Labour and would never have fallen to the SDP had it not been for David Owen's personality. He is constantly to be seen coping with some problem or the other and as an ex-schoolmaster has a particular interest in education. Recently he has taken on the fight to save two residential homes in Plymouth and backed by Linda Gilroy, I am quite sure their voices will carry some weight.

David is especially pleased how dramatically the unemployment figures have fallen since Labour came to power in 1997. In April 1997, 11,880 people were out of work. In October 2000 there were 3,829 unemployed. A great drop and David Jamieson feels there has been a sea of change in the atmosphere in Plymouth. After years of neglect thousands of people are in work, with a focus and direction that makes a vast difference to their lives.

Gary Streeter MP in some ways could be said not to be a Member for Plymouth because his constituency lies on the outskirts of the city and takes in part of the South Hams and West Devon. He essentially belongs to the city however and since I first met him when he was a city councillor he has travelled a long way in the political world. I have always admired his strength of character and his courtesy. When I met him one wet day in October 2000, it was by invitation to his lovely old farmhouse home. The rain was pelting down but he was on the watch for me and graciously came out along the garden path with a big umbrella already open to protect me as I walked towards the house. Who can help warming to such courtesy in this day and age! As a member of the current Shadow Cabinet under William Hague, his political star shines brightly and he brings to his role the honesty and straightforwardness which is so often lacking.

I asked him if he was still enjoying The House of Commons. He was positive in his answer 'Yes' but less than happy about the time it necessitated him being away from home and the loneliness that it engendered. He is a strong family man and hates being away from his wife. One of the things he is currently looking forward to is the extra time they will be able to spend together now that he has a grown up family. At the end of a busy day in The House there is a need to be able to share the happenings of the day and also to prevent one getting hooked on the lifestyle, the buzz and being at the centre of everything British. He has always felt that there is a danger of becoming too protected by the easing of paths when you are an MP and getting too big-headed. Gary says he has little chance of that because his wife and children bring him down to earth every time he comes home.

We talked of the plans for a new town in the South Hams and how he felt very strongly that this should not be. It would be far better, far more sensible to add it on to Plymouth for good sound reasons. Schooling for one. Transport access for another and for the hundred and one problems there are when something totally new is created. He is very aware that a new school will have to be built fairly soon anyway on the edge of his constituency but he does not want it to be isolated which would prevent the pupils taking advantage of all that Plymouth has to offer in the way of recreation, the arts, the theatre etc.

Gary Streeter is a committed Christian and so too is his family. This strength is very apparent in his life. Some time ago he, with two other families, one of them Ian Potts of the Architect Design Group of whom I have already written, bought the large farm house and its buildings together, providing three separate homes and the basis for a full Christian life. They all belong to a church where they meet and worship and literally spread the Gospel. It is a place of worship that has caught the imagination of many. As it grows it reaches out taking the Gospel to the people. Faith is a living thing in all their daily lives. They practice what they preach and Gary firmly believes that working as a Member of Parliament is what God wants him to do.

Writing about Gary Streeter has brought me back to Plymouth City Council of today which is Conservative led and determined to achieve great things. I was lucky enough to talk to Councillor Kevin Wigens who is both Deputy Leader and Chairs the Planning Committee. Here is a man of burning ambitions, not for himself, but for what he believes is right for Plymouth. I really felt that with his determination we really will see Tinside re-born, we will see new life breathed into the city centre. He is not a man to take no for an answer nor to let things slide. He requires prompt action and will undoubtedly get it. Like me, Kevin believes our waterfront is almost unique. He lives in Ocean Court just off Richmond Walk and from his windows he watches the constant movement of naval ships. Not only Royal Navy but French, Italian, Portuguese, and many others who arrive in port to take part in a NATO exercise. These foreign sailors recognise that we have the best navy in the world and they cannot believe their luck when they find out that their home port for the time of the exercise will be Plymouth. With so much Royal Navy activity now Plymouth based Kevin feels pretty confident that we will always be home to the Royal Navy even though in the fifty years of the last century, the service has shrunk in size. With the arrival of Flag Officer Sea Training, the Trident and Vanguard submarines, HMS Ocean and the three other ships of the same size, as well as the normal complement of ships, Devonport is the biggest Naval Base in this country.

It is very pleasing to talk to a councillor who allies sound business acumen to his role as Deputy Leader. Successful business men weigh up the pros and cons, make decisions and then strike out to achieve the objective. This to me is exactly what Kevin Wigens does. The Conservatives were more than a little surprised at their resounding win at the election in May. They thought they might have won by a small margin and were elated at the scale of the victory. I asked him how the newly appointed councillors managed in their inexperience. I was told that it rested on the shoulders of the thirteen seasoned councillors to teach them the art of being councillors. An onerous task which places heavy responsibility on the old hands. It is not a lesson that can be learned overnight but Kevin was very complimentary about his new colleagues and saw them as bright hopes for the future.

We talked about the complicated business of freeholds and leaseholds within the city centre. Some people were concerned that the council were hanging onto freeholds unnecessarily and others that they were giving away what belonged rightly to Plymouth. It is a difficult and emotive subject but I believe we are in safe hands and equally I understand why developers moving in to bring us new business are reluctant to invest unless there is a freehold attached. Much depends on the sensible, rationalisation of the whole and this is happening and will continue to be done.

It was good to hear Kevin Wigens speak so highly of the efficiency and caring of his secretarial staff without whom he could not carry out his onerous role. Most of his time now is spent on Council business and fortunately his own business is sufficiently well organised to run to a great extent on its own. Apart from dealing with the day to day running of a very busy office, Kevin receives somewhere in the region of 150 letters a week, all of which are dealt with promptly. In this he carries on the tradition of the revered and respected ex-Lord Mayor George Creber, who believed that immediate response to a letter, a phone call or a personal request, was essential and prevented anyone feeling disregarded even if the problem could not be sorted out overnight.

Plymouth's Waterfront

Chapter XIV

What's in a name - 46 Plymouth's worldwide

'O dear Plymouth town. O blue Plymouth Sound
O where in the world can your equal be found'

The answer to that couplet in the eyes of a Plymothian is nowhere. Our Plymouth is the mother of towns and cities and she belongs to history, Nonetheless we should never forget the compliment that all these other Plymouths have paid us in naming their town or city after ours.

When I last wrote about other Plymouths in 1993 there were 47 Plymouths worldwide but with the loss of Plymouth on the Island of Monserrat, the number is reduced to 46. Each one has its own story to tell and some of them have been kind enough to write to me. What they have to say has given me pleasure to include in this chapter.

A report from the Business Colony in Plymouth County, Massachusetts tells me that it serves a wide variety of businesses. Virtually all categories of commerce are carried on from high tech to light manufacturing, to retail, tourism and recreation. Doesn't sound too different from Plymouth, Devon does it?

This particular Plymouth is easy to place on the globe and has an international profile because of her unique history. Having sailed from Sutton Harbour, Plymouth, Devon, England on 6th September 1620 with the 102 Puritan Pilgrim Fathers on board, and after a difficult crossing of the Atlantic, 'The Mayflower' arrived at Cape Cod on the North American Coast on 9th November. The stone upon which the party first set foot in the New World is revered today as 'Plymouth Rock'. In recognition of the hospitality they had received in Plymouth, the Pilgrim Fathers named their first settlement 'Plimoth'. Meanwhile on 3rd November 1620, King James I granted to the Private 'Plymouth Company' in England, a Charter licensing the 'Council at Plymouth for the planting, ruling and governing of New England'. It is to this Charter that not only Maine and Massachusets owe their foundation, but also the State of New Hampshire. Later the Plymouth Company was overshadowed by the 'Massachusets Company' which accelerated the settlement and development of New England.

Today Plymouth Massachussets is known as the gateway to Cape Cod and is a perfect place for a New England vacation. You are only 40 miles from Boston, 220 miles from New York and within a 50 mile radius are the market places of Baltimore, Hartford, Providence, Buffalo, Washington DC and Philadelphia. The world famous 'Plimoth Plantation' is a mecca for all visitors, realistically depicting life in the Plymouth Colony of 1627. In addition to seeing Plymouth Rock you can also take a look at the Mayflower II, Pilgrim Hall and the historic homes and landmarks of 'America's Hometown'.

The attractions are more than just historic. There is warm sand on White Horse Beach, the Blue Spruce Motel, great golfing at Plymouth Country Club, deep sea or fresh water fishing sailing, whale watches, cruises to Nantucket or Martha's Vineyard and dozens of excellent restaurants for every taste and budget.

There is something very special about this Plymouth. To travel its 100 square miles is a tremendous undertaking in time and beauty. It is a town of communities, neighbourhoods and housing options that range from thousands of dollars to millions.

Dorothy Wales, the town historian for Plymouth, New York State told me all about 'Plymouth NY'. It is a rural town with dairy farming as the main occupation. The population is less than 1500. There are no major businesses in the township nor are there incorporated villages or other municipalities. The town is governed by an elected supervisor and elected town councilpersons. The children attend Norwich schools in a nearby community. Plymouth residents shop in Norwich and go there to see their doctors and it is from Norwich that they get police protection. Plymouth does have an active fire department and emergency squad, a post office, and a Methodist church. Of historic interest, the Plymouth Historical Society has restored the original depot of the Auburn Branch of the New York and Oswego Midland Railroad, which ran through Plymouth from 1869-1891 and it is now a museum.

Plymouth, Minnesota, has a Communications Coordinator, Helen LaFave, who was kind enough to furnish me with information about this busy place which can trace its history back to the pre-Colonial period, 1400-1500AD. The original inhabitants were the Waspeton Sioux. Their encampment was at the north end of Medicine Lake. Indian burial mounds are still visible there.

It was not until 1848 that the first settler arrived. Antonine Le Counte was a guide and explorer and he carried mail from Red River country to points south, trading trinkets and other goods to the Indians for horses on the way.. LeCounte built the first cabin on East Medicine Lake Boulevard.

The town started growing on the northwest shores, known now as Parkers Lake. New settlers arrived and began organising themselves. A decision was made to call the settlement Plymouth. The name nearly did not survive because during one lot of elections it was decided to change the name to Medicine Lake. The change was recorded once at a town meeting and then for some strange reason was never implemented.

The Sioux did not take kindly to the settlers and an uprising in 1862 caused the townspeople to form a militia. Having regained control the settlers went on to build schools, churches and a post office. By 1863 there were hotels as well. Farming became the trade of most of the settlers and with the building of roads, and Medicine Lake a tourist attraction.

Today it is a well-heeled town with a population of some 50,000 and covers 36 square miles. It has a mixture of residential properties and businesses. The location, combined with Plymouth's lakes and rolling, wooded terrain, continues to attract new residents and businesses, making it one of the fastest growing communities in the metro area. Sounds like a good place in which to live.

Maybe it was a small booklet entitled 'Discover the historic Amador County wine country' that attracted me to Plymouth, California. It is right in the heart of a wonderful wine making area. Numerous wineries can be found along the Shenandoah Road in the

Shenandoah Valley just east of Plymouth. Explore the D'Agostini Winery started in 1856 - a wonderful experience. From here you are not far from Sacremento to the south, Nevada City to the north, and Lake Tahoe to the west. You are also in California's Gold Country which is rich in recreation, entertainment and the arts.

Local historians still question whether Pokerville, Puckervil and Plymouth sprang up at different times, on the same site where Highway 49 meets Main Street today. No matter really, for the town was finally born in 1871 when the Empire Pacific and Plymouth Consolidated Gold Mines promised big dividends. Now, Plymouth is the site of the Amador County fair, started in 1938.

California has deep associations with our Plymouth. On 17th June 1579, during his circumnavigation of the World from Plymouth on board the 'Golden Hind' (originally 'The Pelican') and probably whilst seeking the mythical North West Passage, the Elizabethan Navigator, Sir Francis Drake (1541-1596) landed at 38degrees North on the coast of California (now San Francisco). He named the place 'Nova Albion, and set up a stockade. There too he affixed a 'Plate of Brasse' to a stout post, claiming this land for Queen Elizabeth I of England. The local Indians were friendly but perplexed by the Europeans, ultimately crowning Drake their King, with a Crown of Feathers and much ceremonial. Drake set sail again on 23rd July.

Plymouth Township, Pennsylvania is 315 years old and proud of it. Although English settlers from Plymouth, England, first bought the land from William Penn in 1686, their holdings were purchased by Welsh Quakers before the end of the 17th century. It was the Welsh who were principally responsible for starting the Village of Plymouth Meeting which spans the line between Plymouth and Whitemarsh Townships. The original Meeting House built in 1712 was destroyed by fire in 1867. The present one dates from that time.

On Germantown Pike opposite Hickory Road was situated the Hickorytown Hotel, which was a prominent roadhouse. The village of Hickorytown developed in the vicinity of this centre of activity. In the beginning of the 19th century it was a training place for the 326th Regiment of Pennsylvania Militia and the Second Battalion of Montgomery County. The Friendship Company for Protection against Horse Stealing was organised there in 1807. Hickorytown got its first post office in 1857.

Today's local residents are not aware probably, that they live in what used to be Hickorytown. The completion of the Pennsylvania Turnpike with the major interchange at Germantown Pike has motivated considerable development in the vicinity including a large shopping mall known as the Plymouth Meeting Mall.

In the mid-19th century, Plymouth Meeting was a well known station on what was called the Underground Railroad, the road to freedom taken by escaped slaves. George Corson built Abolition Hall on his property for holding meetings condemning slavery. Towards the end of the century the Hall became a studio for George's daughter and her husband Thomas Hovenden. Hovenden's most famous work was 'Breaking House Ties' which may be seen today in the Philadelphia Museum of Art.

Pennsylvania has another Plymouth in Luzerne County.

Plymouth Connecticut no doubt resulted after a gathering of pious Puritans met in Plymouth, Devon for solemn Prayer and fasting at the City's 'Hospital for the Poor Portion' prior to departure for America. The Reverend John White of Dorchester preached and from amongst the congregation, John Warham and John Maverick of Exeter were chosen and ordained to be their Ministers. The party sailed from Plymouth in the 'Mary and John; on 20th March 1630 and named their landing site Dorchester, in honour of their leader. However they moved to the Wisdom Settlement (the germ of Connecticut) and through their puritan enterprise greatly influenced the development of Connecticut as a State.

Plymouth Connecticut is not so far from Bristol or Manchester! And so it goes on. Carolina has Plymouth in Washington County; Florida, Plymouth in Orange County. The great Elizabethan explorer and mariner came finally to Florida in his travels. He found trading with the Floridans very profitable and when the expedition finally returned to Padstow in Cornwall in September 1565 their bounties included 'gold, silver, pearls and other jewels' in great quantities. They also learned of the crops Maize and Potatoes. Most significantly, John Sparke recorded that 'The Floridans have a kind of herb dried. They do suck through the cane and smoke thereof'. This makes the Hawkins expedition a claimant for the introduction of tobacco to Europe.

Idaho has New Plymouth in Payette County, Illinois, Plymouth in Hancock County. Marshall County is the home of Plymouth in Indiana and there is a Plymouth County in North West Iowa and in Cerro Gordo County. Plymouth is in Lyon County, Kansas and Louisville, Kentucky.

In Maine it is Plymouth, Penobscot County. Maine has a special interest in Plymouth Devon. In 1606 the English King James I granted a Royal Charter to the 'Plymouth Company' licensing its operators to occupy (ahead of the French) new lands in America between latitudes 41-45 degrees (Connecticut-Maine). Prominent in the Plymouth Company were the Popham Family (hence Fort Popham in Maine) and the Gorges. In 1607, Sir Ferdinando Gorges (then Governor of Plymouth) sent out an expedition to settle the area known today as Maine. His tomb in St Budeaux Church, Plymouth, duly bears an inscription stating that 'He found Maine'. Later in 1635, his grandson - also called Sir Ferdinando Gorges - was granted the status of 'First Proprietor and Governor of the State of Maine'

Michigan has a Plymouth in Wayne County, and in Mississippi, Plymouth is in Pontotoc County. In Nebraska it is Plymouth, Jefferson County; New Hampshire, Grafton County has a Plymouth. It is interesting to know that in the year 1623, the first two ships to sail up the Piscataque River came from Plymouth. They were owned by Plymothians, one being Leonard Pomeroy, a wealthy merchant and a business associate of the Gorges Family. The Plymouth Company's Charter of the 3rd November 1620, permitted the settlement in New Hampshire.

Plymouth is in Chenango County in New York State. Ohio has no less than four Plymouths in Ashtabula County, Fayette County, Richland County and New Plymouth. There is Plymouth Park in Dallas, Texas, Plymouth, Box Elder County in Utah. Windsor County, Vermont has Plymouth Union and another simply called, Plymouth.

282

Virginia boasts Little Plymouth in King and Queen County. Finally there is Plymouth in Benton County, Washington and Plymouth Sheboiygan County in Wisconsin.

If you read your Bible all these Plymouth's sound like the Begats in Genesis! Certainly, Plymouth, Devon, England seems to have been responsible for much begatting!

I discovered that Canada also boasts some Plymouths. Four in all in Yarmouth County, Pictou County, Nova Scotia and one in New Brunswick. In New Zealand there is a delightful New Plymouth in North Island.

Perhaps the most unlikely Plymouths are in the Caribbean where Trinidad and Tobago have a Plymouth.

The United States of America, apart from its variety of Plymouths lives on in the lives of Plymothians. There are a huge number of successful companies who have their base, their factories or their offices in Plymouth and not one of them would relocate anywhere else.

To name just a few:-

Acheson Colloids Company	(National Starch Co., New Jersey)
American Express Travel Services	(American Express Co., New York)
Aon Risk Services	(Aon Corporation, Illinois)
Ash Instruments Ltd.	(Dentsply Co., Pennsylvania)
Becton Dickinson Ltd.	(Becton Dickinson Co., New Jersey)
British Filters Ltd.	(Echlin Inc., Connecticut)
Devonport Management Lt.	(Halliburton Corp./Brown & Root, Texas)
Eaton Ltd.	(Eaton Corporation, Ohio)
England Wales & Scotland Railways	(Wisconsin Central Railroad Co., Wisconsin)
Enterprise Rent-a-Car	(Enterprise Rent-a-Car, Missouri)
Environ Europe Ltd.	(Environ Products Inc., Pennsylvania)
Fairfax Communications Ltd.	(Advanced Communication Systems Inc., Virginia)
Gleason Works Ltd.	(Gleason Corporation, New York)
Guildsoft Ltd.	(Datawatch Corp., Massachusetts)
Market Reach Ltd.	(Telelink Systems Inc., Colorado)
Medlogic Global Ltd.	(Medlogic Global Corporation, Colorado)
Paper Converting Machine Co.	(Paper Converting Machine Co., Wisconsin)
Ransomes Consumer Ltd.	(Textron Inc., Rhode Island)
St Mellion Golf & Country Club	(American Golf (U.K.) Ltd., California)
Stafford-Miller Ltd.	(Block Drug Co., New Jersey)
Standard Products Ltd.	(Standard Products Co., Michigan)
S.W.E.B.	(The Southern Company, Georgia)
ToshibaCarrier	(Carrier Corporation, Wisconsin)
Western Equipment Developments	(Aseco Co., Massachusetts)
Western Staff Services	(Western Staff Services, California)
The Wrigley Company	(The Wrigley Company, Illinois)

Plymstock Church. c1890 F. J. Snell

Newton Ferrers/Noss Mayo. c1890 F. J. Snell

285

Hooe Lake and the Royal Oak Public House. c1890 F. J. Snell

Halfpenny Bridge Stonehouse. Shirley Hole

The Royal William Yard – Stonehouse 1947

Chapter XV

Villages within the City

Plymouth has grown from three towns, Plymouth itself, Stonehouse and Devonport becoming larger and larger as the years have gone by. In the course of time the one town became a city and drew into its welcoming folds the various villages and areas today even going as far afield as Ivybridge. Indeed the PL sort code covers an enormous area stretching deep into Cornwall and way into Devon. I like the various villagey feelings you get about some of the urban areas. I live in Stoke which is a lively community in its own right and apart from now being deprived of any form of bank, has just about every kind of shop you need to sustain both the body and the mind. The Stoke Post Office is a regular meeting place for many people who gather there on various days of the week to draw their pensions, get their lottery tickets or even buy stamps! What is so nice about it is the friendly post office counter staff who, without actually prying into your business, seem to know your needs. Much nicer than the cold, austere general post offices. Next door is one of the few family butchers still in being and beyond that a chatty newsagents. Across the road the greengrocer has an amazingly well-stocked shop with equally amazing, sensible prices, closeby is 'Flower Fayre' with gorgeous flowers just waiting to be sold for special occasions. The second hand clothes shop does a good, discreet business in selling your own clothes on a commission basis or finding you excellent quality shirts, skirts, dresses etc that are all in good condition and from which you can very inexpensively replenish a goodly part of your wardrobe. They also rent out exotic hats for weddings, for Ascot, or for any of the various occasions to which hats are still the in thing to wear.

The village has several second hand shops selling bric a brac, motorbike parts, books and heaven alone knows what else. There is a good Indian restaurant, you can acquire a tattoo, go to the barber or to the friendly ladies hairdresser, aptly named 'Ahead of Time'. This is not a posh, up-market salon but the stylists are up-to-date, skillful and imaginative. It is owned by a cheerful woman who with her assistants might well win beauty contests but they are not shining examples for 'Slimmer of the Year ' awards!! It is far cheaper than going to the City Centre and you feel you are not only among friends but kept up to date with what is happening in the village - and who is averse to a little, non-malicious gossip! It's a bit like going to have a cup of coffee with friends with a hair-do thrown in for good measure! You always leave feeling better in spirit, even if it has been a bad day.
A few doors up the street, quite recently, a colourful shop full of curtain and upholstery material, has opened. Good advice is available and your own chairs can be re-upholstered. Next door the moulding shop can supply any type of decorative moulding that one could wish for from cornices to cherubs! Then there is the pet shop which also sells seeds and plants.

The newest venture in the village, just next to the Oxfam shop and the Plymco Store, is 'The Design Bank' an Aladdin's Cave of treasures. It is in the former TSB building and without a doubt has brought an exciting new emphasis on business in the village as well as providing new jobs. It is owned by Brett Squance and Peter Higgins of Plymouth's QFD Interiors who have set up the centre to sell an innovative and exciting range of furniture, fittings and home furnishings at new and nearly new prices. QFD specialises in the renovation and refurbishment of hotel, restaurants, bars and yachts. The company specifies new products, finishes and designs to clients, and when renovation and refurbishments are finished, furniture, fittings and furnishings which have been replaced can be sold on locally.

The old bank has been beautifully converted, as one might expect from such experienced designers. There is a library of fabric samples and reference material. Furniture on offer includes dining tables and chairs from the award-winning avant-garde ironworks company, hall tables, bedroom furniture, occasional tables and large luxury sofas. Garden furnishings, designer lighting, wooden gifts, oil lamps, designer bed linen, voiles, candles and cushions, all add to the attractive range of goods on offer. Many of the things are the sort of objects one does not generally find in Plymouth. If you are looking for something special, this treasure trove will provide it.

The company obtained a £10,000 grant from the city council as part of the Stoke Village enhancement project to help regenerate the old Georgian building which had lain empty and neglected for a decade.

Until quite recently you would have been able to find Trevor Burrows Photography just a little away from the centre of the village in a small lane off Albert Road .The small building was named after Trevor who literally rebuilt the premises which housed his studio, office and darkroom etc. The business is now a limited company and has moved not far away to Millfields where in Studio 8/23, Mary Seacole Road, the business thrives. This talented, professional man has just that something extra that makes people seek him out rather than having to look for work himself.

Trevor will tell you that being a successful, commercial photographer is much more than just taking a photograph. It is a question of balance, in other words knowing about electronics, people, creativity, a business sense and your own limitations, so that you can get the best results for yourself and your clients. Trevor Burrows has proved that this is true. In conjunction with the main thrust of his work within advertising, PR, industry and commerce, he does a lot of work for the local tourism agencies such as the Plymouth Marketing Bureau , amongst others, generally promoting the area. His work over the years has given him a library of photographs which he calls Image File and consists of filing cabinets full of transparencies which can be used as stock shots for brochures and a hundred and one other uses.

Plymouth was lucky that he came here. It was pure chance. Trevor and his wife wanted to come to the South West. Where was almost immaterial so they just stuck a pin in the map and the place pinpointed was Plymouth! He worked for some time in the Plymouth Polytechnic Media Unit, working his way up from a junior position until he found himself in charge. His business sense and organisational ability made him able to implement several worthwhile changes. He wanted to work for himself however and the result is Trevor Burrows Photography. It was certainly the right move, something that was emphasised in March 1992 when he won a merit award from the Institute of Professional Photography at their South Western Regional Annual Print Awards. He was particularly delighted to have won the award because the example he sent them was the only one he submitted! Since then he has gone on to win many other prestigious awards.

If you enjoy the smell of freshly baked bread then your nose will probably lead you to Brimbles,a bakery at 1, 2 & 3 South Hill, Stoke. Ashley and Margaret Newton bought the bakery 14 years ago. The shop was originally three old cottages which were knocked down by the National Trust who owned them. The original plan was for a butchers but it was later converted into a bakery. It is in a conservation area so any possible improvements have to meet with stringent conditions.

The bakery is a great success selling to hundreds of people on a daily basis. The tantalising smell of hot pies and pasties mingles in the air. At lunchtime hundreds of filled rolls are sold every day, in addition to the normal bread, special breads, breadcakes of various types. They also sell hot soup and jacket potatoes with a variety of fillings. Even fresh popcorn.

It is a pleasure to watch Ashley, Margaret and their daughter Janet, at work assisted by three bakers and 5 part time shop assistants. It is a tough life, Ashley starts at 4am, Margaret and Janet are in the shop by 7.30am. Brimbles closes at 6pm.

Mentioning that Brimbles is in a Conservation Area reminds me of the work done by the Stoke Damerel Conservation Society which has Robin Midgeley as its Chairman. It is true that much of Stoke, because of its historical and architectural qualities, is designated as a Conservation Area, within which there are special planning controls, including controls to protect trees. Stoke Damerel Conservation Society is invited to consider and advise the City Council on all planning proposals in the Area. Whilst these controls can limit our freedom, they do give us considerable influence over the shape of the environment. The Society has been successful in many ways. For example it was their work which prevented the demolition of the former Stoke Damerel Junior School and encouraged its conversion to a business park and shoppers' car park; the latter I find a Godsend. It prevented building in the Pleasure Garden behind Nelson Gardens, encouraged improvements in Blockhouse Park resisted, with some success, the removal of large mature trees that help to preserve the elegant townscape in Stoke. They also ensured the retention of a view of Plymouth Sound from Stoke Village centre by securing modifications to a development proposal.

Stoke Damerel Conservation Society would appreciate having more members to give them a greater voice and would welcome anyone who would like to join the Society. The meetings are held on the first Monday of every month at the United Services Officers' Club at Mount Wise. The meetings are open to all members. Membership is £5 per year for a couple and £3 for single members. If you would like more information before attending a meeting, please do contact The Membership Secretary, 19 Acre Place, Stoke, Plymouth PL1 4QR.

Stoke must have more pubs in a concentrated area than most. They all have their virtues and their regulars. I enjoy The Lounge in Stopford Place especially. Largely because it is my local and also because it is a meeting place for a lot of business people who enjoy the genial companionship and the very good, inexpensive, non pretentious food.

Devonport was originally a town in its own right and has always been the home of the Dockyard, now DML and HMS Drake now known as Plymouth Naval Base. Its residents mainly had connection with the Dockyard and the Services, and still has today to a large extent. It is always a busy place and has its main shopping centre in Marlborough Street, now pedestrianised. One of the nicest things about modern day Devonport is the action taken by residents in places like Pembroke Street, Granby Street, who have strong communities who have worked and are working for better lives for their children and themselves. It is good too that companies like the Co-operative Society have opened a new store in the area which is staffed by local people. You get the sense of energy being put into what, at one time was a very run down area. Recently Plymouth City Council have refurbished the swimming pool at Mount Wise which has made a tremendous difference to the children. Many of the children living in this area have also benefited from the Horizon Charity which I have written about elsewhere. Going to sea in boats has given the children a new outlook on Plymouth entirely. Many of them did not even know that Plymouth Hoe was round the corner from their homes.

Keyham is another lively community, right on the Dockyard's doorsteps. They too have wrought miracles in organising a thriving community centre bringing huge benefits to the people who live here.

Peverell is another busy world of its own. Much of the shopping area is on the main road but it does have everything from a big Plymco store to a Post Office, a hairdresser, chemist, florist and greengrocer, a watch repairer, the lively Hope Baptist Church and a branch of Plymouth Library Services. The road behind also has shops and one that you cannot fail to notice .

Children of all ages from three to ninety cannot resist looking into the window of Celebration Balloons in Weston Park Road Peverell. The window is full of exciting balloon arrangements aligned to cuddly toys, cards, ribbons and further behind a dancing array of balloons of every colour and shape designed for special occasions or for the sheer pleasure of a child to clutch firmly in a sticky little mitt. The colourful display demands attention whether you are in a car or a bus and for children walking to and from school their reaction is much like the Bisto Kids of old who used to stand with their noses pressed to the window conjuring up the smells in their nostrils. Today's children simply allow their eyes to take in the magic.

The showroom is tiny but full of fun and a sense of happiness which has much to do with the owner Sarah Onslow. It was her dream to have just such a business as this. The whole thing is joyful. Everyone she supplies has reason for celebration whether it is a birth, a christening, an engagement, a marriage, an anniversary even - dare I say it - the successful divorce! I had never stopped to think about the ramifications of running such a business and found myself listening totally fascinated to Sarah. Whilst I was with her a lady arrived who wanted balloons for a special occasion. She selected the ones she wanted, and then the colour scheme was discussed and finally there was the question of getting the balloons to their destination. Not easy to pack fully blown up balloons into a car - they have a decided will of their own. Sarah has the answer, you bring a large duvet cover to contain them! If the lady had wanted them delivered, Sarah would do it for a small charge. Sarah takes endless trouble to make sure that her customers have the best help and advice possible in choosing their balloons.

I looked through an album of photographs that Sarah keeps in the shop to show customers. The pictures show the most elegant table decorations made entirely with balloons. The artistry is astounding and the colour schemes can be arranged to compliment the room, the clothes etc. One black and white display I thought was stunning and reminded me of My Fair Lady and the Ascot scene.

Not everything runs smoothly in anyone's life and not so long ago the shop was set alight by wanton vandalism and the whole stock destroyed. Sarah was shattered but she has spirit and with the aid of her supportive husband and family Celebration Balloons rose from the ashes and is even better than it was before.

It is great in this stressful life of ours, to find a business which is entirely devised to bring happiness to its customers and to the recipients of these beautiful balloons.

Hyde Park likes to be considered a village in its own right. Surrounded by houses, two schools, Hyde Park Primary School and Plymouth College, a busy shopping street with every conceivable type of outlet, a pub and two churches , one can support its claim. The traders are a united body and every Christmas produce a theme which attracts children and their parents and invariably provides a donation for charity as a result. You will find in amongst the various businesses which include a butcher, a baker, a florist, a small café, a wine merchant , 'A Touch of Class' which has a remarkable story and is something decidedly different. Jacqui Pike and her partner, Mr Jennings, are the inspiration and the driving force within the company.

There are two sides to the business; A Touch of Class is the manufacturing side and Classic Design the retail. The original concept was to make evening dresses for service wives abroad and supply on a mail order basis. Any service wife would appreciate this because formal occasions remain much the same as they were many years ago and evening dresses abroad are not the easiest garments to acquire.

Mr Jennings met Jacqui when he was running 'Start Your Own Business' courses at Enterprise Plymouth and thought she was one of the liveliest people he had ever met. He was invited to help her launch the business and to give general advice. He was happy to help her and also used the DTI initiative for the benefit of the business. This led to Jacqui asking him if he would like to be part of her business. He seized the opportunity although not on a full-time basis and to this day remains a management consultant.

In 1988 Jacqui was offered the contract of making Mess Dress for the Women's Royal Army Corps which she did outstandingly well. About 1990 the army re-organised and redesigned the uniforms. The contract was lost because there was no longer an approved Mess Dress. Eventually the Army approved several of Jacqui's designs and one would have supposed things would have been straightforward from there on but that is not the case.

The rules are incredibly complicated. A 17th-century tradition lays down the rule that the Colonel of the regiment is responsible for clothing his men. Whilst this no longer applies in practice, the decision on which design to adopt is still with each Colonel. A further complication is that the streamlining of the Army has caused 5 regiments to be united into one, but even so the Colonels now have to agree on which design to adopt. This has created delays but it is still good business.

A Touch of Class does make other uniforms and also makes evening wear and ball gowns for the larger lady - the 18+ size. This is sincerely welcomed by those of us who cannot claim to be petite! Jacqui seeks out beautiful materials with glorious colours and creates wonderful ball gowns.

Jacqui finds a large part of her business is manufacturing and supplying nationally to ball gown hirers and of course, special orders. It is quite sad that most of her materials come from Spain, Italy and Germany rather from our own manufacturers. The materials are wonderful, they look expensive and luxurious. To feel the heavy brocades and the rich silks, takes you into a fantasy world.

Jacqui concentrates deliberately on the top end of the market which is not the biggest opening but it is less volatile and provides her with as much work as 'A Touch of Class' can handle. The company deals with all sorts of different orders from a request for Mayoral robes to Elizabethan costumes. An exciting business.

Mutley Plain cannot really be described as a village but it is the busy centre serving the needs of the community living around it as well as many others who stop here on their way in and out of the centre of the city. It has an extraordinary mixture of businesses and probably more pubs and licensed premises than any other street in Plymouth. I have always thought of Mutley Plain as the entrance to the city centre but people who use it regularly would probably rebel at this description. Its wide sweep stretches from the bottom of Townsend Hill with an offshoot at Hyde Park to the beginning of North Hill. As a child I can remember it as the shopping centre for all sorts of products. There were the good old fashioned grocers, Haddy's and Dilleighs where customers would sit on high chairs whilst they gave their order to the person behind the counter. Hardings, an up-market well-established furniture shop was next door. All the banks were represented with Barclays and the Westminster Bank on one side and Lloyds, National Provincial and Midland on the other. There was a wonderfully old fashioned drapers, Wheelers, and a shop that sold knitting wools, a couple of butchers, a fish shop and greengrocers. It is very different now, still good for household shopping but dominated by banks and commerce rather than the retail trade but there is one shop which is still a delight to enter.

A wonderful opportunity arose when in June 1997 Gay Jones and Prudence de Villiers moved In Other Words from a small book and gift shop virtually next door to the Swarthmore Centre on Mutley Plain and took over their new spacious premises a few doors along the road going towards Somerfields Supermarket. Certainly the space allows them to spread their wares more readily and for customers it is easier to browse but one thing they did not leave behind was the warm welcome that emanates from both these charming, knowledgeable women and their staff, and which, in turn, has created an atmosphere that invites people to linger, looking at the books and debating which one, or more, of the many varied gifts to purchase. Gay and Prudence have always had an enormous love of books and this shows in the range which is vast and catholic. If you do not spot the book you want, they will happily order it for you. A further asset is the children's book section. For several years now, the shop has had a specialist buyer, Libby Allman, who has a fund of knowledge about children's books. She can give detailed help with books in the shop, and also takes selections out to local schools, for whom she has also arranged numerous visits from children's authors - helping to inspire a whole new generation with a love of books.

As for the gifts, the greetings cards, postcards and gift wrapping are not just run of the mill and prove that if you come here you are going to find impeccable service allied with inspired purchasing which makes shopping irresistible. Every year, Gay and Prudence take themselves off to the International Gift Fair at the NEC to seek out new and exciting merchandise for 'In Other Words'. A book and a gift shop not to be missed.

St Budeaux has a strong community which has benefited enormously from the bypass which takes the main A38 away from the area. It is still busy but far less fraught. The River Tamar skirts one edge of the 'village' another leads you on the road to Crownhill and towards Dartmoor. Architecturally it is not the prettiest of places but it does have a jewel in the crown in the shape of the old parish church, standing high on the western bank of the Tamar. tucked away off the road. It was here on July 4th 1569 Sir Francis Drake married Mary Newman who came from Saltash. Sometimes known as ' shadowy Mary' she was the least well known of the wives in history of any of our famous men. She died fourteen years after her marriage and was buried in the churchyard. The church also has a wall monument of grey slate to the 16th and 17th century sons and daughters of the old Devonshire Gorges. Sir Ferdinand Gorges was Governor of the fortifications of Plymouth in the 16th century. He organised several colonising parties to North America and in 1635 was appointed first Governor of Maine.

I have memories of St Budeaux church because of the wedding of my great friend, Elizabeth Thomas, the daughter of the much loved local doctor. In those days, during the war, I ' sang for my supper' and spent much of my spare time in a concert party entertaining the troops. Consequently Elizabeth asked me if I would sing at her wedding whilst the register was being signed. I agreed and she chose Handel's 'Where eer you Walk'. A song I knew well and posed no difficulty for me, but I had not taken the organist into consideration. He had no time for a rehearsal other than a hurried few words before the service when I gave him my music. I duly stood to sing at the appropriate moment and we started the walk together! That harmony did not continue; the organist turned over two pages accidentally and it took a considerable amount of 'Where eer you Walk' for us to meet up in a familiar glade!!!

Crownhill on the outskirts of Plymouth and almost the gateway to Dartmoor, is a busy place with the main road from Plymouth to Tavistock cutting it into two. Nonetheless it has a life of its own and its shopping centre which is tucked away in a compact corner, has a variety of shops which are sufficient to deal with most local residents needs, saving them a trip into town.

For me and the thousands of people who have visited it so far, Crownhill has one very special place Crownhill Fort which is steeped in history and was part of Plymouth's hidden defences.   It is the largest and best preserved of Plymouth's Victorian fortifications built between 1863 and 1872. One of the most advanced of Lord Palmerston's forts it was built to defend the country against French attack. Now after a long restoration it stands proud as one of the most important of the country's Victorian forts to remain intact and is open to the public.

I have memories of the Fort which in no way fits in with today's conception. During World War II Crownhill Fort was the headquarters of the Home Guard and commanded by my father, Lieutenant Colonel Bill Northcott. I became a member of the Local Defence Volunteers as we were originally called and later became the Home Guard. It was here on the parade ground that we were drilled, sometimes only using broomsticks as weapons - very much in the tradition of Dad's Army but father, a retired professional soldier, did not resemble Captain Mainwaring! We were a motley crew from all walks of life but we became an efficient and very proud outfit with some members, including my father, taking part in the Victory Parade in London in 1945.

In the early days there was no uniform for women members and all we had were tin hats, gas masks and gold, oak leaf badges. To illustrate this point, my father, no mean cartoonist, penned a cartoon showing a line of naked Home Guard ladies, lined up, wearing their sole uniform, tin hats and with their gas masks slung over their shoulders. Inspecting them were my father and the Brigadier about to pin badges on bare bosoms. The caption read ' My turn now Northcott, you've had yours!'

After the war and for many years Crownhill Fort gradually deteriorated and it was not until the Army's ownership came to an end in 1986 when the Fort was declared surplus to requirements that it was brought back to life. At this point, due to the Fort's significance as one of the most important Victorian fortifications in the country, the Landmark Trust stepped in to save the Fort from an uncertain future.

The massive task of clearing nearly a century of alterations, benign neglect and the passage of time, slowly began once again to reveal the splendour of Crownhill Fort. With the clearance of the dry ditch and the re-instatement of the earth profiles of the ramparts, the Fort once again began to appear as its designer, Capt. Du Cane, had intended.

A European grant in 1993 enabled the Landmark Trust to continue restoration work and to put in place a number of facilities that enabled the Trust to open the Fort to the public for the first time. It was at this time that the parade ground was restored to its original gravel surface and the Landmark holiday apartment was completed, giving people the opportunity to experience the Fort by living here for a holiday.

Restoration was further advanced with the award of a grant from the Heritage Lottery Fund, which has enabled the Trust to implement a range of projects to bring the Fort back to life. This has included the re-creation of the Victorian and W.W.II barracks, the creation of the education resource centre and the installation on the new cannon to be seen in many of the emplacements within the Fort.

To visit Crownhill Fort is a thrilling experience which appeals to people of all ages and has the potential for being a superb 'classroom' for schools wanting to take pupils into an exciting historical world with a 'hands on' approach. There is no such thing as telling children 'Do not touch' at Crownhill Fort. They can handle the equipment the men would have carried, feel the roughness of their uniforms, see the austere barrack rooms in which they lived and hold in their hands the various tin mugs, plates and cutlery they would have used. The strange thing about Crownhill Fort is that it is so hidden that few Plymothians know of its existence and it relies largely on visitors, both schools and the general public, who come from outside the city.

There is so much to see and explore on this 16 acre site. There are nearly two thirds of a mile of tunnels and passages, a veritable rabbit warren, to which children have unrestricted access. A unique collection of Victorian garrison artillery intrigues every visitor but it is the Moncrieff Counterweight Disappearing Gun which has acted like a magnet for many visitors. Crownhill Fort contains two concrete pits designed to mount 'Moncrieff Guns', one of which now contains the only example in the world of a counterweight disappearing gun!

Captain Colin Scott Moncrieff first submitted ideas for a disappearing carriage in 1858 but it was not until 1866 that he presented detailed plans for consideration. The gun was designed to remain hidden below the parapet of the gun emplacement until loaded and ready for firing. Upon the release of a brake a large counterweight would then elevate the gun to its firing position. The recoil then created by the firing gun would be of enough force to bring the gun back down to its loading position below the parapet. Moncrieff explained that the primary objective of the disappearing mounting was to keep the gun detachment and the gun, other than when in the firing position, safely under cover. Some may say that the safety of the gun was deemed more important than that of the detachment!

Moncrieff continued to make improvements on his design and finally in 1871, the MK1 design was approved for use and twenty were ordered to be built. One of these MKI carriages was mounted at a practice battery overlooking Bovisand Beach to the east of Plymouth.

Moncrieff did not stop here. He immediately set about making improvements to his design which, by 1873, had resulted in the much-improved Mk.II carriage, the type used at Crownhill. In 1877 the Inspector General for Fortification agreed to thirteen Moncrieff counterweight carriages mounting 7-inch R.B.L. guns for the Plymouth defences. Two were to be mounted at Crownhill and they were in place by 1885.

In 1900, the last counterweight Moncrieff gun in the country was dismantled at Newhaven Fort in Sussex.

The carriage now seen at Crownhill is a replica made at Irons Bros Foundry in Cornwall under the supervision of historic artillery consultant Austin C. Carpenter. The gun mounted on the carriage, also a replica, is an Armstrong 7-inch breech loading gun. Invented by William Armstrong in the 1850s this type of gun represented a revolution in gun design as one of the first effective breech loading guns to be adopted into the service. The secret of the immense strength of this type of gun was in the method used to construct the barrel. Successive hoops of wrought iron were shrunk onto the gun with the most coils being positioned around the chamber within which the charge ignited.

The guns were rifled with many spiral grooves cut into the bore of the gun. The lead coating of the fired shells bit into these grooves which caused the shell to spin, giving the projectile a degree of accuracy far greater than a smooth-bore and a much longer range. They were first issued to the Navy in 1858 but were however not a success. They were not as powerful as first thought and when tested were unable to pierce the armour of the ships they were designed to attack! The guns were also slow and difficult to operate safely in the cramped conditions on board ship and occasionally blew out their breeches, obviously a very dangerous occurrence. As a result they were rejected by the Navy and were used instead for the arming of land fortification such as Crownhill, to be mounted on ramparts in open, casemated and Moncrieff emplacements.

The tour of Crownhill Fort is an exhilarating and fascinating adventure from which one emerges with a host of information that stimulates ones thoughts of the history of the Fort but equally whets the appetite for learning more about the enormous and far ranging history that Plymouth has spawned.

It is so worthwhile and for many volunteers under the skilled leadership of the Curator, James Breslin and his staff, it has become an exciting way of life. They really do enter into the historical spirit of the Fort which comes alive on selected weekends when its own artillery unit of the 1890s live in the barracks and man the Fort, firing a wide range of the cannon following original Victorian drill. On these weekends, when you can rub shoulders with the unit, dressed in full uniform, the Fort unquestionably becomes the loudest museum in the west-country.

I am indebted to James Breslin for his time and information and his permission to use his words when describing the Moncrieff Counterweight Disappearing Gun.

Just a word of warning. The Fort has many steep steps, grassy ramps and soft paths. It is suggested that you wear sensible footwear and take extreme care. Visitors with young children will find baby carriers preferable to push chairs. Dogs are not permitted within the Fort.

Opening times do vary. From January until the beginning of April it is open for groups and schools by arrangement. From the beginning of April until the end of October the Fort opens daily 10.00-17.00. In November and until mid-December it is again available by appointment for schools and groups and then in December there is a special Christmas opening in 2001 on15th & 16th December from 10.00-17.00. There is free car parking. Ring 01752 793754 for more details or take a look at the web-site www.crownhillfort.co.uk.

Plympton St Mary and Plympton St Maurice are both a mere five miles from the city centre. They both stand on the Torybrook. In olden days the tide of the Laira flowed inland to this point by a narrow creek now covered with meadow and houses. The Roman Ridgeway runs through it, and the story of Plympton goes far back into Devon history, boasting proudly that:

Plympton was a Borough Town
When Plymouth was a vuzzy down.

Plympton St Mary has many beautiful houses and a fine 15th century church standing in a lawn-like churchyard with a bevy of gargoyles jovial and grim and inside a superb vaulted roof. Hearing the melodious peal of bells which hang in the gracious 108 foot tower, is one of the pleasures of visiting Plympton. The church is rich in monuments including one of Sir William Strode whilst under a canopy lies the monument of the armoured figure of Richard Strode of Newnham who died in 1464 and who was an ancestor of the Cobbold family who now live in the Manor house and of whom I have written about in Chapter 9. It also boasts excellent shopping facilities, more than one good school and an abundance of new housing which has developed since World War II.

Plympton St Maurice has a famous son, Sir Joshua Reynolds, England's greatest Portrait Painter who was a son of a master at Plympton Grammar School. It is a quieter place than Plympton St Mary and still very much a village. However one does get a shock when you realise how much has changed even in the last 50 years. I read a description of Plympton St Maurice in W.G. Hoskins' well loved book on Devon, written in the 1950's, in which he says:-

> Plympton St Maurice lies on a by-road half a mile south of the busy road from Plymouth to Exeter. Those who have a special feeling for the small, ancient and decayed boroughs of England will be delighted with Plympton. It has been left on one side in the past two hundred years or so, and one smells cow-dung in the streets instead of petrol fumes; the immemorial life-giving smell of the land from which the little town took its birth in the 12th century'.

It is not recognisable from that description today. St Maurice and St Mary as well as Colebrook are still there but the insidious growth of Plymouth has built new houses, new estates and new industrial areas all around them until they have become part of the city.

Hooe Village today

Its neighbour Plymstock is a very busy place and a very popular residential area of Plymouth. Its grand church is getting on for 600 years. The Harris family who lived in Plymstock for four centuries, have many monuments here. Sir Christopher Harris gave the village its almshouses in the time of Shakespeare. A small number of manors existed here as early as the Norman Conquest - Goosewell, Hooe, Staddon and Staddiscombe. They are now all part of this busy suburb which has also brought in a reluctant Elburton under its wing. Mount Batten which for years belonged to the RAF and which I remember, with affection as a sea-plane station from which its Sunderland flying boats skimmed across Plymouth Sound until they were airborne.

An inspiring sight. Relics of Roman times have appeared at Mount Batten over the years showing that a native trading settlement existed on the south shore of the Cattewater throughout the greater part of the Roman period. During excavations of the present Fort Stamford in 1864, a late Celtic cemetery was discovered.

Hooe now part of Plymstock still has a life of its own. Its lake has been filled in and new homes built but the essence of village life is still there and as you can see from a print, it once was very beautiful and full of history. Sonia Donovan of the Armada Gallery has a great feeling for the place - she grew up there when her parents were the landlords of the Royal Oak.

Turnchapel is somewhere I always remember because of the little steamer ferry which used to cross over to its landing quay from Phoenix Wharf on the Barbican. Those days are long gone but Turnchapel still feels like a small seaside village.

300

Oreston used to be a hamlet close to Plymstock. It is still a delightfully small place in which to live with a true village atmosphere. It was from the quarries here that Plymouth took the stone for its breakwater between 1812-1841 - some 4.5 million tons in all. Robinson Crusoe sailed from Oreston on his last voyage. Robinson Crusoe was of course Alexander Selkirk who was found marooned on an uninhabited island. He came back to Oreston and lived almost like a hermit, in his father's house until he met and married a widow, Francis Candis with whom he lived in Oreston until he died.

Oreston Village.

One wonders in 50 years time how much more development will have taken place in all the many small communities which whilst retaining their own spirit are now Plymouth.

After the Blitz.

Plymouth Rebuilt.

302

Chapter XVI

Commerce and Industry - the Present and Future of Plymouth

What an extraordinary city Plymouth is. Full of surprises, the city hides away all manner of facts and figures, even from Plymothians. We wake in the morning, go out and about, seeing people driving cars, vans, lorries, getting on and off buses and on foot. How often does it occur to us to wonder where they are going and what they do? Until I wrote 'Invitation to Plymouth' in 1992 and started researching this book, it never occurred to me to wonder where they all went, what sort of work they did and how many different industries and businesses made up the whole. Even now, after almost a decade of interviewing people in their workplace, I have only scratched the surface of the range of skills and enterprise. Plymouth continues to excite me and I become more and more thrilled by all that it has to offer, both for those who live and work here and for those who wish to relocate. What a bright future we can offer newcomers.

I think it needs saying that Plymouth's ever growing stature is due to the various agencies who have encouraged investors to bring their companies to the city. It is the constant application and dedication of both the Council, The South West Regional Development Agency, the 2020 Partnership, the Chamber of Commerce and many other bodies who are constantly achieving success.

One man I spoke to, who shall be nameless, told me that he applied to the North, to Wales and finally to Plymouth, for help in relocating his business. The North did not even bother to reply, Wales told him he could call on them if he thought they could be of help. Only Plymouth responded with an immediate telephone call which led to an arranged visit to the city the following weekend. The man and his wife were put up at the Moorland Links Hotel and throughout the weekend were driven around to various possible sites for their business. They were taken to meet some people from the Chamber of Commerce, shown the various schools available and introduced to estate agents. In addition they were told also what help they could expect from the City if they decided to move.

It was not a hard decision to make, aided and abetted by the fact that the weekend was warm and sunny, and Plymouth Sound looked its magnificent best. The firm is now successfully established here and my informant told me it was the best thing they ever did. He also went on to tell me that every possible help was given to him and his family to make sure they settled happily.

I have heard the same story from conference organisers who have found the hoteliers and the council agreeable, efficient and the city a wonderful place to visit. The men appreciate the conference facilities and if their wives are with them, the women enjoy the shopping and the restaurants, the theatre and the various trips that are almost always arranged for them to see the surrounding area.

Probably one of the most important inputs is the millions of pounds that South West Water has spent and continue to spend, in and around the city to improve the standard of the water round the foreshore. Although I have touched on this in Chapter One, I believe there is not a single person in Plymouth who is not appreciative of the work that has been done and is being done to ensure that Plymouth meets the requirements of Europe on water standards.

The most constructive contribution to the renaissance of Plymouth in order to make it of global importance in the 21st century, is the tremendous work done by the various agencies and, in particular, the Plymouth 2020 Partnership, an alliance between Public, private, community and voluntary sectors. Steve Gerry, a strong advocate for Plymouth, operates the Partnership with a determined, quietly aggressive and very enthusiastic approach. He looks for the commonsense approach and winkles out the possible idiosyncracies that he thinks might aid the cause. When I talked to him it was on a very wet day in his office in the old Public Dispensary in Catherine Street. I had no idea of the strength of purpose or the ramifications of the Partnership which was formed in 1993 as Plymouth 2000 Partnership. Its objective has always been to promote economic development and urban regeneration across the City. Since it was formed it has secured six rounds of funding in the Single Regeneration Budget (SRB) and played a key role in securing health, employment and education action zones within the city.

The Partnership is jointly chaired by the Deputy Leader of the City Council, the Chairman of the Plymouth Chamber of Commerce and Industry, and a representative of the community and voluntary sectors. In order to ensure the Partnership board is not unwieldy, membership is restricted to the three core partners plus representatives from the following key organisations: Government Office South West; SW Regional Development Agency; South and West Devon Health Authority, PROSPER, Employment Service and Higher and Further Education. Even a layman like myself can see it encompasses just about every sector of life in Plymouth.

The City was awarded Pathfnder status for the New Commitment to Regeneration initiative in 1998 and this requires the 2020 Partnership to build on the spirit of the partnership and involvement across the City developed by Plymouth 2000 Partnership. And, in recasting the Partnership as the 2020 Partnership, partners have reiterated the need for long-term and lasting regeneration of the city. Each partner brings their own individual commitment to the process, and has agreed to sign-up to the Partnership Principles that underpin it. These are set out below:-

1.   Providing Community Leadership through partnership across sectors
2.   Shared commitment to strategic objectives
3.   Partnership working where value can be added
4.   No single agency solution where joint action is needed
5.   Maximising the investment value of resources; seeking balance between consumption now and investment in the future
6.   An inclusive approach where action involves rather than imposes
7.   Respecting what each partner's contribution is
8.   Acknowledging need for popular understanding and support from the people of the City
9.   Accountability and openness

10.   Giving a stake in the regeneration of the City to each partner, to
       the community, and to individuals themselves.

With so much at stake for the success of the City over the next 20 years. The 2020 Partnership are well aware of the pitfalls but their commonsense and ability to rationalise looks set to ensure that it is not sunk under a tidal wave of disagreement. They have no wish to be hemmed in by bureaucracy but they recognise that their efforts do need to be evaluated and so the programme will be managed by an evaluation consortium, led by the Government Office of the South West.

The 2020 Partnership has a Vision for the City of Plymouth as it moves towards the year 2020.

They see it as a City which has overcome its resistance to change and adopted a new positive attitude, culture and belief of what it is actually capable of achieving and has built its success on:-

·   A clearly focused long-term strategy
·   Inspirational leadership
·   High levels of ambition and aspiration
·   Thinking and acting competitively and innovatively
·   Developing a positive image
·   Being proactive and prepared to take the calculated risk where necessary
·   Partnership working: where it has made a concerted effort to fully integrate; co-ordinate and harmonise the strategies; policies and actions of its Partners in order to fulfil its goals.

Has been prepared to consider and act upon radical solutions to tackle long standing problems.

Has adopted a long-term proactive approach to tackling health and social inequalities and has successfully employed preventative measures which have specifically targeted underlying root causes rather than their symptoms.

Recognises the primary importance of lifelong learning as a source both of self-fulfilment for the individual and of competitive advantage to the City.

Offers an exceptionally pro-business climate to all those prepared to invest in its future, where, in particular, micro and small to medium-sized enterprises are encouraged to flourish and as a consequence have contributed significantly to the City's success in creating employment opportunities and generating wealth to the benefit of all.

Has regained a strong sense of identity in the world, based on its natural and cultivated strengths and international reputation in the maritime and high-tech electrical engineering sectors. It has also used high levels of intellectual capital to seize new opportunities in emerging sectors such as life sciences and the creative industries.
Has maximised the benefits of its geographic links: locally, regionally, nationally and globally. Especially through the development of regional supply chains; its strong North American connections and through trading with its European Atlantic neighbours.

Carefully manages its outstanding coastal and inland natural environment in order to maximise its full potential.

Has thoughtfully developed both its built environment and its transport systems, making the best use of its limited land resources in the most sustainable way.

Provides an attractive international centre for knowledge and learning, tourism and heritage, while acting as a social and economic hub for Devon and Cornwall providing outstanding centres for retail, leisure and the arts.

Offers opportunities and facilities to all and which take into full account the needs of future generations in its decision making, so that they may inherit the same or better quality of life.

A City whose residents are valued regardless of age, ability, economic status, gender, sexuality, ethnic origin, religion or disability.

Have a sense of personal responsibility for themselves and their own future, their community and the environment.

Have a high degree of self-confidence, ambition; good housing, clean air, safe streets and first class education and training facilities

Are involved in identifying local solutions to local crime and disorder problems and are active partners in reducing crime and the fear of crime.

Collectively offer a workforce that is flexible, capable and equipped with transportable core skills.

A City whose communities exhibit strong leadership, while genuinely encouraging participation and involvement of all its people into the decision and policy making processes.

Have access to community facilities, green spaces and employment where new development is distinctive, culturally relevant and of high quality.

Are strong, stable, confident and offer neighbourhoods where people choose to live.

Are confident that community safety principles to reduce crime and the fear of crime are incorporated into all aspects of city life.

No longer exhibit statistically predictable rates of ill health, job opportunities and crime based solely on their location.

A City whose businesses are built on a culture and spirit of entrepreneurship that is ingrained in individuals from an early age.

Enjoy high influential and effective relations with the education sector at all levels.

Are customer orientated and offer increasingly high levels of added-value goods and services in order to compete globally.

Train and develop their staff to be proficient and highly productive in their jobs and where appropriate to become highly skilled 'knowledge workers'.

Are confident and prepared to take risks and to invest in research and development; collaborate in order to compete and which are innovative and rapidly responsive to change.

Collectively offer excellent career progressive opportunities for their employees.

Accept their social and environmental responsibilities and think globally and act locally.

The 2020 Partnership works closely with The South West of England Regional Development Agency - more about them shortly. With the City being intensely proud of its magnificent Plymouth Sound, now a recognised National Heritage, it also realises it cannot live entirely on its surroundings. It is the largest city on the south coast and the second largest in the south-west. The south-west is one of the UK's fastest growing regions. Within that context there are 256,000 inhabitants but the influence of the city spreads further into the region. Some 330,000 people live within Plymouth's travel to work area and the shopping catchment of Plymouth includes over 400,000 people. The work force of the travel to work area is 160,000 reflecting Plymouth's role as the economic motor of Devon and Cornwall. It is clear that the major economic hubs such as Plymouth will play a key role in taking forward the Regional Development Agency's vision for the future of the region, aided and abetted by the efficient and effective 2020 Partnership - an example to other towns and cities throughout Britain.

The dynamic team leading the South West of England Regional Development Agency have no hesitation in recognising that Plymouth is a major player in the need for regeneration. They also recognise that not only does it need help but in its own right the city is facing up to the exciting changes in line, and still to come in the 21st century.

The mission of the South West RDA is to improve the competitive position of the region in order to ensure increased and sustainable prosperity for all. Its vision is of a technologically advanced region where the talents of its people and its environment combine to form a springboard for success. It aims to shape the region's economy and social fabric over the next 10 years. It will aim to deliver Government funding and have a leading role in securing European funding that will enable partner organisations to increase prosperity by improving business competitiveness through improvements in communications and physical infrastructure; by focusing on sectors with the greatest potential; ensuring high quality business support and creating a 'learning culture' for people and businesses.

The South West RDA is actively marketing the region overseas and will directly provide information and advice for foreign-owned businesses locating or expanding operations in the region. This may range from helping to supply suitable sites and premises to the identification of a workforce with the necessary skills and qualifications. The Agency encourages innovation and growth by identifying opportunities and disseminating market intelligence. It supports the work of education and training providers, and assists businesses with workspace requirements and supply and delivery through the South West Regional Office.

The RDA is also committed to addressing social and economic imbalance by helping to reduce the barriers to employment; improving training, travel and childcare and overcoming discrimination. The Agency funds and promotes regeneration programmes in partnership with many different bodies, channelling resources to areas of greatest need. It will improve links between urban and rural areas and encourages joint initiatives, for example combining community regeneration with life-long learning programmes. The South West RDA is also taking a leading role in the major flagship regeneration projects across the region including Plymouth's Royal William Yard and the Plymouth International Business Park at Derriford.

The Agency is also at the forefront in creating a strong and positive image for the South West internally, nationally and internationally and developing quality partnerships.

It was meeting with Michael Roberts, the Director of Marketing and Communications for the South West of England RDA, that made me realise just how important all this is and just how much money the RDA has directed towards Plymouth itself. It is not just a body telling a good story which they believe the South West and especially Plymouth wants to hear. Not a bit of it. Here is a team of people who truly believe that their efforts combined with their know-how will unquestionably contribute to the success of Plymouth. Michael Roberts is a soft spoken man from Northern Ireland who has seen Belfast rise in spite of its problems and knows that the fruition of the projects currently in hand in Plymouth, like the Royal William Yard and the Plymouth International Business Park, will have inestimable benefits. The Royal William Yard is a prime example of somewhere that has suffered for years without a definite future ahead of it. Now the plans show a vision of a prosperous and vibrant cultural village whilst retaining the historic integrity and grandeur of the existing architecture. There will be both luxury and affordable accommodation, restaurants, shops, cafes and bars, as well as commercial and conference facilities, all situated within the present buildings. A great place in which to live, spend an evening and delight in seeing it from the waterfront.

The Royal William Yard plays such a major part in the history of the city. This former naval victualling yard designed by Sir John Rennie in the 1830s, covers an area of 19 acres, providing 47,000 sqm of space in the form of ten buildings, all of which are designed Grade I Listed Buildings. Rennie was asked to remodel the limestone hill at 'Cremyll Point' to provide a level site for the Yard. In addition to factory buildings to provide Navy rations (meat, beer, biscuits), there are extensive storage areas, and a dock from which the stores could be taken to waiting vessels. To create access to the Yard to allow development, extensive infrastructure works were carried out by the former Plymouth Development Corporation. These works included major installations for water, gas, electricity and sewerage services as well as ducts for voice and data. All this previous activity has assisted the South West of England Regional Development Agency, together with its partners, to provide a development framework for The Royal William Yard's exciting future which will create a development of truly global stature.

An example of redevelopment is the Mills and Bakery Building which was equipped as a biscuit and bread factory in 1834. This has been acquired by Prince Charles' Phoenix Trust, and plans for its redevelopment include both luxury and affordable accommodation together with retail outlets. You may be familiar with other Phoenix projects which have turned disused mills into accommodation, retail and sometimes small museums depicting the original purpose of the building. Urban Splash Ltd have been given the go ahead to prepare detailed development proposals for the Clarence and Brewhouse buildings. The former was once a liquid store with a floor each for spirits, vinegar and beer and the latter was purpose built in 1834 but never used as such. As technology allowed quantities of fresh water to be carried at sea, beer rations were abolished. The plans include 91 apartments, a landscaped courtyard, retailing and a high quality waterfront restaurant. It may also have an arts/exhibition centre and museum.

The other major RDA involvement is Plymouth International Business Park where infrastructure work has been completed to create over 40 hectares of serviced employment land on the former Seaton Barracks site. It offers a unique opportunity for major development. Superbly situated between the stunning Dartmoor National Park and dramatic coastline, the site is near the City Centre and adjacent to the City's airport, regional media centre and teaching hospital. It is a new vision for a new future. A spacious, contemporary and distinctive working environment, designed to meet the needs of leading edge companies in advance technology, communication, manufacturing and engineering.

High quality architectural design, careful choice of materials and discreet landscaping combine to provide a modern business park set in natural surroundings. The tone has already been set, with the architecturally striking flagship building of the Western Morning News Company Limited, designed by leading architect, Nicholas Grimshaw, gracing the centre of the site.

Further projects include Tamar Science Park Phase 2 and Plymouth Foyer, just off the Octagon.

Nor must one leave out the energetic approach of the South West of England inward investment team. With their help JDS Uniphase acquired and expanded Sifam Fibre Optic, developing a new fibre optic cable manufacturing facility in Plymouth and expanding an existing site in Torbay. This investment of £5m created 1,000 new jobs in the region.

These are major projects in which the Agency is involved but there are a myriad of other ones in the city and throughout the region. Wherever I go and talk to people I find Michael Robert's name crops up. You will find him on the Plymouth Branding Committee set up by the 2020 Partnership for starters. Rumour has it that the Plymouth Branding Committee is to have Lord Owen as its front man. Wise choice.

In its short existence the South West of England Regional Agency, headed by Sir Michael Lickiss has made an enormous impact and Plymouth is certainly reaping the benefit.

That Plymouth needs men of vision has never been in doubt and the appointment of Neill Mitchell as Chief Executive of the Plymouth Chamber of Commerce and Industry in May 1997 could not have happened at a better time for the city. In a short space of time his talent and energies have been appreciated and recognised and on April 2nd 2001 he takes on another demanding role as the Chief Executive of the Devon and Cornwall Business Council which may eventually be seen as a business-focused shadow Development Agency. First however, before telling you about this quite remarkable man and the aims of the Devon and Cornwall Business Council, lets talk about the purpose of the Chamber of Commerce and Industry and its important role in the city today.

In its 188 years The Chamber has given support and advice to businesses of all kinds and sizes. It has had several homes within Plymouth and now, at last, has its own substantial property at 22 Lockyer Street. Built in 1850 or thereabouts, the building has always been associated with Plymouth's professional and commercial life. It is an excellent location in the City Centre and is a very timely move coinciding with the radical re-structuring of the Chamber which is now being implemented following the Chamber Council's recent Strategic Review. The combined relocation and re-organisation package is exciting and set to deliver greatly enhanced benefits and more focused services to its members in the years ahead, from a high profile HQ in the very heart of the City. A building from which to endorse the Chamber's mission statement which is 'To meet and anticipate the needs of the membership and to proactively represent the private sector to bring about and sustain a favourable business climate, conducive to wealth creation in the Plymouth City-region.'

There can be no better way to explain the beginning and the current purpose of the Chamber than to use Neill Mitchell's own words as they are in the 1999-2000 Year Book of the Chamber.

Plymouth is a maritime city, steeped not only in the Royal Navy heritage (dating from the 15th century and still continuing), but also in fishing and general maritime trade. Thus, back in the Winter of 1813, local shipowners, businessmen and merchants were much pre-occupied with the impact of Britain being at war simultaneously on two fronts. On the Continent the enemy was Napoleon, whilst across the Atlantic hostilities were fully engaged with the emergent Republic of the United States of America, then under the leadership of its fourth President - James Madison (President 1809-17) and his formidable wife Dolley.

On the one hand, Devonport Dockyard was prospering opportunely from working day and night upon the repair and refitting of the Navy's wooden ships. Whilst short-term revenue was also returning to Plymouth in the form of Prize Monies from captured enemy ships and cargoes. However, on the negative side, the Plymouth Fishing Fleet was being deprived of access to its main fishing grounds in Spanish waters; lucrative fur, skins, oil and other maritime trade with the USA had ceased; and corn and stock prices had fallen (post-Waterloo), farm rents were up and Banks were failing. The town's smaller and older industries (textile manufacture/mills/tanning/canvas/sail and rope making) were also in decline and in need of regeneration.

Plymouth was at that time recognised as being near enough a small 'Republic' - self-governed and self-sufficient. So it was on the 7th December 1813, at the old Georgian Guildhall in Wimpole Street (built 1799, bombed March 1941), a meeting of "the Merchants, Ship owners and other Persons interested in the prosperity of the Port of Plymouth and its neighbourhood"was held under the Chairmanship of Henry Woollcombe ' with a view to the furtherance of Trade'. The outcome was a resolution that 'some permanent society be formed with a view to the encouragement of Trade'. Subsequently on 28th December 1813, under the Trusteeship of the Duke of Bedford, the Earl of Mt Edgcumbe, Lord Boringdon and Mr Carew MP, the Plymouth Chamber of Commerce was formed - its annual subscription being One Guinea per annum, and its first Secretary (the Chief Executive's predecessor!) being one William Burt. The Chamber's reassuring motto was (and is) 'Prorsum Semper Honeste' - 'Forwards always with integrity'.

Early objectives were to rejuvenate home and foreign fisheries (notably in Newfoundland waters), to start whale fisheries in Greenland and the South Seas, to establish a West Indian Trade in rum, molasses, sugar and coffee, and regenerate the town's old industries. Preparations would also be made for likely future unemployment arising from defence cutbacks at Devonport Dockyard when hostilities ended. The Chamber was to be housed in the old Exchange Building in Woolster Street, close to Sutton Harbour and only a few yards from the 16th century house at No29 Looe Street - which it occupied in more recent times until 1996.

It is thought that the Plymouth Chamber thus stands as the fourth oldest Chamber in Britain, possibly the World. However by 1860 there were 16 Chambers and in 1893 the number had risen nationally to 78. It was in that year that Plymouth hosted the National meeting of the 'Association of Chambers of Commerce' at the Grand Hotel and so lavished the delegates with hospitality that the Association's later report said that the delegates had been 'charmed beyond measure with the natural beauty of the port and its surroundings, and that they had to confess to having been right royally entertained!' But the gathering was not merely social, as Plymouth businessmen were - as ever - mindful of their extensive international trading interests. The Plymouth Chamber thus proposed at the meeting that the Government should form a Committee to prepare for the decimalisation of the UK's currency and abolition of the Crown and half-Crown and Threepenny piece (an objective achieved a mere 78 years later!)

During the Boer War (1899-1902) some 400 Chamber Members subscribed to a 'Maximum Machine Gun Appeal', in support of the Devonshire Volunteers at the Front - raising sufficient to purchase the Gun in 1900, from Vickers, Sons & Maxim Ltd, for £529.19.6d and later paying a further £1.6s7d for its carriage to South Africa. Amongst recorded donors is one which captures for posterity the spirit of the day, it being from 'a few poor patriots who wish to tell the Boers what Plymouth thinks of them - 3 shillings'! The presentation ceremony was on The Hoe in glorious weather on the 3rd February 1900 and in the presence of a crowd estimated at a staggering 100,000 people. The Mayor duly fired the gun's first shot.

Also during the War, the Plymouth and Aldershot Chambers set up a joint trading monopoly to supply the troops in South Africa with clothing and non-standard issue rations and utensils - an activity which, by 1901, had built up a surplus of 80,000 and was subsequently to form the foundation for the establishment of the N.A.A.F.I. organisation.

By 1910, the 500 Members of the Chamber clearly had high expectations of their body's National importance. For, on 12th November of that year (following the first General Election held in January/February) the Chamber had the audacity to submit a Petition to the Prime Minister - Herbert Henry Asquith -requesting that he should not call a second General Election before Christmas, because such an inconvenience would be 'detrimental to the business men and traders of Plymouth, having regard to the interests of the trading community of the City of Plymouth'. The Petition failed and the second General Election was duly held over the Festive period 2nd-19th December !

During the First World War and the 1920s/30s Depression, the Chamber once again focused upon global trade within a 'Single Market'. Not in Europe one should hasten to add but rather exclusively with the British Empire.

Then came the Second World War - surely the City of Plymouth's darkest hours. The two devastating Blitzes of 1941 and 1943 levelled the old Georgian and Victorian heart of the City Centre, leaving just one building intact (now Waterstones bookshop in New George Street). Inevitably it was the Chamber which pushed for the swift rebuilding of the City, with the specific request that the previous congestion and high density development should be replaced by an ultra-modern open plan scheme designed with convenience for the motor car in mind. So emerged in 1943, Sir Patrick Abercrombies "Plan for Plymouth' - a revolutionary plan which remains evident in the City Centre today.

The 1950s-70s were decades of strong economic growth in Plymouth and the Chamber's main interests were, firstly, lobbying for the building of the Tamar Bridge (opened 1961) and thence upgrading of the A38 to its present standard. Then, in the 1980s and 90s massive cutbacks in the Defence sector hit Plymouth hard and the Chamber became increasingly focused upon economic diversification and the attraction of inward investment --a process which continues. Indeed, the substantial American investment has led directly to the formation of the Chamber's North American Business Club - renewing a transatlantic association which has dominated Plymouth's history, even before the times of the Pilgrim Fathers and the sailing of the 'Mayflower' in 1620 (see website hhtp://www.plymouth-chamber.co.uk/thanks.html).

Today, the Chamber's membership of 560 businesses employing 39,250 people, represents a mixture of ancient and modern. On the one hand it includes Frederick Jacka's Bakery, founded circa 1597 and thought to be the oldest bakery in the UK. Then there is the world famous Plymouth Gin Distillery, whose unique gin has been distilled in its present premises, and widely exported, since 1793. By contrast, the glittering Barbican Glass Works and National Marine Aquarium reflect the modern face of investment in the Sutton Harbour area of the City. As do the Theatre Royal and revamped 'Derry's Department Store in the City Centre and the numerous new manufacturing and business units located on the outskirts of the city - perhaps the most eyecatching being Nicholas Grimshaw's 'Western Morning News' building at Derriford. In short 186 years on and mindful of its colourful past, the Plymouth Chamber is still marching 'Forward' and is, of course, doing so 'always with integrity'.

What of the man himself who has been responsible for implementing the vast changes within the Chamber and the promoting of many other projects? Neill Mitchell has a CV which would have made him a respected and welcome member of any organisation with a much higher profile than Plymouth's Chamber of Commerce. For example if one takes a quick look at his CV and then delves a bit deeper, you discover he started his career in London with Lloyds Bank International, later joining the Civil Service where he worked in the Law Courts and then in the Lord Chancellor's Office in the House of Lords. A move to Margaret Thatcher's Private Office at No 10 in her early Downing Street Years' as Prime Minister (1979-82). A secondment to English Heritage followed and then appointment as Principal Private Secretary to Sir George Young, a Minister in the Environment Department at that time.

Later, Neill returned to the Private Sector and moved into Corporate Public Relations. He specialised in Promotions and Events Management, first at he QEII Conference Centre in Westminster, next with two Royal - Patronised charities and then at BEP Limited where he also served as Company Secretary. Finally, Neill joined the Department of Trade and Industry 'Export Promotion Directorate and headed a specialist team responsible for targeting, organising and hosting the DTT 'VIP Export promotion hospitality programme for top level overseas guests of HM Government. This role included visits to some 2,500 UK exporting companies in all sectors nationwide.

Neill has worked for many causes in the Voluntary Sector, mainly heritage and recreation-orientated, involving Chairmanship and/or organisation of many fund-raising media events. In this context he personally raised over half a million pounds for charitable purposes.

If you add to this his wide ranging leisure interests which include heritage projects, local and naval history, industrial archaeology, horse riding, swimming and watersports, music and wine plus travelling widely in the USA, Europe, the Middle East and India, one can have no doubt that his knowledge is invaluable to a body like The Chamber of Commerce and Industry. To answer the question as to why he accepted the post. He simply says he had done everything he was interested in doing in London and wanted the opportunity of returning to his roots, Plymouth, where his father was a local Landowner, Chartered Surveyor and Devon County Councillor, who had been extensively involved in implementing Sir Patrick Abercrombie's 1943 Plan for the rebuilding of Plymouth. If you ask Neill to describe his career path to 10 Downing Street, he will tell you that he simply followed the line of Isambard Kingdom Brunel's Great Western Railway, i.e born in Plymouth, educated in Bristol and worked in London!

In the space of three years he has achieved much for the Chamber; not the least of which is the rapidly growing annual American Thanksgiving Festival which features four days of celebrations, arts and theatre performances and plenty of transatlantic bonhomie. This is an event which is designed to create a special and permanent 'feel good factor' for Americans. Plymouth with its Mayflower story and other transatlantic links is the ideal and unique place in which to hold such a festival. The purpose is to significantly grow this annual event into a major regional festival. In 2000 it warranted the presence of the Deputy American Ambassador and next year we are promised the presence of the Ambassador himself.

There are some 200,000 expatriate Americans living and working in the UK and probably one million on the Continent who are the market target for the Festival and as a secondary market there is the American tourists who may choose to travel directly from the US to Plymouth to attend the Festival. Obviously this is a boost for the retail sector, transport, gastronomy, sport and communications throughout the entire city and surrounding area. The overall aim is to attract major US investors, by making Plymouth the prime hub for American culture and business in Europe. Already there are over 70 companies in the region with US links.

 Neill Mitchell also started the successful Plymouth and North American Business Club which includes among its members most of the 77 US owned and 7 Canadian companies in the sub-region plus the 308 companies exporting to the US, 221 to Canada and 77 to Mexico.

Now Neill Mitchell is to take on another major challenge in the pursuit of the recognition of Devon and Cornwall. He is the Chief Executive of the newly formed Devon and Cornwall Business Council. It is designed for the promotion of all business in the region and for starters will tackle the improvement of the two counties' transport infrastructure. The pathfinder sponsors of this new initiative are Westcountry Publications, Carlton Broadcasting, PROSPER, Eurobell (South West), Midas Group, SWEB and the NatWest Bank. Neill has always argued that from the viewpoint of the Plymouth Chamber of Commerce and Industry that a single, strong and coherent two-county business voice was needed to ensure that Devon and Cornwall's needs are high on the Regional Development Agency's priority list. This will now be well met by the emergence from the local business representative bodies of the new DDBC. It is an exciting proposition and so well supported that it cannot fail to be successful.

Plymouth Chamber of Commerce and Industry will miss Neill Mitchell's drive and enthusiasm as well as his contacts throughout the world. In spite of being a high flyer one of the nicest qualities about Neill Mitchell is his lack of pomposity which is accompanied by a genuine interest in everything he does, and everyone he meets in every walk of life.

As I complete writing this book at the end of February 2001 all sorts of extraordinary things are happening in the City. At last plans have been agreed for the redevelopment of Tinside. This has been a thorn in the flesh to Plymothians for far too long but it looks as though by 2005 we will have a new Tinside pool and a super redevelopment surrounding it. This can only make Plymouth more attractive to the outside world and provide Plymothians with a facility they have missed out on for years. The acceptance of the exciting and visionary plan came after a long, hard fought battle for acceptance of the scheme planned by a Plymouth Consortium led by the persuasive Brian Gerrish of Currie and Brown who have offices in The Crescent. Currie and Brown's role is Project Manager and Cost Manager - vitally important in a venture of this size. Brian Gerrish gathered round him a team of architects from different firms who collaborated and pooled their ideas. Ian Potts of Architect Design, John Dalton of Dalton and Terry and Graham

Lobb of Form Design, all well known Plymouth architects. Their number was added to by John Allen of the London based firm Avanti, who work a lot in the South West. Lewin Freyer and Partners, who are Civil and Structural Engineers working largely in the Marine sector plus John Brady dealing with Electrics made up the Consortium.

To the lay mind it would seem quite simple to provide Plymouth with a new open air pool as well as an indoor one and all the facilities that go with it. It is not in the least simple because firstly the changing height of the tides over the years now means that a defensive wall has to be built that is high enough to keep out the encroaching sea especially when it is angry. Secondly in order to have a heated outdoor pool it will be necessary to marginally lessen the size of the pool. Thirdly people in this day and age are not prepared to climb up and down a massive number of steps to reach the pool from Madeira Road so an outside lift has to be installed. Then there is the question of facilities, of bars, of restaurants, somewhere for divers to enjoy taking off from heights into clear water. So apart from being functional it must also be attractive to the eye for those approaching Plymouth from the sea. The plan is delightful and makes use of all the natural beauty of the rocks. It may well be in the course of time that the complex will encompass Plymouth Dome as well, giving that a new lease of life.

In Brian Gerrish's mind and those of his colleagues they are creating something very special and much needed. They have been promised the required funding and as each part of the plan comes to fruition they hope that Plymothians will voice constructive opinions so when it is finished there will be a plaque somewhere which will say 'Refurbished for Plymouth by Plymothians'..

The more one talks to people who have a love of Plymouth and want to see it take its rightful place in the country and the world, the more you realise how much is happening; some of it so quietly that it is almost secretive. Perhaps one of the outstanding issues today is whether a new town should be built going towards the South Hams. There are those for it and those against it. One of the most sensible ideas I have heard for a long time comes again from Brian Gerrish who, together with Steve Gerry of the 2020 Partnership and a number of influential people in the City who have joined together to form' Plymouth 1B'. They believe, and I am sure it is right, that to create a town of the size needed would cost something in the order of £1 Billion in infrastructure alone. It would create endless commuting problems apart from anything else. The alternative is to create a better Plymouth. In other words think big and support regeneration projects throughout the City. It would have a superb knock on effect of preventing the death of the City Centre, of creating Plymouth for Plymothians and by Plymothians. Most of us I am sure want to see a revitalised Plymouth in every way and in every corner. The interesting thing is that until Brian Gerrish and his colleagues got together everyone thought it was always the cost that prevented such a regeneration happening. This is not so. If you think big enough and go to outside investors they only begin to get interested if you are talking in billions. Brian discovered this when he started talking to people about P1B's ideas. The group now are in talks with a number of developers and more and more interest is growing.

Successfully brought to a conclusion the imaginative projects would sprout throughout the city providing everyone with a better place in which to live and somewhere that would be the envy of other towns and cities.

Having read Brian Gerrish's report to the Chamber of Commerce in June 1999. I have extracted two paragraphs which spell out the problem and the solution.

'At present Plymouth has many areas which have very poor standards of housing and limited social infrastructure. The City population density is variable, low in the central core and there is concern at a further overall decline in population. Getting to grips with these, and other issues, is difficult due to the overall scale of the problem, and the need to secure substantial sums of money for redevelopment and economic investment.

If £1 billion can be found from all sources to support largely greenfield development and a new town, surely we should be pressing for the same sources to support this level of development in Plymouth where the investment is badly needed.'

Surely the answer is that the solution is there in front of our very eyes, all that needs to be done is to acquire the funding and we know that if one thinks big enough that money will become available without any stress on Plymothians or the Council.

Thank heaven for people like Brian Gerrish and Steve Gerry who are prepared to think big!

Something else that is currently causing an uproar is a leaked document which says that the Council propose to sell off places like the Theatre Royal and the Pavilions together with the very successful Citybus operation. Is it a good idea? It does seem stupid to get rid of good operations. Perhaps the commonsense of the 2020 Partnership will prevail and produce satisfactory solutions. It will be interesting to see what has happened by the time we get to 2010.

Each business I have seen has had an interesting story to tell but few can match the extraordinary tale of Castle Kitchens at Estover. I had simply no idea of the depth of history behind this very modern looking company with its purpose built building on the Estover Industrial Estate. The kitchens they sell and install are superb. Tailor made to suit every customer's kitchen and requirements, they are installed by professionals who are clearly proud of their work. I met Director, Debbie Tait, a bright, intelligent woman with a firm grasp of her business and its needs, but when she discovered my interest in the business she brought her father, Robert Tait, now the Chairman of the company, to talk to me. From that moment onwards I was enthralled by the history of the company which, loosely, goes back to 1660 in Rotherhithe, London where the owner, William Castle plied his trade with his brother Robert and counted among his friends Samuel Pepys. William Castle was mentioned several times in Pepy's Diaries between 1664 and 1666. William was married to Martha Batten, a daughter of Sir William Batten, Surveyor of the Navy, and known personally to Pepys. Their business in those days was mainly the building of ships. The Castles were frequently consulted by Pepys, being recognised experts in the construction of naval vessels, especially third raters. They built the fourth Defiance for the Navy in Rotherhithe in 1666. Coincidentally the company was responsible for the breaking up of the last HMS Defiance on the River Tamar in 1932.

The linking of that William Castle and Henry Castle 1808-1865 who was the founder of the Shipbreaking business, is slightly tenuous, but there is no doubt that they are of the same family. His father George Castle was a well known ship builder and repairer in Rotherhithe. Henry was an adventurer who migrated to Australia in the 1830's before returning to Rotherhithe in 1838. By then he was an experienced shipbuilder, shipowner and repairer and determined to add to this the business of shipbreaking. His first attempts at persuading the Admiralty to allow him to acquire ships of the Navy to break up came to nothing but shipbreaking work of various kinds was carried out from 1845 onwards by Henry Castle when he became occupier of the premises and wharf adjacent to Vauxhall Bridge known as Baltic Wharf. The latter premises became the Head Office of the company until its destruction by bombing in 1941. Notwithstanding the Navy's reluctance to let Henry Castle have their ships for breaking up, he acquired a lucrative contract with the Royal Mail Line ships and broke up several at Vauxhall including the Orinoco, the Severn, the Great Western and the Magdalena.

And so this fascinating story continues when from 1861 onwards major connections with the Admiralty, particularly at Charlton Yard, enabled the Castles firm to successfully tender for the breaking up of a great many sailing ships of the line. The latter were rapidly becoming obsolete owing to the advent of steam and the screw propeller. Over 200 major HM ships have been traced as having been broken up by Castles. Consequently most of the famous of the Last of the Wooden Walls of England and the Navy ended their days at Castles Yards on the Thames.

Apart from their shipbreaking activities Castles have played a significant role in the process of recycling old ships timbers. Henry Castle's son Sidney Nash Castle commenced the manufacture of furniture after opening an additional yard at Longa Wharf Woolwich in 1872. One should remember that much of the wood would have come from the breaking up of ships. By 1887 the company was a recognised specialist in the manufacture of garden furniture and in that year furnished the grounds of Buckingham Palace in celebration of Queen Victoria's Golden Jubilee. Furniture on the Centre and Number 1 Courts at Wimbledon was supplied in the 1920's. Royal Parks, Cricket Grounds and Public Schools all enjoyed furniture with the Castle name on plaques affixed to each item. Even by 1933 when the supply of wooden ships was drawing to a close, the demand for the company's teak furniture made from timber recovered from these ships, was steadily increasing.

All this history must make my Plymouth readers wonder how a shipbreaking company operating on the River Thames finally came to Plymouth. Well here is the story.

In 1904 the firm of Henry Castle & Sons Ltd experienced considerable financial difficulties when breaking up the turret ship HMS Ajax, and the company was reformed in 1906 as Castles Shipbreaking Co Ltd. The Castle family - Sidney Nash and his two sons, Sidney and Philip, continued to work with the new firm. However in 1911 Sidney Castle Jnr, was persuaded to move to Blythe in Northumberland by the newly formed firm of Hughes Bolckow Ltd which later became part of Metal Industries. They subsequently broke up HMS Britannia (removed from Dartmouth in 1916) and HMS Collingwood.

After a period of about seven years working at Blythe, Sidney relocated to Plymouth in 1919 in order to set up his own shipbreaking business at a time when large numbers of surplus obsolete first world war vessels were being auctioned off by the Navy. In

1920 he bought a total of seventeen ships, the majority of which were cruisers and destroyers all of metal construction. He was assisted in this major purchase by the firm of JB Graham Ltd, a firm of metal merchants based in the City of London. The latter company had long established connections with the Castle family dating back to the previous century.

In 1924 Sidney Castle's shipbreaking business was incorporated into a limited company known as Plymouth & Devonport Shipbreaking Co Ltd. In 1931 this company was itself taken over by Shipbreakers Ltd, a company owned by William Ball, a Plymothian, who was also a director of Castles Shipbreaking Co Ltd at Baltic Wharf, Millbank. Ball had become a leading influence in the London based company from 1929. He took a keen interest in matters political and became Mayor of Greenwich.

In 1933 Shipbreakers Ltd had also acquired control of the Thames based business and name. This circle of events finally brought together the different strands of the Castle families activities both in London and in Plymouth which has survived to the present day. The story continues however with World War II when the company's premises were destroyed by the German Luftwaffe but goes on to it's renaissance when Harold Abrams,, a relative of the Tait family, succeeded to the ownership of the company following William Ball's retirement. The Taits eventually acquired the company and set its course in the direction of producing first class kitchens by moving from the old premises at Passage Wharf, Cattedown, which is where Sidney Castle set up his business around 1920, to their current premises in Estover.

The Taits are a remarkable family who have made their mark on the business life of Plymouth, Robert was at one time Chairman of the Chamber of Commerce. He was also Mayor of The Borough of West Devon a few years ago.

I have spent little time telling you about Castle Kitchens but it goes without saying that their standard is high both in the quality of the product and the fitting. They have a respected name in the industry and have flung their net wide working as much away from Plymouth as they do within its boundaries.

Robert and Linda Tait would welcome news from any reader about any information they may have about Castles. The address is Castles of Plymouth, Estover Close, Plymouth PL6 7PL. Tel: 01752 737333.

Architects hold the aesthetic and practical future of every building the city erects, in their talented hands. Their long training, something like eight years, tosses them out into the work place sometimes into total uncertainty. Architects suffer more than most from economic depressions and are then rushed off their feet when the economy bounces back and everyone wants something built. I talked to Ian Potts of the award winning firm The Architects Design Group in Hotham Place, Millbridge, about his role with his other two partners, Marc Nash and Philip Burgess, about the composition of their thriving company. The three men are all graduates of the Plymouth School of Architecture. Men who became very close friends at that time, and have remained so ever since. They are practising Christians who rely heavily on their faith to make sure they are doing the right thing. Ian told me that their faith effects everything they do in life from home to the workplace, and I have no reason to doubt it. Their offices are in a converted chapel in Hotham Place which has a terrific atmosphere, not because of its past use but because of the sense one has of it being a creative environment, designed to stimulate the mind and produce the very best from everyone who works there. They are not afraid to employ older people and have no worries that the varying age groups will not gel. This sense of well being settles on your shoulders and in your mind when you walk in.

Firstly the conversion of the chapel is unobtrusively spectacular and you could imagine every prospective client seeking architects who have vision, would be halfway to signing a contract with them before the job had even been discussed. They are happy to deal with small and large commissions, they listen to people's budgets and design accordingly. They have received an award this year, for their design of celebrity TV chef Rick Stein's new Seafood Cookery School and new business units at Padstow. Recently the company has received a lot of publicity from the media and the press for the commission they landed in London which is for a walkway across the Thames firmly anchored to a bridge, and very definitely not wobbly!! In Plymouth they have been responsible for many buildings and are always pleased to be associated with such projects as the recent ones in North Prospect with a budget of £850,000 to be built by a local construction firm, providing jobs in the area. It is funded by the Government's SureStart initiative. The object is to make the buildings more community orientated. Included are the Halcyon Methodist Church and Neighbourhood Centre which is to be extended to accommodate a community creche and childcare facility, Ham Drive Nursery which will have a large extension to provide space for benefits and health advice - and the baby book library. North Prospect Primary School's nursery will be refurbished and a new adult unit will be added. The buildings will use a variety of materials to give children an opportunity to explore different textures.

Apart from the involvement of the Architects Design Group, this has all come about after many months of hard work by local groups and individuals wanting to improve the prospects of children in this area of the city. It very much underlines all the partnership projects that are going on day in and day out, in which people are determined to do their very best to make Plymouth one of the best places in which to live and work in the whole of the country.

Obviously as architects, Ian, Marc and Phil can design for anyone anywhere in the world. As an example of their versatility, Ian showed me a preliminary design for a project in China. These men have come a long way since they were brave enough to step out on their own, originally with the desire to set up as a team, but with little else except their faith and their talent to help them.

One wonders whether The Architects Design Group would have produced anything similar to the building which was designed in 1991 by the leading architectural practice, Dixon Jones, as a keynote building for Sainsbury's at Marsh Mills. I have to believe that the Millbridge company would have known a bit more about the vagaries of the winds that beset Plymouth before they thought up the theme for the car park 'which mirrors an amphitheatre-style semi-circle, with the erect pin oaks which surround the car park designed to give the appearance of an outdoor room whilst providing shelter from prevailing winds'. The morning that I called in to meet with Mike Booth, their long term General Manager, who incidentally has moved on since then, and the store now has another experienced and dedicated General Manager, the rain was pouring down and the wind gusting - all that was mirrored was a very wet, very unpleasant car park only made up for by the warmth and sparkling colour within the store itself.

One has to give credit to Dixon Jones, who incidentally designed the Sydney Opera House, for a building which is remarkable and memorable. Sainsbury's at Marsh Mills is somewhere that anyone approaching Plymouth on the A38, cannot fail to notice. It stands at the head of the Plym Estuary and across the busy road the backdrop is formed by Efford Fort Hill. More mundanely the adjacent railway line always suggests movement and motion. The most striking element of the store design is the canopy which is visible from all approaches to the store; here an arcaded walkway of eleven translucent PVC sails creates a dramatic focus and echoes the billowing sails of the nautical heritage of Plymouth. It is particularly effective at night when the canopy lighting creates an unusual sculptural effect.

There will be few people who have not at sometime or other over the last 132 years shopped in a branch of Sainsbury's somewhere in the country. It has a history to be proud of and one recorded in a splendid book, ' The Best Butter in the World' written and compiled by the company's archivist, Bridget Williams.

From the very day in 1869 when the first, very small, Sainsbury's shop opened at 173 Drury Lane, Holborn, London, in a poor area, the philosophy then, as now, has always been to give their customers 'The Best Butter in the World' at prices they could afford. I quote David Sainsbury, who wrote in the Foreword of Bridget Williams' book, 'This philosophy of giving customers the best value for money is a theme which runs through the whole history of the Company. The sign on the shopfront of the store we opened in Islington in 1882 read 'Quality Perfect, Prices Lower', and in recent years the same approach has been encapsulated in the slogan 'Good Food Costs Less at Sainsbury's. A commitment to customer service, an obsessive concern about food hygiene, and a belief that well-trained and highly motivated people are the key to successful retailing, are also themes which occur throughout our history'.

There is no doubt that the history of the company has been one of constant and consistent vision. They have embraced every advance in food technology, changes in transport, the invention of the computer, or the development of self-service trading.

Working for a store the size of Sainsbury's at Marsh Mills is like being part of the crew of a very well run cruiseship. A curious analogy you might suppose, but like a cruise ship, customers have to be happy, things have to run smoothly and what is on offer has to be the very best. Some 32,000 people go through the checkout at Sainsbury's in a normal week. By the time they have reached that point, they will have ticked off their shopping list, piled their trolleys high. What happens if you cannot find what you want? All you have to do is ask and help is immediately forthcoming. You will either be taken to the aisle where the elusive product is shelved or a kindly helper will fetch the missing piece in your shopping jigsaw for you. The staff are well trained; next time you are there you may notice that staff do take note of customers and if they see you looking up and down shelves, obviously seeking something, almost always they will ask if they can help.

Staff training is an all important factor and is continuous in the supermarket, or in the company no matter how long you have been with Sainsbury's. Employees of J Sainsbury's plc are given every opportunity to climb the promotion ladder - even to the dizzy heights of Chair!. Apart from the ability to know how to deal with customers, it is a pretty major task to acquire knowledge about the 23,000 items available in the store. I have been at Marsh Mills on several occasions when staff skill has been very apparent. Not so long ago a customer collapsed next to me at the checkout. Quietly and with no fuss help was on hand - the till girl had pressed a button and set the process in motion. The man was carefully and skilfully handled and thankfully recovered quickly. There will have been few people in the store who even knew the incident had occurred. There are times when trolley rage erupts and that too is rapidly dealt with.

We know that Sainsbury's offers value for money, the service is good and it is a friendly place to shop but what about the background in running such a big operation?
The General Manager is responsible for the 500 people employed at Marsh Mills - and has charge of other stores as well, but it is Marsh Mills I want to write about. Sainsbury's as a company has always involved itself in activities beyond the company. It is no exception in Plymouth. When the Marsh Mills site was purchased, in addition to the agreed price, the company gave Plymouth City Council a large sum of money to be spent for the good of Plymothians. This money has been used and re-used successfully. As I understand it, the old Wolseley Home building which was a sort of workhouse, was purchased with this money and turned into units for start up businesses and a piece of its land was sold to the Co-operative Society who built on it their Plymco Store. The profits were then moved on to regenerate part of the land at Millfields, again becoming financially independent.

Plymouth Library has used to good advantage Sainsbury's 'Book Start' campaign which is a national charity and administered in Plymouth by the City Library. Its purpose is to introduce books to babies from a very early age which in turn provides more reading opportunities for their siblings and frequently the parents as well. A highly successful cause. Sainsbury's in turn has funded the creche at Woodford School in Plympton, which has allowed mothers to go to work as well as provide a happy environment for toddlers and babies. One of the benefits for Sainsbury's is that several members of staff are able to leave their children there.

Sainsbury's staff run a charitable operation of their own called 'Side by Side' where they work with small charities needing assistance, not only financial but practical as well. They frequently find themselves painting buildings, or becoming carpenters apart from a host of other events. Every year, what charities they will support are decided upon in advance, usually as a result of letters they have received asking for help. They give generously of their time and the added benefit is the strength of their working relationship which seems to flourish as a result of these outside activities.

Staff are encouraged to 'better themselves' for the want of a more suitable expression. In other words, if any member of staff wants to study a language, take up computer studies, master the art of flower arranging, or indeed anything that, even in the smallest way, might help them to get on with their work, they are encouraged to do so and Sainsbury's will pay the cost of the tuition and for whatever books are required. Second languages for example, have proved very useful within the store because of the influx of foreign visitors especially in the tourist season.

I found myself constantly asking Mike Booth 'What happens if....? With the fully computerised operation what happens if the computers go down? How do they cope with stock control? One has to remember that every time an item is run through the till it is checked off on the stock list by the computer which then determines the ordering level. If this does happen - and it has - the distribution centre uses the forecasted levels to provide the store with goods. When the computer decides to work again, there is a frantic in-store stock-taking to try and work out what quantities of the 23,000 items have been sold. Worse still if the check out tills go down. What if.....? Then Mike, and his colleagues - he never refers to them as staff but always as 'colleagues' - take up their positions by the check out girl or man, with a calculator in one hand and pen and paper at the ready. They have to rely on the customer telling them the price of goods if they can. The amounts are put in the calculator, the items written down, and the customer charged with the total on the calculator.

Distribution has been a worry to Sainsbury's West Country stores from time to time, but this has now been alleviated by the opening of another centre in Bristol. However carefully things are planned the unforeseen or the improbable does happen. Planning way ahead for occasions like Valentine's Day, Mother's Day, Father's Day, all demand special thinking. For example more flowers are sold on Mother's Day than St Valentines - many of them being bought by relatives who take them to the graves of parents who have died. Christmas is always a nightmare. Firstly because although the date remains firm, the days of the week which embrace Christmas itself, change making every year different in its requirements. It is not only the amount of stock that needs forecasting but the additional staff who are required to cover the 24 hour periods which come into play. Mike Booth remembers the days when he used to have a book in which he wrote down his requirements and dispatched the order by post or rang it through. Everything has changed but still the means of being profitable come down to the efficiency and skill of forecasting. Mike says that in his early days he worked as a butcher for a private firm where every penny had to be accounted for, and nothing was done unless it made a profit. That training is still behind the way he works today - and almost always it is profitable!

There are exceptions of course when the improbable happens against the probability which has been forecast. The time of the Total Eclipse in August 1999 is a prime example. 15 months planning went into what supposedly needed to be done. It looked as though the A38 would be grid-locked and in Cornwall there was talk of making the whole county one way - approached by the A30 and left by the A38. To get goods to the Plymouth stores would they need to come in by boat or be air-lifted? Could they find enough portable loos to look after the motorists who would come into Marsh Mills whilst they were grid-locked. Banking, Petrol, and heaven alone knows how many other problems had to be looked at. The planning was neat and thorough, every eventuality covered and then what happened? The whole thing was almost a non-event! A costly, time-consuming exercise.

The laying out of a store was another thing that interested me. One of the infuriating things when you are shopping is the constant changing of the aisles in which you expect to find what you have written on your list. At Marsh Mills this has been very well organised. Everything stays in its rightful place and there are special aisles for special events. Christmas, for example, Easter for another, Barbecues, Mother's Day and all the other occasions. Fresh food is altogether so you can shop quickly if you are doing a small shop. There is a special section towards the back of the store for things like glasses, teatowels, TV's etc. Above all there are wide aisles which make shopping simple and driving a trolley less of a nightmare. The checkouts are also wide. The new Coffee Shop serves good food at very realistic prices - it even has a trolley park.

The great thing about Sainsbury's is its ability to innovate rapidly as it has done in the past and maintain the essential values that it has had since 1869.

Once the barrier is lifted and you are security passed to enter into the world of BAE SYSTEMS in Southway, Plymouth, you become aware of the quiet power and strength of this massive company which in turn owns half of Silicon Sensing Systems, a joint venture formed by BAE SYSTEMS in England and Sumito Precision Products in Japan. Once in the Reception area, where brass plates, beautiful hand made ceramics awarded to the company, add to a sense of well being, it is immediately apparent that here is a company with a distinguished pedigree, with over 80 years experience in the design and development of gyroscopes and accelerometers. This is a joint venture in which the partners have already achieved significant technical and commercial success in a wide range of markets. From its office in Plymouth, Amagasaki, Japan and in the States, it is well placed to deliver solutions to stabilisation, orientation and alignment requirements worldwide. If anything, America is its biggest market place.

At BAE SYSTEMS there is a substantial factory on the site, together with buildings for administration, tool making and research. The thing that struck me most was the sense of ordered quietness that prevailed, whether it was inside the factory or in the various offices. Colin Fancourt, the Head of Business for Solid State Gyroscopes, talked to me about the endless search for improvements in everything they do. He showed me the gyroscope that was the invention of the American, Mr Elmer Sperry, the founder really of all that has happened subsequently. That gyroscope was revolutionary but what would he have made of the low cost solid state gyroscope, no bigger than a thumb nail which is being manufactured at the rate of 2 million a year in a special factory in Japan and is revolutionising the market with its use both commercially and military. It is hoped that a new factory manufacturing this superb piece will also be opened in Cornwall before very long. The market place is enormous and is explored and exploited by a very efficient team who work from the Plymouth site.

For some years BAE SYSTEMS has researched into Navigation sensor technology and one product, Terpromâ looks set to play a major role in the safety of flying. It has the extraordinary ability to be able to define even the smallest ridge on the ground and when a plane is low flying ensures that the moment anything is in the way of the flight path, it warns and lifts the aircraft out of danger. The products and range of the company in the air, at sea or on land cover everything from aircraft and missile navigation systems, gunfire control systems, to electro optic tracking instruments. It first became a British Aerospace location in 1982 when Bae acquired Sperry Gyroscope Company. Sperry themselves had taken it over from Remington in 1975 and had established Plymouth as a manufacturing facility for its main business centred in Bracknell.

British Aerospace acquired the freehold of the Plymouth site in 1983, and it continued primarily as a manufacturing facility until, in the restructure which followed the formation of British Aerospace Systems and Equipment (BASE), it was decided that Bracknell should be closed and Plymouth should become the centre. One of the reasons for the move was the greater ease of recruitment in Plymouth which at that time had a fairly high unemployment record whilst Bracknell was suffering from a 45% attrition rate because of the high employment from 'start-up' electronics companies. This in a sort of a way has backfired because today's employees are almost too stable and have little desire to change companies. I wonder which is the best option? I would plump for stability. However even this may change with Plymouth's successful employment rate to-day and new businesses arriving to compete for staff.
Since 1983 the workforce has more than doubled and the site development has been virtually non-stop. The old style administrative building at the front was completely modernised with a new reception area, board room and office facilities being installed during 1989. Begun in the same year and completed in the Spring of 1990, was the construction of D Building which houses some 300 engineers, as well as a single-status restaurant and some administrative functions. The late Alan Clark, then Minister of State for Defence Procurement opened the building in 1990. Since then an adjoining field has been purchased providing additional car parking for employees.

In 1999 Bae merged with the GEC Marconi company - and the resultant company was named BAE SYSTEMS - the name you see outside the facility today. The site in

Southway is situated amongst the large residential area which has many plus points. In the first place it is close enough for many of the 750 staff to walk or cycle to work, which has to be beneficial. It is in a pleasant area close to Dartmoor and, as it needs to be is surrounded by clean air. The company is firmly rooted in Plymouth and has become part of the community, giving a helping hand to many good causes.

What will stay in my mind having visited there, is the enormous pride Colin Fancourt has in the company and its products, his excitement about the future and the very genuine concern for those who work for the company.

In 1992 when I met John Hanson, the then head of Becton Dickinson in Plymouth, I was very aware of the strength of the company and the man. This strength is even more evident now we are in the 21st century. John Hanson has moved on and is now the Company's European President. On my visit to the Plymouth headquarters this year I talked to Ian Smith, the Human Resources Manager and John Cox, one of his colleagues who has been with the company since its arrival in Plymouth. Their pride in the achievements of the company which celebrated its centenary in 1997, was very evident. Asking Ian Smith to sum up the Company's Purpose, he answered ' It is to help all people live healthy lives. We aim to do this by becoming the organisation most known for eliminating unnecessary suffering and death from disease, and in so doing becoming one of the best performing companies in the world.' As you will discover as you read on, Becton Dickinson today is the legacy of an act of kindness and a shared breakfast over one hundred years ago!

If you read a company profile on Becton Dickinson whose site is based at Belliver, it will say 'Products: Evacuated blood collection tubes and laboratory equipment'. That rather cold statement gives no one an insight into how this giant American manufacturer of health care products started.

The story is simple. Maxwell William Becton and Fairleigh Stanton Dickinson met on a sales trip in 1807. Noticing that bright sunshine pouring through a dining room window was bothering Dickinson. Becton pulled down the shade. The appreciative Dickinson invited him to breakfast, beginning a lifelong friendship.

Within months, the pair formed Becton, Dickinson and Company in New York City. From imported fever thermometers, their line expanded to include hypodermic units and other supplies.
Several years later, to ensure consistent product quality and supply, they moved to a new factory in East Rutherford, New Jersey, one of the first US plants to make hypodermic units. In a few years, Becton Dickinson was producing and marketing a full range of high quality products.

During World War I, the company produced all-glass syringes, a significant improvement over the metal units of the day. Becton Dickinson also developed the ACE brand bandage, originally an acronym for 'all cotton elastic'. For his contribution to the war effort, Dickinson was commissioned as a lieutenant colonel in the Medical Corps and thereafter was called 'The Colonel'. Steady growth followed the war. People who were to make an outstanding contribution joined the company. These included Andrew W. Fleischer, always called 'Doc' even though he did not have a medical degree, and Dr Oscar Schwidetzky. Brilliant inventors, they headed the company's medical products research for decades. Fleischer modernised the stethoscope and invented the first accurate instrument to measure blood pressure. Schwidetzky developed special hypodermic needles and other devices.

In World War II the company was awarded an Army/Navy 'E' for Excellence, for providing quality medical equipment for the armed forces. Dickinson and Becton were instrumental in establishing Fairleigh Dickinson Junior College, now a university.

Following the war, Becton Dickinson continued to develop innovative products such as a glass syringe with interchangeable parts and a device to collect blood in sterile tubes for laboratory analysis. This instrument sold under the Vacutainer brand, opened laboratory medicine to the company.

The founders retired in 1948 and passed on control of the company's future to their sons Fairleigh S. Dickinson Junior and Henry P. Becton. Product lines were broadened and new production capacity built, while international expansion, which had begun in Canada continued.

From the 1950s to 1980s, Becton Dickinson acquired such leading firms as Bard-Parker who developed the first two-piece scalpel, the Baltimore Biological Laboratory, which produced dry culture media in which diagnosticians grow microorganisms for tests: Clay Adams, manufacturer of surgeons' supplies and laboratory instruments; Johnson Laboratories, which developed the BACTEC microorganism detection instrument; and Deseret Medical Inc, a leading provider of catheters, protective gloves and surgical products.

The advent of the disposable hypodermic syringe and needle, introduced by Becton Dickinson in 1961, completely changed the company. This product significantly differed from the traditional reusable type. The needle had to be permanently bonded to the syringe, glass barrels were replaced by more cost-effective plastics and enormous volumes had to be manufactured. This meant huge investment in new equipment, packaging and distribution. Becton Dickinson became a publicly held corporation and in 1963 was listed on the New York Stock Exchange. The family partnership was over, replaced by a new responsibility to thousands of stockholders. Following the floatation Becton Dickinson became a member of the 'fortune 500' in 1970. The corporation has remained innovative and today is a leading, diversified, transnational health care corporation with sales of more than $3 billion and more than 20,000 employees at locations throughout the world. The company brings to millions of people modern medical technology, products made with meticulous attention to quality and a real sense of caring.

Plymouth is one of those locations and here with a multi-million dollar investment, on a 27 acre site in July 1982, Becton Dickinson, Plymouth was officially opened by HRH Princess Margaret. (The Plant actually started manufacturing in October 1981).

Becton Dickinson based its decision for investing in Plymouth on the market potential that lay in Europe and the assurances that were given on the quality and reliability of the workforce. This confidence in the City and its labour force has been justified by the excellent performance of the plant. As Becton Dickinson was expanding, other companies associated with the Defence Industry, were contracting as part of the Peace Dividend. Becton Dickinson were able to offer employment opportunities to many of these highly skilled people.

The Plant at Plymouth has gone from strength to strength with further investment added in 1998 and 1999. The Plant manufactures medical devices and diagnostic products which are exported to all parts of the world.

They are all proud of the achievement at the Plymouth Plant, which has contributed to the success of Becton Dickinson worldwide. John Hanson, as the Company's European President confirms that one of the major contributors to the successful growth has been the quality of the local workforce along with the positive cooperation between local business, Council and Regional Development Agencies.

From a workforce in 1981 of 66 associates to October 2001 Becton Dickinson will have been part of the local community for 20 years. Today it employs over 800 people and is a tribute to its original investors, its workforce and the local community.

From the moment of being greeted by the lively Security man on the gate at Toshiba Carrier UK just across the road from Becton Dickinson in Belliver, I felt the infectious enthusiasm for the company becoming part of my persona. There is nothing flamboyant about this enthusiasm, it simply stems from a remarkable Managing Director, Halsey Cook, who in the space of something like two years has turned a mediocre and some might say dying operation into one of the most successful in the country. For example, from a standing start the company ended the year with an export volume of £14 million pounds. The product entirely air conditioning and its subsidiaries.

The divorce between the original Toshiba operation in Plymouth with its major interest in television, video recorders etc in one factory in Ernesettle and the air conditioning plant in Belliver has allowed the Belliver operation to enter into a marriage with Carrier which some might say was made in heaven. What did the partners bring to the marriage? Toshiba had a first class product in its air conditioning systems and Carrier had the ability to provide the marketing, the sales and the distribution plus purchasing power because of its enormous strength throughout the world. It could not have been a better match. How did Toshiba at Belliver react to the merger? Frankly with a sense of suspicion and caution. They had become almost stagnant, motivation was low and although the rigid, open door policy of the Japanese company had brought new ideas to the Plymothians and others working for them, in some ways the ideas had become a little passe and so the shock waves of American know-how and its get up and go attitude needed to be absorbed before the current success of the Toshiba Carrier operation began to bear fruit. Today the very best of Japanese thinking has taken on the mantle of the American ideas happily. The staff wouldn't wish to work anywhere else and how successful it has all been is evident when you look at the export figures of £14 million for the last year, and UK sales up by 20% with a further 15% projected in year 2001.

When I talked with Lisa Birch, the Personnel Manager, her frank opinions of what had happened since the merger, made me eager to learn more about this vibrant company which has a set of standards which are willingly adhered to. Every newcomer to the company is given a pack which in a comprehensive but succinct manner spells out what is expected. Under the heading Performance comes a series of requirements. It means good practices - moving towards best practices - in finance, in recruiting, in product performance, quality implementation, delivery schedule, distribution, marketing, manufacturing - everything. A performance is about continuous improvement, so its starts with admission of defects, which is the only way you ever get better at anything. It also means the willingness to confront change openly, clearly, with courage, being innovative and taking risks, while using good judgment and common sense. The reality is that what won last year will not win this year! Customers' expectations are rising all the time and competition is moving very fast. Under Ethics comes 'A performance organisation also means playing by the rules; no short cuts on ethics and integrity ever. Environment Health & Safety confirms that 'Protecting the safety of our employees, and the environment, is a core value within the company which will not be satisfied until its workplace is safe from hazards, its employees are injury free, its products and service safe, and its commitment and record in protecting the environment are unmatched. It is a company of Equal Opportunity.

Number 6 on this document sprang out at me as being almost, if not entirely unique. The heading was UTC Employee Scholar Program. It means that any employee who has the drive and energy to go back to school and register for full credit courses from a recognised institution will have the company backing. The company will pay one hundred per cent of all course-related books, registrations and academic fees as well as up to three hours paid time off per week, regardless of the field of study chosen, i.e. even if they are not related to the job. There are no exceptions provided course requirements are met. In addition graduates from a recognised institution will be awarded shares of the UTC stock. The reason for this programme is simple in the words of the UTC President, George David, 'Our goal is to have the best-educated work force on the planet..'

The company also believes in its Dialog Program. It is keen to provide communication channels that encourage self-expression and open dialogue relative to employee opinions, attitudes and concerns.

In addition to the traditional communication channels, through peers, supervisors, management, human resources, or employee representatives, Toshiba Carrier has established with the DIALOG programme, a confidential way of handling any question, suggestion, comment or concern any employee may have. If, for any reason, the employee wishes to remain anonymous, the question or comment will be forwarded by the DIALOG administrator to the appropriate member of management or to the manager designated, and in a timely fashion, the employee will receive a detailed response. The identity will be totally protected.

Thousands of questions, comments or concerns have been channelled through the Dialog programme at Carrier which has allowed the Company to improve a number of its policies or procedures, solve issues of inequities, uncover questionable ethical practices and help make Carrier, a better place to work.

The obvious care for employees, the constant, motivated drive from Halsey Cook down to the most junior employee makes Toshiba Carrier an exciting place. My good fortune was the opportunity to take a look at the immaculate factory where the workers themselves, following the rules, keep the factory clean - no cleaners are employed apart from the sub-contractors who see to the loos, the rest rooms and vacuum the carpets of the administrative offices. It was amongst a number of short blue jacketed men (the jackets were short - not the men) that I met Denis O'Connell, the General Manager of the Factory. A powerful job but quite obviously carried out with great efficiency, and like everyone else here, a hunger for success. His open plan office had various different areas each with movable screens carrying every bit of information about what was happening in the factory. Nothing is hidden here. You could read how many days had been lost by illness, how much they had exceeded target, what was needed to keep the wheels of industry turning over. Each morning for about ten minute there is a gathering here of people who have reports to make, people who have ideas to put across. Everyone stands, not even the boss man sits. It is held at 10am on the dot and is an example to many companies who waste hours of manpower time sitting round tables at meetings which go on far too long and are frequently unproductive. At 8am there is also a meeting of sections on the factory floor who come to discuss what has been written on a Flip Chart the previous day. The subject matter can be anything that an employee believes needs to be done to achieve target. While I was there one man wrote 'Hoist required'. Simple enough but without it no doubt productivity on his section would be held up.

This is a factory where everything has a place and is marked out accordingly. Everything is replaced where it should be and the whole essence of neatness makes for efficiency. I was amused by the 'Red Tag' bag. This is a little polythene bag in which notice of anything which is left in the wrong place gets noted. It is then pursued to ensure the offenders take back what is rightly theirs and don't get their knuckles rapped again!

In a time of high employment levels in Plymouth, Toshiba Carrier, who do not profess to pay the highest wages, are ensuring they have a stable and contented - but not complacent - work force.

It has been an excellent marriage.

Incidentally I was fascinated to discover under the umbrella of the Plymouth Manufacturers Group that Lisa Birch, Toshiba Carrier's Personnel Manager, and a number of Personnel and Human Resource Managers of Industrial and Retail companies in the city meet together to discuss wage structure, staff management etc. If you have never heard of the unobtrusive but immensely powerful Plymouth Manufacturing Group, it is made up of 25 group members who are represented by their Chief Executives. The requirements of membership are simple; they must be manufacturers, they must have over one hundred employees and that whatever they talk about is totally confidential.

The group does not have an office, but they do have a secretary who organises the group's meetings which take place at different venues, six times a year. They also have social occasions but the main purpose is to talk about generalities in their world without betraying the individual confidentiality of each company. The conversation will range over current trends, the consideration of annual wage increases, new regulations and amy other topic which is beneficial to the group. They also unite as a pressure group to encourage the city or the county to act in a way they think is necessary for the good of the whole. There is no question that they are immensely powerful. Quite rightly when you consider that between them they spend in excess of £30 million annually on goods and services provided by other businesses within the city. Many of their members are to be found in influential positions on committees striving to achieve greater success for Plymouth as a whole.

It is known that every job in manufacturing creates another four in other services including sub-contracted work. We should also remember that a great deal of the new investment in supermarkets and leisure facilities would probably not have taken place without this new wealth injection into the local economy.

Doctor Graham Stirling Chief Executive of the Barden Corporation (U.K.) Limited, part of the Barden Corporation of Connecticut, U.S.A, is one of the leading members of the Plymouth Manufacturing Group and amongst his many other roles he is the energetic Chairman of PROSPER which has done much to help the prosperity of Plymouth. I enjoy meeting Graham Stirling because he has a zest for life which he marries well with his flair for the business of his company. He is a sincere fan of the virtues of Plymouth and in the time since I met him in 1992 the Barden Corporation has tripled in size and now is the leading manufacturer of super precision ball bearings in the world. These have applications in many individual sectors, including textile machinery, high performance vacuum pumps and machine tools. The company machines to near frictionless perfection, providing an engineering service which is the envy of other International ball bearing manufacturers. Barden's advanced bearing technology is specified throughout the aerospace, medical and computer industries.

The company's underlying principles are product quality, precision, excellence, performance and availability, and that is repaid by the loyal workforce in terms of versatility and adaptability. Graham Stirling is proud of the record of the lack of absenteeism in Plymouth and the non-stoppages which people experience in other parts of the country.

I reminded Graham Stirling of our meeting in 1992 when he told me how reluctant his American parent company were to invest more money in Plymouth, which they deemed to be a backwater. He persuaded the hierarchy to come to Plymouth and see for themselves, arranging a splendid dinner at 3, Elliot Terrace. They came, saw the magnificence of Plymouth Hoe and the Sound, had a wonderful meal in this historic house. They fell in love with the city and the £3 million Graham Stirling needed for expansion was promptly forthcoming. A good example of why Lord and Lady Astor's gift to the city of their home, needs to be used for just this sort of purpose.

This time talking to Graham Stirling made me green with envy!! The Barden Corporation manufacture precision ball bearings for Formula I clutches, wheels and gear boxes and as a result Graham gets to visit many of the circuits - purely for ensuring that the product works! A wonderful excuse in my view. I am quite passionate about Formula I and I will never watch a race again without taking an intense interest in the bearings and any failure. It must be equally thrilling for the Barden workforce.

I asked Graham Stirling if he had any reservations about manufacturing in Plymouth. His only regret is that we do not have a better airport that is not only too small but is also regularly affected by fog. This is a reservation that is not from just a single voice.The question is where could another airport be sited?

The Gleason Works Limited are virtually next door to the Bardon Corporation. It is very pleasing to know that a Plymothian, Robert Ball, is now the Vice President of this vast American Corporation and also the Chief Executive of the Plymouth operation. He is a man who, having left the Dockyard, looked for a company which could offer an exciting and challenging career. This he certainly found and along the way has, like Graham Stirling, done much to further the cause of Plymouth including being Chairman of the Chamber of Commerce and Industry.

Gleason were once based in Watford and in 1964 found themselves needing to expand. It was not possible to do so in that area because of Government restrictions. They had to find a Development District and visited every area in the United Kingdom recommended by the Board of Trade. In each locality an in depth survey was carried out and Gleason met with the local Board of Trade representatives, councillors, industrialists and, where appropriate, trade union representatives.

At that time, everywhere available in England, Scotland and Ireland offered government grants and local incentives but this was only one of the considerations in choosing an appropriate site. Such a move, by a company whose skilled operators and engineers manufactured a high precision product, necessitated the re-location of a nucleus of key Gleason employees.

An attractive area was important and Gleason wanted to ensure they chose the best location which met, not only their present needs, but those for the foreseeable future. Therefore they compiled a shopping list.

1. A green field site on which to build a factory and office with land for future expansion.
2. An area of unemployment without being depressed.
3. A pool of labour which would become a committed and loyal workforce and who would be willing to be trained, spending several months in Watford prior to the move.
4. An area with good employee relations
5. A helpful and co-operative local government
6. A college or organisation qualified to assist in the training of apprentices
7. Council houses available until employees found their own homes.

Plymouth became the yardstick to which all succeeding areas were compared. Nowhere achieved the same standard. Plymouth was not actually on a government list of places available but the City Council were so keen to have Gleason move to the county, they moved heaven and earth to achieve this.

331

Gleason for their part, liked Plymouth, liked the site on offer at Estover, found the Council extremely co-operative and other local managing directors helpful in outlining the advantages and also the disadvantages in the area such as communications.

In August 1967, the factory was transferred from Watford to Plymouth and Robert Ball was one of the engineers who returned to the city with the company. Gleason have never regretted the move. That was just over thirty years ago and the Plymouth plant is now the major gear tooling and cutter blade manufacturing site for the entire Gleason Corporation.

The history of the firm is quite interesting. It was established by William Gleason, who began his apprenticeship in America in 1851 on arrival from Ireland. He worked in a Rochester, New York, machine shop and when the Civil War broke out took his mechanical skills to Colt's Armoury in Hartford, Connecticut. He returned to Rochester in 1865 and formed the firm of Connell and Gleason. From his invention of the bevel gear planner, the company grew to world leadership in the production of gear making machinery. In 1919, the first Gleason cutting tools were manufactured in the United Kingdom under licensing agreement with Buck and Hickman, long time representatives of Gleason.

We already know of the move to Plymouth and from that time onwards they extended their area of business from Europe to the Far East as more and more machines were brought in. In 1969 it became necessary to extend the factory by a third. By 1973 the decision was made to build an extension at the rear of the factory across all three bays.

Gleason Works Limited was one of the first companies in Britain to obtain the National Training Award and in 1989 received the British Standards Award, BS 5750, in recognition of its quality standards. Winning awards has continued ever since.

In 1991 three separate product groups were created to further improve and strengthen Gleason's position in the market place. These were the Standard Products Group, the Special Products Group and the Tooling Products Group.

Robert Ball, who by now was the Director and General Manager at Plymouth, became Vice-President of the Tooling Products Group responsible for operations worldwide.

The Plymouth plant today is the major gear tooling manufacturing site for the Group concentrating on the manufacture of workholding equipment and cutter heads. CNC technology and computerisation increasingly play a part in consolidating the forward thrust of the Plymouth operation, as does the design, research and development of tooling equipment.

With continuous re-design work on its products, together with major patents granted and pending as well as major investment in manufacturing equipment, it is clear that Gleason will ensure market leadership.

The streamlining which has taken place on both sides of the Atlantic has placed Gleason in a very strong position in today's volatile and competitive market place. It is well known that Gleason responds quickly and effectively, not only to present, but also to predicted customer demands, and as a consequence, now exports more machines and tooling to Japan than any other company in the world. The Plymouth operation exports 95% of its production to the Far East, Europe and the USA leaving just 5% for the UK market.

Gleason is a true creator of wealth in the Plymouth area since raw steel is the only bought in part of the product. Even the steel is supplied from the UK.

The company also invests heavily in the training of its employees through apprenticeships and ongoing training. It takes a great interest in welfare and education in the city, and the Gleason Memorial Fund has donated to various organisations and schools, such as the RNLI and Age Concern and have provided a technology room at Southway School. The Memorial Fund also donated £47,000 to Coombe Dean School for a business centre equipped to train pupils and adults in the type of skills needed in today's high-tech world.

The Wrigley Company was the very first occupant of a site in Estover. Between 1953 and the mid 1960s, The Wrigley Company had expanded the London factory three times and had reached the point where it either had to build a new factory or set up a subsidiary plant.

The decision was made to build a new factory and a firm of management consultants was brought in to survey the country.
The company needed access to engineering skills because many of its factory employees are associated with engineering in one way or another and it also builds its own high-speed wrapping machines.

It also needed good housing for its key workers and to be confident that the staff moving from London would like their new environment.

Another vital requirement was clean air - chewing gum quickly absorbs obnoxious odours from the atmosphere.

Plymouth was an obvious choice and, during negotiations with the city council for the Estover site, a clean air covenant was written into the agreement. This requires the council to confer with Wrigley when industry is brought into the surrounding area to ensure there is no contamination to the production process.

The management at Wrigley will tell you that Plymouth City Council was fantastic when the company came to the city and has been ever since. Only one employee who made the move disliked Plymouth and returned to London.

The company has enough land at Estover to cope with all the expansion for the foreseeable future so it will never find itself in the same situation as it was in Wembley.

Wrigley is one of Plymouth's biggest success stories of recent years with production growing steadily every year since the late 80's. In 1999 the factory produced more than 1.2 billion packets of gum.

The company employs around 680 staff, 89% of which work at Estover, the remainder being Wrigley's field sales force with members located all over the UK.

The story of the growth of the Wrigley Company, which began in the USA, is one of a man with a mission and $32 with which to carry it out.

William Wrigley went to Chicago in the spring of 1891 and, with the only other commodities he possessed (energy, enthusiasm and salesmanship), started selling Wrigley's Scouring Soap from a basket.

The enticement he gave to purchasers proved more popular than his initial product so he switched to selling baking powder, offering two packets of chewing gum with each can.

Everyone loves getting something for nothing and once again the appeal of the free gum overtook the product it was supposed to promote. Though at the time there were already a dozen or more gum companies, William began marketing it under his own name and carrying on with the principle of offering free gifts with purchases.

In 1907 business in the USA experienced a general slump and slashed expenses, including marketing activities. William Wrigley was a pioneer in the use of advertising to promote sales and, instead of cutting back, he saw that spending more and increasing this activity would put him ahead of the competition. By 1910 Wrigley's Spearmint gum was America's favourite brand.

There is a story told about William Wrigley that sums up his philosophy. He was travelling on a train to the West Coast of America with a young accountant who questioned the large sums the company was spending on advertising. The accountant suggested that Wrigley's bottom line profit would improve considerably if the advertising budget was reduced.

William Wrigley responded by asking the young man how fast he thought the train was travelling. About 70 miles an hour, the accountant retorted.

'What do you think would happen if they took the engine off?' asked Wrigley.

'The train would come to a stop,' replied the puzzled accountant.

That explained exactly what would happen to Wrigley's business if there was a cut back in advertising. One of the things that William Wrigley used to say was 'Tell them quick and tell them often'., meaning it was essential to keep your name in front of the public at all times.

That policy is adhered to today and Wrigley spends more than £19 million in the Uk each year to keep its products in the public eye.

Factories were established outside the USA and business boomed until the outbreak of the second World War meant the top grade materials used to make the gum dried up, and the entire output was shipped to the troops abroad.

Even then, although no gum was available for sale to the civilian market, a unique advertising campaign,, featuring an empty wrapper with the slogan 'Remember this wrapper', ensured that Wrigley's gum remained in the forefront of people's minds, if not their mouths.

The site at Estover covers 45 acres although only six have been built on. Land availability and a good supply of skilled workers were the two main reasons for choosing Plymouth and, although the majority of Wrigley's UK production is sold outside the South West, gum is a relatively compact product so freight charges are not excessive. Plymouth is, therefore, an ideal location.

The Wrigley family, based in the USA, has retained overall control of the business which now has manufacturing facilities in 17 countries, and sales offices all over the world.

Today over 20 million people in the UK, chew gum for many reasons; for breath freshening, for dental benefits, to teeth whitening, for nasal clearance and throat soothing and for simple pleasure.

In the UK, Wrigley produces the nation's top selling sweet - Wrigley's Extra. Retail sales of this brand reached 400 million packets in 2000 - an all time record for the company and a chewing gum product.

And the staff at Estover can also claim credit for creating the enormously successful dental care campaign which has made millions of people aware of the dental benefits of chewing sugarfree gum to help prevent tooth decay.

After eating, plaque acid is produced which can attack teeth for up to two hours. Chewing sugarfree gum after a meal or snack stimulates saliva to neutralise this acid and strengthen teeth against decay.

Wrigley's Orbit is positioned as the dental brand in the UK and is recommended by over 90% of the dental professionals. It is recognised by the World Dental Federation, British Dental Association and the Health Education Authority for its contribution to oral health.

Latest product developments include Ice White for helping to keep teeth clean and white, Airwaves Vapour Release for nasal clearance and Airways Honey Lemon to help soothe a sore throat.

The future looks extremely bright for Wrigley Plymouth which is playing a key role in developing business throughout Europe. The company is taking full advantage of the opportunities offered by the global market and is on course to meet its ambitious plans for production and profit growth in the new millennium.

Estover breeds success for firms and none more so than Fine Tubes, a specialist tubing firm. They manufacture seamless and welded tubing in stainless steel, nickel and titanium alloys in straight lengths and coils. Size range is from 0.3 to 50.8mm outside diameter with principal markets being the oil & gas, nuclear, semi-conductor, aerospace and medical industries.

As I write Fine Tubes has a turnover of £20 million a year, occupy more than 215,000 sq ft and employ 380 people. Now they have announced that there is to be a £2 million expansion which in turn will create a further 10 jobs. They are delighted to be expanding at a time when some in the manufacturing sector are experiencing difficulties. The programme envisaged covers a complete new tube production mill and associated handling equipment which is aimed at the production of stainless steel and nickel alloy small diameter tubing for the oil and gas and semiconductor industries.

The specification for the tube mill had to ensure its ability to compete on a global market in terms of quality efficiency and cost competitiveness. Fine Tubes Sales and Marketing Manager takes great pride in the fact the the tube mill is of UK manufacture. Fine Tubes exports approximately 60% of its production.

The Estover based Japanese electronics firm Murata came to Plymouth in 1990 as a result of the work of the then Devon and Cornwall Development Bureau. At that time they had an office in Tokyo where they worked hard to entice companies to come to Devon and Cornwall. I was amused when I learned that they always tried to arrange for visiting potential investors to come to Plymouth last after they had been to the North, Wales or Scotland. By this time the visitors were always tired and not inclined to be enthusiastic until they saw how superb Plymouth Sound was and how awe inspiring the ruggedness of Dartmoor. Add to this a traditional cream tea and possibly dinner in 3, Elliot Terrace after which there was no contest - Plymouth had won!

That is simplifying a complicated business but who can deny that Plymouth is a wonderful place in which to live and work!

When I went in 1992 to take tea with Yoshitsugu Fujiwara, the managing director of Murata at Estover, he expressed how delighted he and his wife were to be in Plymouth and how happy he was about the way in which he and his Japanese colleagues had been welcomed into the life of the city.. However liking Plymouth would not have been sufficient reason for the setting up of Murata at Estover. The package had to be right. What Plymouth had to offer was entirely acceptable to the Murata Manufacturing Company Ltd, whose headquarters are in Kyoto, Japan. They are a world leader in the production of electronic components and the many tens of millions of pounds original project was the largest ever inward investment into Devon at that time.

The arrival of Murata demonstrated the success of the partnership approach employed in Devon to attract new investment.

In this case it was a two year operation by the Development Bureau which succeeded in bringing Murata to Plymouth together with the key assistance from the City Council. The Council had secured the Texas Instrument site two years earlier in readiness, rather than letting it go for warehousing or distribution services, until a new job-creating project could be attracted to replace the employment lost when Texas Instruments closed its Plymouth operation.

Murata purchased the former Texas Instruments' plant from Plymouth City Council and set about refurbishing the 47,000 sq ft factory to the high standards required by themselves. From the small staff of 150 in 1990 it has steadily grown.

The gentle colour schemes and the peaceful atmosphere within the building belie the amount of production that is achieved here. Murata is one of the largest manufacturers of ceramic capacitors in the world; indispensable parts of virtually every electronic circuit.

I always thought that ceramics had something to do with pottery! I know now better. Mr Fujiwara taught me that historically mankind has created various civilisations. Each civilisation was driven with 'basic materials'. There was the Stone Age, the Age of Earthenware, the Bronze Age and the Iron Age. Today three types of materials in particular support modern civilisation. They are polymers, metal and ceramics, surprisingly the newest material on the list is also one of the oldest.

Today's ceramics are called fine ceramics. They are inorganic substances, with the exception of metals, and because of this they are the most plentiful of all resources on earth and in the entire universe. Though in the past they were often used for utilitarian purposes, now they are in the spotlight as the latest technological discovery serving today's rapid progress of the electronics industry. Their features include what conventional materials lack, and they have become one of the most widely used materials in every type of electronic equipment, from household appliances to industrial machines.

Murata supplies an amazing number of ceramic-based electronic devices,

Princess Yachts plc until June 2001 Marine Projects (Plymouth) Ltd is a company of which Plymouth is intensely proud. Today it is one of the most successful companies in the world, renowned for the perfection of its products. Plymouth provides it with the perfect waterside site for its factory and offices, in Stonehouse Creek. In this age of mass production, it is unusual to find a major boat builder building each craft from start to finish with a single team of craftsmen. The Princess for example, in styling design, technology and craftsmanship, sets an example that others can only aspire to. The advanced hull forms have won international acclaim for their consistently outstanding performance, exceptional all-weather handling and economy.

One of the most important considerations in the design and performance of a powerboat is correct trim. It is a matter over which Princess Yachts plc takes particular care, in order to achieve the best possible ride, handling and drive efficiency. For this reason every new  Princess undergoes a painstaking programme of development and sea trials to establish the optimum choice and layout for engines, shaft geometry, propellors and weight distribution. Few other builders can match the depth of development undertaken by Princess Yachts plc in relation to this critical factor, and the outstanding performance that results is probably the single most important element in the company's reputation as one of the world's leading exponents of power cruiser engineering. For equipment and fittings, experience has shown that the best way to ensure consistently high standards of quality is to produce as much as possible themselves. That is why all hull and super structure mouldings, interior joinery, upholstery and most window assemblies are all manufactured within the company. Princess Yachts plc insist on the highest standards so who better than the company itself to ensure they meet them?

In 1993 I wrote that it would be interesting to take a look in ten years time at S.R. Vosper, Electrical Contractors. I am happy to say that my instincts were correct. The firm has grown in stature and has expanded. The expansion has been done steadily and lessons have been learned along the way. Some have been painful experiences but the present success has come from the fruits of that learning curve.

The business is owned by Stephen Vosper and his wife Karen who has given him every support from day one. She will tell you that she drew the line at digging trenches and chasing walls, but she does all the bookkeeping for the company and deals with suppliers. She has also become adept at helping Stephen when he is tendering for jobs. Today they are skilled and organised enough to take on substantial work and do so regularly. They have no need to advertise because most of their work comes from recommendations from satisfied clients.

How did the business start? Stephen is a Plymothian born and bred who served his apprenticeship with T. Clark and Co. of London after which he joined Devonport Dockyard in 1978. A little over ten years later there was a great deal of unrest within DML, and the threat of many redundancies. Stephen decided to ask for voluntary redundancy and then set up in business for himself. The redundancy was refused but his mind was made up and he left the Dockyard with just a week's pay in his pocket.

It is his straightforwardness and ability to complete a job skilfully and on time that has won him many contracts - not all of them in Plymouth. He and Karen have found that life is tough, the hours long but gradually the investment he made of one week's pay packet, has become a thriving business producing a good standard of living for himself, Karen and their two boys Matthew and Adam.

Stephen and Karen are both enthusiastic about their business. They want to be part of the growth of the city and give as much as they can to the community. This is the sort of business which deserves success and is a fine example of what can be achieved from small beginnings.

Another business which has grown from very small beginnings is The Kitchen Factory which operates out of a building in Faraday Mill. It started when two men who had a dream. Kevin Grearley and Paul Kirsten came to Plymouth from Manchester. They wanted a growth business and decided that there would always be a need for new kitchens and especially if they could align quality with a price that was affordable. At first it was to be a do it yourself package with the carcase and the other equipment ready for the customer to have installed. They achieved quality, their marketing methods kept the price down but at the end of the day more and more customers wanted their kitchens fitted. Slowly a team of fitters became part of the business and with more and more satisfied customers spreading the word, allied to realistic prices, the company moved into more spacious premises in Faraday Mill.

Today the Kitchen Factory no longer deals only in kitchens but sells and installs the most beautiful bathrooms as well as fitted bedrooms. Walk into their factory and you are surrounded by well laid out kitchens, bathrooms that ooze luxury and the sort of bedroom furniture that is both functional and very attractive. Kevin told me that they are busier than they have ever been and very happy with the way the business is growing. It has not come easily. Fitting bathrooms is the hardest job - and is the most expensive. The Kitchen Factory is open seven days a week and it is rare that Kevin is not to be seen there on any of the seven days. Success does not come without sacrifice.

Plymouth has surprised Kevin. When he first arrived he was not at all sure that the city was ready for this sort of business but he now would recommend it to anyone wanting to relocate.

One message that Kevin would pass on to anyone starting a business like his. Don't forget the power of advertising. I am not sure he even knows the William Wrigley story on the essential needs of advertising but Kevin consistently advertises using every medium the city offers from the buses to the papers, the radio and occasionally the television. It is a costly exercise but without it the business would go backwards, and not continue to climb the ladder of success.

Just round the corner from The Kitchen Factory in Prince Rock is the Acheson Colloids Company (Acheson Plymouth). The word 'Globality' is a term used by Acheson Colloids Company which is a division of Acheson Industries (Europe) Ltd, which is in turn the European Headquarters for Acheson Industries Inc. headquartered in Port Huron, Michigan, USA. On May 29th 1998 the Acheson family, which had owned the Company since its inception at the start of the last century, sold the assets to the National Starch and Chemical Company, a United States company headquartered in Bridgewater, New Jersey. Acheson joined the EEM (Electronic and Engineering Materials) division of National Starch & Chemical. National Starch itself was bought by ICI from the Unilever Group in July 1997 as part of ICI's global strategy to convert itself from a Commodity Chemicals Company to a Specialist Chemicals Company. Thus, Acheson Colloids Company today is a Company within the ICI Group by virtue of its membership of the EEM Division of National Starch & Chemical.

That then is the background, but Acheson Colloids has enormously deep roots with Plymouth. It first set up its base here in 1910 after some short months in Camborne, Cornwall. The factory was one of the few that survived two world wars and especially the blitz from the German Luftwaffe in 1941. Of course it has been modernised and is an important part of Acheson Europe.

The story of the company is very interesting. To protect his patents Dr Acheson decided to set up manufacturing bases throughout Europe, and sent over a young engineer, Fernley Banbury, to locate sites for these plants. In 1910 a small initial production facility was set up in Camborne, Cornwall, but very quickly the Company moved to its present Plymouth site where it has been ever since. Plymouth offered real advantages for the United Kingdom plant; it had soft water, low rates, was a Channel port and was served by two railways. What may have tipped the scales in Plymouth's favour was that Banbury had trained as an engineer in his native Cornwall and at Bickles, the engineering firm in Millbay Docks. He also married a Bickles girl. In any case, the Prince Rock factory opened in July 1912. In those days Elliot Road crossed the railway line by a bridge, turned sharply left (as it still does) and Acheson Colloids was built at the end of the road. More roads have been added since those days.

By 1913 the factory was already being extended. It was briefly closed down on the outbreak of war in 1914, when all the employees went off to the forces, but it was soon back in business. Its name, Oildag, roused suspicions in the police. It has a German ring, and they came investigating. Acheson replied furiously, the Western Morning News wrote a leader defending the Company, and all was forgotten. A young son George Acheson, was appointed to manage the Plymouth plant and he lived with his new English bride near the Prince Rock factory. It was an experimental as well as a manufacturing plant and by the end of the war was the only Acheson factory in Europe. The Acheson plant still continues on the same site, although it has been enlarged and rebuilt a number of times, and it is now one of a total of four plants in Europe, three speciality chemical, and one engineering. In 1966 Acheson had a payroll of 120 but as a result of changes in the market, and increases in productivity the present Company membership stands at 65.

The company restructured itself in 2000, on a Pan-European basis with previous operational sites now functioning as part of an integrated European Unit. This matrix structure permits Acheson in Europe to respond to its customers, which are themselves increasingly operating on a Europe wide basis. I talked with Acheson's Tony Parry, formerly General Manager of the Plymouth site, but now responsible for expanding Acheson's products for the metal forming industry in developing economies linked to the European Union. Tony has had a varied career, and was an expatriate for 15 years of his career. He tells of the time he went to Korea, and set up a company, which was the first British manufacturing joint venture set up in Korea. He made many friends, made a success of the business for the company, and found himself a frequent visitor to the British Embassy in what he describes as a 'Rent-A-Mob' role. There were so few British people in the capital, Seoul, that everyone had to be rounded up for Embassy parties and VIP visits in order to show the flag!

He has also worked for British companies in Mexico, the Far East and is now very much involved with Acheson's sales development in India, the Middle East and South Africa.
The Acheson Company is a speciality chemical producer, with products sold into metal forging and casting companies producing components primarily for the automotive supply chain. The company is also involved in the electronics and speciality coating business, such as electromagnetic shielding coatings, black matrix coatings for the television industry, inks for printed circuit boards, and friction minimising coatings for a variety of automotive applications, such as window channels, seat-belt buckles and windshield mounts. The firm's 'Dagâ' brand is globally recognised as a mark of quality.

In addition to its excellent products Acheson research and development efforts are focused on providing novel and environmentally friendly products for their customers' current and future requirements. With technical facilities located in Japan, Europe and the United States, the Strategic Business Units can rapidly respond to the customers' needs. The Acheson world-wide technical network provides for communication among their technologists and allows an exchange of ideas and knowledge, thus keeping technical staff abreast of the newest developments and emerging technologies around the world.

Acheson is dedicate to a global research and development effort with the goal of helping customers succeed in the international marketplace.

One of the most quietly successful businesses in Plymouth has to be Lang and Potter who have their factory in Galileo Close on the Newnham Industrial Estate. Ask what they do and David Potter, their Chief Executive will tell you that they will tackle anything that needs cutting, stitching and finishing!. This means that they provide flooring, upholstery, soft furnishings and canvas for a niche market which takes them to establishments like the Army at Bovingdon, the Royal Navy at Yeovilton, ships at sea, schools, universities, completing the interior furnishings for Marine Products, recovering furniture for private customers like myself, and a host of other outlets. It is a business that has been passed down from father to son and now the younger of David Potter's two sons as well as his married daughter are part of the business.

The company has 120 employees and a fleet of 41 vehicles. It is another stressful business but David Potter clearly thrives on what he does and is never willing to sit back on his laurels; he is always looking for new possibilities and new outlets. He rightly says that you must acquire new clients to sit on top of the pile, allowing for the possibility that some of the older ones will no longer be there.

That philosophy is sound. What Plymouth is achieving now is the result of never leaving any stone unturned to find new investors in the city. The old adage that 'Success breeds Success' is very true.

New stones have been turned over with a vengeance with the arrival of Call Centres in the city. In the case of ONdigital and Orange they are amongst the largest employers in Plymouth and have introduced a totally new work culture. With a desire to know more about these companies I sought the help of ONdigital's General Manager in Plymouth, Alan Lawson, who is responsible for a staff of some 1420 people who all work out of Ballard House in West Hoe Road. Like most people I have read some of the stories in the press about the slave labour treatment meted out by Call Centres to their staff. Having been in the offices of ONdigital at Ballard House and seen the working conditions and also having met one or two members of staff in the course of every day life, I cannot stress too much that such bad press is unwarranted at ONdigital. Also from what I understand from Alan Lawson, bad practices do not prevail among the companies who are part of a group known as the PCC - no not the Parochial Church Council but Plymouth Call Centre Conference. Much like the Plymouth Manufacturer's Group, this is a gathering of those involved in Call Centres in Plymouth including ONdigital, Orange, First Western, TMA Global, Market Reach and others who get together roughly every two months to discuss matters relating to their business, recruiting, training, wage structures etc.

The PCC is chaired by Alan Lawson, a no nonsense man who speaks his mind firmly and without fear or favour. He is a refreshing tonic to talk to.

What happens in a Call Centre. How do they recruit, how do they train? These were some of the questions I talked to Alan about. He, of course, can only speak about ON digital, but they are an exemplary example of how such a centre should be run.

First of all ONdigital is dealing with Customer Service for its subscribers, who telephone to get assistance of some kind in the main. One has to accept that a programme which has gone down in the middle of transmission is almost as emotionally devastating to the viewer as a breakdown is to the car owner. The customer needs tender loving care, an understanding of the problem and the information which will enable the programme to be restored. Therefore recruitment has to be a thorough and selective business. The company needs to employ bubbly people, with good telephone voices and a liking for the human race. People who will not lose their temper if the customer is awkward. So from the outset the company knows what sort of recruit they are seeking. Having got past the interview the candidate then goes through a rigorous six weeks training - three weeks in the classroom learning about the company, its products, technicalities, billing etc, the next three weeks in practical training on the telephones.

Call Centre staff at ONdigital earn £5.15 per hour which is enhanced by bonuses for team performance at the end of every month and can at its best be an additional 20% but more realistically is likely to be around the 12% mark. There is also additional money to be earned for Bank Holidays, Christmas etc and for overtime. The latter is the choice of the worker. When they join they can stipulate that they will only work 371/2 hours a week, or a laid down number of extra hours, or work extra time whenever they are asked to do so. This means that the work ethos covers the needs of all sorts of people from mums with small children to those who want to make more money for whatever reason.

The working conditions are excellent at Ballard House - who could not enjoy looking out of a window onto Plymouth Sound? On each floor the working areas are light and airy, crammed with computers of course! The staff have an excellent subsidised restaurant, there are vending machines on every floor. Rest rooms for those who cannot do without a cigarette - there is a very strict no smoking rule in the offices. Nurses are employed to care for anyone who does not feel well and they will visit the homes of those who call in sick if they are needed. Staff working late at night also have the benefit of Security men who will escort them to their cars in the car park to ensure they are safe. Being late for work is not acceptable - and why should it be?

Yes, there are firm rules laid down for conduct. Time-wasting is not permitted and now being developed and shortly to be installed is a system in which everything a call centre operator does is recorded throughout that person's shift. This has a twofold purpose. For the company it will allow them to monitor what is happening and for the operator there is the comfort factor of having all that they have said or done recorded so that there can be no come-backs. It is surprising how many callers will try to wriggle out of contracts for all sorts of spurious reasons including the one that starts 'Your operator said.......' Monitoring will stop that.

Alan Lawson acknowledges that with Call Centres being new to Plymouth, recruiting is comparatively easy. There are many would be operators who join the company not fully appreciating what they will be doing and sometimes this backfires when the recruit discovers it is not what he or she want at all. One of the reasons that ONdigital and Orange for that matter, decided to come to Plymouth was because of the potential workforce already here.

ONdigital may not manufacture widgets, they may not, according to one manufacturer contribute to the GDP of Plymouth, but they are here to stay and Plymouth is richer for them.

Devonport Dockyard 1947.

343

Cawsand Village near Plymouth

Chapter XVII

Within easy reach of Plymouth

One of Plymouth's greatest assets is the additional benefit of the wonderful countryside, beaches and the moors, all within easy reach. It does not matter whether you strike out towards the ruggedness of Dartmoor, seek out the gentleness of the countryside and the villages of the South Hams, collect your passport to gain entry into Cornwall by crossing the River Tamar to Torpoint, or the sweeping structure of the Tamar Toll Bridge to Saltash. Everywhere has its own charm and its devotees.

The main road from Plymouth to Tavistock will lead you very rapidly to the beginning of Dartmoor. You either love or hate the moor; there is no half measure. Most people fall in love with it and it is a bit like a good marriage, sometimes turbulent, sometimes inexplicable, mysterious, exciting, infuriating, but always beloved. Within its encompassing arms you wake in the morning never knowing what the day will bring.

People who live on the moor are a breed apart, generous enough to want to share their love affair with outsiders and astonished if your reaction is not the same as their's. No intrusion of man, since prehistoric times, has managed to conquer the wildness of this granite mass, some 130,000 acres in all.

There are fundamental lessons to learn about Dartmoor before you start exploring. It is a National Park, but that does not mean you have unlimited access. For example, it is an offence to drive a car more than 15 yards off the road.

You are asked not to feed the ponies because it encourages them to stray onto the road, putting themselves and road users into danger. There is a severe fine for those who do not heed this request. One other important point is to take note if red flags are flying on the north side of the moor. This means the army is at work. Disobey the warning and you could get shot!

It is not a place in which to take chances. People have died of exposure on Dartmoor. The weather can change in minutes from glorious sunshine to impenetrable mists. On a summer's day it looks as if butter would not melt in its mouth. Do not trust it. It is easy to get lost and very frightening. In heavy rain it becomes almost sinister.

If you have only a little time in which to explore, a round trip that will take you from Yelverton to Princetown and Tavistock and then back through Horrabridge to Yelverton again, is ideal. There is constantly changing scenery, rugged moors, isolated small moorland farms, rough coated ponies and grazing sheep belonging to the hardy farmers. In places the land is lush, in others sparse and riddled with gorse and heather. You will see the tors and valleys as you wend your way until you arrive at the isolated Princetown, the home of Dartmoor Prison. The forbidding prison walls were first raised in 1806 by French prisoners of war who were forced to erect their own gaol. It must have been appalling. Even on a summer's day Princetown is never the warmest of places and in the swirling mists of winter, penetrating rain eats into one's very soul. The poor prisoners must have hated the guts of every Englishman.

In 1812, the French prisoners were joined by hundreds of captured American sailors, who were given the task of building the church. Its beautiful east window lights up the greyness of the interior. It was donated by American women in memory of two hundred of their kin who died in captivity. There is also a memorial inscribed to Sir Thomas Tyrwhit ' whose name and memory are inseparable from all great works on Dartmoor'. It was this wretched man who suggested Dartmoor prison should be built, a memorial of which Devon is not proud. A prison sentence for the offender to be served in this barren fortress, sends shudders down the spine of the most hardened criminal.

Nonetheless there is happiness to be found in Princetown. Visit the Plume of Feathers with its welcoming warmth. Run by James Langton and his family since 1968, it is charming, the food is excellent and the ale plentiful. The inn is full of atmosphere with beamed ceilings, slate tables, copper lamps and log burners. The Plume was the first building to be erected in Princetown in 1785 during the reign of George III.

Without in anyway detracting from the antiquity of the pub, the Langtons have a camp site for Dormobiles and tents just across the car park. In a sort of hostel known as the Alpine Bunkhouse, you can stay in what are effectively two dormitories with ten beds in each, a kitchen, dayroom, toilets, showers and drying room - something that is an essential on Dartmoor. If you prefer something a little more sophisticated there are charming letting rooms within the Plume. Children are welcome and a special adventure playground has been designed for them.

A meandering road will take you down into Tavistock, a fine old Stannary town and the birth place of Sir Francis Drake. Here is a place steeped in history, which will give you a great deal of pleasure, whether you explore the parish church with its magnificent windows and its great sense of history - Drake worshipped here - wander amongst the array of shops or pop into the old Bedford Hotel which is full of character and a meeting place for almost everyone in the surrounding area. The river runs at one end of the hotel and on its banks are the ruined walls of the abbey. I love the shops and especially Crebers, an old fashioned grocer's that smells of sugar and spice and all things nice and has an array of delicacies with which to tempt any gourmet.

Tavistock Abbey to all intent and purpose governed the little town and its markets so when Henry VIII gave the Abbey estates to his friend, John Russell, the first Earl of Bedford, it must have meant considerable change. Only the ruins of the abbey remain. You can still see the stones in the heart of the town around the square laid out by the Duke of Bedford, who spent his mining royalties in doing so.

In the vicarage next to the hotel are the most picturesque fragments of the abbey and the Great Gate with the abbot's prison in the ruined tower above it. Betsy Grimbal's Tower is also here. She was a nun who was loved by a monk. He, perhaps from a sense of guilt, perhaps from rejection, murdered her.

The abbey saw much history in the making. One of the young abbots became so great he was chosen to crown William the Conqueror. One of the first printing presses in the country was set up here, and in the medieval church, with its wonderful pinnacled tower, wide nave and glorious gables, I have witnessed the sadness of death when a young American friend of mine buried her mother and her happiness some years later when she came from the States to have her marriage blessed . One of the three aisles was built for the Clothworkers Guild, with a lovely roof of carved beams and bosses. The font is over 500 years old. Who knows, Sir Francis Drake might have been baptised in it. The church is a place of peace and exploration and worthy of your time to look at its treasures.

If you have time to spare before you start the journey back to Plymouth you might drive out of Tavistock on the Okehampton road and take a look at the the Tavys, Mary and Peter. Twin villages which grew out of the settlements on either side of the River Tavy. Each has a church linked by a bridle path and a little bridge. Peter Tavy has an old and very attractive hostelry, which provides good food, warmth and a great atmosphere. Mary Tavy has the Royal Standard Inn, standing on the main road. It is full of history.

Just a little further up the hill from the Royal Standard you will see the engine house of Wheal Betsy, which was part of the extensive workings of an old lead and silver mine. Women worked on the surface of this mine breaking up the ore. They were known as Bal Maidens. Bal is an old word for mine which is more often in use in Cornwall than Devon.

At one time Mary Tavy housed Wheal Friendship, the largest copper mine in the world, later producing arsenic which was exported from Morwellham Quay, now a tourist attraction just off the Tavistock-Callington road and well sign-posted.

As you come back into Yelverton on the Tavistock road, you will find the village divided - not against itself - but because the main road has created the barrier. Tucked away in one section is Leg O'Mutton Corner which has a good pub, a busy newsagents which seems to sell everything, a super restaurant and my favourite, The Yelverton Paperweight Centre. When I first went there some years ago I had no idea what to expect. It was the radiance of the colours that first struck me. The room is full of well-lit cabinets and showcases, housing paperweights of every conceivable shape and size, weight and origin. After looking for a while at each individual piece, I wanted to know more. It was started from the collection of the late Bernard Broughton. His whole life was devoted to the collecting of these beautiful objects. He first started showing his collection in St Tudy, Cornwall in 1968 and later moved to Yelverton. On his death, the business was purchased by his assistant Kay Bolster, who had found Bernard's enthusiasm infectious. She expanded the collection and after working here for some years, she has sold the business on.

The collection today has over 800 paperweights on permanent exhibition and is reputed to be the largest private collection in Europe. Among these beautiful objects are many from the factories of Baccarat and St Louis who make the finest French paperweights.

I fell in love with the Millefiori weights, which consist of a great variety of ends of fancy canes cut sectionally, at right angles, with the filigree cane to form small lozenges or tablets. These, when placed side by side, and massed by transparent glass, have the appearance of a series of flowers or rosettes. If you think I am an expert on paperweights, you are very wrong! After my first visit I was so enchanted that I went home and read avidly anything about paperweights that I could find. When you see all the different types, the flowers, the whirls, the butterflies - even reptiles - all encapsulated in beautiful glass, I am sure you will be as eager as I am to learn more.

Collecting paperweights need not be a costly business, although the most expensive one that I have read about cost £99,000 in 1990. At the Yelverton Paperweight Centre one can start collecting for the modest price of £5 rising to somewhere over £1,600. The place is unique. It attracts collectors from all around the world. Admission is free and there is also free parking.

There is a nice hotel tucked away in Harrowbeer Lane. You can almost see Harrabeer Country House Hotel from Leg O'Mutton Corner. The owners run it as though they were inviting guests into their own home. Many business people come to stay and rapidly become friends, bringing their families back to stay at a later date. Sometimes the house at night becomes International with a house-party including Swedes, Germans, French, Welsh and English. It is a comfortable place, full of fun with good food, a friendly bar with a vast log fire, where most guests seem to congregate.

I have a different memory of this fine house. It used to be the Officers' Mess for the RAF Squadrons flying from the aerodrome during World War II. The aerodrome spread right across a vast area and was the cause of many houses in Leg O' Mutton Corner having to lose their gabled roofs because the planes needed the height to land on the runways. My memory is of super parties in the mess tinged with sadness - never admitted by the squadrons - when pilots did not return from their sortie.

193 Squadron who flew Typhoons, were based there and they had a live duck as their mascot. The duck was taken every evening for a trip to the nearest hostelry - usually the Royal Oak at Meavy. Here the duck would dip his beak into any beer mug he could reach and frequently ended up absolutely legless. I never understood why he remained free of hangovers!

Someone once said to me that the icing on life's cake is having good memories. I am quite sure anyone who stays at Harrabeer House will leave with very happy ones.

You pass The Moorland Links Hotel on your right as you return from Yelverton to Plymouth. I have already written about the hotel but this gives you the opportunity to take a look at it yourselves.

If you were to leave Plymouth on the Kingsbridge Road you would come to the village of Yealmpton where Old Mother Hubbard lived and to the Kitley Estate. I have already written about the Kitley House Hotel but not about Kitley Caves which attract thousands of people every year. I talked to Mark Bailey, the marketing manager for Kitley Estates who has been instrumental in turning the enterprise into such a success. Firstly let me tell you about the 'Farm Shop' . This started as a small business in a shed set up to sell the produce from the estate. This quickly developed into a substantial business and is now a very large shop selling a wide range of produce, including honey from bees who find the fruit crop ideal for their needs! There are some speciality goods and what is really a delicatessen, although I do not suppose Mark Bailey would describe it quite like that. Whatever the name this is a superbly run enterprise. It is clean, absolutely professional but not quite what one would envisage as a 'Farm Shop'.

Attached to the shop is an enormous conservatory housing winter and summer bedding plants for sale. It really is an absolute must for gardeners. I am told that between 35-40,000 people come here every year and the number is growing, thanks largely to Mark Bailey's ability to get things moving. He keeps house and thoroughly enjoys living in this area although he hails from Shrewsbury.

Also under his aegis are Kitley Caves which were undiscovered for many thousands of years until local quarrymen accidentally uncovered a cave entrance whilst blasting off limestone in the early 1800's. Since then much has been discovered and is being discovered still, about how the caves were formed, the extent of the system, about the creatures that have lived in the caves and those who have died, even about the quarrymen and the part limestone played in the local economy.

It is one of the most fascinating places to visit in the area and a splendid booklet written by Mark Bailey, is available for your use when you visit. It is able to trace how the caves were formed. It is a little unnerving to read that the limestone from which Kitley Caves were started off by the skeletons of billions of living creatures. Caves such as these at Kitley are the result of acids contained in water dissolving the rock and carrying the solution away; typically caves start as tiny holes dissolved out of the rock and as these grow so they can carry more water which, in turn, can dissolve greater volumes of material.

Throughout much of the period of cave development animal and plant debris found its way into the caves. There are still bats there today, but it is suspected that other animals actually made their homes in the caves. It could have been hyenas and bears; the fossil remains of both have been found on the site. Kitley C aves are endlessly exciting to scientists because of the information they unveil about themselves, the ever changing environment and, because of the light thrown on cave development. For laymen it is equally enthralling. The colours of the calcite formations are exquisitely beautiful - sectionalised formations are on display in the museum.
Excavation is still continuing. The cave passages illuminated for the safety of visitors, form only a fraction of the cave system. The caves sit on a block of limestone covering an area of over two square miles and from the evidence of trial digs and geological surveys, the area is honeycombed with cavities.

Kitley is set in beautiful countryside with a Woodland Trail starting just outside the museum. A year or so ago I went to an open air concert on the estate, on a balmy summer's night and listened to the Royal Philharmonic plus two soloists. It was enchanting. The audience spread themselves about the ground which rose gently away from the auditorium. Everyone brought picnics plus candelabra or lamps, and as the evening drew on so the original sunlit scene was replaced by the magic of a thousand twinkling lights.

The woods are alive with animal life, flowers and insects. You can walk alongside the river as you make your way to the car park. At a little wooden bridge which spans the River Yealm, you should take a moment or two to absorb the beauty that surrounds you. In summer it is peaceful but in winter the storms can turn the trickling river into a raging torrent that rises to within three feet of the bridge. Whole trees are caught up and swept down the frothing, angry cataract. The rise in water level also has its effect on the caves' interior where sections become inundated.

The River Yealm rises in the foothills of southern Dartmoor and the source of the Yealm is a notable beauty spot. It is particularly attractive to those fond of walking in rugged and beautiful seclusion.

At one time many salmon were found in the Yealm but now, sadly, hardly a salmon makes its way upstream to spawn. The salmon population has been disrupted by widespread netting both inside and outside the estuary, which has hit the Yealm pretty badly. You may still be lucky enough in autumn and winter to see a salmon swimming powerfully upstream to a suitable gravelly spot in the headwaters where it makes a shallow depression, called a redd, into which it lays hundreds of eggs. There are still trout to be seen which attract the avid kingfisher - the most spectacular angler of all the birds! The river is always entertaining and beautiful no matter what time of the year, just as Kitley is. A day spent in this extraordinary place will stay in your memory for a very long time. Make the most of the chance and pamper yourself with a night or two at the Kitley House Country Hotel.

After you leave Yealmpton it is just a short car journey to the pretty villages of Newton Ferrars and Noss Mayo where time has stood still and only brought into the present by the modern yachts which lie at anchor on the river at the head of the creek.Apart from the tranquillity of the villages which have excellent hostelries, Noss Mayo has a wonderful church that was built in the 14th century and boasts a tower and a chancel of the 13th century. The villages are beloved by artists and many of the houses are now the homes of non-villagers, who come here to stay to recharge their batteries and sail.

Now back to the A38 and Ivybridge once a small village just ten miles outside Plymouth, and now one of the fastest growing small towns in Europe. It still manages to hang on to its local traditions and at the same time provides a good life style for all those who have come to live in the new housing estates which now surround the original main street. On your way back into Plymouth from Ivybridge you will come to the well known Endsleigh Garden Centre which has grown in size and stature over the years and is now a favourite place for people in the surrounding areas to enjoy an outing and at the same time be sure of assistance from the intelligent and helpful staff.

Robin Taylor is the owner and the driving force of what must be the most successful enterprise of its kind in Devon. Originally Robin and his brother bought four acres in 1972 in order to establish a garden centre outlet for plants raised on their father's nursery at Endsleigh, Tavistock, but it has grown. Enlargement to twice the acreage could have meant a hotch potch, instead it is laid out superbly and logically.

I am always impressed by the helpful and intelligent staff who are to be found everywhere as well as in the four information centres. These are people who do not mind a simpleton like me asking questions which are quite trivial. They are as helpful to my small needs as they are to a serious gardener spending a lot of money. This team work is part of the philosophy taught by Robin Taylor who is insistent that courtesy is shown to every customer. He is the sort of man who does not expect anyone to do anything he would not do himself.

Talking to him, one would expect to find an ardent gardener but he will tell you, quite openly, that it was not his love of plants which brought him into the business. It was strictly as a viable economic proposition. I believe it was this approach that has brought him so much success. He is objective and not a dreamer. Something that many would-be entrepreneurs should apply to their dreams!

Just behind Ivybridge lies one of the most popular sporting venues in Devon. Dinnaton Sporting and Country Club has just about everything and is a club to belong to. Used a lot by local people whether it is to play golf on a challenging course or to take the family swimming, it is good value. The 25 metre indoor swimming pool is kept at an enjoyable temperature within fully air conditioned surroundings. There is a versatile gymnasium equipped with its Powersport Multigym and Power Jogger which allows for everyone's keep fit requirements - from females in need of a little light exercise and 'tone up', to the experienced athlete training for a competition.

There are sauna, steam and solarium suites. The relaxation area allows you to unwind or maybe enjoy the beauty care and massage available. You can play squash on one of the four courts, which include three glass backed Perstorp Championship Courts. On the same semi-sprung wooden floor there are two Badminton Courts waiting to be played on.

All this is only part of what Dinnaton is all about. Behind the sporting area there is a delightful block of buildings nestling round an attractive courtyard. Here you can stay in comfortable rooms, use the facilities and enjoy the fun of the club. The Courtyard also contains the pleasant restaurant and various rooms equipped for business conferences or seminars. It is also used for weddings and other functions.

Perhaps after lunch instead of swimming or playing squash you might decide to take the family to Dartmoor Wildlife Park at Sparkwell. The park s situated on the south western edge of Dartmoor in thirty acres of beautiful Devon countryside, three miles from Plymouth and one and a half miles from the A38. It has been developed in the grounds of Goodamoor House, an old country mansion once the home of the Treby family whose name lives on in the Treby Arms at Sparkwell.

Sparkwell has one of the most comprehensive 'Big Cat' collections in the South West, a falconry centre second to none and a very successful animal breeding programme. If the weather is not too kind the barn is the venue for 'Close Encounters of the Animal Kind', a 'hands on' talk, touch and learn session, which is fun, informative and educational. Children of all ages respond to it.

Before returning to the centre of Plymouth, no one should miss visiting Saltram House belonging to the National Trust. It is a place of great beauty and at the same time beset by the traumas that make keeping our National Heritage safe, such a difficult task.

You approach it along a sweeping drive which prepares you for the wonder of this Grade I Listed Georgian house, built in the 18th century by the Parker family.

The National Trust does not like to think of Saltram as a museum, but as a home. It is their wish that visitors should feel that they have arrived whilst the family is out. Everyday silver is left out, as if it were going to be used, and everything has been arranged in the house as it would be if it were lived in. You can wander along the stone flagged floors,marvel at the beautiful and ornate pieces that adorn the walls, ceilings and floors. It is quite blissful but a nightmare for those who have to care for it.

The Administrator will tell you that the National Trust has had to become more commercially aware. It is quite obvious that increasing sums of money are needed if we are to conserve this magnificent heritage. The sad thing is that the greater the public's interest in our wonderful houses, the more people visit them, and the influx of people can cause more harm than monetary gain because of the resulting damage to the buildings and their contents.

How are the National Trust handling this problem at Saltram? By treating it in many ways as families would have done in the great days of country houses. Often they were only lived in for a few months of the year and the remainder of the time shutters were closed and furniture covered. Practically the same thing occurs at Saltram. The house is open from April or Easter, whichever is the sooner, and closes for winter months from October.

Saltram over the years has suffered much wear and tear, more so now with such an increase of visitors than previous times. A lot of the furnishings have been damaged by sunlight. The silk wall hangings, Chinese wallpapers and original carpets are very fragile. These carpets cannot be walked upon so special carpets are laid down for visitors.

To protect the colours of the carpets, upholstery, paintings and textiles, the windows are fitted with ultraviolet filters and the light is controlled by drawing Holland blinds. Every evening the shutters are closed and all the silver is put away. Every morning just before opening, the shutters are opened. This is just one way of conserving these wonderful historical artefacts.

The humidity of the house has to be kept constant all year long. It has to be monitored every day. If the level rises suddenly this can result in untold damage.

The house is spring cleaned from January until opening time, by specialists taking the utmost care. In the time of the Morleys (the last family to live at Saltram) nine carpets used to be dragged out early every morning on to the grass, turned over and pulled across the dew to clean them! There is no ordinary use of furniture polish, which contains acrylic and would ruin the wood. Special polish is used just once a year. Scaffolding is erected to allow the high shelves and ceilings to be cleaned. The vacuum cleaner has a piece of netting attached to it to catch any precious pieces that might fall off the ceiling, ornaments or paintings. The offending piece is then rescued and taken to the restoration room for repair.

Contingency plans against any eventuality have been taken by the National Trust. The Library contains irreplaceable material; the oldest book being the Nuremberg Chronicle, and there are some superb Rembrandt etchings. The greatest of all English portrait painters, Sir Joshua Reynolds, who was born in Plympton St Maurice, was a frequent visitor to Saltram. If, God forbid, any of the paintings or anything else of beauty, antiquity and value, were in danger of being damaged by water following a fire, then Saltram has the co-operation of a blast freezing company who would blast-freeze everything that was damaged by water and remove them to cold storage until such time as the conservationists could use their special techniques to dry them out.

Most of us have no idea what a complex task it is caring for this sort of property. It was an eye opener and has made me even more appreciative of all that is done to allow the general public the sheer joy of sharing our wonderful heritage.

One of Saltram's major assets is the park. As the house becomes more and more fragile, entertainment is transferred outside. Saltram hosts Anglo-American fairs, The Lions Club, one of Plymouth's very active fund raisers, takes advantage of the setting, and pays for the privilege of course. More and more companies are using the grounds for product launches and associated occasions. The courtyard and stables are an added attraction. On most days the park is free for use by anyone, but it is closed from dusk to dawn.

The National Trust are imaginative and hard-working in seeking monies to help maintain this beautiful house. One of their fund raising enterprises is a series of concerts with a mixture of classical music and Jazz. Listening to classical music in the Saloon by candlelight or in the Orangery is magical. Imagine the tones of a harpsichord playing Mozart, with fragile light flickering over breathtaking scenery, and the stillness of an autumn evening catching every note. Parts of the house are lit by candles for these splendid occasions and visitors are allowed to look around.

Crossing the river from Admiral's Hard in Stonehouse to Cremyll on the Cornish side is a voyage I have explored with you in Chapter 12 but that has not touched on the exquisite beauty that is to be found as one steps ashore from the little ferry, walks up the hard, through the gates and there, ahead of you is the entrance to Mount Edgcumbe Park. This gift to Plymouth by a former Earl of Mount Edgcumbe has given thousands of Plymothians the opportunity to revel in its quiet beauty and its splendid walks and the chance to explore the house. If walking is not your forte and you prefer a gentle wander in the park then add to that enjoyment by indulging in a lunch time snack or a mouth-watering cream tea in The Orangery. It is a charming café in lovely surroundings and run by the Hadlingtons who have The Brasserie at Mayflower International Marina. The Orangery is also a popular venue for wedding receptions.

Before I start off on the exploration of the house and the park, I am always tempted to stop at The Edgcumbe Arms, just beyond the ferry landing. This fine old hostelry dates back centuries and is rumoured to have 15th century antecedents. Its age is unmistakable when you step onto the old stone flagged floors, see the old beams and remember from time to time to duck ones head to avoid the low ceilings. It is a warm, inviting inn, where the very Cornish landlord David Rowe with his friendly wife Amanda are the essence of good innkeepers. It is not only their welcoming smiles and the courteous behaviour of their staff that makes this inn special, it is everything about it. It smells of lavender polish and local flowers, its brasses gleam, its well-stocked long bar ensures that there is a beverage of some kind that will please both locals and visitors. The food is traditional and cooked to a high standard using local produce and vegetables whenever possible. You can stay here, if you wish, in comfortable bedrooms, waking each morning to the sounds of the countryside and the life of the busy river. It is an ideal base for anyone wanting to explore Plymouth and at the same time be able to take in the glory of the Rame Peninsula.

It is entertaining to sit in the bar watching and listening to the very varied clientele. Locals use the pub regularly and that means a lot of lively, entertaining banter, quite frequently started by David Rowe himself. He has a rich Cornish accent and a personality to match. Visitors flock off the ferries in summer time and add to the fun of the bar. Sundays sees a regular gathering of Plymouth people who come across the ferry for a walk and then into the Edgcumbe for food, drink and the surety of good company.

Now for that walk through the park to Cawsand and Kingsand, two old smuggling villages joined together by a simple sign on the wall of a house between the two villages.

Looking at Mount Edgcumbe House rising majestically above the tree-lined avenue from Cremyll, is quite wonderful and it is almost impossible to believe that you are looking at a building that lay in ruins, a victim of the Second World War. Over the last forty years it has been rebuilt and once again its grace adorns the park. It is equally interesting and quite moving to know that it was the vision and determination of Kenelm, sixth Earl of Mount Edgcumbe, and his architect, Adrian Gilbert Scott, that caused the ancestral home of the Mount Edgcumbe family to rise, like a phoenix from the ashes. I am always moved because Kenelm did it knowing that he had no son to inherit and the line would pass to the New Zealand branch of the Mount Edgcumbe family. Kenelm's son was killed in World War II and is remembered in the private chapel of the house dedicated to him some ten years ago. I like to think that the whole restoration was started by Kenelm and continued by others after his death in memory of Piers Richard who was killed at Dunkirk in 1940. It was such a courageous act. Kenelm with no direct heir, could have walked away from the ruins.

My first memory of the Mount Edgcumbe family was in the thirties when, as a child, I was occasionally taken sailing with my father in the sleek dark green, ocean going-yacht which lay at anchor just off Cremyll, belonging to the 4th Earl, another Piers. Afterwards I would be given tea in the big house, perched on a chair with my small legs trying hard to reach the floor. I have nothing but happy memories of this great house.

When you walk into the entrance hall you will find some interesting pieces of furniture, two tables thought to be of the 18th century, cannons of the 17th century and a small George III cannon used for signals. There are late 17th century chairs, straight backed and upholstered Coronation chairs used at the Coronation of Queen Elizabeth II. This really gives you an immediate insight into the collection of furniture that has been gathered to furnish the house. Much of the furniture was saved and this was later augmented by additions from Cotehele, the Edgcumbe family's other estate on the banks of the Tamar just before it reaches Calstock, and the Edgcumbe's London house. It all has an interest and is set off by the lovely warm colours on the walls, apricots and blues, showing off the fine plasterwork. There are some fine portraits but none to compare with those lost when the Germans destroyed the house. The house then contained an oval dining room hung with portraits of the family going back in unbroken succession to Piers Edgcumbe of the Civil War. Only one of these survived, Richard the second Lord Edgcumbe (1716-1761), who had been the black sheep of the family - his portrait was stored in the basement and survived to outlive his more respectable relatives. Three beautiful seascapes by William van de Velde are probably the best of the other pictures to survive.

It is the joy of wandering through this house and catching glimpses of the stunning views that makes it so appealing and in another sense it is the great effort that has gone into recreating the original house for the benefit of Plymothians. I just wish more of them took the trouble to visit the house. Even the park does not get the number of people it should and yet it is free. For those of us who do use the park and love it, we are probably blessed by the fact that it is not crowded. Here you can walk for miles and seldom see anyone.

Now when I walk through the formal gardens towards the house, I love every moment; the English garden, so called because it is the picturesque shaping of the beds that earns it its name, not the exotic plants! Then, what is now the Italian Garden, containing the Orangery, where you can get a very good cup of tea and excellent home-made cake. The marble fountain, the stairway, the statuary, all make it enchanting. The French Parterre Garden like all of them is protected by large hedges of evergreen, oak, laurel and bay to provide essential shelter.

The great green sweep of manicured grass takes you up the drive to the house. This was probably laid out sometime in the 18th century and now consists of lawns, terraced walks and shrubberies. The lawn area to the east has been returned to its mid-Victorian beds, and one of the three summer houses within the Earl's Garden has been beautifully restored by the 'Friends of Mount Edgcumbe'. This one is the Cedar Seat which looks across Barn Pool to the Hamoaze and Plymouth Sound.

The Shell Seat, a fragile dome like structure also in the Earl's Garden, has been restored. Shell grottoes were much in vogue in the latter part of the 18th century and because of Cornwall's interesting geology and its many mines, a number of grottoes and seats were built using a mixture of both minerals and shells for internal decoration. Sadly now only two remain in the county. The Mount Edgcumbe Shell Seat is all the more precious for this reason.

Just before the Spanish Armada threatened this country, Admiral Sidonia Medina, Phillip of Spain's admiral in command of the Armada, was asked by the King what he would like as a reward for defeating Sir Francis Drake and the English. Without hesitation, Sidonia Medina replied. 'The Estate of Mount Edgcumbe, sire - the most beautiful place in the country.' The man had good taste, the estate is beautiful with fabulous scenery in every direction, an abundance of wildlife and birds, flora and fauna.

There are many walks which will give you ample opportunity to enjoy Mount Edgcumbe Park and revel in the glorious views. Cremyll to Redding Point, for example, will take you about 11/2hours and goes via the Avenue to Barnpool, Milton's Temple and Lady Emma's Cottage, originally a small thatched house built in the 'picturesque' style of the early 19th century. Emma was the daughter of the second Earl of Mount Edgcumbe (1764-1839) and she used the cottage to entertain her weekend guests. It was rebuilt about 1880, and is now leased to a private resident. From here the route zigzags uphill to the Earl's Drive and Redding Point returning to Cremyll Lodge Visitor Centre via the top of the Amphitheatre.

The easiest route is the three miles around the coast via Maker into Kingsand and Cawsand. I walked this way many times in my childhood but I doubt I took in the beauty around me, more than likely I took it for granted! Follow the track towards Maker and you will see Maker Church, or to give it its proper name, St Macra's. The church is first mentioned in 1121 but during the second half of the 15th century it was almost entirely rebuilt. The 70ft tower is a landmark for miles around and one I see from my bedroom window in Stoke, every morning. It was used as an Admiralty signal station in the 18th century when its own crew passed messages by semaphore to Devonport Dockyard and Mount Wise.

Before long you find yourself looking across the Sound to the Mewstone jutting out of the water near the Devon coastline. Follow the track as it slopes into Hooelake valley - a misnomer because there is no lake! Almost immediately you get a superb view of Cawsand Bay ahead of you surrounded by the eastern coastline of the Rame Peninsula, and terminated by Penlee Point with the fog warning station below.

You just keep on going, passing Hooe Lake Cottage, originally a huntsman's home and now a private house. From the road the view back to the left includes the Breakwater and the Lighthouse, and in the meadow nearby is a white navigational beacon. Opposite the cottage there is a stile on the left hand side of the road. Cross the stile and follow the footpath around to the right, where you enter a dense copse of evergreen oaks, known locally as Dark Trees. This track is part of the Earl's Drive which extends from Mount Edgcumbe House to Penlee Point, where in the 19th century, there was a liveried gatekeeper.

Coming out of the copse you have a clear view of Kingsand and Cawsand. Between Cawsand and Penlee Point a terrace, of what were once coastguard cottages, stands out. A few hundred yards further on you pass by a footpath branching off to the left. This gives access to the tidal Sandway Point and the beach below. It is here you will see the remains of some of the old fish cellars where catches of pilchards were sorted and packed in cases for overseas shipment.

Before you reach the village of Kingsand you will have to climb the steep slope of Minadew Brakes rising to over 400ft at a point inland just beyond the still threatening walls of the disused Grenville Battery which dominates the skyline. Pass through the gate, turning sharp right almost immediately opposite the road, Lower Row, onto Devonport Hill. As the summit is approached the views of Plymouth Sound, Staddon Heights, Bovisand Bay and Wembury are unsurpassed, and beyond the rolling Devon Moors.

Your reward for this walk, if the beauty was not sufficient, will be a visit to the Rising Sun, an inn which is not only hospitable but has some of the best crab sandwiches to be found anywhere. They use crab caught mainly off the headland or the Eddystone Rocks. The pub was once a former Customs House and is a listed building dating back to the 1700's, when the Royal Navy 'revitalled' from Cawsand Bay to avoid the temptation of the flesh pots of Devonport for the largely 'pressganged' sailors. Henry Tudor is said to have used the path outside the Rising Sun during his clandestine visit to England whilst in exile. Kingsand is believed to have derived its name from this visit and because during the 1700's and 1800's the Kings Men or Revenue men as they were better known, were based here to patrol Cawsand and Cornwall - Kingsand in those days was in Devon.

The adjoining villages of Kingsand and Cawsand are so much part of my life that I tend to go towards them like a homing pigeon. I spent the greater part of my childhood there in a house on the hill overlooking Cawsand beach and leading into the Square. A blissful life for any child. I had my first boat, a small rowing dinghy with lightweight oars by the time I was five and progressed from there to a larger dinghy with sails. Every free moment was spent in my boat. I remember the summer before the war

started, lying at anchor under the lea of Penlee woods whilst I studied for my School Certificate as it was called in those days. I remember the young midshipman from the giant aircraft carrier Hermes and the battleship Rodney, sailing their whalers into the bay at weekends, and usually taking several of them home for tea.

Whenever I go there it is always a case of 'I remember'. I will never forget the sunlit mornings when the sound of waves, gently lapping, were the first things I heard when I opened my eyes. I remember the storms when the wind blew so strongly that one could not stand up on the hill and the rains would come tumbling down the hillside, right through the backdoor until they found an escape at the front. I remember the old fishermen, the Hancocks, the Williams, the Wilcocks and Sam White, a great character who taught me how to fish. I remember the occasion when we caught a small shark in his nets and had to bring it ashore. The nets were ruined but Sam and I thought up a scheme whereby we took it into a boatyard by Cawsand beach, mounted it on a trestle, polished the now very dead shark, and then opened the doors to the public, charging them one penny a time to look at the monster. We got a severe wigging from the local bobby but Sam collected enough to buy new nets! I can also remember helping him with his ice-cream stall on hot summer days. The pay as much ice cream as I could eat in wafers that always ended up a soggy mess before the ice-cream was finished. Wonderful - I can still conjure up the taste of the ice-cream. I remember going to church in St Andrews church and sometimes in the little Norman church at Rame Head, which to this day has no electricity and is the most atmospheric church I have ever been in.

As a child Sundays would have been a lot happier for me if I had been allowed to go to the Congregational Chapel in the village, especially on Sunday School Sundays when the girls all had special, frilly, brightly coloured satin dresses and wore straw hats with flowers and ribbons. To dress similarly was always my ambition but my attire was far more austere and the Church of England did not have these wonderful Sunday School specials with the outings as well. I remember too the days of the Maypole in Cawsand Square and a sort of Floral Dance which was danced from the top of Kingsand village, in and out of the houses, right down to Cawsand Square. It is strange what one remembers.

Perhaps most of all I remember the Sunday morning when World War II started. I stood in the doorway of the sitting room and heard the solemn words of Neville Chamberlain on the wireless. We were at war and so ended my childhood and my idyllic life in Cawsand.

There is a fine old pub at the top of Garrett Street in Cawsand called The Ship Inn. In my young days it was owned by a colourful character called Fred Eteson who counted Gracie Fields as a great friend. She was a frequent visitor to the inn.

Because of the geographical position neither of these two villages has ever suffered too much from the last century and I cannot see much changing in the 21st century. The streets are still narrow, the houses and cottages charming and the people who live there seem to be able to stand back from today's frenetic pace. Of course, because of the position. it was the most wonderful place for smugglers who carried out their nefarious trade almost unnoticed in spite of the Revenue men. At one time every house in the village was in some way part of the activity. I believe there are still tunnels leading from Cawsand beach into caverns, blocked today, of course.

My late father, who was a total pillar of society and declared absolutely everything when he returned from abroad, thought nothing of a little smuggling in my childhood days. He would not have considered it so. He merely carried on a tradition started by his father and grandfather before him. The French crabbers sailed into Cawsand Bay regularly and when they came ashore, they brought water casks. They would arrive at our house, the contents of the casks would be decanted into suitable containers, then refilled with their rightful contents and the Frenchmen would depart with smiles and some money! My father's dinner parties were renowned for fine wines and brandy!

If I had come across the Torpoint Ferry to reach Cawsand I would have driven through Torpoint and along the winding leafy lanes up to Tregantle and then taken the coast road to Rame and down into Cawsand. The views when you reach Tregantle are spectacular, right over Whitsand Bay stretching as far down as Downderry. The cliffs drop steeply below the road and it is quite a climb down to the beaches but the long stretches of golden sand outweigh the energy expended.

Had you not taken the fork at Antony towards Tregantle, the road would have taken you on its winding way, with sudden and unexpected glimpses of the River Lynher, through Sheviock with its splendid church, the old village of Polbathic and then to a point where you join the main Plymouth-Liskeard road at Trerulefoot.

You can eat well and inexpensively at Windy Ridge Eating House, a remarkable business which has grown from the time when it was just a stopping place for lorry drivers, into a good, well run restaurant where the food is plentiful and ideal for families.

If I am wanting an evening out in a special place then I would choose Heskyn Mill just off the Trerulefoot-Saltash road. It nestles in the Tiddy Valley and is a beautifully converted 19th century corn mill. The restaurant is unusual, warm and welcoming and has a good reputation for its lunch and dinner menu. Part of its charm is the machinery which is still intact and in working order. The large chimney beside the building was to aid a steam engine, housed in the adjacent barn; its purpose to keep the mill wheels turning during water shortages.

A wood burning stove gives a cosy atmosphere to the bar area, where a small menu is available at lunchtimes. Upstairs, amongst the wheels and machinery, is the restaurant, where a full a la carte menu is served all week apart from Sundays and Mondays.

Continuing into Plymouth, having looked at the charms of the old village of St Germans first, you will go up hill and down dale until you come to the Saltash bypass. There before you will be two great feats of engineering, the modern Tamar Bridge opened by the Queen Mother in 1961 linking Cornwall and Devon by road, and the other, one of Isambard Kingdom Brunel's masterpieces, the Brunel Railway Bridge built over a hundred years earlier in 1859.

Brunel Railway Bridge and Tamar Bridge.
Linking Devon and Cornwall.

PLYMOUTH THE WATERFRONT CITY

INDEX

| Vern Allen | Exeter | 01392 273305 | p108 |
| Western Morning News | Derriford | 01752 765500 | p 93 |

Chapter Six – Money makes the City go round

Bond Pearce	West Hoe Road	01752 266633	p124
Business Personal Finances		01752 675197	p123
Curtis, Solicitors	Mutley Plain	01752 204444	p125
David Rice	Ridgeway, Plympton	01752 348834	p124
Nicola Ellis & Co.	5 St. Laurence Road	01752 227428	p125
Enterprise Plymouth	Somerset Place	01752 569211	p120
Financial Management Services		01752 221133	p122
Foot & Bowden	Derrys Cross	01752 675000	p124
Lloyds TSB	Royal Parade	01752 668281	p116
M&L Associates	Mutley Plain	01752 261596	p126
Nash & Co.	Beaumont Road	01752 664444	p125
NatWest	St. Andrew's Cross	01752 226226	p118
PriceWaterhouseCoopers	Notte Street	01752 267441	p 70
Prince's Trust	Intercity House	01752 251051	p120

Chapter Seven – Plymouth and the Church

Christian Centre	Cattedown	01752 661019	p142
Hope Baptist Church	Peverell	01752 772809	p138
Jewish Synagogue	Catherine Street	01752 773309	p136
Methodist Central Hall	Drake Circus	01752 660997	p140
Mutley Baptist	Mutley Plain	01752 203346	p139
Pilgrim United Reform	Keyham	01752 544969	p143
Roman Catholic Cathedral of St. Mary & St. Boniface	Cecil Street	01752 662537	p141
St. Andrews Church	Royal Parade	01752 661414	p133
St. Budeaux Parish Church	St. Budeaux	01752 351087	p140
St. Peter's	Wyndham Square	01752 222007	p141

Chapter Eight – The Importance of Education

College of Further Education	Kings Road	01752 305300	p163
Coombe Dean School	Elburton	01752 406961	p160
Devonport High School for Boys	Millbridge	01752 208787	p155
Devonport High School for Girls	Outlands Road	01752 705024	p155
Hyde Park Infants	Hyde Park	01752 225364	p158
Internet Co-op	University	01752 233722	p162
Kings School	Hartley	01752 771789	p158
Peninsula School Of Medicine	Tamar Science Park		p163
Pixieland Day Nurseries	Hartley	01752 770550	p146
Playzone	Whitleigh		p147
Plymouth College	Ford Park	01752 228596	p151

Chapter Sixteen – Commerce and Industry – the future of Plymouth

Chapter 17 – Within easy reach of Plymouth

Heskyn Mill	Tideford	01752 851481	p359
Kitley Caves & Estates	Yealmpton	01752 880202	p348
Kitley Country House Hotel	Yealmpton	01752 881555	p348
Mount Edgcumbe House	Mt. Edgcumbe	01752 822236	p353
Plume of Feathers	Princetown	01822 89240	p346
Rising Sun	Kingsand	01752 822840	p357
Saltram House	Plympton	01752 336546	p351
Windy Ridge Eating House	Trerulefoot	01752 851344	p359
Yelverton Paperweight Centre	Yelverton	01822 854250	p348

*First Thanksgiving in Plymouth England 1988
by Liz Jones.*